Hubris

ALSO BY JONATHAN HASLAM

Soviet Foreign Policy, 1930–33: The Impact of the Depression

The Soviet Union and the Struggle for Collective Security in Europe, 1933–39

The Soviet Union and the Politics of Nuclear Weapons in Europe, 1969–87: The Problem of the SS-20

The Soviet Union and the Threat from the East, 1933–41: Moscow, Tokyo and the Prelude to the Pacific War

The Vices of Integrity: E.H. Carr, 1892–1982

No Virtue Like Necessity: Realist Thought in International Relations Since Machiavelli

The Nixon Administration and the Death of Allende's Chile: A Case of Assisted Suicide

Russia's Cold War: From the October Revolution to the Fall of the Wall

Near and Distant Neighbours: A New History of Soviet Intelligence

The Spectre of War: International Communism and the Origins of World War II

Hubris

The Origins *of* Russia's War Against Ukraine

JONATHAN HASLAM

An Apollo Book

First published in the UK in 2024 by Head of Zeus Ltd
This paperback edition first published in 2025 by Head of Zeus Ltd,
part of Bloomsbury Publishing Plc

Copyright © Jonathan Haslam, 2024

The moral right of Jonathan Haslam to be identified as the author of this work has been asserted in accordance with the Copyright, Designs and Patents Act of 1988.

All rights reserved. No part of this publication may be: i) reproduced or transmitted in any form, electronic or mechanical, including photocopying, recording or by means of any information storage or retrieval system without prior permission in writing from the publishers; or ii) used or reproduced in any way for the training, development or operation of artificial intelligence (AI) technologies, including generative AI technologies. The rights holders expressly reserve this publication from the text and data mining exception as per Article 4(3) of the Digital Single Market Directive (EU) 2019/790.

9 7 5 3 2 4 6 8

A catalogue record for this book is available from the British Library.

ISBN (PB): 9781804548233
ISBN (eBook): 9781804548202

Cover design: Matt Bray | Head of Zeus
Maps © Jeff Edwards

Printed and bound in Great Britain by Clays Ltd, Elcograf S.p.A.

Bloomsbury Publishing Plc
50 Bedford Square, London, WC1B 3DP, UK
Bloomsbury Publishing Ireland Limited
29 Earlsfort Terrace, Dublin 2, D02 AY28, Ireland

HEAD OF ZEUS LTD
5–8 Hardwick Street
London EC1R 4RG

To find out more about our authors and books
visit www.headofzeus.com
For product safety related questions contact productsafety@bloomsbury.com

For Karina and Timothy, as always

"So, what was the collapse of the Soviet Union? It was the collapse of historic Russia under the name of the Soviet Union."

Vladimir Putin, 12 December 2021

"When it rains on the post-war Soviet part of the Novodevichii cemetery, it seems as if tears are pouring down the bronze or marble faces of the monuments – the scientists, the officers, the members of the party, the managers, the intelligence officers, the builders, the writers, the actors and all those who constructed and defended the Soviet Union commemorate a country that disappeared in shame, condemned and misunderstood."

Dmitry Ryurikov,
Yeltsin's national security adviser

"The belief that it was the world's sole superpower led America into one diplomatic misjudgement after another over the next three decades [from 1991]."

Sir Rodric Braithwaite, Britain's ambassador to the Soviet Union and Russia (1988–92)

Contents

Maps		x-xv
Preface		xvii

Part I

1	Pax Americana	3
2	Russia Elbowed Out	37
3	Western Europe Caves In	83
4	NATO Goes to War	99
5	Face to Face with Putin	114

Part II

6	Regime Change	151
7	Obama in Office	175
8	Maidan	193
9	The Road to Damascus	220
10	Trump Fails	227
11	Paying the Gas Bill	246

Conclusion: The War of the Russian Succession?	254
Sources	271
Endnotes	291
Acknowledgements	334
Index	335
About the Author	350

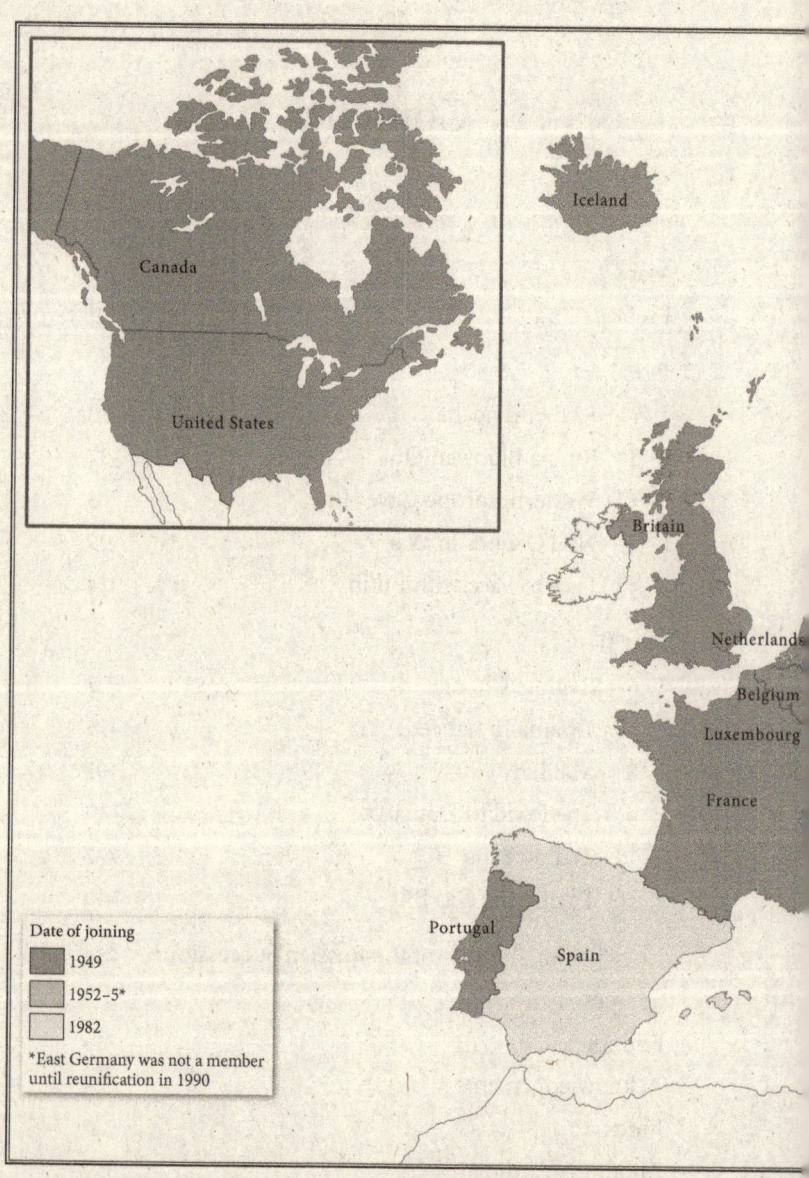

NATO Europe 1994

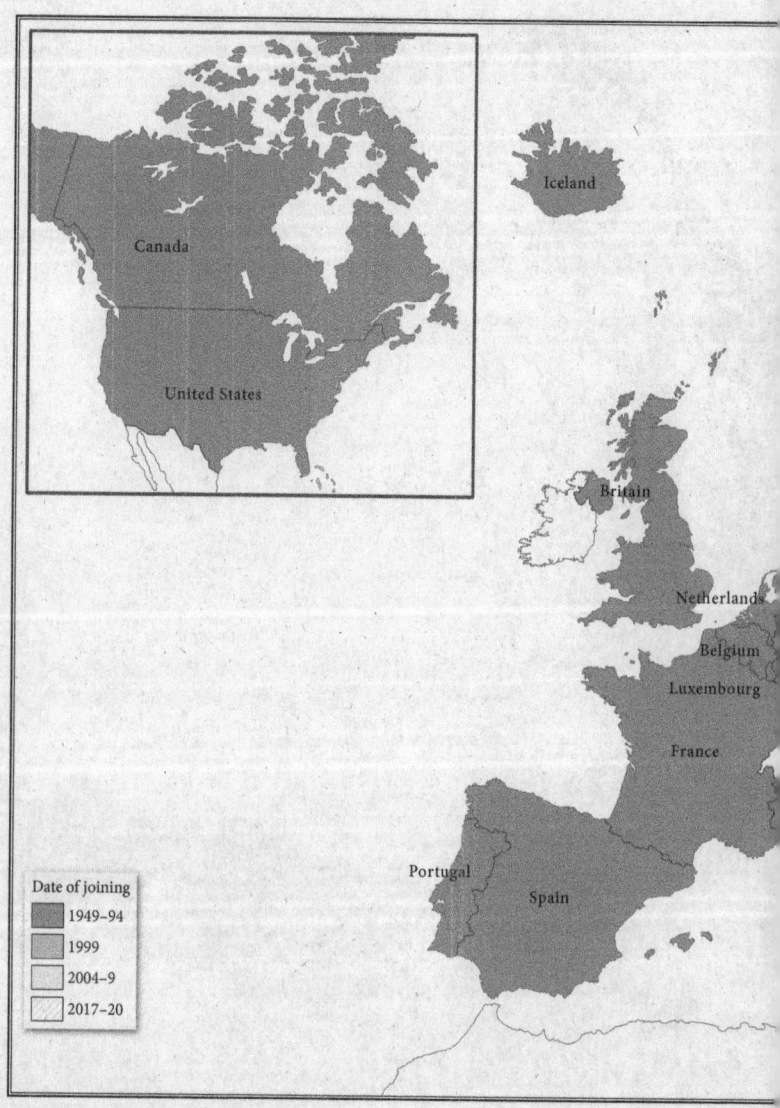

Expanded NATO Europe 2022

Russia-Ukraine, indicating Donetsk, Luhansk and Crimea

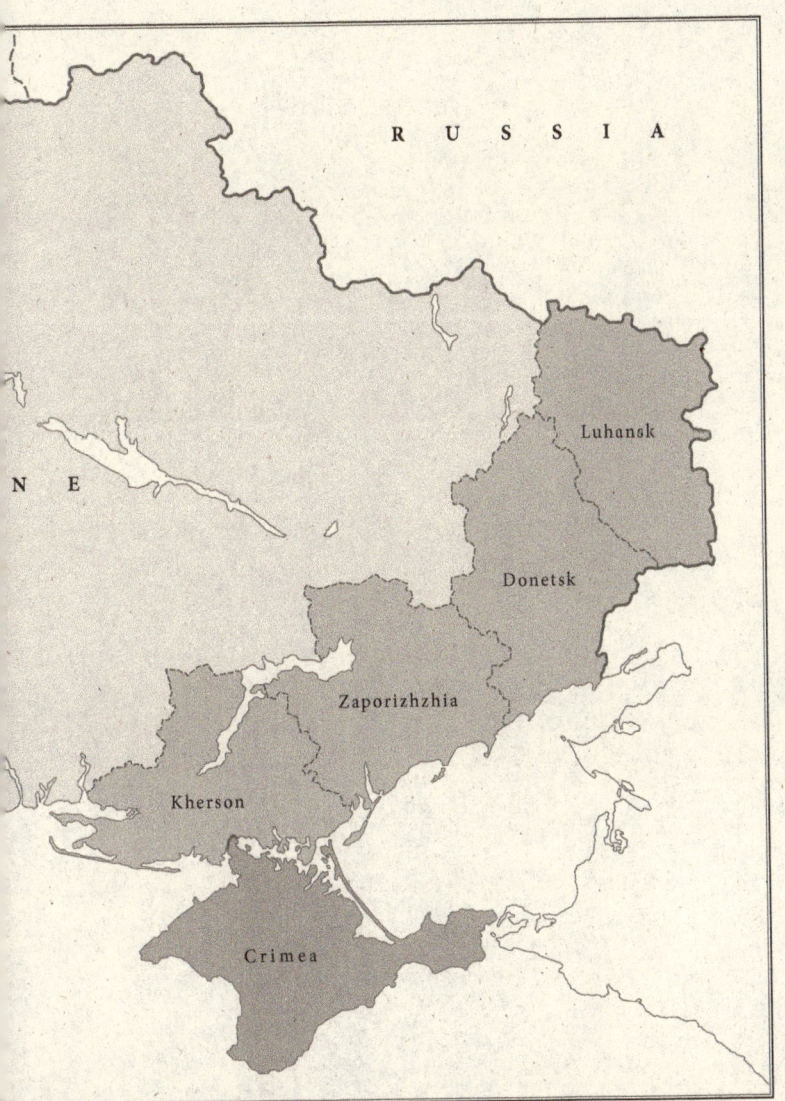

Preface

You might have thought that a book about the origins of Putin's war against Ukraine is all about *them*. But, certainly in the first instance, paradoxical though it may appear, it is also about *us*. And *us* means the United States and its allies in Western Europe.

How could this be so? The Cold War ended abruptly, and the Soviet Union collapsed in on itself. The foundations of Russia's communist empire had long been unsound. And it had weathered badly. Undoubtedly pressure from the West made its continuation increasingly difficult. But we did not bring the empire down. It fell of its own accord, at our feet. And how we responded was bound to make a great deal of difference to what rose up in its place.

The situation was complicated by the fact that the states of Eastern Europe liberated from the Nazis were reconstructed in the Soviet image after the Second World War. They were now unsurprisingly not content to wait and see what would emerge, given over forty years' subjugation to Soviet rule. Russia had always been an empire, in fact if not in name; it had no experience of democracy in our meaning of the term; and not since 1928 had Russia experienced even minimally a market economy as we would understand it.

Eastern Europe, which the Germans hastily renamed Central Europe in a diplomatic gesture of respect, did not hold the initiative, however. That lay with others, above all the country that remained the sole Superpower: the United States. But potentially also it lay with what had now become the European Union, an aspirant entity dominated by the Germans and the French. Germany reunited was distracted, however. It was preoccupied with economic and social reconstruction, so it was not in a position to create a new security architecture that would find a place for Russia. France on its own lacked heft. Britain invariably deferred to the United States. And the United States was afraid that if Western Europe reconstructed the continent along its own lines, the Americans would sooner or later be shut out.

To avert this alarming scenario, the North Atlantic Treaty Organization (NATO) had to be given new purpose. The former members of the Warsaw Pact – excluding Russia – were already looking for military integration with the West; something seen as more reassuring than being merely distant appendages of the European Union. An additional issue was whether former republics of the Soviet Union, which were determined to go their own way, would remain aligned with Russia, and, if so, at what cost to themselves. Ukraine, the most important of these, promptly decided on undiluted sovereignty, but also on non-alignment between Russia and the West. The problem was that neither Russia nor the United States was prepared to see this happen.

Part I

1

Pax Americana

> "I think the world is counting on us today as it has in the past... And they look to America not just to engage, but to lead... We do believe there are no limits on what is possible or what can be achieved... The United States can, must, and will lead in this new century."
>
> – Secretary of State Hillary Clinton, 8 September 2010.[1]

Signs that war is imminent are unmistakeable; impossible to conceal from prying eyes. Viewed from above on 23 February 2022, beneath tell-tale clouds of smoke Russians could be seen hurriedly burning classified papers in the courtyard of their embassy in Kyiv as they prepared for evacuation. A massive cyber-attack hit Ukrainian government communications systems. At 5.30 a.m. on the following day a pre-recorded announcement from Russia's President stated that a special military operation was under way to topple the government of Volodomyr Zelensky in Ukraine.[2] The assessment of the US Central Intelligence Agency (CIA) was that he intended a speedy, two-day Blitzkrieg.[3] Later, reporting from similar sources indicated that Russia's Federal Security Service (FSB) had penetrated the Ukrainian state apparatus, which Putin believed ready to launch a coup d'état as Russian troops entered Kyiv.[4]

In Washington DC the assessment was not very different. A year later, Under Secretary of State Victoria Nuland recalled that "virtually every analyst as they watched Putin get ready for this battle—and you'll remember that President Biden, Secretary Blinken, Secretary Austin began warning that Putin had this plan as far back as November of 2021. Most people predicted that if Putin invaded, he would have control of Ukraine, he would have control of Kyiv, he'd have control of the government within a matter of weeks."[5]

The briefings relied upon by the Kremlin and picked up by the Americans, however, turned out to be utterly misleading; indeed, wildly optimistic for the Russians. Women in Ukraine did not turn out to welcome their "liberators" with colourful bouquets, as some notoriously greeted the Germans in June 1941. At least one Russian-speaking grandmother in the countryside of eastern Ukraine, who had accumulated an arsenal of her own, took to shooting down Russian drones instead of ducks.[6] Meanwhile, complacent Russian military planning in northern Ukraine resulted in 40 miles of slow-moving vehicles in a queue on the main route to Kyiv. The bleak prospect of a rout then resulted in a vengeful campaign of unflinching ferocity and primeval savagery on the part of the Russians, recalling what had been inflicted on the Soviet Union by Nazis.

The halcyon days of optimism after the Cold War were long gone. Yet few, if any, seriously anticipated a war in our lifetime between two sovereign states, even on the margins of Europe. To understand why this happened and to focus purely on Vladimir Putin and his psychology is not enough, tempting as it is, even though from the outset the Russian media identified their president alone as the sole instigator of the war. His ill-tempered presence loomed over a bizarre meeting of the country's Security Council that was broadcast from the Kremlin on Russian television. Putin was seen publicly berating those officials who had evidently urged caution and wanted to avert a perilous war.

Putin as Consequence as well as Cause

One man is not an army, however. Biography, though essential, takes us only so far. There is certainly more to all of this than merely the sinister person of Putin, however powerful he had made himself. Radosław (Radek) Sikorski, Poland's former foreign minister (2007–14), can scarcely be accused of being pro-Russian. He wrote, well after Russia invaded Ukraine, that:

> Putin did not become today's Putin immediately, although the potential for violence was always there. He started as prime minister with a program of Russia's modernization with which we could live with and support. For some years he was on a convergence course with the West and was willing to spend political capital for the sake of economic integration with the European Union. After Chancellor Merkel [of Germany] told him that Poland had a veto power over Russia's association agreement with the EU, he tried to fix our relationship… But then, in 2011, when his return to the Kremlin was greeted with mass protests in Moscow and St Petersburg, he concluded that the West was trying to do to him what the West had done to Kadafi [Gaddafi]. He decided to create an alternative and rival pole of integration, the Euro-Asiatic Union, and he correctly concluded that it would not be a serious organization without Ukraine.[7]

In other words, Putin's stance was never completely rigid, even if his character was unwavering. There is much we still have to learn of his upbringing in postwar Leningrad. All we do know is that until he fixed upon a career in the KGB and was apprised of the need to succeed academically, he showed more aptitude and interest in developing his skills in martial arts than in his studies. But he was nonetheless ready to compromise when needs must. He read law at Leningrad University in spite of the urgings of his sole patron, a Judo instructor, because he was advised that this was the best route into the security services. After the collapse of the Soviet Union, he also rapidly adjusted to the reality of capitalism red in tooth and claw. But more of this later.

Western policy certainly played a role in Putin's balance of mind and that of the inner circle around him. After all, he succeeded to the presidency of Russia back in 2000. It took him more than a decade, until 2014, to seize Crimea, and even then only in retaliation for his loss of Kyiv. And, despite doing so, the balance of power on the continent still failed to move in his direction. Putin did not finally seek to conquer Ukraine proper and topple its government until 2022. So if it were merely a matter of personal ambition, why the delay? As we have seen from the battles fought in the course of this war, it is not as though most of Russia's armed forces were in a much better condition in 2022 than they had been two decades before; morale was a good deal worse, and the Ukrainians could not believe the primitive state of Russian tanks.

The decision to resort to war is not usually taken lightly, even where the chance of success is within reach. So what exactly occurred in the years between that brought Putin to this point? What problem did he imagine that he was trying to solve? And how is it that in so doing Putin has largely carried his collaborators with him – at least those that did not flee to neighbouring states, succumb to an obscure poison, fall out of high-rise windows or die in an adventitious plane crash – even in the face of calamitous setbacks that, to say the least, call into question his judgement and that of those he has relied upon most?

The United States certainly knew that Putin identified the West as a threat. After the annexation of the Crimean peninsula from Ukraine on 20 February 2014, the National Intelligence Officer for Russia under President Barack Obama, Eugene Rumer, suggested that:

> Russia's actions in Ukraine were entirely logical, perhaps even inevitable, as an extension of Russian threat perceptions. Seen from Moscow, the rapid changes in Ukrainian

politics – the collapse of the presidency of Viktor Yanukovych and the coming to power of a political coalition advocating Ukraine's pro-European and Euro-Atlantic orientation, including eventual membership in the European Union and the North Atlantic Treaty Organization – carried with them profound political consequences… they signalled the emergence of new threats right at its doorstep, threats that no Russian leader is likely to tolerate without a wholesale change in the country's ideology and understanding of its national security.[8]

So we are at once transported into the psychology of "threat perceptions". How real were they? Was Putin the only figure who took this view? The fact that Russia's main enemy, the United States, persistently sustained and enhanced its presence in post-Cold War Europe is not something that should be dismissed out of hand. In Moscow it very quickly became an obsessive fixation.

The best reputed National Intelligence Officer for Russia under President Reagan was Fritz Ermarth. He commented: "Putin, Putinism, and the behavior of the Putin regime are very much a product of, as a backlash to, Russian developments in the late 80s and the 90s…"[9] Ermarth always deserved to be taken seriously. Putin's rise to power is to be understood not as some whimsical act of fate but as a product of Russian conditions, which most certainly did not evolve in an international vacuum. They were intimately bound up with, and largely dependent upon relations with the West. Russia was weak and internally divided following the collapse of the Soviet Union. These events occurred well before Putin acquired a leading role in his country's foreign policy, when the country was still in turmoil after the empire unravelled.

On 24 February 2022 Putin asked why Russia had been so consistently disdained by the West for more than two decades. It was, he had no doubt, all about power and the balance of power. "The answer is clear;" Putin said, "everything is understandable and obvious. The Soviet Union at the end of the eighties in the last century became weak and then completely collapsed." As a consequence Russia suffered "a paralysis of power". "It cost us when for some time we lost confidence in ourselves and that was it—the balance of power in the world was broken."[10] No country is more conscious of the critical importance of power than when that power has abruptly been swept away. For Putin, and he was not alone in this, loss of power fast became a fixation. And this has so often been the very point at which a state is potentially at its most menacing to immediate neighbours.

On Putin's view, it was not just the fact of the Soviet Union's sudden collapse that caused so much damage, but also the reaction to it from its former adversaries. What exacerbated defeat was the unconstrained outburst of triumphalism that the United States found so hard to resist. The élite in Washington abjured the spirit of Lord Castlereagh who made peace in 1815 by including defeated France within the new Concert of Europe; the advice of the Liberal economist Keynes to prop up Germany economically after its sudden, unexpected collapse in 1918, instead of imposing draconian reparations; or the enlightened attitude that could be summed up in Winston Churchill's wise words after the next great conflict in 1945: "In victory, magnanimity".

Matters were made worse by the fact that Russia had never been a "normal" state. It had always been an empire of some kind. The word Tsar, after all, means Caesar. Losing an entire empire at one fell swoop is a devastating blow to the self-esteem of any proud metropolis. This resonates with the Spanish, the Portuguese or the Dutch, as the rulers of the known world in earlier times. In the early 1960s France under President Charles de Gaulle grudgingly let go of an overseas empire and became a country obsessed with national prestige where even the survival of its language had to be defended to the last against the "cultural imperialism" of the Anglo-Saxons. Margaret Thatcher's war to defend and recover the Falkland Islands/Las Malvinas after Argentina's invasion in the early 1980s resonated through the home counties of England with the evocative spirit of post-imperial revenge.

Why should we expect Russia to be so different? US Secretary of Defense and former director of CIA Robert Gates, an experienced Kremlinologist, long accustomed to Russian ways, certainly understood. He put his regret on record: "The arrogance, after the collapse, of American government officials, academicians, businessmen, and politicians in telling the Russians how to conduct their domestic and international affairs (not to mention the internal psychological impact of their precipitous fall from superpower status) had led to deep and long-term resentment and bitterness."[11]

The Russian people were utterly baffled at the lightning speed with which their apparently mighty country – a cradle to the grave welfare state, however threadbare – completely disintegrated around them, to be reconstituted into an array of independent states desperate to be free of Russian control. Its trauma was made all the worse because it was a contiguous land empire. In Putin's words, "millions of Russians [who] went to sleep in one country... woke up abroad".[12] The sum total was estimated at 25 million. It left Russia's ruling class shaken as liberated nations and their sponsors in the West popped open the champagne. The Americans and their allies at long last witnessed what had always been intended to happen through four long decades of sustained sacrifice.

The objective had originally been defined in NSC-58/1, a memorandum written by George Kennan, the architect of US containment of the Soviet Union, in December 1949 when heading the all-powerful Policy Planning Staff at the US State Department. It finally bore fruit almost exactly four decades later when the Berlin Wall collapsed. The division of Germany that had scarred Europe since 1945 had finally ended, paving the way to German reunification. President George Bush ('41)[*] was blunt: "The Soviet

---

[*] Hereafter I have followed the current American practice of distinguishing between George Bush senior ('41) and George Bush junior ('43) by the dated sequence of US presidents.

Union did not simply lose the cold war; the Western democracies won it."[13] Not without reason the more reflective Secretary of Defense Les Aspin, under President Clinton, lamented: "America crows that it won the Cold War".[14]

Stephen Hadley became Special Advisor to President Bush ('43) for National Security Affairs on 26 January 2005. He never laid claim to be a Russia specialist. Yet Hadley, too, came to see clearly the fundamental nature of the problem, even if it did not attenuate his recommendations when in office:

> This humiliation narrative, this fall from power, this lack of respect, it's in Putin's perceptions, but it's also in the perceptions of the Russian people. And when people many times overstate how much Russian foreign policy is Putin's policy, and how much is he reflecting actually the impulses, the anxieties, the frustrations, the sense of loss of respect, of humiliation of the Russian people, I think you have to see Putin as someone who is, yes, shaping public opinion in Russia, but also reflecting public opinion in Russia. And to simply say the problem with US-Russian relations is just about Putin is a very inadequate explanation.[15]

Hadley had it right, at least in retrospect, though not at the time. Voices from Moscow have consistently confirmed as much. "With the end of the Cold War", *Nezavisimaya gazeta* recently pointed out, "the West decided that the former approach to international relations through the prism of geopolitical interests was over. The world must be constructed by asserting universal values important for all: human rights, the struggle with climate change, freedom of trade and the universal extension of the appropriate institutions." This has not worked, however. "The fundamental mistake is based on the impression that the West in its role as victor of the Cold War would decide not only the rules of the game but as victor of the self-same game; if one cannot for some reason win by the rules."[16]

"Forgive and forget" does not generally happen for generations unless an entirely new and greater common threat has suddenly emerged to blot out the past. It would be well to remember this unpleasant truth about the relations between states.

The collapse of the Soviet Union as a Superpower marked a stunning victory for liberalism globally, an unintended and unanticipated gift to the capitalist order. But it also brought its own problems. In Russia the black market became *the* market, never entirely disconnected from organized crime even if across the rest of the world it inaugurated an era of extraordinary opportunity for those with access to ready capital. For the first time since 1914 the world market was restored and the USA was the country in the best position to benefit from it. Was it not inevitable that the Americans, the Soviet Union's main rivals who had invested so much treasure and shed so much blood in the destruction of communism, would seek to dominate at every turn in the aftermath? Perhaps. But was it also inevitable that the United States would seek to move bag and baggage into the Soviet sphere of influence and, indeed, onto former Soviet soil in what became known as "the near abroad", when Russia had packed up and was on the point of leaving? Those Americans who were engaged in this enterprise knew exactly what they were doing. The US government was made keenly aware at every stage of the negative impact on Russia of NATO expansion to the East. Indeed, it acted consistently against the best specialist advice within and outside government, most notably in the teeth of strong opposition from the hitherto mighty Pentagon.

Attitudes towards Russia were mostly dismissive, enough to appal Clinton's second Secretary of Defense, mathematical physicist Bill Perry, a veteran of the Cold War since the Cuban missile crisis of October 1962. When those in the administration repeatedly heard that the Russians objected to US policy, Perry reports that the dismissive response was: "What could they do about it?"[17] It had evidently not occurred to those who derided Russia as of no account what trouble the former enemy, wounded but still alive, could cause; what humiliation would do to those managing Russian foreign policy, nostalgic for past prestige, who had to answer to an elected legislature voted into place by a massively disillusioned, bewildered and disgruntled populace.

It might be said that most victorious states would have behaved in the same way as the United States did. Machiavelli implies as much in *The Prince*, on the assumption that most men "are not good".[18] In the American case, however, it was a little more complicated. And this leads us down into the rabbit warren of US domestic politics in the 1990s, following the decisions of one insecure and distracted president preoccupied with gaining a second term – Bill Clinton – through to an even more indecisive president, George Bush ('43), frightened of making bad judgements and answering to dominant and more experienced neo-conservative elders arguably possessed of no greater wisdom. It is here in Washington DC that reasons of state meet and dissolve in the face of opinion expressed through Congress; so much so that any notion of a foreign policy freely conducted by the executive as a rational response to external conditions – much beloved of conventionally minded political scientists wedded to "rational actor theory" – is to say the least an idealization of grim realities.

For these reasons the war in Ukraine has to be seen in the context of the tension that re-emerged between Russia and the West with the assertion of US global hegemony and the failure to design a post-Cold War security architecture in Europe. It helps explain an intriguing and sobering paradox: why, once Russia finally invaded Ukraine in 2022, and in spite of well publicized atrocities by Russian forces, equal to those committed in Syria and the remnants of Yugoslavia, almost to a man Putin's administration, including all but one of his entire diplomatic corps, fell in lock step behind him despite deep personal misgivings about the resort to war. And it was almost certainly not just from fear for personal safety, though that was and is real enough, because even under Stalin at his most brutal in the late 1930s, diplomats and intelligence officers defected to the West, even when they were terrified for their own survival and that of their families back home. Only former generals and retired colonels spoke out in condemnation, led by rabid nationalist Leonid Ivashov, driven into early retirement by Putin back in 2001 at the age of 57.

When war broke out, a credible witness at the very centre of events, Andrei Kortunov, General Director of the semi-official Council for International Affairs, acknowledged that many of his colleagues in the Russian Ministry of Foreign Affairs at Smolenka were, like him, "totally astonished, shocked and stunned".[19] However shaken, the Ministry none the less supported the war in the firm belief that the West had long ago turned its back on Russia at the time of its greatest vulnerability, in order to expand into the countries of the former Soviet Union, its "near abroad".

We have, therefore, to explain how it came about that interminable difficulties in East-West relations underpinned Putin's war, however hard this is to comprehend. What, then, were the turning points down this road to perdition?

The sudden and unexpected declaration of former President Clinton that it was, indeed, he who from the outset had initiated the expansion of NATO to the East is of considerable significance; particularly given the additional claim that the war against Ukraine showed just how farsighted he had been. This assumes of course that NATO's eastern enlargement had played no role in what Russia had become and what it did in 2022, which, of course, Clinton had necessarily to deny.

"Lately," Clinton asserted on 10 April 2022, "NATO expansion has been criticized in some quarters for provoking Russia and even laying the groundwork for Vladimir Putin's invasion of Ukraine. The expansion certainly was a consequential decision, one that I continue to believe was correct."[20] Former Secretary of State Warren Christopher comfortably took the same view: "the historical record ought to give Clinton a lot of credit for NATO expansion. It would not have happened without him, and it would not have happened nearly as rapidly without his pushing it."[21] "I think", added Deputy Secretary of State Talbott, "that perhaps

– not entirely objectively – that having our cake and eating it too with regard to NATO enlargement and the NATO-Russian partnership was one of the important accomplishments of the Clinton presidency."[22] But gluttony invariably has unpleasant consequences, as we all know; if not immediately, then not long thereafter, which was surely true in this particular instance.

Condoleezza Rice served as Special Advisor to the President on National Security and later Secretary of State to President Bush ('43). Confronted with the disaster of Putin's war on Ukraine, she indecently hastened to acquit herself and, indeed, it seems, everyone else in Washington DC, of being even remotely at fault in the handling of post-Soviet Russia. At the Aspen security forum, where the like-minded gather for mutual reassurance, in July 2022 Rice confidently dismissed all doubt, asserting that "everyone from the Clinton administration to the Bush administration, to the Obama administration, to the Trump administration did everything possible to try to integrate Russia into the international system".[23]

Really? Distance certainly lends enchantment. The dispassionate observer might be forgiven for thinking that perhaps Rice protests too much. The expansion of NATO, the most important innovation of US foreign policy in those years, scarcely enhanced Russia's integration into the international system; indeed, the Russians vehemently objected to it, repeatedly and for one very simple reason. It left Russia firmly out in the cold, against every assurance, assurances that were repeated time and again. Amid the embarrassing chorus of self-serving justification there was only one glaring exception: former Foreign Minister of France Roland Dumas, who did not hesitate to remind us that back in the days of German reunification: "The West had promised that NATO would not extend to Russia's doorstep."[24]

It is thus not as though Clinton and Rice were never warned. Because no war of this kind ever appeared likely on their watch, they blithely assumed such an outcome was never possible; and not for want of repeated misgivings expressed by

European statesmen. Had not that same complete lack of imagination as to the threat posed by al-Qaeda exposed the United States to 9/11? French President Jacques Chirac reminded the Americans more than once that, although Russia had swallowed much without striking out, there could well be adverse consequences down the road: "the future is very long", he cautioned. No one could plausibly claim that the Russia policy of these administrations met with universal acclaim or easy acceptance even within the United States or among its closest allies; and certainly not among those best acquainted with the Soviet Union as an adversary, whether in or out of government. America's best known and most authoritative Russianist was George Kennan, the originator of containment, the strategy to block Soviet expansion across the postwar world; he later held a Chair at the Institute for Advanced Study in Princeton. At the beginning of 1997, by which time it was already too late, having lobbied incessantly those he knew in government to no avail, Kennan went public with the argument that "expanding NATO would be the most fateful error of American policy in the entire post-cold-war era". He predicted that "Such a decision may be expected to inflame the nationalistic, anti-Western and militaristic tendencies in Russian opinion; to have an adverse effect on the development of Russian democracy; to restore the atmosphere of the cold war to East-West relations, and to impel Russian foreign policy in directions decidedly not to our liking." Kennan added "It is, of course, unfortunate that Russia should be confronted with such a challenge at a time when its executive power is in a state of high uncertainty and near-paralysis."[25]

Although invariably Olympian in his judgements, Kennan was by no means unique in his objections. The dramatic, public advice against "a policy error of historic proportions" was repeated on 26 June in the strongest terms by means of an open letter addressed to Clinton by fifty former senators, ambassadors and civil servants. Prominent among them were former Chairman of the Senate Armed Services Committee, the hard-nosed Sam Nunn, former ambassadors to Moscow Arthur Hartman and Jack Matlock, who advised Reagan, former Secretary of Defense Robert McNamara, Eisenhower's notoriously Machiavellian national security adviser Bob Bowie, and Reagan's trusted arms control negotiator and the author of NSC/68, the blueprint for the militarization of the Cold War with the creation of NATO in 1950, that wily survivor Paul Nitze.[26] Even as hard-headed an analyst such as Tony Lake, the Special Advisor to the President for National Security under Clinton, acknowledged Russia's "psychological trauma".[27] The former national security adviser Zbigniew Brzezinski, invariably a Pole at heart, was unperturbed and stood apart from the rest: utterly dismissive of what he contemptuously derided as "misguided psychotherapeutic theories regarding how to deal with the Russians".[28] Yet even he argued for a far more limited expansion of NATO than actually occurred.

Moscow Reassured by Word of Mouth Alone

The fact that while the Soviet Union was still visibly crumbling the Russians were promised authoritatively that NATO would not expand to the East has been repeatedly denied; and these promises have been cloaked and muffled in a veritable fog of evasion, half-truths and equivocation.[29] Russia subsequently published an embarrassingly long laundry list of the empty assurances given at various times by the great and the good.[30] On 2 February 1990 German Foreign Minister Hans-Dietrich Genscher outlined German plans for reunification to Gorbachev, letting him know that "NATO would not extend its territorial coverage to the area of the GDR [East Germany] nor anywhere else in Eastern Europe". Taking the lead, a week later, on 9 February 1990, Secretary of State Jim Baker told Soviet Foreign Minister Eduard Shevardnadze that, following German reunification, there would be "iron-clad guarantees that NATO's jurisdiction or forces would not move eastward". Mikhail Gorbachev was assured later in the afternoon that "there would be no extension of NATO's jurisdiction for forces of NATO one inch to the east" if Germany reunified.[31] On the following day Chancellor Kohl told Gorbachev: "We consider that NATO must not expand its sphere of action. We need to find a reasonable way of regulating this. I fully understand the Soviet Union's security interests..." On 6 March John Major, Britain's Prime Minister, was more explicit: he "does not foresee conditions currently or in the future under which the East European countries could be in NATO". Only President Mitterrand of France, inveterately suspicious by nature, disrupted the earnest chorus of reassurances. After a conversation with Gorbachev on 6 May, he noted that he could foresee former members of the Warsaw Pact signing up with NATO. But he warned that this would "reinforce a sense of isolation, encirclement even, in the Soviet Union. I am certain that such a direction would not be right for Europe."[32]

With understandings in place, on 23 August 1990 German reunification was settled between the interested powers. The Soviet government – now on its last legs – had tried to insert a clause precluding a united Germany's membership of NATO but Gorbachev, by now worn to the bone, gave up the idea as unrealistic. None the less the Russians remained nervous at the likely long-term consequences of reunification. Lt General Brent Scowcroft was Special Assistant for National Security to President Bush ('41). He acknowledged that even membership of NATO by a reunited Germany was "the Soviet Union's worst nightmare"[33]; let alone further expansion of NATO to the East. Of course, nothing "iron-clad" was ever formulated on paper, let alone by treaty.

The multiple reassurances were, however, never forgotten by the Russians. Every new accession to NATO came as a needling reminder of what had been so sincerely promised and so casually tossed away. Russia felt it had been stood up at the altar with not even a ring to prove it had been there. Inevitably trust was severely undermined and this gap between word and deed inevitably undercut the US-Russian relationship. Seven years later the fact that previous undertakings had been broken was raised by Moscow when negotiating the establishment of a NATO-Russia Council with the Americans. Foreign Minister Yevgeny Primakov, who had been head of foreign intelligence in 1990, not surprisingly insisted that any new agreement between the two parties be legally binding, unlike the previous undertakings on NATO expansion.[34] Moscow's persistent demands on this point took fully into account the fact that US administrations had shown that they did not feel bound by commitments entered into by their predecessors when they were not in writing, let alone those not ratified by the Senate.

Indeed, it was in recognition of such concerns that at a meeting in Brussels in May 1990 NATO's Secretary General, the former German Defence Minister Manfred Wörner, had announced the "main objective in the next decade", which "will be the construction of a new European security structure encompassing the Soviet Union and the Warsaw Pact. The Soviet Union will play a significant role in the construction of this system. If you take into account the Soviet Union's current dilemma, having in effect no allies any longer, then one can understand their reasonable desire not to be pushed out of Europe."[35] The image of integration was beguiling, and the European partners in NATO seemed to be reliable guarantors. In March 1991, for example, Genscher reminded Baker that "At the 2+4 negotiations [between West and East Germany plus the Soviet Union, the United States, France and Britain] the Soviet Union was given to understand that there is no intention of NATO expanding to the East."[36] In conversation with the German permanent representative to NATO, Hans von Ploetz, a month later, Wörner explained the situation in Russia. The fear in Moscow was that even acceptance of NATO's continuation over the long term would strengthen Gorbachev's opponents. And Wörner, in talks with the Russians, had "already made clear that NATO was not seeking a change in the balance of power or enlargement of the military boundaries to the East".[37]

In May a Franco-German conference of ambassadors reviewed

the situation. Klaus Blech, Germany's ambassador to Moscow, pointed to "the development of a new security problem" that was not so much objective as it was rooted in the Russian "state of mind": the belief that matters had been allowed to slide over the past two years. "For the future it is important for the west that the Soviet Union does not turn back on its way to Europe", he insisted. The danger that it would lurch into isolation was real. "The outlook is for a truly nationalistic greater Russia with the collapse of the Soviet Union." [38]

Meanwhile the states of Eastern Europe were undergoing an identity crisis. Looking to the distant past provided few guidelines, in that the problem of national minorities had plagued the region. These were not homogenous nation states from 1919.[39] Far from it, the existence of German minority populations, for example, had presented Adolf Hitler with ready opportunities to pursue a strategy of divide and conquer. In 1939–40 and later in 1945 Stalin had redistributed territory in the region to Russian, Byelorussian and Ukrainian advantage, no doubt calculating that maintenance of the new order would rest on Moscow's enforcement.

One clear sign of Russian insecurity was a clumsy proposal echoing the Rapallo Pact of 16 April 1922 put forward by Foreign Minister Alexander Bessmertnykh, an Americanist by training and now a deeply resentful nationalist. He made a pass at the Germans, suggesting the creation of a firmly rooted alignment – "*Kernlinie*" – between the two countries without which, he claimed, Europe could have no future, but with it, the two could become "a significant factor in world politics".[40] Such seductive suggestions were, of course, precisely why Germany's allies were so insistent on it remaining at the centre of NATO and why Germany was so committed to that reassurance. But the approach was not as odd as it might seem at first sight. The Germans never assumed that the Americans would remain in Europe. When he visited St Petersburg in 1991, Chancellor Kohl met the young Vladimir Putin at the Mayor's office, then heading its department for foreign relations. Putin asked for his perspective on the future of relations between Germany and Russia. Kohl said that in twenty to thirty years China and India would be strong and the United States would be going its own way.[41]

Nothing, however, could have been further from White House thinking. And its consequences for the future of Russia were momentous. Himself a thorough-going realist, Secretary of State Baker's counsellor Robert Zoellick recalls that none of those managing US foreign policy ever had any intention of working with the Russians. The Secretary was instead, as Machiavelli would have expected, intent on drawing maximum short-term advantage: "in Baker's terms, kind of gather what you could, put it in your basket while you can".[42] Which was, of course, exactly the opposite of what Baker had led the Russians to believe he would do. Indeed, on 9 February 1990 he had purposefully assured Gorbachev that "neither the President nor I intend to extract any unilateral advantages from the processes that are taking place".[43] The deception continued for over a decade. And Gorbachev, desperately clutching at straws, was trusting enough to believe that the Americans were sincere.

Under Bush, the West Divided

Not that NATO was of one mind. What emerges from declassified archives and direct testimony is that, from the outset, the allies were divided as to what should be the best future course of action. Germany struck out in one direction, the US administration in another. The resourceful and ever-confident German Foreign Minister Hans-Dietrich Genscher had no doubt that a solution to the security issues could be found "with a bit of European imagination". He took the view that the former satellite states of the Soviet Union would very soon become members of the European Economic Community. Russia was not likely to object. The situation with respect to NATO, however, even as to "the little East European countries", was entirely another matter.

Their membership "would severely irritate Moscow, which was in no one's interest". Instead, he had assured the Czech Foreign Minister, Jiří Dienstbier, that the Soviet Union would be integrated "as an equal partner in a European security structure" (*Friedensordnung*) while the countries of Central and Eastern Europe would join pan-European institutions ("also not NATO") for their security. The Conference on Security and Co-operation in Europe (CSCE), which harked back to the Helsinki declaration in 1975, seemed a convenient vessel for that purpose. It would become an organization in its own right. "It is very important for Moscow", Genscher continued, "that a satisfactorily integrated security policy is found for Poland and for the Czechoslovakian Socialist Republic outside NATO, otherwise there would be too great a fear that republics leaving the Soviet Union would also want to join NATO. The USSR would never accept this."[44]

On this matter Germany and France were agreed, initially at least. The Americans, however, felt slighted at this vision of an exclusive post-Cold War European order that threatened to shut them out. But early American attempts to hijack the process were not appreciated. At a routine NATO meeting, the former French Foreign Minister Roland Dumas vividly recalls, President Bush ('41) confidently suggested that he deliver a speech about the future of the alliance: the transformation of NATO into a more universal body for defence against the sum of all dangers to the world. The French President bristled at anything even remotely suggesting that NATO take on commitments "out of area". He could barely contain his fury. "If you wish to change it [NATO], we would need an additional meeting", Mitterrand said, "a big conference with it up for discussion. But we do not want to give our agreement today, just like that, off the cuff [*à la sauvette*]... Are you out to recreate the Holy Alliance?"[45] He added: "If you wish to modify the Treaty, let us summon a peace conference, if you like; we're ready. But today, given how things are, it is something that hasn't been discussed; it looks too much like reviving the Cold War. Out of respect for the President of the United States, we won't vote against; we will abstain."⁴⁶ With that, the French effectively kicked the ball firmly into touch.

It is telling that no such conference ever took place. Instead Bush, undaunted, eventually confronted Mitterrand in person over what divided them. The airing of French objections at the US attempt to bolster NATO led everyone to suspect that they would have preferred the Americans to leave Europe altogether, Bush suggested. After all, France under General Charles De Gaulle had abandoned the integrated military structure of NATO in 1966 precisely to escape American control over its defence planning. President Lyndon Johnson had promptly moved NATO bag and baggage out of Paris and deposited it outside Brussels, also leaving France at the tail end of intelligence sharing.

For his part Mitterrand did not hold back from attacking Bush: "Since the collapse of the Soviet Union, I haven't understood the reasons why you're trying to give NATO a new content. At the time that the threat of war is receding, it seems you want NATO's mission to expand. Why is this? You never discussed it with us. What does the US want more [of] than it had before?" Taken aback and tongue tied, Bush lapsed into a stunned silence. Baker's hastily scrambled, inarticulate improvisation to cover for the president scarcely rang true.⁴⁷

Behind it all lurked the undeniable fact that the ultimate aim of rolling back the Russians from their postwar occupation of Central and Eastern Europe had finally been achieved. The "Defense Planning Guidance" drafted by Under Secretary for Policy Paul Wolfowitz and issued under Secretary Dick Cheney's hawkish and watchful eye at the Pentagon found it deeply reassuring that "for the foreseeable future the continued fragmentation of the former Soviet state and its conventional armed forces have altered so fundamentally the character of the residual threat as to eliminate the capacity to wage global conventional war or even to threaten East/Central Europe without several months of warnings."⁴⁸

The anomaly, however, was that the Americans were

determined to remain in Europe come what may, even where no apparent need could be found. Once the daunting threat from Soviet military power collapsed, the rationale for NATO as a standing alliance, an historical anomaly by any standard, was hard to sustain. It was the resolute determination of the United States to hold fast regardless that requires explanation, as much as the adverse Russian reaction to it.

On 8 March 1990, with German reunification on the horizon, Mitterrand was invited to lunch at the White House. Brent Scowcroft, the Assistant to the President for National Security Affairs, was "looking for some kind of initiative that they [the Americans] could launch to justify their role in the new Europe. They are worried at the prospect of their military presence becoming unjustifiable."[49] He was certainly not alone. The United States permanent representative to NATO, Robert Hunter, a veteran of Washington DC, once pointed out that allowing the US to leave would have been a disaster for American interests. "In fact, we'd gotten to the point where we couldn't withdraw from Europe without doing fundamental damage to ourselves. Economically, as much as anything. On the economic side, during the Cold War, the strategic glue helped us over economic problems. Since the end of the Cold War, economic glue has helped us over strategic problems, because we have a three trillion dollar annual relationship, we can't damage that."[50] This was also how Britain's Foreign Secretary Douglas Hurd saw matters. The veteran *Washington Post* journalist Michael Dobbs took the view that "Supporters see NATO enlargement as critical to preserving the institution that has guaranteed an American presence in Europe for the past half-century."[51] Note his choice of terms: not guaranteed the peace, but guaranteed a US "presence".

All was not lost, however. Scowcroft had a solution in mind: "We need to create a political framework that would enable us to justify our military presence despite the absence of an enemy."[52] And what would become of NATO? As of 1993 Clinton's incoming Secretary of State Warren Christopher worried about the alliance "decaying", given that the very reason for its existence had disappeared.[53] This was also very much the preoccupation of Tony Lake, Scowcroft's feline successor at the White House, who talked Clinton into unveiling an ambitious international agenda that dwarfed his predecessor's idea of an out-of-area adjunct to the alliance. Deputy Under Secretary for Defense Walter Slocombe took one determined step further. The end of the Soviet Union did not pose "the familiar problem of averting or containing or reversing a threatening development, but of how to make use of an opportunity".[54]

For their part, at that moment the Russians had no time to fret much about the external world. They had an overwhelming array of tasks to undertake at home, and in foreign trade they tended to wait for their former partners to come to them. Russia made a great mistake in not re-engaging with the countries of Central and Eastern Europe as equals, at the very least to renew pre-existing trade arrangements, now that the Warsaw Pact had dissolved and the Council for Mutual Economic Assistance (Comecon) along with it. A vacuum enveloped relations with Eastern Europe at a seminal moment in Russia's economic and political regeneration that was entirely to its disadvantage.[55]

Moreover, Russia seriously underestimated the massive reputational damage inflicted by Gorbachev's bloody attempted coup in Lithuania in January 1991, which had the immediate effect of driving the Balts, and not only them, in the direction of NATO.[56] In Czechoslovakia Václav Havel, the heroic dissident of Charter 77, the anti-communist resistance in Czechoslovakia, was now president of his country. He complained to the Germans that the dissolution of the Warsaw Pact left Czechoslovakia in a vacuum without being a part of NATO. This baffled the Germans, given that the threat had disappeared. Berlin was thus completely unreceptive. Officials at the Auswärtige Amt were insistent that the Czechs should understand the "damaging" impact of their complaint on "conservative political and military circles in Moscow" and that "without the involvement of the Soviet Union security in Europe can only be confrontational and not co-operative".[57] Germany thus fully understood the state of mind in Moscow. But was anyone listening?

Entirely in character, Havel ignored the German plea to move carefully on Russia. Instead he continued to insist that the countries of Central and Eastern Europe "do not feel themselves to be part of Russia's sphere of interest, of its 'near abroad', and they are upset by certain sounds which have of late been heard in relation to Russia's foreign policy to the effect that there should be more specific relations between our countries and Russia, and so forth".[58] Invited to a high level meeting at NATO in the autumn Havel drew the obvious conclusion that his hosts were not ready for: "We would like some sort of institutionalisation of relations with NATO and would accept some form of associate membership." At which point Secretary Baker, caught off guard, stepped in awkwardly to blurt out that he was "not sure it [NATO] will go so far".[59] Havel therefore had to await a change of administration in Washington DC before his project could be realized. He had as yet little or no public support for this. At that time only 36 per cent of the Czechoslovakian population backed the idea of joining NATO, and even after entry the number did not rise above 56 per cent.[60]

Moreover, it is not as if leading Russians failed to discharge a warning shot across the bows of NATO. On 14 December 1992 at a meeting of the Conference on Security and Co-operation in Europe, Russia's frustrated young Foreign Minister, Andrei Kozyrev, startled the assembled company with a satirical rendition of policy were the communist and ultra-nationalist opposition to come to power:

> First: while fully maintaining the policy of entry into Europe, we clearly recognize that our traditions in many respects, if not fundamentally, lie in Asia, and this sets limits to our rapprochement with Western Europe. We see, along with some degree of evolution, essentially unchanged strategies

on the part of NATO and the WEU [West European Union], which are drawing up plans to reinforce their military presence in the Baltic and other regions on the territory of the former Soviet Union, and to interfere in Bosnia and the internal affairs of Yugoslavia. Clearly sanctions against the SRY [Socialist Republic of Yugoslavia] were dictated by this policy. We demand that they be lifted, and if this does not happen, we reserve our right to take the unilateral measures necessary to defend our interests, especially since they cause us economic damage. In its present struggle the Government of Serbia can count on the support of Russia as a Great Power.

Second: the lands of the former Soviet Union cannot be seen as a space for the complete application of CSCE norms. Essentially, this is a post-imperial space, in which Russia has to defend its interests, using all available means, both military and economic. We shall strongly insist that the former republics of the USSR join without delay the new Federation or Confederation, and there will be tough negotiations about this.

Third: all those who think that they can disregard these distinctive features and interests, or that Russia will undergo the fate of the Soviet Union, should not forget that we are talking of a state capable of standing up for itself and its friends. We are of course, ready to play a constructive part in the work of the CSCE Council, although we shall be very cautious in our approach to ideas leading to interference in internal affairs.[61]

A stunned silence descended. Everyone stared at their shoelaces; no one quite knew what to say. But in the end Kozyrev was easily dismissed as a lightweight, a diplomatic *ingénu*, at a mere forty years of age barely halfway upstairs. His ruse did not go down well. It simply left a bad taste in the mouth. The text was not even published in the Russian press. It could, however, easily have been penned by Putin on assuming power nearly a decade later. Predictably the warning, like the many others to come, went unheeded.

The Clinton Administration

That such omens were casually dismissed most certainly had nothing to do with the intelligence of those targeted. There were other reasons. Clinton had absolutely no sense of direction in foreign policy. He had little more at his disposal than parting words from Bush ('41) that he should seize the initiative and prevent the United States from drifting into self-imposed isolation. The US mission, Bush declared, was to further the cause of democracy across the globe. "The advance of democratic ideals reflects a hard-nosed sense of our own American self-interest", he had insisted. "Strategically, abandonment of the worldwide democratic revolution could be disastrous for American security."[62] This was to be the mantra of the next two decades.

Clinton's drift in foreign policy was not allowed to continue indefinitely. "In the aftermath of the collapse of the Soviet Union", notes Eric Edelman, then Under Secretary of Defense for Policy, "... there was this search for... the animating principle of US foreign policy."[63] Predictably, after nearly a year in office, Clinton echoed his successful predecessor and embraced "the concept of enlarging the world's free community of market democracies as a major organizing principle of American foreign policy". Specifically, the ultimate objective was a "common European-Atlantic system" at the end of "an evolutionary process that potentially embraces Russia, Ukraine and Eastern Europe".[64] Of course no Europeans, East or West, were invited to offer a considered opinion on their fate, or to clarify the part they were destined to play in this grandiose vision of American hegemony.

The problem had less to do with this grand design inspired by

Jefferson's Empire of Liberty – a bold declaration of policy not yet operational – than with who exactly was to decide upon the details of its construction, and how others were to be convinced of the need for it. Meanwhile, following their self-imposed retreat to their 1921 borders, the Russians had ceased to be an immediate, credible, conventional military threat to the security of Western Europe, even though their thermonuclear arsenal still matched that of the United States. And mutual annihilation was never a credible option. The plain fact was that as soon as Russian armed forces had moved out of Germany, any sense of urgency about reassuring Moscow of NATO's benign intentions quickly evaporated.

During the election campaign Clinton had eagerly seized the opportunity to lambast Bush for not intervening in the crumbling state of Yugoslavia to forestall "ethnic cleansing" (a euphemism for genocide). A vicious war of secession had broken out, pitting Serbs against Croats and Bosnians. Yet the President had won office largely because the Democrats focused on domestic problems, not those of other countries—and he therefore gave little priority to Russia's rehabilitation. The Clinton strategy was brilliantly encapsulated in 1992 by the Democrats' witty strategist James Carville with a catchy quip that he hung on a board in the campaign headquarters at Little Rock. It resonated like no other throughout the campaign: "The economy, stupid." This, insisted Leon Panetta, chief of staff from June 1994, was "more than a campaign statement. It reflected what the president wanted to focus on… He really cared about domestic issues."[65] After the inauguration the board may have gone, but its sentiments still prevailed.

The US economy had, after all, just emerged from recession, and President Yeltsin "was clearly anxious… that the US might take its eye off Russia due to its economic challenges… at home", as Clinton's adviser Tony Lake noted.[66] The massive military buildup by President Reagan in the 1980s designed to intimidate the Soviet Union had sacrificed good housekeeping in public finances to excess borrowing for an avaricious defence budget. The options now of cutting defence and assisting Russia were entirely complementary. The American population, however, looked to enjoy the benefits of victory in the Cold War: a peace dividend to reward them for their sacrifices in the form of excessive taxes and high public debt. In that event, how much would be available to help Russia? And what might happen if in the end they decided not to do so? Indeed, was foreign policy a priority?

The Under Secretary of Defense for Policy, Slocombe, was certainly right in his judgement of the impact made by the end of the Cold War and the advent of the Clinton presidency: "As a consequence of this massive change in the world, Bill Clinton expected to be the first [US] president since Herbert Hoover who would not need to be preoccupied with foreign and security problems."[67] Joan Baggett, the Assistant to the President for Political Affairs, a no-nonsense activist who hailed from rural Alabama and had forged close ties with industrial trades unions, made a revealing comment that reached the press: "Presidents do get a foreign policy bug. We'll just have to make sure he [Clinton] doesn't succumb to it."[68] Soon after the inauguration, in February 1993, for the *New York Times* Thomas Friedman reliably reported the following:

> During a meeting of the President's top economic advisers last week, the Deputy Budget Director, Alice M. Rivlin, was describing areas of the country that would be affected by the withdrawal of a Federal timber subsidy when she found herself being corrected by President Clinton over which trees were found where.

> A short time later, Mr. Clinton's top foreign policy advisers were gathered in the Roosevelt Room poring over a map of Bosnia, in a nearly four-hour session intended to establish the Administration's policy for the Balkans, its first major foreign-policy initiative. The President did not correct anyone about details on Bosnia. He did not attend.[69]

The compass thus pointed towards a foreign policy drifting along on cruise control.

Moreover, Russia had effectively all but disappeared over the horizon. Its dire condition did not prompt the delivery of timely economic assistance on anywhere near the scale commensurate with the immense size of the former Soviet Union and its problems; if anything the opposite was the case. Harvard economist Jeffrey Sachs, summoned to Warsaw to help the Polish transition to capitalism on the strength of his experience with Bolivian debt relief, recalls the startling contrast between the Bush administration's eagerness to forgive post-Communist Poland what it owed and its stubborn resistance even to consider the idea for the former Soviet Union. The "grand bargain" worked out by Sachs and his Harvard colleagues based on the Polish model was discarded. And whereas one could plausibly argue that at least in dealing with Poland one was turning the pumpkin back into the coach it had once been, with respect to Russia, where no one alive had direct experience of living under capitalism, the task was much greater: that of turning a pumpkin into a coach for the first time.[70]

Deputy finance ministers from the leading economies (G-7) had arrived in Moscow on the eve of the Soviet collapse at the invitation of Gorbachev's leading economic reformer, Yegor Gaidar, in November 1991. But Bush showed little interest, as he was facing new elections. Deputy Secretary of State Larry Eagleburger told Sachs bluntly in March 1992 that an economic plan to freeze Russia's debt or anything else to help the Russians was just not going to happen. To make matters worse, in Russia itself the reformists took Sachs's advice only *à la carte*. They eliminated controls over prices but carried on subsidizing production and printing more money to pay for it: a recipe for runaway inflation. They also failed to deregulate energy or foreign trade—which opened up enormous possibilities for corrupt personal enrichment, from which those in the right place at the right time (like Putin in St Petersburg) could benefit.

Persuaded to stay on in Moscow after Clinton won the

presidential election in the United States, Sachs found the attitude of the new administration no different. Those who advised on Russia, like Strobe Talbott, had no understanding at all of economics; and those at the top of the Department of the Treasury, such as Larry Summers, knew next to nothing of Russia. The atmosphere was one of drift. Alarmed by rising opposition in the Duma, Yeltsin then called a halt to the policy of "shock therapy". It had resulted in massive short-term inflation when prices were allowed to find their market level while the Central Bank pumped out money to keep production afloat.[71]

How was the Clinton White House seen by Russia's pro-Western Foreign Minister? The best that could be said was that America's attitude appeared to be one of benign indifference. It was, Kozyrev recalled, "a friendly but self-centred administration".[72] Clinton was seen as weak, unable to deliver what Russia so desperately needed. The rhetoric on aid to Russia was never matched by deeds.[73] An early indication of his lack of interest in Russia was that when Clinton received an enthusiastic invitation from President Yeltsin to visit Moscow, to the dismay of the Russians he had to be pressed into it, and did not make the trip until he had been in office an entire year, in January 1994.[74] At a summit held nowhere near troubled Europe but in mellow Vancouver, Clinton committed merely $1.6 billion to Russia while simultaneously pressing Yeltsin to accept stronger economic sanctions against Yugoslavia, when he knew full well that their cost to the Russian economy ran "into the billions".[75] This kind of chronically inconsistent thinking was a tell-tale sign that neither Clinton nor his closest advisers ever kept their eyes on the Russian problem when the time was still ripe. The President was also, at a personal level, far too easily distracted.

In the words of Kozyrev, Yeltsin "knew well that Russia needed substantial assistance from the West for a successful transformation [of the economy]". It depended on Clinton. Here Yeltsin had serious doubts as the American president was seen as a "foreign policy lightweight" focused on the domestic front and unable to deliver what Russia needed.[76] Kozyrev explains: "Yeltsin... denounced the IMF's demand that Russia freeze fuel prices and wages, arguing that such a move, besides being a political death knell, would trigger a general price rise. Because even meeting milder demands, as a condition for receiving assistance, estimated at $24 billion, couldn't be achieved without serious assistance in place to do so, a vicious circle was promptly created, effectively blocking any large-scale material aid. The highly publicized 'helping hand' of the United States and its allies in the interest of strengthening democracy in Russia degenerated into little more than empty and humiliating talk, and gave the opposition in parliament and the executive bureaucracy an opportunity to gloat over the clumsy failures of the 'hapless schoolboys' who were trying to negotiate aid from the West."[77]

No doubt this partly explains why Talbott later dismissed Kozyrev a little uncharitably as "one of God's original whiners".[78]

No Marshall Plan for Russia

When countries are overwhelmingly defeated by the United States – as were Nazi Germany and imperial Japan – the consolation prize of full-scale aid and economic rehabilitation at least in part compensates for the humiliating impact of defeat, in return for the requirement to restructure society in superficial imitation of the American model. But the Cold War was not the kind of war that resulted in the rubble that modern airpower and artillery leave in their wake: blood-soaked corpses and hungry children pulling on the heart strings of the world. The poorest among the elderly in Russia suffered silently in private where even the World Salvation Army could not reach them. It was in this sense an invisible defeat with invisible consequences; certainly one unseen on television by the American public. But it was no less traumatic for Russia.

It was without question true that the very idea of large-scale economic and financial assistance – in the words of the incoming Secretary of State, the ultra-cautious lawyer Warren Christopher – "obviously cut against the priority of eliminating the [federal budget] deficit...".[79] He felt that it was for the Russians to do more to encourage inward investment (as though, entirely new to capitalism, they knew how). There was no lobby for a Marshall Plan aid programme inside government. And it was not just the administration's fault. Congress, which would have to vote the funds, was still congenitally anti-Russian, and now isolationist as well; fixated, of course, on the public benefits of peace for its constituents.

Amid the chaos of the White House, which Panetta began putting to rights on his arrival in June 1994, entirely inexperienced and ambitious young aides such as George Stephanopoulos (another Rhodes scholar at Oxford) epitomized the new spirit of the times in their casual indifference to foreign policy priorities. He also very much objected to assisting Russia on the grounds that it would be both politically controversial and fiscally damaging.[80] "Did anybody want to sacrifice moving ahead on our economic agenda for foreign policy?", Stephanopoulos asked rhetorically: "No."[81]

Matters were not helped by the fact that the United States, on its own account and through the International Monetary Fund (IMF) and the World Bank (IBRD), did embark on several simultaneous aid programmes to put the Russian economy on the path to the free market. So did the EU, through the European Bank for Reconstruction and Development (EBRD), but these programmes lacked coherence without an expert coordinating hand at the wheel and sustained commitment to a successful outcome in the face of unanticipated obstacles emerging from an alien culture. The Americans would have labelled such a person a "Tsar". Larry Summers, later Secretary of the Treasury, was unlikely under Clinton to enhance a promising political career by focusing too much on Russia. Beyond the beltway, college economists who studied the country lacked standing because their line of work was in the tradition of political economy, unsupported by high status mathematical theory. Orthodox free market economists succeeded in getting themselves appointed as advisers on privatization, often to the irritation of some Russian counterparts who believed that they knew their own economy and its immediate needs much better. And some of those most familiar with the problem were found to have mishandled funds allocated by the United States for aid to Russia.[82] It began to look all too like an American show, but an off-Broadway production with no great backing.

For all the attention they received, Russians saw themselves as victims rather than beneficiaries, even when in receipt of significant international attention and financial assistance. During the 1990s large amounts of aid money were inevitably diverted from laudable objectives through rampant crime and corruption, from which local officials such as Putin – then in St Petersburg – greatly benefited. The legal system was like a grim caricature from Charles Dickens' *Bleak House*, the banking system dangerously fragile. It was hard for the government to know what production and distribution actually were because of under-reporting to evade swingeing taxes by multiple collectors, who pocketed the proceeds for themselves. And even when aid did reach the right destination, no one liked to see themselves as recipients of charity, though the population enthusiastically welcomed its return to Russian life.

Assistance was especially needed to dismantle the massive, ageing military-industrial infrastructure and replace it with inward investment, most evident in the Leningrad region and in Ukraine's Russian-speaking Donetsk basin. But it was not to be found; certainly not in the quantity needed. And when the Russians inevitably expanded arms exports as a way of giving a new lease of life to a sector deprived of high domestic demand and to relieve the burden of foreign debt of the entire former Soviet Union, which was now carried solely by Russia, they were systematically blocked *by* the United States either because they clashed with US foreign policy goals – as in the case of its sanctions against fundamentalist Iran and the containment of Serbia – or because they created new competition for existing US arms sales to the Third World.

And one blockage to the massive riches of the American market through most favoured nation status – the Jackson-Vanik amendment to the Trade Act of 1974 – remained in place indefinitely, held hostage by a self-serving Congress for favourable deals furthering US agricultural exports to the Russian market. This amendment was kept in place despite the two-decade long disappearance of the problem it was supposed to solve: Soviet government discrimination against Jewish migration to Israel. Nothing was more symbolic of Americocentrism than this. In conversation with the US ambassador Putin "was scathing on Jackson-Vanik. 'You've been teasing us on this for years.' It was 'indecent' to keep prolonging the process or levering Jackson-Vanik to settle agricultural trade issues. Even Soviet era refuseniks, he said, were insulted by the continuing of the policy."[83] Not until December 2012 was the amendment removed, when finally Russian entry into the World Trade Organization threatened to place the United States in breach of its obligations. If one thing was clear, it was that Russia was obviously not a priority for jobbing congressmen unless some kind of reward, electoral or financial, was in sight.

Unsurprisingly, resentment at the treatment received in these years has remained visceral in Russia to this day. Even moderate newspapers look back at this decade with deep resentment: "Russia went through the 'daring nineties' with Michel Camdessus, then managing director of the IMF, as the piper; the tune's unforgettable context was the burial of the Soviet Union."[84] Anders Åslund, a tough-minded Swedish economist working alongside Sachs, recalled that "the West didn't lift a finger for Russia". The G-7 countries did little and handed the problem over to the World Bank and the IMF. John Odling-Smee, overseeing Russia at the IMF, complained that the G-7 expected his organization to observe its rules on lending but then bend them when the

Yeltsin government met political trouble.[85] The IMF was, as it still is, largely funded and directed by the United States. Ultimately it effectively threw in the towel. Britain's Prime Minister John Major was certainly not alone in thinking more could have been done. He even expressed the generous wish – to the horror of his officials – that Russia join the European Community.[86] As the main player, the United States of course took the blame for failure.

So the world had at one and the same time a new US president with a fine-sounding "grand strategy" in foreign policy but little time or inclination to give much attention to the detail of its implementation, let alone attend to the long-term impact on relations with Russia; except, that is, where it intersected with the demands of various domestic lobbies. Having conceived the design, a busy president thus delegated detailed implementation to others. And he stuck resolutely to the path he had mapped out.

2

Russia Elbowed Out

"We cannot accept NATO membership for the Central/East European states" (a reference to the Soviet reaction and the promise in the 2+4 talks, that the NATO area would not be extended to the East).

– Foreign Minister Hans-Dietrich Genscher,
11 October 1991.[1]

However loudly Russia called attention to itself, it had long ceased to be of any great significance to the United States. Europe, on the other hand, unquestionably remained central to American priorities. At the Senate Committee on Foreign Relations Subcommittee on European affairs, its former and future chairman, Richard Lugar of Indiana, described the core challenge as that of "'how' to anchor the United States in Europe". For him only NATO enlargement could do this.[2]

And as to the Russians, Joachim Bitterlich, Chancellor Kohl's adviser on foreign policy, gave the Americans the benefit of the doubt. On his view "Our [US] friends were convinced of the need to reach out to the Russians, but at the same time kept [their foot] on the brake."[3] In fact the Americans were less inclined to reach out to the Russians than Bitterlich presupposed. While the current administration was good at making self-interested decisions kitted out in Jeffersonian rhetoric, in Russian eyes Uncle Sam offered little more than tea and sympathy; and, at times, even that seemed to be in short supply, certainly from Warren Christopher, who was beset with problems beyond his limited capacity to resolve. It took a decade for this fundamental contradiction between bland reassurance and underlying intentions to become clear. And by the time it did so, the policies responsible had become too entrenched to allow for serious reconsideration, leaving once influential critics from within the administration howling impotently into the prevailing wind.

NATO Expansion, or Not?

The "new" Europe not unreasonably had every expectation that it would become part of NATO. Czechoslovakia's President Havel was never a man without hope. He had allies within the Visegrád group (Poland and Hungary) that was formed in February 1991 and possessed a huge reservoir of popular sympathy in the West. The Poles had had their own NATO enthusiasts for even longer than the Czechs; indeed, some were senior communist military officers serving the Warsaw Pact. At the Canadian embassy in Warsaw in the late 1980s the diplomat Eric Bergbusch was startled to hear Polish strategic planners openly enthusiastic about NATO. They saw its influence "as an indirect constraint on Russian behaviour and they believed it might have a further role to play in achieving and sustaining a Europe that would be free and open and no longer divided into armed camps".[4] But was any European leader in NATO willing to speak out? Robert Hunter recalls that "Of all the initiatives that led up to the recreation of NATO in the 1990s, the only major one that came from elsewhere was the NATO-Russia relationship, though the German defence minister Volker Ruehe did press for enlargement as much as anyone within the alliance."[5]

On 26 March 1993 the ambitious young Christian Democratic politician Volker Rühe, an original thinker and an independent figure in his own right, purposefully broke ranks to deliver a clarion call demanding NATO's eastward expansion. He launched his initiative at the International Institute for Strategic Studies in London. It was the anniversary of Chancellor Schmidt's call to arms against the threat of the Soviet SS-20 missile that had been designed for a pre-emptive counterforce strike on US forward-based systems in Europe. The idea that there could exist any parallel between the two interventions was far-fetched. Rühe's speech was authorized neither by Kohl nor Genscher.[6] Indeed, it was also delivered in the face of opposition from Germany's generals.[7] Bitterlich, Kohl's national security adviser, was none too pleased. He assured the Americans that Rühe was "on his own on that one". And to underline that fact, at a private dinner for five US state governors, the Chancellor himself, sure that he would be widely quoted, said "As I told Clinton, NATO can exclude taking in countries of Eastern Europe."[8] Genscher, too, "simply did not want to do it".[9]

The Germans were too late, however. In April 1993, during a ceremony to celebrate the opening of the Holocaust Museum in Washington DC, the Presidents of the Czech Republic and Poland, Havel and Lech Wałęsa, seized the opportunity to suggest to the President that membership of NATO be extended to their countries. On returning to the White House Clinton was surprised to find Warren Christopher and Tony Lake to be in favour, though his friend (and Russian specialist) Strobe Talbott was fundamentally opposed. And so, more importantly, was the Pentagon. Here the mercurial Les Aspin, his deputy, Bill Perry and – a hangover from the Bush administration – the congenitally cautious Chairman of the Joint Chiefs of Staff Colin Powell were more concerned about Russia's likely reaction.[10]

Clinton's administration was floundering. Matters came to a head on 25 May with an Overseas Writers lunch at the Foreign Service Club addressed off the record by Peter Tarnoff, Under

Secretary of State for Political Affairs, the number three at State. He discounted the idea that the United States would take a leading role in world affairs. Tarnoff emphasized instead that it would operate within a multilateral framework. "It is necessary", he emphasized, "to make the point that our economic interests are paramount."[11] Once the story was out, on 7 June his embattled superior, Christopher, was reduced to despatching a circular to US embassies that sounded like a complete confession of failure. He inadvertently indicated from the outset that as Secretary of State he had been unable to cope in his new post: "When we took office on Jan 21, we found the agenda overflowing with crises and potential disasters. A substantial proportion of time and energy have gone to navigating between submerged rocks and whirlpools on every continent…"[12]

The administration not surprisingly believed it had good reason for caution. After talks with Havel and Wałęsa, Clinton asked that Lake look into the issue of NATO enlargement. Meanwhile, Christopher, having tried to reassure everyone that the United States was, after all, still in charge, chose a NATO foreign ministers meeting on 10 June 1993 in Athens to forewarn the European allies that "at an appropriate time, we may choose to enlarge NATO membership. But this is not now on the agenda."[13] The chief interest in enlargement, which very soon became "the centerpiece of the first administration", was to establish a firm rationale for a continued US presence in Europe: "you needed NATO to be relevant in order to keep the United States engaged", recalled James Steinberg, Director of Policy Planning at the State Department and later deputy to Lake at the National Security Council. "There was always the option that NATO could wither away."[14]

Christopher's novel suggestion to the European members of NATO, effectively that the alliance should expand or die, had come entirely out of the blue. And coming from someone with the uncongenial manner of a Dickensian undertaker, it inevitably met with a cool reception as the allies were not at all ready for this new departure, certainly not the offhand manner of its delivery. Taken aback, they made clear that any public discussion of the issue would be damaging. Somehow the Americans expected to predetermine the fate of Europe under their own leadership for the foreseeable future and without consulting the Russians, yet they were at the same time entirely content to leave the acute problem of Yugoslavia's bloody dissolution solely in German hands. Moreover, the French had yet to recover from the shock of German reunification. Their own status in Europe had been severely reduced. Even the nuclear *force de frappe* was now dismissed in Bonn as of no further use. So it was not exactly a judicious moment to introduce further complications into NATO Europe when no one could work out the future purpose of the world's first standing alliance; if, indeed, it had one. No other alliance had ever possessed a permanent bureaucracy, so the disparity between its size and absence of purpose verged on the embarrassing.[15] Much came to hinge on events in the former Yugoslavia. In the case of that bloody conflict, if one looked at what the Americans actually did instead of what they said, their future in Europe remained a matter of doubt.

The Yugoslav Tangle: NATO à la Carte

No other issue took up more time or caused more trouble within the Clinton administration than the disintegration of Yugoslavia and its consequences. The unparalleled number of files dedicated to it in the Clinton presidential archive testifies to that. On 18 October 1990 a US secret intelligence assessment accurately diagnosed the problem:

> Strong centrifugal forces are driving the 70-year-old Yugoslav state apart... National pride, economic aspirations, and an upwelling of ethnic-based religious and cultural identification will continue to push Slovenia and Croatia toward

independence. Secessionist sentiment has been powerfully stimulated by Serbian attempts to dominate the federal political process.

It also predicted perfectly much of what would happen:

Yugoslavia will cease to function as a federal state within one year, and will probably dissolve within two. There is little the United States and its European allies can do to preserve Yugoslav unity.

At first sight the United States therefore had no incentive to get involved. For Europeans and Americans alike the two liberal principles of democracy and national self-determination were in direct collision as majority rule in the republics seeking statehood left national minorities – notably the Serbs – in urgent need of protection. CIA warned that "Statements by US officials on behalf of national self-determination will be used out of context by republic leaders to rally support within their national constituencies against central controls... European powers will pay lipservice to the idea of Yugoslav integrity while quietly accepting the dissolution of the federation."[16] The trouble was that this deadpan assessment was immediately leaked to the *Washington Post*.[17] And there was no shortage of Yugoslavs across the various republics who could read English.

As the country began to submerge under a tidal surge of competitive nationalism, ethnic minorities simultaneously jumped ship for the lifeboats or into the gunboats. The Serbs, with long memories of massacres at the hands of the Croat Ustaše, fascists backed by the Nazis in the Second World War, sought to save themselves at the expense of everyone else through pre-emptive conquest and what was euphemistically called "ethnic cleansing", the displacement and massacre of rival communities. Britain's ambassador in Belgrade at the time, Sir Peter Hall, recalls that "pressure should have been applied on Croatia to assuage the fears of the quite substantial Serbian minority in Croatia. Instead there was a sort of triumphalist new Croatia using the sort of chequer board symbols that had been so popular there in the Second World War. Indeed everything was done to make the Serbs in Croatia alarmed."[18]

Encouraging Croatia to believe it would have its independence immediately recognized, given this background, made no sense. But 700,000 Yugoslavs now lived in Germany, two-thirds of whom were Croat.[19] Croatia had once been a reliable ally of Nazi Germany. At first Chancellor Kohl resisted the idea of recognizing Croatian independence. But he was under heavy pressure from Austria, Hungary, Poland and the Vatican: a right-wing Catholic alignment evoking unpleasant memories of the past. The French were opposed. For domestic reasons Kohl was leaning towards recognition. Then in October 1991 Cardinal Giovanni Lajolo, the Nuncio in Bonn, upped the stakes and pleaded on behalf of Pope John Paul II personally that the Chancellor recognize the independence of Croatia. Bitterlich, Kohl's national security adviser, recalls that the Chancellor "was appalled at this blatant faux pas in the Vatican's foreign policy".[20]

This left France more than a little uncomfortable at the assertion of German interests, even as Berlin went out of its way to ensure that Paris was on side in such matters. Kohl recognized that "for France German unification was to some extent a 'blow'".[21] The French, he noted, were tempted to say that "a national policy is being pursued to acquire areas of influence in Central and Eastern Europe and the Balkans".[22] It mattered a great deal, therefore, that Germany did not act alone.

Meanwhile the United Nations was making arrangements for peace observer teams to be sent to Yugoslavia on behalf of the European Community (and Russia). The Americans, true to form, ostentatiously stood to one side: "the Yugoslav problem was essentially one for Europe", they declared. Simultaneously the United States warned in private of its "real concern... that the UN peace-keepers should not be stuck there in a war situation".[23] Baker warned the Germans that "The USA wants no internationalisation of the conflict." But Genscher, still elated at reunification, felt that Europe had no need of an American presence in the Balkans. He was comfortably complacent about what counted in the post-Cold War world. A military presence was unnecessary. The power of money would solve everything. "In Europe", Genscher declared triumphantly and prematurely, "no state can exist without the support and co-operation of the European Community."[24]

Robert Badinter, a Jewish professor of law and member of the French Senate, whose family had been wiped out by the Nazis, had the challenging task of arbitrating between the various Yugoslav republics. He was of course insistent on the human rights of the minority populations. The Croat constitution was a particular problem in discriminating against the Serb minority. At the very least it was hoped that diplomatic recognition would be held hostage to the institution of a protective regime for minorities in Croatia despite Vatican indifference to such concerns. The Conference on Yugoslavia was chaired by the deceptively languid figure of the former British Foreign Secretary Lord Carrington. Peter Carrington believed "that the Germans will ignore or override Badinter and recognize [Croatia] anyway, probably pulling all or most of the E[uropean] C[ommunity] with them. He is disturbed by this prospect because such an act on the part of the EC could have negative consequences for a resumed conference." It would, in Carrington's words, be "an act of bad faith".[25] The Montenegrin gambler Slobodan Milošević, president of Serbia, held most of the important cards while negotiations were conducted to find a Solomonic judgement allowing Croatia and Bosnia Herzegovina to break away while safeguarding the rights of their Serb minorities, even while fighting continued. But Belgrade's hold over the Bosnian Serbs was increasingly tenuous as negotiations collapsed. The danger for Milošević was that they would appeal over his head to the people of Serbia, the largest and dominant ethnicity of Yugoslavia. It is at this point that Germany bolted out of the stable in recognizing Croatian independence. But Kohl was as ever determined not to remain alone.

The member states of the European Community had agreed previously that before recognizing any constituent republic of Yugoslavia as an independent state, every attempt to create a fully acceptable compromise between all parties should be exhausted. Germany's well-advertised determination to break ranks by prematurely recognizing Croatia, which had declared independence in June 1991, worried all the other states. Secretary-General of the United Nations Javier Pérez de Cuéllar wrote to the President of the European Economic Community's Council of Ministers Hans van den Broek: "More than one of the high level interlocutors described the possible consequences of such a development as being a 'potential time bomb'... I believe therefore that uncoordinated actions should be avoided."[26]

In the last three months of 1991 the capture of the Croatian port of Vukovar by the Serbs and their bombardment of Dubrovnik played into German hands. Genscher predictably secured very little support from fellow ministers at their meeting on 17 December. Yet by hook or by crook Kohl managed to turn the votes around at a subsequent meeting by granting various favours all round, just as Carrington had feared. Genscher converted Foreign Secretary Douglas Hurd, for example, by agreeing to allow the British to recuse themselves from the social chapter of the Maastricht agreement on European Union.[27]

The turnaround of European élite opinion made war in Bosnia inevitable. Germany formally and unilaterally recognized the independence of Croatia – without insisting on the observance of minority rights – on New Year's Eve 1991. The remainder of the European Community reluctantly followed suit on 16 January 1992. Slovenia's recognition mattered less because it had no significant Serb minority. Bosnia-Herzegovina – the next in line – was, however, another matter entirely. As Pérez de Cuéllar's successor, the Egyptian diplomat Boutros Boutros-Ghali, notes, the cataclysm that unfolded was not caused entirely by diplomatic recognition, but recognition did ignite the explosion that followed.[28]

As an example of what Europe's conduct of international relations promised for the post-Cold War world, Germany's *force majeure* and the subjugation of EU members to its wishes certainly failed every test. Madeleine Albright, then US permanent representative at the UN and later Secretary of State, commented that "the big mistake, if you talked to anybody, was the Germans moving to recognize Slovenia without consulting with anybody else [the United States] and turning an internal issue into an international issue and then expecting everybody to pick up".[29]

German actions were confidently underwritten by the Gladstonian assumption that economic power would predominate and make for peace in former Yugoslavia. Surely the free market and the economic power of the European Union would prevail? This economistic cast of mind was prelude to an astonishingly short-sighted German policy a decade later that led Chancellor Angela Merkel to assume that Ukraine would eventually give way to an association agreement with the EU, in spite of Russian opposition, because material interest dictated it. And, when that failed, on the back of her predecessor, Gerhard Schröder, she allowed her country to become fatally dependent on Putin's Russia for two-thirds of its energy supplies. The consequences of economistic optimism for the population of former Yugoslavia were also predictably catastrophic.

The German belief in the overwhelming power of money more than met its match then and later. What is so striking and what the Germans found hard to comprehend about the former Yugoslavia was how, for those caught up in the maelstrom, emotions overrode all material interests. The leader of the Bosnian Serbs, whom Milošević rightly labelled "the mad doctor", the psychiatrist and one time comedian Radovan Karadžić, declared in February 1992 that "until two or three months ago we were hoping to be able to play the 'Yugoslav card'[...]. This is slipping out of our grasp. That's why we started on another track: a

Serbian Bosnia and Herzegovina. Our sovereign right, our army. We are preparing the constitutional framework to be able to have immediately... a national guard, to have our own police force, to have a government, to turn the Yugoslav army into the army of the Serbian Bosnia and Herzegovina."[30] So began the siege of the Bosnian capital of Sarajevo on 2 April 1992, a city sunk in a linear valley locked in by the surrounding hills.

Colonel Colm Doyle, an Irish officer heading the EEC monitoring mission in Sarajevo, has described the situation:

> The JNA [Yugoslav People's Army] was a formidable fighting force, among the largest and best equipped in Europe. Bosnia, protected by its high mountains and situated in the interior of the federation, had been a principal armoury for Yugoslavia. While the Bosnians took for granted its important defence role, they had never imagined that the very army that was there to defend them could become aggressors. We hoped, and many Bosnians believed, that they would remain impartial... It was, however, long suspected that Milošević had given instructions, as far back as January 1992, to have Bosnian Serbs serving in the JNA throughout Yugoslavia transferred to units in Bosnia, thereby effectively turning part of the JNA into a de facto Bosnian Serb army loyal to Belgrade... By the time that the Federal Republic of Yugoslavia (consisting only of Serbia and Montenegro) was created on 27 April 1992, the renegade Republika Srpska would inherit a professional army, complete with weapons and equipment and consisting of about 90,000 well trained and disciplined men already in Bosnia.[31]

Yugoslavia fell within the purview of Steven Meyer, who was CIA deputy chief for the Balkans. But like many country specialists, he despaired of the amateurs in charge of foreign policy at home. In his view "US policy has never understood this region... the depth and importance of ethnic identification."[32] Britain's

Prime Minister John Major, a pragmatist, entirely agreed. Intricate solutions were in fact devised to reconcile the ethnic patchwork of former Yugoslavia with demands for the independence of its constituent republics: the Cutleiro Plan, and the Vance-Owen proposals advanced by Carrington. They meant accepting the facts on the ground – the displacement of populations and the creation of enclaves like Republika Srpska – and were therefore all summarily rejected by Warren Christopher without offering any workable alternative to replace them. Everyone knew that what former foreign ministers Cyrus Vance (United States) and David Owen (Britain) proposed was imperfect. It meant accepting the results of forced depopulation at the hands, mostly, of menacing Serbs. Aggression was thus rewarded in order that further aggression be curtailed. And the fly in the ointment for the Americans was that some 30,000 US troops would be required to enforce the agreement. This was far from ideal. But what exactly was the practicable alternative? Who had the will and the power to roll back the outcome of a brutal civil war?

For all its intemperate criticism of Bush during the election campaign, the Clinton team actually had no idea at all what to do. "We wanted to go in not by assigning a brigade or division of UN forces, hoping for the best", Secretary of Defense Perry recalls. "In the beginning we said if we went in it would be as part of a NATO force."[33] London, accustomed to spheres of influence as its frame of reference, and convinced this was in essence a civil war, looked on in horror at any prospect of NATO intervention confronting a Serbia armed by Russia. In practice it also meant that any policy recommended by Perry was impossible to enforce, because the British and French did not believe that public opinion would accept the idea of their own soldiers risking death to glue together the fractured state of Yugoslavia.

Russia, though a shadow of its former self, nevertheless demanded a voice over the fate of Yugoslavia as a matter of prestige; its policy makers were now in the unaccustomed role of playing to the gallery, from which pan-Slavic invective was being hurled. The Russians asserted historical continuity with their influence in the Balkans, which they had liberated from the Ottoman empire in the late nineteenth century. And the Red Army did, after all, liberate Belgrade in 1944. But there were other forces also at work. The vivid parallels between the breakup of Yugoslavia and the simultaneous breakup of the Soviet Union, both multi-ethnic mosaics, were hard to miss. Russia had a strong interest in forestalling further precedents for unilateral secession. It therefore clung rigidly to the international legal principle that had become dominant in post-colonial Africa. Built of artificial states devoid of nationhood and haunted by the perpetual fear of tribal separatism, the prevailing doctrine of the Organisation of African Unity was *pacta sunt servanda*, treaties must be observed – no changes should be made in the territorial status quo.

To the Russians the outlook was not uniformly bleak. On the positive side, they also spied opportunity. Lt General Yevgeny Barmyantsev of the GRU – military intelligence – had served in the United States as deputy military attaché running agents out of the embassy on 16th street in Washington DC from 1977–83 and then directing operations across the English-speaking world from Moscow before being posted as defence attaché to Belgrade in December 1996.[34] His very appointment was a startling indication of Moscow's new order of priorities. Everywhere else in Europe lay within the American sphere of influence, he noted. And "only one blank patch remained – Yugoslavia".[35]

The dominant nationality, the Serbs, formed a significant minority of the population within several, though not all, the other republics. So when these republics broke away to form their own nation states, they took with them a segment of the once dominant Serb nation; and in each instance the chauvinist lobby sought to re-assert the privileges of the minority by resorting to violence. And were there not now 25 million Russians stranded outside the homeland and a stream of other ethnicities stranded within what were now new nation states? Ethnic conflict in former Yugoslavia set an ominous precedent for Russia, unless pre-empted from the centre. The war to prevent Chechnya breaking away from Russia's southern flank in 1994, soon abandoned as a grievous failure, highlighted that fact.

Yeltsin, having in an act of unthinking opportunism promised that they could go their own way in order that he might take power in Russia, was then unable to persuade the former republics of the Soviet Union to regroup as a voluntary federation under Russian auspices in 1991–2. He also appeared impotent when confronted with Russia's own potential dissolution. Wörner's successor as NATO Secretary General, Javier Solana, noted that, although the Soviet Union did not collapse into civil war, "Russia in a way experienced the Yugoslav process as a second chapter, albeit in miniature, in what began to be seen as a process of historical humiliation of the old Russia."[36] When in August 1991 Yeltsin's press secretary, Pavel Voshchanov, declared that Russia would revise its frontiers with former republics of the Soviet Union who did not join the newly proposed post-Soviet union, he had to be hastily disavowed.[37] Russia's ambassador in London from 1994, Anatoly Adamishin, once very much a supporter of Gorbachev, took the same view as Foreign Secretary Hurd that Yugoslavia was engaged in "a civil war", which meant that any form of armed intervention from outside was fundamentally illegitimate. At the same time, however, he also saw the Serbs as allies.[38]

The collapse of Yugoslavia was not the only test faced by Yeltsin. But it was one of the first foreign policy crises that would determine where Russia stood with respect to a crucial issue of principle. Responding to the Serb siege of the Bosnian capital of Sarajevo, on 30 May 1992, and with Kremlin support, the UN Security Council did reluctantly vote to impose economic sanctions on the Serbian-controlled rump of Yugoslavia. But this single act of solidarity with the NATO powers sparked fury from the populists in the Russian Duma. The vacuous ranting of the communists and nationalist hotheads encouraged by former general and now Vice President Alexander Rutskoi, who had demanded that Ukraine return the predominantly Russian-populated Crimea, threatened to suck the air of freedom out of the Kremlin. At the Russian Security Council and with baiting by the press, the young, mild-mannered Kozyrev had to fight his ground with unaccustomed ferocity against accusations from Rutskoi of turning Russia into "a banana republic", until Yeltsin belatedly came to his aid.[39]

The persistence of Serb aggression simultaneously exposed the absence of consensus within the White House and between the United States and Western Europe. The British and the French had boots on the ground in former Yugoslavia, now joined by the Russians – 1,130 of them – organized through the United Nations Protection Force (UNPROFOR), but collectively hampered by the fact that the UN "force" had no heavy arms at its disposal, no rules of engagement, nor its own intelligence organization.[40] Rather than deterring the Serbs, UNPROFOR reluctantly stood by, at best rendering humanitarian assistance to the victims as Serbs roamed at will torturing, murdering and expelling Croats and Bosnians from towns and villages they had lived in for centuries. Meanwhile, the incoming Secretary-General, Boutros Boutros-Ghali, gave partisan observers – such as US permanent representative Madeleine Albright – the impression of an unpleasant air of haughty indifference to the Balkan crisis. This was a diplomat whose priorities were clearly directed rather more at the Third World to which he belonged, and who at times appeared casually dismissive of Bosnia as a European sideshow. Africa, after all, looked a good deal worse; not just the war in Somalia, but also with the first massacres of the horrific Congo war from October 1996.[41] Boutros-Ghali's diary summed up his view that UNPROFOR was "being used by the Europeans and the United States to show that they are doing 'something' about the hell that Bosnia has become; and that the United Nations Protection Force serves as a scapegoat, because we cannot stop the horror".[42] In short, the hopes raised by the international community could not be met given the limited resources provided by the UN.[43]

Rather NATO Expansion than Intervention in Yugoslavia

It was really up to the Americans to take a stand in sorting out the Yugoslav mess if they did, indeed, wish to lead the post-Cold War order in Europe. Former Senator Al Gore as Vice President was charged with oversight of foreign policy "in an administration plagued by disorganization and indecision".[44] And Gore followed the Secretary of Defense in blocking any option that would place US troops in harm's way, which implementation of the Vance-Owen plan required. He also had the ear of those on Capitol Hill, his former domain. Instead Gore, never a headstrong leader, tended to listen rather than lobby; after all, he was the Democrats' heir apparent, and assumed that his aspirations at the very least depended upon his ability to avoid making unnecessary enemies among former colleagues on the Hill. Thereafter the administration spent years wandering around in circles and came up with no agreed consensus until events finally forced their hand to deploy military power to counter Serbia in 1995, and, later, in March 1999.[45]

The administration was certainly not a model of good order. Had not Clinton been responsible for the ill-thought-out despatch of Delta Force troops and Rangers into the Somali civil war, independent of the United Nations, on 3 October 1993? Thousands of Somalis died in the ensuing chaos: men, women and children. And in revenge the dead bodies of American soldiers were dragged through the streets of Mogadishu, the United States humiliated in the process as its citizens watched the ghastly spectacle on CNN.[46] Then in 1994 the President invaded Haiti and ended up inadvertently replacing one despot with another, with various parts of the administration backing different sides. "The State Department, the Defense Department and CIA each seem to have its own policy to conduct in Haiti", commented Boutros-Ghali sourly in his diary.[47]

The administration was therefore not exactly enthusiastic to repeat either experience on a much greater scale in former

Yugoslavia. As already mentioned, Warren Christopher, who had been Vance's deputy in the Carter administration, had rejected out of hand the only existing remedy for the war in Yugoslavia – the complex tapestry of the Vance-Owen plan for Bosnia introduced on 2 January 1993 – because he claimed it rewarded the forceful annexations of 1992. Christopher and other senior figures such as Tarnoff, who also once worked for Vance, could not find a good word to say about the plan. Worse still, the Secretary decided "to tour western Europe with a plan so hedged with nitpicking reservations that it was inevitably rejected by America's allies. Washington then attacked the Europeans for their inadequate response. But, as the crisis worsened, Christopher repeatedly argued with his colleagues that American military involvement must be kept at the lowest possible level."[48] As Boutros-Ghali noted: "From the outside, the policy the White House is conducting in this matter appears the consequence of an obscure and Machiavellian calculation."[49] And he was not alone in this regard, though pure prejudice and plain incompetence might have been closer to the truth.

Instead of directly participating in UNPROFOR, and in order to circumvent Christopher's aversion to intervention, the White House in utter frustration secretly turned instead to covert operations directed against the Serbs. In 1994 "tacit approval" was given for arms smuggling to Bosnia from Iran and elsewhere, and before long the Iranians were running a military training camp in the country under the auspices of Bosnia's head of secret intelligence, an American protégé.[50] By 1995 the Americans were also surreptitiously training the Croat military.[51] All of this was, of course, clearly visible to Russian military intelligence, present within UNPROFOR and well established at the embassy in Belgrade.

Tony Lake came from Henry Kissinger's stable, although something of a prodigal son. He had opposed the extension of the Vietnam War to Cambodia, a war which Kissinger desperately sought to prolong as a means of enhancing the US bargaining position for an eventual settlement. But Lake was also a firm believer in Realpolitik. Like his erstwhile master, he was convinced of the need to expand NATO to the East and determined to persuade the president of its merits. Reports from the West European capitals could not be ignored entirely, however. On 17 July 1993 Lake's memorandum on "European Attitudes Toward NATO Enlargement" indicated difficulties that lay ahead. "A number of allies... including Germany and the UK, differ with us in [our] wanting to exclude Russia *a priori* from membership. The British also believe that enlarging NATO to include the Baltic states will be too sensitive due to Russian objections..." Lake had no illusions "how sensitive the Europeans are to the Russian angle" and expected "West European apprehension may grow as Russian pressure increases."[52] But Lake was nothing if not persistent.

Now deprived of its outer defence perimeter formed by the Warsaw Pact, which kept NATO at a distance if not at bay, Russia obviously feared lest the alliance encroach from the West and, indeed, from the South. It appealed instead for a NATO redesigned as a collective security rather than a collective defence organization – which required Russian membership rather than exclusion. To put it crudely, from being a target of NATO, Russia hoped to play a leading role in determining – and potentially vetoing – whatever targets emerged. A redefinition of NATO objectives and the establishment of an effective pan-European security structure were, on Moscow's view, a necessary prelude to any extension of NATO eastwards if expansion were, in the end, unavoidable.[53] In August Yeltsin allowed for the fact that Poland and Czechoslovakia might seek to join the alliance. But he qualified this by accepting it only as part of a process of Pan-European integration in which Russia participated. This was outlined by Yeltsin in a letter to Clinton on 15 September.[54]

The problems for Russia were several. Persistent use of its right to refuse consent at the UN Security Council, from its very foundation, did not exactly encourage the West to believe that granting Moscow a veto in any European security framework would be wise. Yeltsin no longer had any leverage in negotiating such a framework as his power base had all but vanished. And NATO had in no way altered since the end of the Cold War, in either structure or purpose. The alliance carried on as normal both politically and militarily. The Russians remained the only enemy in view. Moreover, NATO apparently showed no likelihood of or interest in changing its purpose or practices; which the Russians increasingly realized to be the case, but were powerless to change.[55]

For the United States NATO was, of course, its sole justification for remaining in Europe, though its original purpose was on one view now a matter of history and its actual military effectiveness was on this view seemingly redundant. For their part, however, the Germans and the French were not much interested in refurbishing an establishment that had outlived its purpose because they looked instead to supersede the alliance with an all-European confederation – at the very least a European security and defence identity. Scowcroft had claimed the Americans did not oppose the idea, except, and this was not a minor matter, for one vital proviso: "we fear lest such a project pushes us out of Europe".[56] That is, of course, why it never came to pass.

The Americans had a major advantage. The Franco-German vision of Europe was not without its problems. Helmut Kohl was no Otto von Bismarck. He had hastily conceded the transformation of the European Economic Community into an integrated European Union. This was a quid pro quo for German reunification for his French counterpart, François Mitterrand, in defiance of Margaret Thatcher, with the signature of the Maastricht Treaty (1991).[57] Thereafter Kohl had his hands full. Foreign policy was not at the top of the list of priorities. Genscher took the lead. Kohl's adviser on national security, Joachim Bitterlich, recalls the Chancellor saying: "I will sign all the initiatives you are preparing with your comrades-in-arms on Foreign and Security Policy, but the completion of this area will be the very last step of European integration because of the remaining traditions and the history of some of our important partners such as France and the UK."

To Kohl the extension of the EU rather than NATO to the East would provide the foundations for a new European security architecture. Bitterlich explains: "The West European nations thought that the process would happen first via the EU, without saying when or how, while it was becoming clearer that some of the new democracies in Central and Eastern Europe that wanted to become part of the EU and NATO were focused much more on the protection offered by the Atlantic Alliance."[58] It mattered because, with respect to Russia at least, the Americans took the view that "Germany is perhaps our most important European partner."[59]

The stages set for entry into the European Union were established at a meeting of the European Council in Copenhagen (21–22 June 1993), agreeing that four years of preparatory negotiations to meet the criteria for entry were necessary. For the East European aspirants the prospect loomed of interminable paperwork, the inevitable product of Napoleonic bureaucratic practice. By the time of admission anything could have happened inside Russia, where price controls had been lifted in January 1992, leading to hyperinflation of over 2,500 per cent; the fate of its transformation into a market democracy was hanging by a thread and the spirit of revanchism was rampant in the Duma. Not surprisingly former members of the Warsaw Pact were not prepared to take anything on trust from a country that had impoverished and oppressed them for at least four decades. NATO seemed much the safer option, even when the inflation rate dropped and more normal economic life began to pick up in Russia.

Strobe Talbott

At least some Americans were listening intently to what Moscow was saying. And although countries like Poland and what was now the Czech Republic thought an unreformed NATO an adequate guarantee of their security, Lake had to overcome sceptics even within the United States. Implementation of Russia policy was intended to fall largely upon the slender shoulders of Clinton's erstwhile house-mate as a Rhodes scholar at Oxford University (1968–9), Strobe Talbott. Clinton appointed Talbott Ambassador-at-Large and Special Advisor to the Secretary of State on the New Independent States and then, within a year, Deputy Secretary of State. This inevitably stretched him well beyond his original brief, which was in and of itself the most demanding of all. When Talbott was appointed it was agreed that he chair an inter-agency committee, the Former Soviet Union Steering Group. This would consist of Under Secretaries from the various departments, including the National Security Council, involved in Russia. In mid-December 1992 Clinton, exuding his accustomed charm, disingenuously assured Talbott that he – Strobe – was "his man" in the inter-agency policy-making process.[60] That did not last long. The quick-minded, headstrong and ambitious economist Larry Summers, Under Secretary at the Treasury, accustomed to the cut and thrust of Harvard, immediately sought to undermine his authority.[61] And Talbott's problem, crucially, was that he did not have a seat on the all-powerful National Security Council, which Lake chaired, and which had the penultimate word.

A more than competent Russianist, Talbott had speedily produced a condensed translation of former leader Nikita Khrushchev's unpublished memoirs, which proved a sensation when they appeared in 1970. On the back of that early success he made his name as a *Time* foreign correspondent focused on the Cold War under the Reagan presidency, where his access as an outsider was second to none. But apart from his undoubted academic talents, and he had the looks and manner of an Ivy League Professor, he was not an ebullient personality. New to the system, it did not take too long before his better judgement was ruthlessly undermined by those more skilled in bureaucratic warfare but far more ignorant and far less scrupulous than he was. A trimmer by nature, his misfortune was that he appeared to be less than comfortable with open confrontation. Christopher, too, was not normally confrontational, with the demeanour of an arbitrator rather than a prosecutor, though he could be extremely stubborn. It undoubtedly helped in the introduction of new ideas, that Christopher saw himself as the efficient functionary working within a consensus forged by others, rather than as the bold initiator of a policy that he had personally conceived. So the kind of intense battles that had played out in the 1970s between the Secretary of State and the Special Advisor on National Security, the alpha males Kissinger and Brzezinski, were avoided. *Boutonné* is the word for Christopher; an American Douglas Hurd, perhaps, minus the droll witticisms and the trademark pin-stripe suits; though his manner certainly suggested that he would not have been entirely uncomfortable buttoned up in one.

Partnership for Peace

The Pentagon, as ever, had interests at stake. Though bereft of much else, Russia alone still had the thermonuclear capability to threaten the American homeland. This was an issue the Republicans continued to work on in opposition by advocating an effective system of ballistic missile defence, the Reagan project that re-emerged at the end of the Clinton presidency and alarmed the Russians still further.

The US military pre-emptively took the initiative in forging a new relationship with the Russian armed forces. The dynamic Polish-born John Shalikashvili, Supreme Allied Commander Europe, took the lead. "The role of Russia's military was key", wrote Perry, Secretary of Defense and Ashton Carter, a fellow physicist and Assistant Secretary of Defense for International Security Policy, "because it was the institution that would endure, whatever might happen to Boris Yeltsin's democrats or their successors."[62] In 1993 they began a military-to-military programme named the Pragmatic Partnership. Regular meetings were held between officials on both sides led by Carter that went well beyond pro-forma ritual. Fundamentally averse to the admission of Central and East European states to NATO, the Pentagon came up with an ingenious idea designed to delay entry and ease Russian anxieties at the prospect of NATO's untimely arrival on their doorstep. It was called the Partnership for Peace (PfP). This the ambitious and impatient Republican senator Lugar derided as "Partnership for Postponement". The project was unveiled at a meeting of NATO defence ministers convened in Travemünde, Germany, on 20–21 October 1993. It was inaugurated in Brussels on 11 January 1994.

The idea is usually attributed to Vietnam flying ace Major-General (USAF) Joseph Kruzel, Deputy Assistant Secretary for Defense for European and NATO Policy; though many inevitably claimed credit after the fact. Shalikashvili adopted it and summed it up as a means of changing the Russian mindset of confrontation with the West. "The best way to do that", he explained, "is to embrace them as forcefully as possible so that they would have no reason to think of their defense against us, but think of their defense in partnership with us. So it was at first [a matter of] convincing the Europeans that [it] is in their best interests too."[63] Shalikashvili's approach had all the subtlety of Egon Bahr's embrace of East Germany that paved the way for détente in Europe during the Cold War, acidly caricatured in East Berlin as "aggression in bedroom slippers". "We wanted to slow the ball," Carter recalled. "The phrase we used at the time was we don't want to create a 'Weimar Russia'."[64] Carter, who had written a senior thesis on medieval history at Princeton, though a physics major, was referring to Germany's humiliation at the Paris Peace Conference (1919) and its ostracism. Together with economic collapse, it was the Versailles settlement and its draconian economic reparations that boosted extreme nationalist sentiment and eventually launched Adolf Hitler to power in 1933. At least someone in the administration knew his history, which was not elsewhere apparent in the White House.[65]

At the Office of the Secretary of Defense, US military

intelligence was long accustomed to stepping into Russian boots to see the world from the Kremlin's angle of vision. They still had much to learn, however, as they discovered when debriefing their counterparts in the 1990s. Robert Conquest, the noted historian of Stalin's terror, visited Russia for the first time in his life as an ex-communist after the fall of the Berlin Wall, and in the company of senior US army officers. When they finished their extensive tour of war monuments and arrived at the Voroshilov Military Academy, the American generals were invited to describe teaching at the National War College. They duly presented a lengthy outline, which included a sparkling array of fashionable social sciences. Then came the turn of the Russians. And what did they teach? "War!" came the blunt response from the other side.[66]

General Wesley Clark, another Oxford graduate and still a resolute cold warrior, was at that time director of strategic plans and policy on the Joint Chiefs of Staff. He developed contacts with former enemy counterparts in the early 1990s and, not entirely convinced they had changed one iota, very quickly sensed "their continuing sense of ownership and privilege in Eastern Europe".[67] On the Russian view this was, indeed, their sphere of influence from time immemorial, as the Americans had held sway over Latin America since 1823 with enforcement of the Monroe Doctrine. The Russian stance was made clear to the US deputy chief of mission in Moscow by Georgii Mamedov, the Russian Deputy Foreign Minister, who, though Azeri by birth, was temperamentally as well as by vocation very much a dedicated Russian diplomat.[68] Mamedov insisted that "NATO should not proceed as if nothing has happened to the East-West relationship. NATO needs to deal with the East Europeans in the context of the fundamental change in the relationship between East and West, and between Russia and the US."[69]

As late as 1 July 1993, Wörner, hosting a delegation from the Russian Supreme Soviet visiting Brussels, "stressed that the NATO [North Atlantic] Council and he are against the expansion of NATO (13 out of 16 NATO members support this point of view)."[70] The reassurances mattered. Hardline opposition to Yeltsin's market reforms was only temporarily suppressed at the beginning of October, when he resorted to force against armed resistance to a new constitution and new elections due in December. So the last thing he needed was for the West to rock the boat. On 22 October Christopher flew to Moscow with Talbott for the purpose of assuring Yeltsin that the new idea for a Partnership for Peace would be a non-threatening solution to the demands from Eastern Europe, and the equally pressing concerns of the Russians that their former subordinates should not join NATO. Yeltsin, however, was not always an attentive listener and understood his visitors to have said that Partnership for Peace was actually a substitute for NATO expansion. The Americans present, faced with the unaccustomed prospect of telling a foreign leader that he had got the wrong end of the stick, and anxious not to spoil the atmosphere by correcting him, left Yeltsin with a dangerous delusion.[71]

The situation worsened still further. Not for the first time, Christopher was holed below the waterline just before reaching port. Opinion in Washington DC was already hardening against Russia. In Madrid Wörner addressed delegates from all the main European organizations, supposedly off the record – as the proceedings were nowhere briefed to the press – and completely undermined the credibility of what Yeltsin had been told by insisting that the main task of the alliance was still the maintenance of the balance of power in Europe and looked to NATO expansion much further East.[72] Against whom, exactly, was power to be balanced? There was no balance after the Soviet collapse. So the objective observer could be forgiven for concluding that he had to mean nothing less than a bid for NATO to reach across the Caucasus, through Russia's "near abroad" to the south and on into Central Asia.

The Kremlin was certainly not about to let that go without a challenge. The minutes of the meeting fell into Russian hands. Return fire took the form of a long briefing paper from Major

General Dmitrii Dmitriev, head of the Information-Analytical Directorate of the SVR (civilian Foreign Intelligence). The SVR under director Yevgeny Primakov was something of a Soviet sanctuary that had been saved from the kind of demoralization that plagued the Foreign Ministry. Indeed, Vyacheslav Trubnikov, himself a former director of the service, recalled that Primakov "not only preserved but strengthened its authority in the new Russia". Everyone was paid on time, there were shops where food could be bought to take home and the canteen was said to be the cheapest and best in the country. Moreover, Primakov saw to it that the SVR sustained its ties with its counterparts throughout the former Soviet Union.[73] As a means of counteracting Kozyrev's Panglossian optimism, Primakov presented Dmitriev's memorandum to Yeltsin on 15 November 1993 to show that he, the president, had been badly deceived. It was assembled from secret intelligence and open sources. Yeltsin told him to publish it, which he promptly did, with the necessary excisions, in the national press.[74]

Two leading Russian newspapers, *Nezavisimaya gazeta* and *Izvestiya*, each published an article eleven days later focusing on Wörner's speech. If it were, indeed, the case that along with the defence of its members, "the main goal of the alliance in the current situation is the maintenance of the balance of power in Europe", then "advancing the limits of the North Atlantic Alliance to the frontiers of Russia requires either bolstering its military, which clashes with the solution to the problem of economic development, or agreement on asymmetry in the sphere of security, which is also against the interests of the Russian Federation". Wörner had suggested that NATO look to Central Asia for further expansion: evidently the alliance thereby now wished to close in on Russia from the south as well as from the West. The writer warned of the impact on Russian public opinion: "the internal political situation in Russia and the Russian state of mind". What was needed instead was "a synchronisation of the process of enlargement of NATO's zone of responsibility with a change in the character of this alliance; an adjustment of its functions to the particular needs of the current stage of historical development".[75] This document was to have been a joint position agreed between the SVR and the Foreign Ministry, but at the last moment Kozyrev, who evidently suspected that he was its most immediate target, had disowned it.[76] Had the Americans known of this, it would have emboldened them to press ahead. And it certainly began to look as though they did.

President Clinton had a schedule of visits taking in NATO (9–10 January 1994) and then (11–12 January) the Visegrád countries (Poland, the Czech Republic, Slovakia and Hungary) who were the most eager to join NATO. On the eve of this marathon run of summits, and after the elections in Russia showed the strength of the nationalists, Lake counselled against any over-reaction that might alter the course they had set for themselves. "The Russian elections notwithstanding, we should not abandon Russian reform, which is what too rapid or overtly preferential treatment of the V[isegrád] – 4 in the process of NATO expansion would mean. Doing so would play into the hands of Russian hardliners and thus likely make C[entral and] E[ast] E[uropean] states less secure." In Brussels Clinton argued that NATO, while open to membership from other European countries, would "launch a major initiative through a Partnership for Peace, in which we invite Partners to join us in new political and military efforts to work alongside the Alliance". The NATO communiqué also made reference to "fuller integration of the countries of Central and Eastern Europe and of the former Soviet Union into a Europe whole and free", thereby satisfying America's partners that no preference be expressed in support of the countries of Central and Eastern Europe as against Russia.[77]

Even after a year into his presidency, however, Clinton was still unsure of himself in this new arena, skating uncertainly on thin ice. And his image suffered as a consequence. He had no experience in or instinct for foreign affairs, his administration squabbled among themselves to an unusual degree, and on top of this he had a fatal flaw: the populist politician's eagerness to please, which abroad could be easily interpreted as deliberate disingenuousness. Clinton was, as the *New York Times* castigated him, wobbly, inconsistent and indecisive but simultaneously obsessed with the appearance of his foreign policy.[78] Thus came the perfect moment for the right person to flip him around. The President stopped off in Prague en route to Warsaw and Moscow and then executed an astonishing volte face.

The Visegrád group were the countries that the imperious US permanent representative at the UN, Madeleine Albright, daughter of a Jewish refugee from Prague, was sent to canvas in the New Year. A Brzezinski protégé, she could not be expected to give the benefit of the doubt to the Russians. As was her custom, she liked to form clear impressions from her meetings and then issue recommendations in a tone that brooked no refusal. She bluntly reported "their fear that we are naive about the Russians, and that we are willing to sacrifice their security to preserve our relations with Russia". No less important was the fact that everyone she spoke to was "concerned about how Ukraine fits into the picture and understood the danger of leaving it out". She added that, "down the road, they want themselves in NATO and the Russians out".[79] Mention of Ukraine made its impact in Washington DC.

To say that this did not fit in well with the existing NATO consensus would be an understatement. In Brussels on the first leg of Clinton's European tour, "most Western officials (as well as those in Moscow) believed that the idea of NATO enlargement had been shelved in favour of the Partnership for Peace [PfP]".[80] But in Prague on the second leg of the President's visit, Havel insisted to Clinton that PfP "must be the first step toward membership". In responding and as yet uncertain which path to take, Clinton remarked defensively that "there is no consensus now among NATO allies to extend formal security guarantees for two reasons. First, it is not clear who could contribute to the common defense. And second, the reaction in Russia could be the reverse of what we want, especially after the last election." Clinton added a concern that the alliance did not want just to redraw the East-West line a few hundred miles further East; "not least because Ukraine does not want to be pushed back into Russia's orbit".[81]

On the following day, however, and with Lake at his side, it suddenly became apparent that Havel had made a momentous impact on the President. Ukraine was no longer a blockage. Clinton reacted immediately by abruptly shifting position. He dropped any concern at all about reactions in Russia. In what proved to be a fateful moment, he now assured one and all that PfP was not "a permanent holding room. It changes the entire dialogue so that now the question is no longer whether NATO will take in new members, but when and how".[82]

It now became increasingly apparent that the Americans were intent on going their own way. The course for a new policy had been set regardless of what their allies, however important, including the Germans, might think. Needless to say, this came as an unpleasant surprise to NATO Europe. When they learned of the volte face, they were infuriated. Jenonne Walker, a tough former CIA analyst who had fought her way up the ranks against all the odds as a woman of her generation, was the Senior Director for Europe on the National Security Council. This was very much her own domain. Walker was convinced that in NATO "few wanted to move as rapidly as President Clinton" and that "Chancellor Kohl was urging President Clinton to slow down lest he damage relations with Russia".[83] "Some West Europeans", Walker recalls, "felt they'd been misled."[84] That is an understatement.

NATO Enlargement Takes Priority

Back in the White House the President's sudden change of tack took immediate effect. The PfP was now effectively brushed aside in favour of NATO enlargement, though as a slogan it continued in place, but increasingly gutted of any significance. No one would stand up to Clinton. Talbott had, however, identified with

PfP and that could potentially slow things up. But, adjusting seamlessly to the President's new commitment, Talbott's superior, Christopher, "brought Dick Holbrooke back to be Assistant Secretary of State for European Affairs [26 August 1994]". The Secretary recalled "feeling that our European affairs needed a more aggressive approach, I brought him back with two thoughts in mind. One was Bosnia [wars of ethnic separatism following the collapse of Yugoslavia in 1991] to be sure, but the second was NATO, and Dick deserves a lot more credit in his way for taking a very aggressive role in pressing for the expansion of NATO and getting it on the agenda for the semi-annual meetings of the NATO council and just driving forward the timetable that meant by the end of 1996 we were clearly on track for an expansion of NATO and an expansion in a way that permitted an overarching relationship with Russia."[85]

Yet the primary means of keeping Russia on board with that process – the NATO-Russia partnership – was, as Lake's deputy Samuel ("Sandy") Berger readily confessed, "a bit of a fig leaf".[86] Christopher himself had no appetite for appeasing the Russians. Indeed, he did not care for them at all. At Policy Planning Steinberg recalled: "He felt that the initial approach, which was to be rather deferential and solicitous of the Russians, rather than producing more forthcoming attitudes, encouraged the Russians to be even more demanding."[87] The initiative, however, lay not with State, even after Holbrooke's arrival, but ultimately with the National Security Council, where Lake had already won the traditional battle between the two as the dominant voice in foreign policy making.

Holbrooke was obsessive and also notoriously intimidating. If it were within his power he would secure whatever the president needed at whatever cost to the self-esteem of anyone less enthusiastic, however many stars a general had. He did not hold back from humiliating the much-decorated Major-General Kruzel, for one, in the presence of his colleagues, just to win the argument. As television viewers will know, when Air Force One carrying the

President descends, it is announced that "the Eagle has landed". Holbrooke's inflated sense of self-importance was such that when a plane brought him down into former Yugoslavia, those on the ground who knew him well joked that "the Ego has landed". That mattered little to those who brought him back to the State Department, however, as long as he delivered.

On enlargement the Americans were to set the framework, while the Russians and those who pleaded their cause – including Talbott and the Pentagon – would in the end just have to live with it. As far as Clinton was concerned – and he "would not be deterred" – "moving to the center of Europe [under pressure from Kohl, Poland, Hungary and the Czech Republic were now redefined as Central Europe] with NATO was essential and that did not need to cause an eruption in Russia".[88] The opponents of expansion beyond the corridors of power, by contrast, consistently argued, as did the military, that it would, indeed, create turmoil in Moscow. For them the maintenance and development of good relations with Russia were a higher value.

Throughout 1994, however, the White House was relieved that, having failed in Bosnia, it could at last be seen to get something done somewhere. For Clinton the issue of NATO expansion was a matter of timing only. And he was notoriously impatient once his mind was made up. It was something of a habit for the National Security Council bureaucracy under Bush ('41) to respond to a position paper with the words "A question for the future, not now." "From the beginning, however," Special Assistant Walker, recalls, "any paper sent to the President with these words would be returned with his left-handed scrawl in the margins: 'why not now?'"[89]

What was seen as temporizing over enlargement under Jenonne Walker at the National Security Council was thus no longer acceptable. The White House was set on what Steinberg called "a relatively rapid expansion of NATO".[90] Walker was quietly relegated to Prague as the next ambassador. Losing no time, while she was still taking lessons in Czech, Lake dislodged the normal process of inter-agency consultation and ushered in as Walker's replacement a tough-minded Russianist, Alexander (Sandy) Vershbow. Vershbow was chosen because he "was as forward-leaning as he [Lake] and President Clinton on NATO enlargement". Together with two others – Daniel Fried, Senior Director for Central and Eastern Europe, and Nicholas Burns, Senior Director for Russia and Eurasia, Vershbow put together a roadmap for "Moving Toward NATO Expansion". Reflecting the spirit of the Prague meeting, it suggested a more rapid admission of new members than others in the administration ever envisaged and included, controversially, Ukraine and the Baltic states.[91] Everyone else was now cut out, including Clinton's point man Talbott, who was benched for the rest of the game, as he was now outnumbered by others of a different opinion and inhibited from seeking direct access to Lake, let alone the President.

Christopher said of Clinton that NATO expansion "would not have happened without him, and it would not have happened nearly as rapidly without his pushing it".[92] But why exactly did he now push it so hard? A salty realist who had worked her way up through the ranks, Walker subsequently explained: "A less admirable reason for some to push NATO enlargement was to distract attention from Washington's unwillingness to oppose Serbian aggression in Bosnia. Enlargement was to make NATO seem vigorous on the move, despite its absence from Europe's worst conflict in the Alliance's history. The shadow of war loomed over everything. One senior political-level official in the State Department even drafted a speech arguing explicitly the need to 'enlarge NATO to save it,' but was dissuaded from being so blunt in public."[93] There was no threat assessment that demanded NATO enlargement. Inevitably the Russians were inclined to assume that some kind of larger strategic imperative existed, a Machiavellian inner meaning; not merely a distraction from more urgent matters but a strategy that had everything to do with cementing US supremacy over Europe. They were totally mistaken in this assumption.

Had there been a military rationale, then the Pentagon would have been on the front line pressing for enlargement instead of spearheading opposition to it. Then a young Russianist Jim Goldgeier, briefly serving at the National Security Council during what was for him an unexpectedly disillusioning time, recalls on the contrary that "In the early Clinton years, there were fears that Russia might abandon its efforts to reduce dramatically its nuclear arsenal or that a domestic backlash would lead to the return of Communists to power in the 1996 elections."[94] Indeed, a Russian, Colonel-General Leontii Shevtsov, attached to the allies in former Yugoslavia later remarked on his own surprise at being unable to find even one American general who actually favoured NATO expansion.[95]

The misgivings of the Pentagon, including Perry – Secretary of Defense from 2 February 1994 – and Shalikashvili – Chairman of the Joint Chiefs of Staff from 25 October 1993 – had certainly not dissipated. That they were not listened to should be seen in the context of Clinton's "rocky" relationship with the military. Whereas notable right-wingers who evaded the draft – John Wayne, Ronald Reagan, Dan Quayle, George Bush Jr, Dick Cheney, Donald Trump and John Bolton – were speedily forgiven their apparent reluctance to risk their lives for their country, indeed admired for their bellicose rhetoric, this was not the case with Clinton. He preferred a smart suit to bomber jackets, and he had been pilloried during the election for evading military service in Vietnam. He had then, after his election, also put his reputation on the line by seeking to legitimize the status of homosexuals serving in the armed forces when Aspin was still Secretary of Defense.[96] So the Pentagon was marginalized, if not shut out entirely from the crucial decisions made on NATO enlargement.

Opposition within the structure of power was thus neutralized; above all from those who knew Russia best, and at the very time the early negative consequences of the new line began to show through. For instance, Kennan's much publicized objections – originally expressed in private – were unsurprisingly fully shared by the US embassy in Moscow.[97] Thomas Pickering was the ambassador and, although no Kennan, he was very experienced and had also turned out to be the most assertive ambassador for many years. Pickering recalled that "once we got wind of NATO enlargement as a serious policy option... we wrote back quite serious, quite strong telegrams to Washington, saying that they had to calculate the effect of NATO on the Russian policy. Rarely, if ever, did we get answers... Could we have done it differently? And I say, yes, quite probably."[98]

His talented young political counsellor, William Burns (at the time of writing director of CIA), was well equipped, being a fluent Russian speaker and a very quick learner. Burns was not slow to detect a new assertiveness in Russian policy, "Born of a mood of national regret over the loss of superpower status and an equally acute sense that the West is taking advantage of Russian weakness." The honeymoon in relations with the United States was definitely over, he wrote. The tougher statements from Yeltsin in the autumn of 1994 against NATO expansion "were an unsubtle reminder of Russian angst about neglect of its interests in the process of reconstructing European security institutions".[99] It is not as though the Clinton administration could say that it was not properly informed. Every US administration had invariably possessed far more information and insight on other countries offered up by its bureaucracy than it knew what to do with – on both sides of the Potomac –but the great and the good just chose to ignore intelligence when inconvenient.

Those in London with direct experience of Russia agreed with their American counterparts. David Logan, Assistant Under Secretary for Eastern Europe from 1992 to 1994, wrote that "Russian membership of NATO may have been impossible but only with a security institution in which it was on an equal footing with the United States might we have avoided the tensions and suspicions, rooted in fear of Western expansionism, manifested in the Ukrainian and Georgian crises."[100] Moreover, the EU was of far greater value at a time of economic reconstruction than

NATO. Indeed, the Assistant Under Secretary for Eastern Europe in London – formerly the number two in the Moscow embassy – took the view that "too much emphasis was being placed on the expansion of NATO, which bothered the Russians a lot".[101] And this attitude persisted for some considerable time.

When Yeltsin arrived in Washington DC at the end of September 1994, unknown to him the die was already cast. True to form, however, Clinton was not exactly candid and extended further empty reassurances that he had given no thought to keeping. Moreover, when Kohl's national security adviser Bitterlich reached Washington DC for his usual consultations in October, he arrived believing that it was as yet still undecided who might join NATO. Bitterlich had three key questions in mind: "which countries would be members in the future? Under what conditions, exactly? What 'compensation' would there be for Russia?" The Germans assumed, for example, that the Baltic states, Bulgaria and Romania would be neutralized as Austria had been in 1955.[102]

The Germans React

When Bitterlich reported back on his return to Berlin, however, Kohl was horrified. Yeltsin had seen both Clinton and Major. Updated on these conversations, and with no sign that domestic political instability in Russia had settled down, Kohl, in the words of Bitterlich, "unequivocably criticised these two important NATO allies about their stance on NATO enlargement".[103] Evidently it was this that prompted the Chancellor to write to Clinton mid-month in support of enlargement but including the important caveat, which was entirely wasted on the President, that "An important element will be Russia's greater integration into the European security structures."[104] Wasted, because the Americans never had any such plans or intentions, as soon became evident.

The Chancellor saw it as essential to have an open discussion with the Russians "since an enlargement of NATO should be a contribution to security and stability throughout Europe". Kohl's idea was that Russia should be more closely involved in European security structures, possibly through the CSCE (Conference on Security and Co-operation in Europe). This could be worked out in Budapest where the Americans and Russians were due to meet in order to finalize the fate of Ukrainian nuclear weapons systems.[105] Bitterlich has since explained their thinking: "The Americans had from the beginning suddenly pushed for a large scale, while we, with the support of the French, bearing in mind the situation overall in Europe and the fragility of developments in Russia, as well as other countries of the former Soviet Union, wanted to work in stages. Our interests were also unfortunately oriented towards different countries."[106] The problem separating the United States from Germany and France was thus not just one of orientation, and scale, but also of timing.

Kohl was destined to be disappointed. None of Germany's partners showed any real interest in the further development of CSCE to alleviate Russian anxieties. The Americans kept their distance. And even that stalwart supporter of CSCE, the German Foreign Ministry, dropped the idea.[107] Whatever Talbott would now have us believe, he was very much the moderate at this stage; every so often discreetly tapping the brake, though never so hard as to bring everything grinding to a halt. James Steinberg at Policy Planning, an advocate of NATO expansion, disagreed with Talbott: "initially he [Talbott] was much more reserved about it. He wanted to go slowly, and he was concerned about the impact on the outside world and on the evolution of democracy in Russia."[108] Steinberg recognized that "the people who wanted to go slowly said, 'Precisely because things are not consolidating well in Russia, we should not put more stress on the system'".[109]

In Washington DC, the Minister for Europe at the British Foreign Office, the crusty working-class, former SAS officer, David Davis, told Talbott that his government's "thinking on

NATO expansion was very close to our own". NATO should be contextualized within "a broad European security Architecture". But Davis feared the United States "might be moving forward too quickly and too publicly".[110] Talbott was also briefed by Pauline Neville-Jones, the forthright Political Director of the Foreign Office, on the following day. It became apparent that enlargement was supported "as long as this avoided setting criteria for admission, establishing timetables, and identifying candidate members".[111] Which was, of course, what the White House was already in the process of doing behind everyone else's back.

In the first week of December Talbott realized that he had been cut out of top-level discussions on enlargement. A crucial shift of principle had been made to include Ukraine, along with the Baltic states, as potential members, but to leave Russia out. Clinton ineptly announced his intention to expand NATO at a hasty summit with Yeltsin in Budapest to sign a memorandum devolving Ukraine's nuclear stockpile to Russia. Kohl's notion of incorporating Russia into a larger security system remained on the shelf. Taken by surprise, Yeltsin reacted in fury at Clinton's declaration that "NATO will not automatically exclude any nation from joining. At the same time, no country outside will be allowed to veto expansion."[112] The Russians had deliberately been elbowed aside. Enraged, Kozyrev promptly announced that the Russians would not now sign up to PfP, a threat which left most of the Clinton people merely shrugging their shoulders with indifference.

For Russia there could be absolutely no doubt where all the decisions on the future shape of European security were being made: in the United States. Clinton had departed after a very brief appearance. Yeltsin had no alternative but to vent his indignation at Vice President Gore, who had been left behind to pick up the pieces. "If you do this, what is Russia's relationship to NATO?", he demanded to know. Gore, who had absolutely no idea and was left scrambling for words, replied implausibly, "Well, on one extreme, conceptually we have not ruled out that Russia could be a part of

NATO." No fool, Yeltsin immediately dismissed this out of hand. Gore also claimed, equally implausibly, that the United States wanted to see "an undivided Europe". But he did not actually say whether he considered Russia a part of Europe or realize that this could be an issue, as every Russian knew it to be, certainly among its neighbours to the West.

Gore's only consolation for Yeltsin was that "The process will be conducted in parallel with a deepening of the [US-]Russian partnership and your partnership with NATO."[113] The problem was that this turned out to be yet another insincere and meaningless reassurance, as the Americans could never be bothered to work out how to square an all-NATO policy towards Russia with a parallel Russo-American entente, a measure of equality that Moscow desperately sought.

Talbott Reacts Badly

Yeltsin was not alone in his fury over what had just happened. By the time he discovered just how far others had run ahead with NATO expansion without consulting him, and that Clinton had announced the plan at Budapest, Talbott was finally driven to write a *cri de coeur*: an explosive memorandum addressed to Christopher, which should really have been copied to, if not directed at, his old friend Bill. He was responding directly to Lake's memorandum to Clinton of 9 October, which took a much tougher line on Russia than a previous memorandum for Christopher of 12 September. The October memorandum, "Moving Toward NATO Expansion", spoke of consulting the Russians throughout the process "but without giving Russians a veto over NATO decisions". Critically, for the first time a National Security Council document suggested that the "Possibility of NATO membership for Ukraine and the Baltic States should be maintained; we should not consign them to a gray zone or a Russian sphere of influence." Lake also referred to an "'Insurance policy'/" strategic hedge' rationale (i.e. neo-containment of Russia)" to be "kept in the background only, rarely articulated." Thus the possibility of Russia joining NATO was not to be ruled out "explicitly", which clearly meant that it was to be ruled out implicitly.[114] It also meant that a renewal of the Cold War was not to be impossible.

It is at this point that the United States made a fight with Russia over the future of Ukraine inevitable. It was merely a matter of time.

Ukraine now had its own identity and fixed sense of purpose as a "permanently neutral state". The Russians found this hard to adjust to, and not just to the loss of the Crimea, the historic home of the Black Sea fleet at Sevastopol since 1783. All attempts by Yeltsin to create a new union at a meeting in Belarus on 7–8 December 1991 had failed completely. It was too late. Only a week earlier Ukraine's Leonid Kravchuk had been elected president with 90 per cent of the vote, with a turnout of 86 per cent. Much to Yeltsin's surprise even voters in the ethnically Russian Donbas region showed little interest in a renewed union. The Commonwealth of Independent States was no substitute. It encompassed most but not all of the former Soviet republics but was in reality no more than a talking shop.

The Russians, however, had by no means given up seeking to re-establish what would effectively have been a post-Cold War alliance with a subordinate Ukraine. But they were to be sorely disappointed. Effectively a cold war now ensued between the two countries, worsened by the fact that both fledgling democracies struggled with the countervailing tide of populist nationalism. Vice President Aleksandr Rutskoi, a former air force colonel, demanded the return of Crimea to Russia. Under his supervision, on 21 May 1992 the Russian Federation's Supreme Soviet issued a judgement "On a legal evaluation of the decisions made by the highest organs of state power in the RSFSR [Russian republic] in changing the status of Crimea, taken in 1954". It claimed that in transferring Crimea to Ukraine from the Russian republic, the Soviet authorities had breached the Russian constitution. The

Russian government insisted talks be held and that the population of Crimea be separately represented.[115] Of the roughly 2.5 million population of the peninsula, 67 per cent were Russians and 97 per cent were Russian speakers.[116]

There were other controversial issues at stake. Lurking behind them was the fact that US planning for war with the Soviet Union using forward-based systems included aircraft carriers in the Eastern Mediterranean, which could send in nuclear capable jets flying low through Ukraine, the soft underbelly, to attack Russian defences.[117] Crucial parts of Russia's nuclear capability were also stationed within Ukraine; though the keys were tightly held in Moscow. The borders between the two countries had never been demarcated. Not only had Ukraine been an integral part of the Soviet military industrial complex, it was also still a nation state in the making, having been enlarged to the West twice by Stalin, in 1939 and 1945. It thus partook of a complex patchwork that lacked inherent homogeneity in respect to religion and language as well as national identity. Native Ukrainians made up only 73 per cent of the population, and it did not take long for cracks to begin to appear in Ukraine's body politic. The legacy its leaders had to grapple with was by no means a simple one. It was this that gave the Russians hope that, if worse came to worse, its near neighbour could be partitioned, and much of that lay in the divided loyalty of the Russian-speaking population to the east and the south.

In a heroic attempt to patch up relations between Moscow and Kyiv, on 23 June 1992 the two sides began negotiating a treaty of friendship, co-operation and partnership. It was seen as setting the tone and creating an atmosphere in which detailed questions at issue between the two sides could be settled reasonably if not amicably. The awkward issue of the Black Sea fleet was not the least of the obstacles encountered and effectively surmounted by postponement. The Russians continued to command the fleet, yet it remained in full display anchored in Ukrainian waters. Negotiations, at times fraught with emotion, took an unprecedented length of five years – until 31 May 1997 – and only succeeded once the treaty was bundled up with three agreements concerning the Black Sea fleet providing for a twenty-year lease of Sevastopol.[118]

On 10 July 1994 the second round of Ukraine's presidential elections had taken place. With only three days to go, the headline on 7 July in *Pravda Ukrainy* said it all in framing the choice the country faced: "With Russia or Under Russia". The accusation levelled at Leonid Kuchma was that he posed as the candidate who would act more assertively against Russia yet "cannot intelligibly explain to journalists why Russia's military industrial complex is banking on him in particular".

Kuchma won against Kravchuk. His voice seemed one of restraint, focused on the prospects for trade. Kuchma called for "normalising relations" with Russia, "our strategic partner".[119] Symbolically, the first foreign ambassador he received was Russia's, Leonid Smolyakov. Kuchma in turn called on Yeltsin to pay a state visit. And he secured a compromise constitution two years later that provided for "the consolidation" of the nation while deftly recognizing the status of Russian as a minority language alongside that of others. To say the least, relations between Kyiv and Moscow were a minefield. Given continuing sensitivities on this score, any direct American interference was bound to create severe problems in the country's relations with Russia.[120]

Whatever one thought of the merits of the positions held by the two sides, no one had a better understanding of the Russian sensitivities than Strobe Talbott and no one was more deserving to be in on the initial decisions on NATO expansion than he was. Yet he had been deliberately excluded from the process. His infuriated response was thus uncharacteristically robust. Talbott wrote: "We're seeing diplomatic reporting and intelligence now suggesting that the Russians believe that NATO expansion and the $25 billion plus-up of the defense budget are just two of many signs that we're abandoning partnership, engagement and integration and adopting instead a strategy of preemptive containment. In fact, quite a few Americans, including some of our own colleagues, believe we should do something of that sort. That would be a catastrophic mistake. Our policy would become a self-fulfilling prophecy." Everyone knew that Russia was "a country in a state of confusion and transition". The "big question" was "transition to what? What will Russia be like a generation from now?" Talbott did not stand with the pessimists. "It is in the vital national interest of the US that Russia remain on a reformist course." NATO expansion had "direct implications for peace-keeping in the Transcaucasus: if the Russians become convinced that we are locking them out of an expanded Europe, they'll be all the more proprietary about what they see as their sphere of influence, all the more heavy handed in 'the near abroad,' all the less amenable to UN and CSCE involvement in their peace-keeping activity". NATO expansion also had implications for Bosnia, discussion of which had plagued the administration. Here "NATO's role, especially when it comes to air strikes, is hard enough for Russia to adjust to now; it will be all the harder if that issue plays out against the backdrop of an ongoing dispute over NATO expansion." The bottom line was that "the prospect of NATO expansion provokes some of the most basic Russian reflexes to twitch: their fear, rooted in geography and history, of encirclement and of exclusion; their sense of being neither truly European nor Asian nor modern". The Russians had been under the misleading impression that PfP was a substitute for NATO enlargement. "As somebody put it in a meeting recently, we had a second track but there was no train on it." They had "a concept but no blueprint". As to the allies: "The French have always been cool on it; the Germans, or at least some Germans, switched from being advocates to skeptics. The Brits have consistently tried to play both sides."

The issue and timing of enlargement had, in Talbott's opinion, been conditional on the bigger picture. "A year ago we said that the expansion of NATO would depend in part on the 'security environment' in Europe. By that we meant – and were clearly understood to mean – that if Russia 'went bad' we'd hasten the entry of the CEE [Central-East European] states to protect them from newly aggressive Russian behavior."[121] Russia had certainly not yet gone "bad", but what had just happened would undoubtedly contribute to its doing so.

That same day Perry, who had also taken alarm at Russian outrage, had with some urgency managed to arrange a top-level meeting with the President and foreign policy makers, believing it yet possible to persuade them to slow down the pace. His declared preference was still to work on the NATO-Russia track before going ahead with enlargement. Perry felt strongly that a prevalent "disrespect for Russia" underlay decision-making.[122] Thus enlargement should on his view be deferred.[123] The gains were long-term, he insisted. It would be a mistake to rush the fences. But he was too much the rationalist. And it was as though Talbott's memorandum had never been written. The objections of Secretary Perry and General Shalikashvili also counted for little. Perry later came to realize that "It was a done deal before the meeting."[124] The mid-term elections on 8 November had seen the Democrats lose the House of Representatives for the first time since 1955. Clinton was not going to wait on events. Now every vote counted.

Arnold Horelick Warns Congress

The United States is not France. The conduct of and responsibility for foreign policy in the United States is not purely the prerogative of the executive. It is shared with Congress even during a national emergency, when time is of the essence. But it does require someone on Capitol Hill to take the initiative. He or she can do so only with inside knowledge as to what the White House is up to. Access is essential. And in this instance the legislators were out of the picture while the key decisions were made on NATO expansion.

Closing down internal exchanges of opinion meant that the "national discussion and debate" that should have taken place earlier "did not precede the administration's decision at the end of last year [1994]". This is what Arnold Horelick, a perceptive but dyspeptic former National Intelligence Officer for the Soviet Union and Eastern Europe (1977–80) and still a consultant, complained about in testimony to Senators in the New Year. "Last December [1994], for reasons that [US] officials have not yet made clear to the Congress or to the public, the administration sought to accelerate the process, declaring the question of whether to expand now settled but denying that expansion had anything to do with a 'Russian threat'." At the prestigious and authoritative RAND Corporation, and implicitly speaking not only for himself but also for fellow Russianists denied a voice on a crucial issue within the deep state, Horelick subjected the policy to intensive forensic examination in testifying to Congress: "Frankly," he testified, "it is my very strong impression that the proposal to expand NATO owes a great deal of its appeal to the paucity of other ideas in circulation about ways to revive the fortunes of the flagging Western alliance and to overcome the torpor that has afflicted it. In the presence of this conceptual vacuum, virtually the entire burden of reviving NATO has been laid on enlargement." He caustically likened the situation to that of a troubled couple who sought to salvage their wreck of a marriage not through therapy but by having another baby in order to revive the relationship.

And what would be the result for Russia? Horelick dramatically highlighted the "undesirable, unintended consequences that could outweigh the benefits that we are seeking". It was in the American interest, he insisted, to enhance the likelihood of the "revolutionary transformation" in Russia succeeding "or at least our interest in not inadvertently harming its chances: it is obvious – and I do not have to belabor the point – that a Russia that emerges from its transformation with a stake in the stabilizing European order can make management of Europe's future security problems a lot easier. A revisionist Russia that feels itself shut out would make European security management much harder and far more danger-prone, and, of course, it would also have a tremendous impact on defense budgets in all of the Western countries."[125] The fact that Horelick could never have been mistaken for a naïve Russophile made his critique all the more credible.

And what of Ukraine? When President Kuchma visited Washington DC on 21–23 November 1994, having negotiated Ukraine's transfer of its thermonuclear weapons to Russia under American pressure, Clinton assured him that "the US does not want to see Ukraine caught between NATO and Russia".[126] But this calculation simply did not add up: at once expanding NATO, and depriving Ukraine of its only ultimate means of self-defence while, as his own officials had covertly provided for, engineering Ukraine's accession to NATO in the longer term. It meant that Ukraine would now depend upon the United States – with policy dependent upon the shifts in domestic opinion – for its future security against Russia. Horelick hit upon the dilemma that NATO expansion created for the newly independent Ukraine – and he did not yet know that Lake had already included it on the list as a NATO candidate – the second largest republic of the Soviet Union and a major segment of its armaments industry. "Pressure on Ukraine to move beyond economic integration toward security ties with Russia would surely follow with consequences that could threaten Ukraine's independence and security or both." People had talked of a security vacuum opening up in Eastern Europe after the disappearance of the Warsaw Pact. Horelick was not reassuring: "Would there be a net benefit to European security from trying to fill one security vacuum at the expense of deepening insecurity in the adjacent one?"[127]

As to a solution, Horelick believed that what was needed was a Marshall Plan for Russian economic recovery rather than NATO enlargement. What the advocates of enlargement blithely ignored, but which the US military were only too well aware of, was that Russia was tottering on the brink, with exceptionally high inflation, complete social disorientation and Yeltsin's unsteady hand on the tiller. Worse still, Russia's President had just had a heart attack.

3

Western Europe Caves In

"...the U.S. intends to remain an important element in the European balance of power to lead NATO's expansion to include Central Europe."

– Richard Holbrooke to Hungarian Prime Minister Horn.[1]

US reassurances to Russia on NATO expansion were accompanied by the claim that the organization was changing: it was no longer the war-fighting alliance that it had been during the Cold War. If that were so, it was not unreasonable to ask, why then did the Visegrád countries seek membership of the alliance? Apart from the troubling issue of the motives driving those seeking to join, it was a claim bluntly contested by director of foreign intelligence Yevgeny Primakov. Primakov, codename Maksimov, had once spied in the Middle East undercover as a journalist before becoming an academic.[2] He told Yeltsin that "We had absolutely reliable evidence that strategic military planning at NATO headquarters as before includes a 'worst case option' for the use of nuclear weapons". Against whom? Primakov asked. "Russia, China?"[3]

In March 1997 at a summit in Helsinki, Clinton had been in office for more than five years, and he was as charming but as unhelpful as ever. He readily acknowledged the problem raised by Primakov with a belated plea: "I'm trying to change NATO".[4] He had still made no effort to do so, however.

Much in politics is, of course, to be explained by established bureaucratic inertia and the enduring power of vested interests, not least those of the US Department of Defense. Instead, the tricky task of tackling departmental obstructiveness and reforming the order of battle fell to President George W. Bush ('43), Clinton's successor; at least to his Secretary of Defense, Don Rumsfeld, an old hand who was eager to get started. Bush's cynical consigliere, Karl Rove, of course, had no illusions: "Here was a system that was clearly designed to meet the challenge of 5,000 Soviet tanks coming through the Fulda Gap in Germany that wasn't there any longer. Yet it took an enormous amount of muscle to kill it, raising questions about how difficult it was to modernize the military."[5] The Russians were not much impressed by the results of these changes: "NATO prefers to 'keep its powder dry'," the Foreign Ministry's specialist on arms control noted, "and the old functions from the time of the Cold War – guaranteeing readiness for a confrontation in Europe with a major adversary – have not been removed by anybody. They have merely been displaced to a secondary position."[6]

Arming the Bosnians

From all sides the military within NATO opposed enlargement for various reasons, not least because it would ultimately mean change, though not of the kind that the Russians were looking for. Full-scale expansion entailed dilution of a compact alliance that had been solidified – and not without difficulty in accommodating bitter rivals Greece and Turkey – over several decades. It also brought with it responsibility for territory, the defence of which was impracticable (like the Baltic states), certainly given the existing order of battle. And while the White House was pushing ahead on East/Central European membership, the military was simultaneously arguing about the impracticability of intervention in former Yugoslavia without being encumbered by UN control. Yet the use of NATO out of area for offensive purposes inevitably aroused Russian misgivings, because whereas it had a veto at the UN Security Council it had none within the alliance. In addition, it highlighted Russia's utter irrelevance to the solution of the Balkan problem.

In the face of resistance from the CIA, which had tried to work through the Serbs and continued to liaise secretly with Milošević's head of secret intelligence (*Državna bezbednost*), Joven Stanišic, the White House, State Department, Department of Defense and CIA began arming Muslim resistance to Serb ethnic cleansing, including Mujahadin fighters.[7] The arms came by way of what was called the "Croatian pipeline" from Iran, Turkey and Pakistan, and were financed by Saudi Arabia. Even Ukraine, Israel and Greece were implicated. (The Croats were then colluding with the Bosnians against the Serbs.) This of course deliberately undercut the British-sponsored UN ban on arms for Bosnia sponsored by Foreign Secretary Douglas Hurd, which had been introduced on 25 September 1991, and which the Americans were officially tasked with enforcing by air but which they now did their level best to undermine.

US policy was freed from remaining British constraints by the massacre at Srebrenica. The town had been designated a UN safe haven protected by a Dutch battalion, but the Dutch were speedily disarmed and 8,000 Bosnian males, including those as young as fourteen, were rounded up and shot by Bosnian Serbs in July 1995. It was a blatant act of genocide; the most horrific individual consequence of the intensification of this extended ethnic civil war. The subsequent bombing of Sarajevo's marketplace on 28 August (by whom remains a matter of doubt) resulted in NATO air strikes – Operation Deliberate Force – against Bosnian Serb targets from 30 August through to 14 September, including the dropping of depleted uranium munitions.[8]

The fact that the bombing took place as the Croats and Bosnians were launching a joint offensive against the Serbs, which inter alia lifted the long siege of the Bosnian capital of Sarajevo, certainly suggested that all this amounted to much more than mere retaliation. But it did finally succeed in bringing Milošević to the negotiating table before the year's end. Arguably, though, the bloodshed could have been avoided several years earlier if Christopher had not sabotaged the Vance-Owen plan, since the peace conditions did not differ much from those originally proposed by Vance and Owen and dismissed at the time as immoral. The key difference, of course, was that Clinton now faced re-election.

The hypocrisy of it all did not escape the participants, and those relegated to the sidelines, namely the Russians. In Moscow Talbott found Kozyrev desperately trying to cool the temperature as everything seemed to be spinning out of control. Prime Minister Viktor Chernomyrdin had even indulged in loose talk of Serbian genocide. Had the Vance-Owen Plan succeeded, of course, NATO need not have been mobilized; however necessary in 1995, this served only to aggravate Moscow's abiding sense of exclusion and deep-seated sense of grievance. The Americans, however, were scornfully dismissive of Russian dismay. "I know all this makes you sigh heavily and perhaps, if you're really annoyed, roll your eyes", Talbott wrote to Christopher, appealing for empathy. "I can just hear you thinking to yourself. There they go again. And there goes my trusty deputy, making the case not just for tolerance but for accommodation of the big babies in Moscow... once again, I think we've got to go about the conduct of diplomacy as adolescent (if not abnormal) psychiatry where Moscow is concerned."[9]

In London the Russian ambassador's concerns were by no means trivial. The US military attaché told him that NATO was needed to preserve peace in the Balkans. Adamishin's reaction was that "this alters the mission of the alliance from defensive in principle to something different. In practice – offensive, both beyond the limits of its borders and also in favour of one side.

NATO power is substituting for UN peace-keeping operations". At the Foreign Office Adamishin was advised that "for the West, Bosnia was not important, but how they pulled together within NATO. Wow!", he wrote: "It means they bombed the Serbs for the purpose of preserving and strengthening NATO."[10]

For the first time since his arrival in London, on 17 September Adamishin expressed his unease in a memorandum destined for Yeltsin's eyes only. "Dear Boris Nikolaevich," he wrote, "the extreme nature of the situation that has come into being as a result of the bombardment by NATO of the Bosnian Serbs, intervention by force into a civil war, obliges me to turn to you in person. Russia is protesting against the bombing, but NATO does not hear her. Moreover, it is escalating; a solution is being pressed into being by force." Adamishin went on: Russia's participation in the Contact Group looked like appeasement of NATO's military action. "This is doing great damage to the prestige of Russia as a nation state." He added: "I have already proposed and once again propose that we declare the program of co-operation by Russia with NATO at an end; cease Russia's participation in the Contact Group until the bombardment ends. Sooner or later NATO will have to do that. Let everyone see that it has been done under pressure from Russia… It is a matter for the Serbs whether they take part in talks or not. Our interests extend further than that. In any event a solution will not come from our side."[11]

Within two days the ambassador was excited to receive a call from Yeltsin's main aide, Viktor Ilyushin, summoning him to Sochi by the Black Sea, where the President was still on holiday. Expectations rose, but just as quickly crashed to the ground. After the debriefing with Ilyushin, Grachev and Kozyrev, nothing came of Yeltsin's hint at a tougher stand towards NATO. Adamishin felt frustrated that he had not made his case. Yeltsin was tired after a rambling and detailed briefing from Kozyrev and a more self-disciplined presentation from Defence Minister Pavel Grachev. The tête-à-tête with Yeltsin that Adamishin had prayed for never happened. "Dima" (Dmitrii) Ruryikov, the President's national security adviser, who was very much old school in his thinking and deeply nostalgic for the glories of the Soviet past, had apparently expected Kozyrev – whom he had seriously concluded was an "American agent of influence" – to be sacked. On the following day he expressed his acute disappointment to Adamishin that this was not on the cards.[12] The "Serbian allies" thus failed to find themselves a Russian umbrella, and for the time being the Bosnian war ended with the so-called Dayton agreement, initialled in Ohio but signed in Paris on 14 December.[13]

The same concerns raised and pressed by Horelick in congressional testimony were subsequently echoed in numerous diplomatic despatches. With Russian presidential elections due in the summer of 1996, Italy's permanent representative to NATO Amedeo De Franchis emphasized the need "to avoid feeding Russia's sense of marginalisation from Europe's security procedures at an extremely delicate phase in its history" with the democratization of the country.[14] Relations with the West were not made easier because of the war Yeltsin had unleashed in November 1994 on rebellious, separatist Chechnya in the North Caucasus, beginning with the bombardment of the capital city, Grozny, under the command of Defence Minister Pavel Grachev. It was done to sustain Russia's uncertain territorial integrity. It was not just an abject failure – in 1997 Yeltsin gave up the effort and signed a peace – it was also a bloody fiasco for his badly led troops and the unfortunate Chechens.

It could have undermined entirely the arguments of anyone in Eastern Europe that Russia posed any immediate threat to their security in the foreseeable future. Judging by the Chechen war, even a domestic insurgency within Russia was apparently impossible to suppress in the face of difficult terrain. Instead, its impact on those in the region only served to confirm their fears of living with Russia without a protective military canopy that only NATO could provide. Moreover, for at least nine months the crisis played into the hands of those at home who questioned Yeltsin's judgement. From the US embassy in Moscow Burns noted how the war spluttered on into the summer of 1996 with a fatal combination of aggressive assertion, crass ineptitude and wilful savagery; a godsend to the countries of Central and Eastern Europe in need of a justification for entry into NATO as an insurance policy.[15]

Overcoming Scepticism in Europe

Remarkably, and against the odds, both Yeltsin and Clinton won re-election in 1996, the former on 3 July, the latter on 5 November, both with a little help from their friends and some very deep pockets; in Yeltsin's case oligarchs such as Vladimir Gusinsky and Boris Berezovsky, now media moguls who owned the two leading television channels. They naturally expected and received something of material value in return.

The NATO summit had been scheduled for July 1997 in Madrid. The decision was to be taken on the first new candidates for admission. But the European allies were as uneasy as ever on the subject of Russia and enlargement. The late timing of the summit was not fortuitous. Arriving first in London, on 13 January, Talbott had a meeting with British Foreign Secretary Malcolm Rifkind. Here he also met Jeremy Greenstock, the robust Political Director of the Foreign and Commonwealth Office. He was confronted with the paradox of reassuring the Russians that NATO enlargement presented no threat, while at the same time acknowledging that those in Central and Eastern Europe "see enlargement as actually directed against Russia".[16]

The uncomfortable line of conversation certainly did not get any easier a day later when Talbott called on the French President, an old-fashioned Gaullist who was most emphatically not in a charitable mood. Jacques Chirac chided his visitor for the fact that the issue of NATO enlargement had been "poorly handled" during the US presidential elections the previous November. The Americans had not taken "full account of Russian sensitivities". "If one imposes NATO enlargement on the Russians," Chirac said, "the Yeltsin regime will not be able to resist the public reaction and will not remain in power for very long." Looking further ahead Chirac insisted that "you shouldn't underestimate the consequences... you should not blind yourselves to the possibility that this could lead to a resurgence of deep-rooted Russian nationalism". Talbott pushed back. On his view this was incorrect. Talbott insisted that his own knowledge of Russian opinion came from "reliable polling", which only prompted Chirac's dismissive rebuttal that no reliable polling system – even Yuri Levada's inexpert outfit subsidized by the Americans – existed in Russia. "Russia's leaders are becoming increasingly nervous", he added; there had been "more and more opposition to NATO enlargement over the past six months." "Do not forget that, if there is a new drama in Russia," Chirac warned, "it is the continental countries in Europe who will feel the consequences most, not the United States." His parting words were: "I repeat that to impose something on Russia would be a big ask. NATO enlargement is not urgent... When you want something, you cannot humiliate the other party."[17] But the Americans seem not to have been listening. And Talbott had already lost that argument back home.

Having been boxed about the ears, Talbott escaped with the impression that Chirac was unsure whether he would even attend the Madrid summit. Talbott then visited Kohl the following day to find that the German Chancellor, too, was emphatic about how frightened the Russians were. Kohl recalled a European Union Council meeting in December 1992, to which Yeltsin had been invited. The atmosphere was not propitious. Kohl recalled: "Under the table, he [Yeltsin] took my hand and said: 'Helmut, they don't like me, they don't like us [the Russians].'" "You can tell Yeltsin that his fears and insecurities are not grounded in reality," Kohl added, reassuringly, "but in fact, there is some truth in what he senses." Kohl was concerned that Yeltsin was the best that Russia had to offer, but because of his poor health he did not have long to go: "we don't have much time left", Kohl warned.[18] The Europeans sensed that there was worse to come.

John Major was Talbott's last port of call by return flight on 19 February. The news was no better. "Major said he was struck the last time he spoke with Yeltsin, how much his opposition to NATO enlargement had hardened. Two years ago [1995], Yeltsin had been concerned but when pressed at the end of a long conversation, had admitted that his main concern was about rapid expansion; if the process unfolded gradually, Yeltsin had said that it could have a tolerable political cost." Since the presidential elections in 1996, however, his attitude had hardened. "Major judged that Yeltsin was most concerned about possible plans to expand NATO right up to his borders. Yeltsin wanted to know where the process would stop." In answer to all this Foreign Secretary Rifkind floated the idea of building an interlocking system of security that "transcended Russian sensitivities".[19] This had also long been the Franco-German solution. But, though Talbott was too diplomatic to say so, the Americans had no intention of moving in that direction, and for his part Rifkind certainly had no intention of pressing them to do so, as soon became evident.

The United States remained the only global Power. Africa was the single notable omission from its vast overseas military presence. The fundamental aim, from Bush ('41) to his son Bush ('43), was to use NATO as an instrument for the enforcement of a Pax Americana that stretched well beyond the boundaries of Europe. For that it had to remain an alliance. So an integrated system of collective security for the continent alone that included Russia, as the Europeans kept suggesting, was certainly not seen as being in US interests. The United States, of course, was not only not a European Power, it was above all extra-European in the vast array of its interests, economic and political.

Faced with the prospect of the first wave of admissions to NATO – Poland, the Czech Republic and Hungary – which he had been unable to stop, Russia's new Foreign Minister Primakov was clearly most alarmed at what could follow in the Baltic states and Ukraine. In London on 27–28 February 1997 Primakov had talks with Rifkind, in the full understanding that it was not the

British who made the decisions. The Foreign Secretary, invariably emollient, appeared to sympathize with his position, though later in Washington DC he took an entirely different tack. A bad omen, in the words of the Russian ambassador, was that he "completely evaded our accusations that they had obviously not carried out the gentleman's agreement not to expand NATO 'by an inch'". Moreover, "article 5 [an attack on one is an attack on all], critical to the military alliance, remains obligatory, and this is not the transformation of the alliance that was proclaimed. They are now sowing the wind, and will reap the whirlwind".[20]

A week later Primakov warned Talbott that, although the NATO-Russia documents under negotiation could not touch upon alliance membership, the two presidents would have to include them in their discussions on enlargement: "if any countries of the former Soviet Union are admitted to NATO, we will have no relations with NATO. I know that can't be in the document, but it must be a common understanding." And when Talbott jibbed at this, Primakov, speaking from his detailed knowledge of NATO's order of battle, shot back: "let me be very frank. NATO is a military alliance. Its main task is collective defense against aggression. We know that the planning for the worst-case scenario involved Russia."[21]

At the summit with Clinton in Helsinki on 21 March, and under heavy pressure at home, it was Yeltsin's turn to make a last-ditch appeal for the Americans to meet the Russians halfway. He insisted that "Our position has not changed. It remains a mistake for NATO to move eastward." The reason why he would sign up to a NATO-Russia Final Act on co-operation was that he "had to take steps to alleviate the negative consequences of this for Russia". It was "a forced step". Yeltsin added: "Decisions by NATO are not to be taken without taking into account the concerns or opinions of Russia. Also, nuclear and conventional arms cannot move eastward with new members to the borders of Russia, thus creating a new cordon sanitaire aimed at Russia."

And one issue was of particular importance, "enlargement

should also not embrace the former Soviet republics. Especially Ukraine." Once more Ukraine was marked out by Moscow for special attention. Yeltsin was emphatic that, were the former Soviet republics admitted, the Duma would pull out of the agreement. In ten years' time it might be a different matter. To which Clinton insisted that "no one is talking about a massive, all out accelerated expansion". Yeltsin took a moment to vent his innermost fears about the fate of the near abroad. He suggested that "regarding the countries of the former Soviet Union, let us have a verbal, gentlemen's agreement – we would not write it down in the statement – that no former Soviet republics would enter NATO. This gentlemen's agreement would not be made public."[22] To this Clinton astutely and predictably said "no"; not least because, he said, in his experience nothing ever remained secret for long. What he did not also disclose, of course, was what no other member of NATO knew: that the Baltic states and Ukraine had been on the list of potential candidates ever since NATO expansion was tabled at the White House in 1994.

The residual hope that the Russians clung to was that before NATO gathered in Madrid the NATO-Russia Final Act would lock in security guarantees on two fronts: adjusting the agreement limiting conventional weapons in Europe to compensate for its loss of the former Soviet republics, and compensation for the increased force levels it would face from NATO's enlargement; and banning the basing of nuclear facilities in the form of missile sites on the territories of former Warsaw Pact allies. But after an illusory moment of hope, NATO Secretary-General Solana clarified that none of this was in fact on offer.

Russia's Boom and Bust

The talks in Helsinki resulted in the NATO-Russia Founding Act on Mutual Relations, Co-operation and Security of 27 May 1997. This created a Permanent Joint Council. It was intended to lighten the blow of the first stage in NATO expansion. But it scarcely lived up to the hopes that were vested in it, as the Council did nothing to compensate for the emerging military imbalance. Moreover, the Russians appear to have believed that an exclusive bilateral arrangement with the United States would at least implicitly slow down the process of further enlargement. In American eyes, however, Russia was never as important as the geopolitical advantages afforded by the incorporation of the border states.

The fast-crumbling Russian domestic consensus on foreign policy was scarcely alleviated by the condition of the economy. Throughout the 1990s, as NATO mopped up Russia's neighbours as members, the Russian economy was on a rollercoaster ride. Having escaped the straightjacket of central planning that gave predictability at the expense of growth, it had now plunged into a market system that promised but failed to deliver growth, and sacrificed secure, if low living standards. Meanwhile vague promises of assistance once made by Secretary of State Baker had given way to grim reality as the international organizations responsible for aiding the reform effort alternated unpredictably between excessive trust and stern severity in the conditions they laid down for the release of funds.

At the bottom of the pile the Russian population was subjected to unaccustomed inflation and job insecurity as the heart of the welfare state was ripped out and replaced with nothing but uncertainty, a new form of alienation and rampant corruption at every level. State assets, along with dollars, fast became the preferred medium of popular exchange. People lined Gorky street (formerly Tverskaya) in Moscow desperately selling whatever came to hand from under the counter or off the back of a delivery vehicle. You could easily be poisoned from eating the unrefrigerated cans of caviar on sale in the sunshine. No one had any assurance when anything would stabilize. It was for the privileged few, as Western bankers found on arrival in the Russian equivalent of the gold rush, the wild East, where everything was on sale, including those responsible for financial regulation.

Major, who, as a former Chancellor of the Exchequer, was not unfamiliar with economic matters, believed that Bush could undoubtedly have responded to Russia's needs with greater dexterity had he so wished. Major suggested that "the IMF might have looked slightly less harshly at helping Russia in the early Yeltsin years. The IMF applied strict economic criteria and asked Yeltsin and Russia to do things in return for their loans in a situation of chaos that no secure Western democracy would have been able to do at a time of peace. He might have looked more critically at that and it might have had a different outcome."[23]

Initially, radical economic reform led by Russia's first Prime Minister, economist Yegor Gaidar, was obstructed by the Duma. It had only managed to privatize 70 per cent of the smaller enterprises through a scheme of certificated share distribution among employees, who promptly fell prey to sharks – including Western diplomats – offering ready cash during rampant inflation because the holders had no idea that hanging on to these shares would eventually prove profitable. The Duma answered to the vested interests of giant state monopolies like Gazprom for the gas industry, epitomized in Gaidar's immediate successor, Viktor Chernomyrdin (1992–8), perhaps best known for his aphorism: "We hoped for the best but things turned out as they usually do." That was why the energy industries were not liberated from state control. Not until the constitution was reformed in December 1993 to give the presidency greater powers did the centre and the economic reformers have a chance to dictate the process of change, but by then Yeltsin had grown wary, until he realized that the power of big money could secure his re-election.

The complication ahead was that those driving the reform process in 1995, led by Anatoly Chubais and under the influence of the *nouveaux riches*, initiated a transparently corrupt form of marketizing Russia's huge conglomerates to ensure that capitalism in Russia was there to stay. Out of this emerged enormously wealthy oligarchs, like Mikhail Khodorkovsky, as head of Yukos, a powerhouse in the oil industry. Some of them kept the records of shares in obscure locations on the other side of the country in Siberia and ripped out the entries of shareholders to grab everything for themselves. They hired former KGB officers to ensure their own security and as enforcers to collect debts. It was not unknown for foreign businessmen to disappear from the airport on arrival having taken unlicensed taxis, never to be seen again. The oligarchs then deployed their considerable resources to evade taxation (which bankrupted the treasury) and mobilized them to influence the parallel process of political change.

The political side effects were for a time eclipsed by the first sustained growth spurt Russia had experienced when in mid-1997 inflation was effectively banished and the tiny Moscow stock market suddenly blossomed to become the best performing in the world. Only a year later, however, it crashed as the underlying weakness of the Russian banking system showed itself. A crisis erupted on 17 August 1998.

The financial world was now truly global for the first time since 1914. The causes of Moscow's financial collapse emerged as an extension of the Tom Yum Kung crisis that broke out in distant Thailand the year before. Hot money that had accumulated in a Thai boom began fleeing for the exit when expectations of further growth dropped. The Thai Baht dropped its dollar standard and fell by 50 per cent in value. Dollar denominated debts doubled and, unable to meet payments, firms went bankrupt. Before long most Asian markets were struggling in anticipation of a flood of cheap Thai exports even as the IMF stepped in to stabilize the situation. As investor confidence in developing countries' markets fell, Russia experienced unprecedented capital flight and rising interest rates, forcing a devaluation of the rouble and a moratorium on debt repayments. By 1999 inflation had reached 85.7 per cent. No one knew how much worse it could get; memories of the early 1990s were still all too fresh. Nothing discredited economic reform more than this disaster. It was effectively the terminal crisis of the Yeltsin regime.

Although triggered by events far afield, the catastrophe was also due to a severe deterioration in terms of trade for Russia's main exports, which were raw materials, particularly oil and gas, amounting to at least 85 per cent of the country's export earnings. This was, of course, also not something Moscow had any power over. But what was unquestionably within its grasp – financial stabilization in the form of tax revenue – had fallen victim to the manifest greed of the oligarchs to whom Yeltsin was now beholden; particularly those who paid for his re-election in 1996.

Under Chubais the state had sold off its assets in casual disregard for the world prices of the commodities concerned. From boom in the 1970s, commodities hit bust in the 1980s. Energy prices, in particular, lay at the lowest end of the curve, which in a handful of years began to shoot upwards in yet another boom. What was Chubais' excuse? In a conversation with the *Financial Times*, he argued "We did not have a choice between an 'honest' privatisation and a 'dishonest' one, because an honest privatisation means clear rules imposed by a strong state that can enforce its laws. In the early 1990s we had no state and no law enforcement."[24]

The least one can say is that, like most economists, Chubais was not so good at looking ahead. Disgracefully, state revenues now amounted to only 16 per cent of GDP. By July 1998 debt interest payments were 40 per cent higher than government income.[25] On 17 August Russia was left with no choice but to default on its debts. The Russian stock market fell off a cliff. The ultimate dangers of external dependence were frighteningly apparent, with untold consequences for living standards at home. To Yeltsin, by then increasingly inebriated while the walls caved in around him, it came as "a fantastic shock", as former aide Georgii Saratov recalls.[26]

Behind closed doors Yeltsin's instinctive response was to jettison the leading free market reformer Boris Nemtsov as his intended successor. In his place he brought in former foreign intelligence chief, foreign minister Primakov. He became Prime Minister in September 1998. The free market, which had until very recently smiled on Russia, had now shown its teeth. Dismayed at liberal radicalism, Yeltsin instead moved to firm up what little had already been achieved in respect of economic reform. But other dangers emerged. Primakov had presidential ambitions of his own and, along with the corrupt mayor of Moscow Yuri Luzhkov, epitomized former Soviet officials who would later become identified as the *siloviki* – the hardliners.

The US ambassador at the time was James Collins. He well remembers "how absolutely paranoid the entire elite was at what might happen as a result of the collapse of the ruble and the collapse of the economy... There was a real worry that there was going to be a huge uprising and chaos. Everybody from the farthest right to the farthest left in the political spectrum in Moscow at that time was out trying to keep a lid on things. I remember this was [a] serious business."[27] The Yeltsin era was thus widely seen at home and abroad as a busted flush. Out of ignorance the President had squandered opportunities. People clung on to him only for fear of something worse. In the bitter memory of reformer and former Gorbachev aide Viktor Kuvaldin: "At the end of October 1991 Boris Yeltsin promised that in three to four years our country would be counted among the prosperous and securely provided for. But we fell into such a deep pit that we are to this very day digging ourselves out of it."[28]

4
NATO Goes to War

*"Our cooperation came to the brink of collapse with Kosovo.
If we had not kept in touch and dealt honestly, and openly
with one another, it would have gone over the brink."*

– Yeltsin to Clinton, 20 June 1999.[1]

Former Yugoslavia did not remain quiescent for long. Douglas Hurd, who helped secure the end of sanctions on Serbia at Dayton, breakfasted with Milošević in the following summer on behalf of NatWestMarkets to advise on the lucrative privatization of Serbian Telekom. Pauline Neville Jones, whom he had just taken on board at NatWest, took the notes for her former and now current boss. The company was by no means the first choice – which was UBS – but the subsequent Italian parliamentary board of enquiry notes that NatWest was "chosen personally by Milošević (as an extension of his friendship with Douglas Hurd)".[2] The Serbs were, indeed, very grateful for the "salvage anchor" – as the Italian enquiry called it – provided by this exorbitant deal.[3] Italy paid far too much for its share despite the fact that the ambassador in Belgrade warned them of the dangers. The Serb regime had as a result more money to suppress the opposition and used the proceeds to fund the crushing of the Muslim Albanian rebellion in the province of Kosovo.⁴ Kosovo's capital lay inside Serbia. Pristina was the most industrially developed part of the country and, crucially, it was also central to the medieval birth of Serbian identity, though it was now peopled predominantly by Muslims, a situation not unlike Jerusalem. Here the (Kosovan Albanian) liberation army, the KLA, operated with the backing of foreign military supplies as the United States turned a blind eye to shipments of arms from the Islamic world. On 28 February 1998 the KLA proclaimed a war to liberate Kosovo. The Serbs responded with customary savagery. A ceasefire was arranged on 12/13 October 1998 courtesy of the Organization for Security and Co-operation in Europe and a monitoring force – the Kosovo Verification Mission – was put in place under someone closely associated with the CIA, a former ambassador to El Salvador, "Bill" Walker. But instead of facilitating mediation, which was the ostensible purpose of the monitoring force, CIA personnel aided and abetted the KLA to force out the Serbs with the result that the Kosovans gained the advantage over them by early 1999. On 15 January Walker claimed there had been a massacre of civilians at Račak in southern Kosovo, when in fact the Serbs had launched a classic punitive assault on the town in retaliation for the murder of three policemen, which resulted in the deaths of several dozen KLA fighters.⁵

Casus Belli

Suitably packaged for his superiors in Washington DC and the compliant media, the incident was seen as just the reason for war that Madeleine Albright, the new Secretary of State, had been seeking. Albright, much the same as Holbrooke in terms of character, but forthright in acknowledging that she was "not a diplomat", had a mind to teach Milošević a lesson.⁶ And Sandy Berger, not about to stop her. But first they had to win international support, and for that purpose negotiations at Rambouillet were conducted. They collapsed in mid-March when Serb intransigence predictably refused to allow what was effectively the occupation of their country as the means of enforcement.

It was also clear that the Russians would block action in the UN Security Council. Albright had tried her best in Moscow with Primakov, who was otherwise something of an admirer. They could speak candidly if not bluntly to one another – in English – without causing offence. On 26 January, for instance, in Washington DC, when they were deep in discussion on the Russian economy, Primakov had blurted out what haunted him in utter frustration: "We [the Russians] are moving through a narrow corridor between chaos and dictatorship."[7] But the Americans failed to heed such warnings or indeed take any Russian warning seriously. Russia's resistance to US wishes was therefore increasing. And when Britain's permanent representative to the United Nations suggested in private to his Russian counterpart that they back the US demand that the Serbs sign on to Rambouillet, Sergei Lavrov, although intelligent enough to see the sense in it, insisted that this would be "too great a capitulation to US policy. The lines had been drawn."[8]

Robert Hunter, the US permanent representative to the alliance in Brussels, looked back regretfully: "NATO has often not been inclined to consult Moscow even when Russia has believed its interests were involved", he noted. "Following Russia's acquiescence to the first NATO expansion, and its possible role in the Implementation Force for Bosnia, the issue came to a head with the US-led NATO decision in 1998 to use airpower against Serbia over Kosovo. To Russia Serbia's humanitarian transgressions were not as important as the West's ignoring Russian concerns about attacks on Serbia, the provocations of the ethnic Albanian Kosovo Liberation Army and the absence of a UN Security Council resolution. From Russia's perspective stopping aggression against Bosnia-Herzegovina had been one thing; attacking Serbia over Kosovo, which was part of Serbia, was quite another."[9]

Albright, however, was determined to have her way on Serbia, whatever the odds against success. She was out to avenge the failure of the administration to act at the earliest moment – by lift (the arms embargo) and strike (striking Serbian forces from the air) – to save Bosnia, which she had for years vigorously advocated. Unknown to the Germans, who came in to support the Americans, the State Department was also pro-Albanian under Albright, which Bitterlich – as usual, handling matters for Kohl – learned about only later in Brussels.[10] Allied airpower was the obvious instrument for attack. Sandy Berger recalled: "NATO had been created in the late 1940s and never really used except in Serbia for a brief period of time. This was the first war that NATO had fought."[11] And Russia believed it had good reason to suspect that it might not be the last. *The Economist*, invariably well briefed from Whitehall, shed light on events: "The Kosovo war was not fought for conventional reasons of national interest, nor yet was it quite the humanitarian venture that western leaders proclaimed it to be. Rather it was a war they stumbled into by miscalculation when their diplomacy failed; it then became not just a war to end Serbian injustice, but also a war to preserve NATO's credibility."[12]

On 24 March 1999 NATO launched Operation Allied Force. It was intended as a short, sharp shock. But, as so often happens, it turned out to be nothing of the sort. It became a seventy-eight day bombing campaign against Serbia aimed at halting Milošević's campaign against Kosovars.[13] Primakov was onboard a plane heading for major economic negotiations in Washington DC. Vice President Gore had called him en route to forewarn him of the likelihood that Holbrook's last-ditch attempt to get the Serbs to accept the Rambouillet agreement would fail. And when the bombardment of Belgrade was ready to be unleashed, Gore updated him. Primakov consulted Yeltsin, refuelled at Shannon in Ireland, and flew straight back to Moscow. There he called Milošević in an attempt to persuade him to accept Rambouillet, to no avail.[14] Primakov's lame argument for halting the bombardment was the fallacious one that it would not force the Serbs to the table. In truth even the most westernized Russians saw the

Serbs as brothers and blinded their eyes to the atrocities inflicted by them.

When the bombing began, Russia's Foreign Minister Igor Ivanov, formerly ambassador to Spain, froze all co-operation with NATO. But it was an empty gesture. The Kremlin was powerless in the face of NATO's air war. It never had the leverage over the Serbs that others thought it might have had. On 14 April Yeltsin appointed Chernomyrdin to negotiate a way out, which he failed to do because Milošević still believed the Americans were bluffing. Finally, on 19 April the two presidents, Yeltsin and Clinton, spoke to each other by phone. Yeltsin said that "quite frankly… anti-NATO sentiment in Russia keeps growing like an avalanche. Great pressure is [being] exerted on me and the Russian leadership as a whole in favor of taking measures to help Yugoslavia, all the more so since NATO has helped the Albanian fighters. We continue to oppose Russian involvement in the conflict, but our ability to counteract those demands are limited." He found it "increasingly difficult to resist sentiments here".[15]

The Russians were worried not merely about the state of relations with NATO, as Talbott discovered from his conversations with Yeltsin's key advisers: Ivanov, Chernomyrdin, aide Alexander Voloshin and, now Prime Minister, Primakov. "Russia was concerned about the 'many Kosovos' in the F[ormer] S[oviet] U[nion] and even inside Russia." And it was equally clear that "Kosovo policy had become caught up in feuding between Yeltsin and Primakov." The impact on Russian domestic opinion could not be ignored: NATO bombing boosted the nationalists and the communists ahead of the Duma elections in December. Russian prestige had to be restored before then. Talbott told the North Atlantic Council "that Russia was worried about the possibility of a permanent protectorate run by NATO… If the West were to take part in an international troop arrangement, Russia wanted to be there too."[16]

Seizing Slatina Airport

Ripping a leaf from the American book, the hardliners in Moscow were not about to wait for an invitation. They resolved that only by direct action and the threat of force could they secure Russia a place among the UN peacekeepers in Kosovo.

Anatoly Kvashnin, the tough chief of Russia's General Staff, had contacted NATO's Supreme Allied Commander Europe, General Clark, and Lt General Mike Jackson (commander of the Allied Rapid Reaction Force in Kosovo) through military attaché Lt General Barmyantsev. He told them that ground forces should not go into Kosovo without the explicit consent of the UN Security Council. Jackson, who had read Russian at Birmingham University, was much the more reasonable on this matter – "I do not want to start World War III", he famously said – than Clark, who, still very much in Cold War mode, bluntly told Kvashnin that Russia was not wanted. At which point his Russian interlocutor retorted that "along with your forces, ours will come too". Thereupon Kvashnin called on Vladimir Putin, who had risen to become director of the FSB (counter-intelligence) and secretary of the Russian Security Council. The belief was, as Barmyantsev recalled, that what was going on constituted "an attempt to remove Russian participation from questions of global significance for European security".

Kvashnin suggested to Putin that they seize Slatina airport, 15 kilometres outside Pristina, the capital of Kosovo. Putin asked why. Kvashnin replied that "we would have to leave but we would be there to bargain". Putin said that if he thought it worthwhile, then Kvashnin should go ahead after further consultations in the Ministry. But Kvashnin deliberately cut out his own minister, Grachev, and Foreign Minister Igor Ivanov. "I feared a leak", Kvashnin recalls. "Because there were around them many comrades whom I called agents of influence. To use the language of the Great Patriotic War, 'A chatterbox is a godsend to a spy.'" The operation, worked out under director of the GRU Valentin

Karabel'nikov, was planned with men from the General Staff, the Main Operational Directorate and the UN peacekeeping contingent.[17]

As soon as it became known that a UN peacekeeping force was due to arrive from neighbouring Macedonia at Slatina airport, a small group of eighteen Russian special forces moved in under deep cover as the advance guard. News of the movement by at least forty Russian military vehicles in the direction of Kosovo soon reached the Americans and precipitated a hasty flight by Talbott to Moscow to find out where these forces were headed. But on enquiry no one seemed to know anything. The fact was that the Russian military attaché in Belgrade, Barmyantsev, was in overall command of the operation on the ground, and in direct communication with the General Staff. It was he who guided the convoy through the Bosnian-Serbian border. In Moscow, answering for the operation of which he was nominally in overall charge, Major General Valery Rybkin was asked what his orders were. But his instructions were entirely oral, deliberately so. Rybkin was ordered three times by Yeltsin, almost incoherent with rage, to turn the column around, which Rybkin said flatly that he was completely unable to do. Contact was none the less made with Barmyantsev. His goal in sight, however, and infuriated at Moscow's latest messages, Barmyantsev recalled how he "was taken aback!... To accomplish a forced march that had taken many hours, of more than 600 kilometres and then, almost at the target, call a halt?! So that NATO forces seize the aerodrome before we do?" He reported that this was just not possible. The battalion was in the Kosovo hills and out of radio contact, Barmyantsev claimed, which was entirely untrue. He was playing for time. Meanwhile the Americans, not far away, blandly assumed that the Russian battalion was just heading towards the railway station for a regular troop rotation.

Finally, at 2.00 a.m. on the night of 12 June 206 Russian troops rolled into Slatina airport from Bosnia and were handed over to General Viktor Zavarzin, who had been the main military representative to NATO, while Barmyantsev, job done, drove back to the embassy in Belgrade. They had been caught on camera, however, by CNN, to the amazement of Kosovo Force (KFOR) commander Jackson as well as senior officials in Moscow. Almost immediately Clark phoned to instruct Jackson to secure the airport before the Russians arrived, using force if necessary. Clark was, to say the least, itching for battle. "I am always reluctant to go *ad hominem*," Jackson said later, "but I think, in some quarters, there was still a sense that the Cold War was inbound. That the Russians weren't the Russians of 1999, but the soviets of 1979. This underpinned the approach taken." Clark's orders were more easily issued than implemented, given that a truce had just been secured with the Serbian army, who were far from defeated and were positioned between the British and the airport. Moreover, news soon came in that 1,000 more men were heading their way on six troop transports from Russia. Before action could be taken, instructions came in from the United States ruling out the use of any American troops and, given that the French had also announced that they would have no part in any fight with the Russians, this would effectively leave the British alone in the line of fire.

It did not take long for Western forces to seize command of the air, however. Romania, Hungary, Bulgaria and Ukraine simultaneously refused permission for Russian troop transports carrying reinforcements to fly through their air space. After a great deal of wrangling the British finally made use of the terms of service in KFOR by contacting the Chief of the Defence Staff in London to refuse implementation of Clark's orders. Even then it took the Chairman of the US Joint Chiefs of Staff to call off Clark, who was punished by early retirement not long after.[18] But it was a close-run thing with generals with Clark's mindset literally calling the shots.

The Americans had spent the past decade misleading the Russians: at first, that NATO would not go east; then, at the end of the decade, reassuring them that although it would, indeed, expand eastwards it was no longer the old alliance and that Clinton was changing it. And then came the NATO bombardment of Kosovo as a direct instrument of US foreign policy. So it was not altogether surprising that Russia should have turned sour. The impact in Moscow, the American ambassador recalls, was "the most profound turn against Yeltsin and the Americans" that he had experienced. "It went deeper even than the economic issue and it went far down and became a cause for all of those critics of Yeltsin and the reform process, and those who thought that Yeltsin had done away with Russian greatness…"[19] It adversely affected even those on the front line of economic and political reform such as Chubais. Symptomatic of the breakdown in trust was the fact that the main lobbyist in the Soviet Union for the reunification of Germany and the retreat from the Baltic, Vyacheslav Dashichev – formerly a GRU colonel and a protégé of Marshal Zhukov – vehemently opposed American intervention. "It is not a secret", he wrote, correctly as it turned out, "that the separatist movement of the Albanians was itself inspired, financed and armed by CIA."[20]

If there was one incident that ensured that Putin and the forces of the deep state – the *siloviki* – would inherit Yeltsin's Russia, it was this. Prestige was everything. The Russians had little else. They had symbolically stood up to NATO and, by refusing to give way, they had at least won a place at the table and with that some self-respect.

The imbalance of economic power between East and West became all the more apparent in that after two terms in office Clinton had cannibalised Republican policies and achieved unusual economic success; notably from the peace dividend yielded by expanded trade and investment in China and elsewhere. The Russian government, on the other hand, had failed to raise revenue and achieve badly needed institutional reform of the economic infrastructure. This was rightly interpreted by the IMF as resulting from "the lack of political consensus".[21] And few could dispute the fact that the political consensus was seriously disrupted by Clinton's all-out pursuit of NATO expansion at Russian expense.

The problem, which the Americans exacerbated throughout, was that they were telling the Russians that NATO was no longer directed at them, while simultaneously tacitly reassuring former members of the Warsaw Pact that they would be protected from the Russians by joining the alliance. To Western Europe, enlargement not only made no sense strategically, it also created tensions with Moscow at a time when the latter was being encouraged to press ahead with essential and risky market reforms while retaining a democratic form of government.

When, at delicate moments, indiscretions leaked to the press that revealed the vacuous core of Clinton's NATO-Russia policy, the whole structure looked all too like an opportunistic enterprise undertaken wholly for domestic political purposes. Certainly, few in NATO who knew the United States from the inside had any illusions. On 10 July, behind the scenes of a summit, two statesmen fell to discussing Clinton's motives for expanding NATO to include the Baltic states. It is a little-known secret that no country is so intimate with Pentagon policies and plans than Canada. Its embassy personnel had long had an open door into the Pentagon. The Prime Minister of Canada Jean Chrétien's comments were picked up by a stray microphone. In the course of the conversation he told Belgium's Foreign Minister Jean-Luc Dehaene: "What is shocking [about American politics] – and I follow this problem, I know the rules – is that nothing's done for reasons of state, it's all done for short-term political reasons, to win elections. Take the quarrel over whether to admit the Baltic states [into NATO]. That has nothing to do with world security. It's all because in Chicago, Mayor Daley controls lots of votes for the [presidential] nomination... The American system. In your country or my country all the politicians would be in prison for selling their votes."[22]

To the extent that the Clinton administration wished to see Russia become a healthy market economy, it should have taken fully into account the impact of its own foreign and defence policy on Russian opinion. But it did not do so. Instead the Americans merely grew irritable at any Russian objections to US behaviour. They could not claim that they had not been warned. Chubais, the economic reformer, patiently explained to Albright that the "Russian people did not understand the rationale for NATO expansion. The issue of enlargement brought the entire range of the Russian political spectrum together in opposition... There was no support among the Russian people for NATO enlargement. Russians would need time to heal from the wounds of cold and hot wars. We did not need NATO enlargement to exacerbate the problems in Russia." And why was enlargement pressed ahead at such speed? "What was the danger? What was the threat?"[23]

The Russians invariably saw American policy as more purposeful than it actually was. But in the United States the left hand had little idea what the right hand was doing, and, to the extent that it did, it did not care; larger domestic political and personal preoccupations overrode the longer-term objectives and any interest in keeping US-Russian relations stable, which should have been important given Russia's massive thermonuclear firepower. No serious thought was given to the underlying instability within Russia. Yeltsin was seriously ill and by now so deeply unpopular that some estimated his support as low as 5 per cent. He was none the less the only stable point in Russia's turning world and stunned everyone by announcing his resignation on New Year's Eve 1999.

The Irresistible Rise of Mr Putin

The surprise for all but Clinton was to learn that Vladimir Putin was Yeltsin's heir apparent as acting president. At their final summit in Ankara Yeltsin had disclosed that his newly adopted protégé, the relatively unknown, small *khudinki* (skinny one), Putin, the very man who signed off on the Slatina airport escapade, would win the forthcoming elections to the presidency.

It was here, too, that Yeltsin appears to have imagined himself in Stalin's seat at the Livada palace, Yalta, crown of the Crimea, determining the fate of the postwar world with Roosevelt and Churchill in February 1945. Inspired by the grandeur of the occasion, Yeltsin had a bright idea. Clinton should get out of Europe. "Just give Europe to Russia", he calmly suggested. "The US is not in Europe. Europe should be the business of Europeans. Russia is half European and half Asian... If you... take all the other states and provide security to them, I will take Europe and provide them security. Well, not I. Russia will."[24] If anything showed after Kosovo just how far apart Russian and American thinking was, it was this strange moment.

Putin now signed a decree exempting the president and his family from prosecution, civil or criminal. The young pretender had joined the KGB in 1979 after studying law at Leningrad University. Following training under the *nom de guerre* Platonov, he was sent to the GDR in the mid-1980s, heading the Soviet-German House of Friendship in Leipzig as cover. When the Berlin Wall came down in 1989 his entire world had collapsed. Putin found work within the KGB overseeing Leningrad University. This brought him into direct contact with his former law professor Anatoly Sobchak, once dean of the faculty, who was looking for someone hungry like Putin at his modest rank (major) from the security services. And when Sobchak became mayor of Russia's second city, he took Putin on in 1991 as a trouble-shooter in the post of deputy and very soon first deputy. St Petersburg was at that time, as economic reformer Chubais noted, "ideologically sterile". It also had a well-established criminal underworld. The city, at the core of the old Soviet military industrial complex, with men like Putin in charge, had banned the word market "because it sounded anti-Soviet".[25]

As was obvious to even a casual visitor speaking Russian, the oppressive atmosphere in the old city – which had previously always seemed more relaxed than the capital – was utterly unlike that prevailing in Moscow. Putin's people gave place to the city's criminal protection rackets – the baseline price for protection was fixed at $25 an hour covering the person, business and apartment for anyone selling on the street or inside the covered market – which made it most unlike the capital's plurality of criminal gangs, where at least some degree of freedom and price differentials for protection could be found. Putin also took charge of incoming foreign investment, with German interests to the fore – most notoriously *St Petersburg Immobilien und Beteiligungs AG* (SPAG) – aided by former GDR intelligence officers he had cultivated. Sitting on the mayor's advisory board in regular contact with Russian and foreign directors, Putin appears to have taken his slice of the proceeds; though, unlike others, such as the first deputy prime minister in those days, he scrupulously avoided asking for money up front and in person.[26] On the External Relations Committee of the city council alongside Putin sat others who would rise to the top with him: Dmitrii Medvedev, Alexei Kudrin, Alexei Miller, Igor Sechin and Viktor Zubov. One city councillor, Marina Sal'ye, who managed to secure an investigation of these activities – notably cut-price sales of Russian minerals to the world market in return for foodstuffs that never arrived – was blocked at every turn and ended up having to flee into the silent obscurity of the countryside to escape the dread consequences of her damaging revelations.[27] A close friend of hers, Sergei Yushenkov, was murdered after registering an alternative liberal political party. And journalist Anatoly Levin-Utkin was beaten to death on 24 August 1998 for asking too many questions about these murky affairs.

Putin was never idle. His was a post with long hours of arduous work, including regular travel to and from Germany. After losing a bid for re-election in 1996, his patron Sobchak eventually fled to Paris to avoid prosecution for corruption. This left Putin stranded. All his eggs had been placed in one basket. Putin moved to Moscow at around the same time as the free-market economist Aleksei Kudrin, also a deputy to Sobchak, whom Putin had assiduously cultivated. Their children and their labradors played together out at Archangelskoe in the south-western suburbs near Moscow's ring road, where they both now lived, conveniently close to foreign intelligence headquarters in the woods at Yasenevo across the road. Kudrin was well connected with the Ministry of Finance, with whom he worked closely in the St Petersburg years. He had also been a late entrant to a discussion group of enterprising economic reformers headed by Chubais who were taking full advantage of Gorbachev's perestroika in 1988-9.

When, in July 1996, Chubais unexpectedly replaced Yegorov as head of the presidential administration, Kudrin was invited to come on board as deputy head.[28] But what was good for Kudrin was bad news for Putin. Putin had been recommended to Yegorov by Pavel Pavlovich Borodin, at one time the larger than life, dynamic young mayor of Yakutsk, who had impressed Yeltsin in the course of the President's travels in Siberia: Moscow's shops were bare in 1991, his were full. Down on his luck, Putin was then offered second best: to deputize for Borodin, head of presidential property management, a source of considerable personal enrichment from corruption in refurbishing the Kremlin, but essentially an unexciting job focused on finance. Putin had, however, been recommended to the former head of the administration, Yegorov. And Yegorov was sacked by Yeltsin and replaced with Chubais. And Chubais did not hesitate. He moved to block Putin's appointment.[29]

Once Chubais had left office, however, and the President's son-in-law, Valentin Yumashev, took over in March 1997, Putin found the opportunity he had been waiting for and gave friends to understand that the job he had was "not completely to his taste".[30] His rise thereafter accelerated at dizzying speed. In July 1998 Putin was given command of the FSB (counter-intelligence and domestic security), which meant that he had the book on everyone. It was also under his authority that a specialized FSB unit – the Department of Counter-Intelligence Operations (DKRO) – was formed to tighten surveillance over foreign diplomats and officials living in Russia, deterring espionage and subversion by means of intrusive intimidation.[31] Yumashev was finally forced out on 11 December 1998, enmeshed in a web of corruption that led directly to Yeltsin. In March 1999 Putin took charge of the Security Council, and then replaced the former fireman, Sergei Stepashin, as Prime Minister in August. Little was known of Putin's political views, however, and only so much could be surmised.[32] It looked very much like a stitch-up. At the Ankara summit in November Yeltsin confidently predicted that Putin would win the forthcoming elections to the presidency.[33] And Yeltsin was no clairvoyant.

5

Face to Face with Putin

> *"There had been a real hollowing out of British expertise on Russia, because Russia wasn't seen as a problem. British politicians also didn't realise how different their Russian counterparts were – they're intelligence officials not politicians as the west understands them."*
>
> – A senior British defence adviser, April 2022.[1]

In the United States the Democratic candidate, Vice President Gore, very narrowly lost the presidency to the novice Republican candidate George Bush ('43).[2] Bush was inaugurated on 20 January 2000. Putin, long confined to the shadows, was determined to make his own public relations splash. On the morning of 9 February the FSB swept in and cleared Novodmitrovskaya street, the site of the popular tabloid, *Komsomol'skaya pravda* and its elder sister, the communist daily, *Pravda*. A cocker spaniel called "Richard" was led into the offices to sniff for bombs. Then at 12.15 p.m. Putin arrived to take calls on the newspaper's phone-in programme, *Pryamaya linaya* (direct line). He hung in there for two long hours patiently answering random questions, great and small, from a veritable procession of potential voters and jobbing journalists.[3]

Putin had yet to make a formal announcement that he would stand for election. But since he had taken everyone else off the airwaves and his main backer was Boris Berezovsky, who controlled mass media outlets such as ORT, this was evidently his exclusive moment unless people could be persuaded to vote for a return to the past under the communists. Here Putin coined a carefully nuanced slogan: "he who does not regret the destruction of the Soviet Union has no heart, and he who wants to see it recreated in its previous form has no brain". Inevitably, inquisitive listeners at home and abroad were curious to know what "form" he therefore envisaged in his only promised undertaking: that of "recreating a union state".[4] Were these just empty words, and, if not, was membership to be voluntary or compulsory? This was certainly never made explicit. And however generous one's interpretation, its implications for relations between Russia and its near neighbours and the West were ominous, given Putin's determined character and the steadfast commitment to independence among the former Soviet republics, including that of Ukraine, which the Americans had been actively encouraging.

Recreating "a union state" without Ukraine would, of course, have been completely impossible. Putin's main aim implicitly collided with the long-term American aim of bringing Kyiv into NATO, let alone the opinion of Ukrainians, which was at this stage unknown. Polling of Ukrainian attitudes towards NATO in 1998 found little support for joining the alliance.[5] Putin's ambition also potentially clashed with the "Defense Planning Guidance for Financial Years 1994–1999" drawn up under Defense Secretary Dick Cheney's supervision in February 1992, which stated that "Our first objective is to prevent the reemergence of a new rival, either on the territory of the former Soviet Union or elsewhere, that poses a threat on the order of that posed formerly by the Soviet Union."[6] After all, had not Zbigniew Brzezinski argued in 1994 that "It cannot be stressed strongly enough that without Ukraine, Russia ceases to be an empire, but with Ukraine suborned and then subordinated, Russia automatically becomes an empire"?⁷ These forthright words were, as to be expected, picked up and distributed by Russian intelligence.⁸

Brzezinski was never irrelevant. He was, aside from his continuing role in retirement as an influential foreign policy publicist at the Center for Strategic and International Studies, the mentor of the hawkish Madeleine Albright. And it was no accident that from 1990 the United States gave more aid to Ukraine than any other former republic of the Soviet Union, though most of it one way or other ended up in the ample coffers of the local oligarchs. Aware of all this, one of Putin's first acts as president was to visit his counterpart, Kuchma, in Ukraine on 18 April 2000. Here they argued about much more than the cost of Russian gas and the fact that Ukraine was hosting oppositionist Chechen media outlets. The inter-relationship between Russia, Ukraine and NATO inevitably also arose. Putin immediately fired a shot across the bow. "No, Russia is not welcome there [Brussels]", Putin said. "And if we are told that we are not welcome there, then we will object to NATO getting closer to our borders."⁹

In other words, Russia's attitude to NATO enlargement was contingent upon Russia's acceptance into the Western camp. The British certainly knew as much. How exactly they were certain of this is as yet unknown. But they had made the crucial decision on their own account to make the Russians feel welcome.

The Honeymoon with Tony Blair

In London, where the Labour Party had won office in a landslide in May 1997, Prime Minister Tony Blair's foreign policy adviser was a young high-flyer, the former MI6 officer John Sawers (later 'C', the director). He had previously worked as Hurd's Principal Private Secretary. Evidently based on hints from Russian intelligence sources, Sawers encouraged Blair to reach out to Putin before the forthcoming Russian presidential election.[10] At MI6 'C' – Richard Dearlove – was equally encouraging.[11] At that time the sister service for communications intelligence, GCHQ, had seen expenditure on Russia crash to 16 per cent from 70 per cent of their budget. It fell further to a new low of 4 per cent by 2006, at the very time when relations with Russia began seriously deteriorating.[12] Similar falls were evident for MI6 and MI5. But someone was too embarrassed ever to release the numbers. Career prospects in intelligence and diplomacy were in secular decline for Russianists; the EU or Middle East terrorism were the way to go. And judging by the quality of some of those employed at the embassy in Moscow, the quality had already deteriorated.[13]

Some months before, Clinton had also indicated to Blair that "Putin has enormous potential... I think he's very smart and thoughtful."[14] An invitation gave Blair the tactical advantage when he made a controversial private visit to St Petersburg with his wife on 10 March 2000, a fortnight before Russia went to the polls. They were shown around Peter the Great's glittering summer palace, Petrodvorets, and the magnificent Hermitage art gallery, before being escorted to see Prokofiev's opera "War and Peace" at the Marinskii theatre in the evening. It struck Blair that Putin very much wanted to be liked.[15] This, of course, was unlikely to have been entirely spontaneous, given the intensity of individual psychology in KGB training. Looking back, Blair felt it was a relationship "that began really well" and, succumbing to imagined empathy, felt "an initial warmth". Even on the issue of repression of the rebellion in Chechnya, which was the subject of considerable controversy back home in Britain, Blair showed himself to be "sympathetic to the fact that this was also a vicious secessionist movement with Islamic extremism at its core..."[16] It mattered that Putin enjoyed foreign policy, as did Blair.[17]

Lord Robertson, formerly Labour's Defence Minister and now Secretary General of NATO, followed suit, in the hope of resurrecting the links with NATO broken by the Kosovo crisis. His mission met with some success. "I wish to renew relations with NATO", Putin said. "Step by step, but I wish to do so."[18] "When are you going to invite us to join NATO?", Putin asked. Robertson dryly replied that "we don't invite people to join NATO, they apply to join NATO". This was simply not true according to article 10 of a treaty that Robertson appeared not to have read. "Well", Putin tartly retorted, "we're not standing in line with a lot of countries that don't matter."[19] Yet they did, of course, matter, as they were to have a vote and were before long fully capable of reducing Russia's room for manoeuvre vis-à-vis the alliance.

Putin enlarged on the crucial strategic issue that bothered him most in an interview with David Frost on the BBC: "Let's assume there is a desire on the part of those who perceive the chance to install new mechanisms of ensuring international security. But pretending – or proceeding from the assumption – that Russia has nothing to do with it and trying to exclude it from this process is hardly feasible." He did not rule out joining NATO "if and when Russia's views are taken into account as those of an equal partner". But it did not just have to be about membership. Putin also made clear that "We believe we can talk about more profound integration with NATO but only if Russia is regarded an equal partner. You are aware we have been constantly voicing our opposition to NATO's eastward expansion."[20] Conversations with Putin continued on his first official visit to Britain after election as president in mid-April.

Blair's success appeared to augur well when the time came for the newly elected George W. Bush ('43) to meet Putin on neutral ground in Slovenia on 16 June 2001. Putin seemed very down to earth. Showing tactical flexibility, he had notified the British that he would not exert pressure to delay further NATO enlargement. In this, however, he was flatly contradicted by his Defence Minister Igor Sergeev. Off his own bat, Sergeev told his NATO counterparts on 4 December that "further enlargement would be a major political error, in response to which Moscow would 'take appropriate steps'". Moreover, as 10 Downing Street noted, the "Russian intelligence presence" in Britain was "at Cold War levels, and they continue to try to post active and hostile officers to work against British interests worldwide." Clearly there was still some degree of dissonance among leading figures within the Putin administration, and between what they said and what they did. But Sergeev did not last long; he was abruptly supplanted by a much smoother personality, the former senior KGB officer Sergei Ivanov, in March 2001. London thus congratulated itself that "Our engagement in 2000 gave the opportunity to influence him, and those around him, during a formative period." Moreover, the British also had an eye to the long term in the "need to continue to engage across the spectrum of Russian society, through our assistance with education, retraining, democracy-building, broadcasting, commercial enterprises and so on. This will help the slow process of de-Sovietization and promote the sort of society we want to see."[21]

The Blair government was not slow to back up its overtures to Moscow with enticing incentives. Selling armaments to other states requires standard individual export licences and end lease use agreements. In 1999, the year war against the Chechens renewed after bombings in Moscow, Britain granted Russia twenty licences. They increased to more than 500 per cent. Sales took off, in particular, from 2003 at a time when the Prime Minister was most anxious to secure preferential treatment of British Petroleum in the exploitation of Russia's rich energy market.[22] But more importantly, perhaps, it also underwrote an earnest attempt to win over Putin as a potential member of the Western camp. The trouble was that the Prime Minister placed excessive reliance on inter-personal contacts and a blind eye was turned to the emergence of domestic repression in Russia, though it was widely publicized in the Western press. Blair's working assumption was that the war in Chechnya was merely an aberration. It was also wrongly assumed that the Americans were as pragmatic as the British, or at least, when charmed by Blair, could be persuaded into becoming so.

Across the Atlantic, the new US administration that Blair's foreign policy adviser Sawers was about to meet certainly augured well in that it had every appearance of being peopled more by grown-ups than the Clinton transition team had been. Thereafter, perhaps, the differences appeared less promising. Who exactly was in charge? One could scarcely have described Bush as a forceful personality. He was too much of "a people person": prickly when confronted with press corps snobbery, not unlike his Republican predecessor Richard Nixon had been. Moreover, unlike Clinton or Nixon, he was never the kind of chief executive who could happily absorb his brief at a glance and lose himself in further detailed exploration of an issue on his own. And he ventured into detailed discussion with a foreign statesman only after very close advice. As Bush's consigliere Karl Rove noted: "The foreign policy stuff he readily recognized was not his forte."[23] Indeed, Deputy Secretary of State Dick Armitage formed the distinct impression that it took two years before "the President started feeling that he was really the President".[24] Everyone seems to have expected his younger brother, Florida Governor Jeb, to lead the Republican Party until he thought better of it. And George Bush had, after all, won election on a Supreme Court ruling by a tight margin against the favourite, Gore, who was reputed to be well-versed in matters Russian. Russia, however, now counted for even less than under Clinton. Putin was not in for an easy ride.

The Bush Team

The old guard working for the president were led by Vice President Cheney, whose own chief of staff and national security adviser was Lewis "Scooter" Libby. Cheney had been "a central figure in the transition" and was expected to "turn the Vice Presidency into a real powerhouse". From the outset he was set to be "the power just behind the throne".[25] Rove used to refer to him as "management".[26] From the outset Cheney insisted on actually attending the National Security Council. Here he was careful not to speak out at meetings but, as soon as everyone else had left, he had private words with Bush. Cheney also brought on board fellow hardliner Don Rumsfeld, an old friend with whom he had previously served, to counter-balance the more emollient centrist Colin Powell as Secretary of State. In the scathing words of the former President Bush ('41), the current incumbent's father, he "built his own empire".[27]

As to the Assistant to the President for National Security Affairs, Condoleezza Rice, she had apprenticed under Scowcroft on the National Security Council during the earlier Bush administration. In 1989, it was on her watch and with Cheney as Secretary of Defense when intelligence information came into the White House from the Office of the Secretary of Defense indicating, well before the fact, that the Russians were seriously considering ending the division of Germany. The implications were extraordinary. But the intelligence was effectively suppressed and the culprit duly hounded out of the military because he purposefully broke the line of command.[28] The example could not have been lost on Rice. The system is unforgiving; it takes no prisoners. Being prematurely right within government is an unpardonable sin, as others were to discover with respect to the al-Quaeda attacks on 9/11; whereas playing safe within the prevailing consensus and being wrong with the majority is a certain guarantee against failure.

There also prevailed "a feeling among some of the bigger players that Condi Rice will not be able to hold the ring at the NSC against these big beasts".[29] Albright, whose father – Josef Korbel at the University of Denver – had been Rice's early mentor, predicted as much. Albright uncharitably remarked "that she was worried that Colin Powell would not be a heavyweight player as Secretary of State, at least compared with the Cheney/Rumsfeld combination. Nor was Mrs Albright sure that Condi Rice would prove much beyond a comfort blanket for the incoming president, briefing him on geopolitics."[30]

Progress made at Blair-Putin meetings had thus been a touch premature given that everything hinged upon decisions taken not in London but in Washington, where the British ambassador had instructions to get up the administration's backside and stay there.³¹ And all Blair had done thus far to win over Putin looked to be at risk, without support from the senior partner. The omens were not good. Almost as soon as Rumsfeld breezed into the Pentagon on 14 February 2001, he seized the initiative and lashed out at Russia as "an active proliferator" of nuclear weapons for "selling and assisting countries like Iran and North Korea and India and other countries with these technologies which are threatening... the United States and Western Europe and countries in the Middle East".³² It was not that this was untrue. The question was whether megaphone diplomacy was the right way to go about solving the problem. But it fitted in with the pre-election promise to be tough on the Russians and as such it clashed head-on with Blair's drive to keep the Americans "engaged" on Russia.³³

The Secretary of State, Colin Powell, had more in common with the British. His job, not for the last time, was to pick up the broken china. "With respect to Russia, we do have some strains as a result of this issue. But I think that with Russia, we'll be able to deal with this and it won't be any kind of even short-term damage to our relationship", Powell lamely suggested.³⁴ It was very apparent that hawks – the "vulcans" as they were called – were definitely in charge at the White House. A veteran of the Clinton administration, Sandy Vershbow, himself no dove and now permanent representative to NATO, accurately warned that Moscow's objections to further expansion "would not deter the Bush people; they were more likely to encourage them".³⁵

The United States had become accustomed to looking down on Russia as a defeated power of little or no account. Robert Hunter, previously US permanent representative to NATO, noted that "the prevailing view in the George W. Bush administration was that, since the Soviet Union had lost the Cold War, the US and NATO would do as they please".³⁶ Rice did not have much direct knowledge of Russia. Czech was her main foreign language. She could manage to speak Russian but lacked practice, having seldom visited the country. To her Russia was always more of an abstraction, an armoury of dangerous weapons systems, and now, with the Cold War ended, and careers devoted to Russia a liability rather than an opportunity, studying the country further was certainly no way to spend one's evenings.

Rice had instead joined the presidential campaign banging the drum for Reagan's dream and the Soviet nightmare of an effective anti-ballistic missile defence system. Before assuming office she had audaciously dismissed Russia in print as "mired in inaction and stagnation"; pockmarked by "weakness and incoherence".[37] Summing up, Russia analyst Jim Goldgeier correctly notes that "In the first half of 2001, the Bush administration was less concerned about Russia's reaction [to NATO expansion] than the Clinton team had been in 1996, because the new US foreign policy team did not see Russia as central to American diplomacy."[38] Indicative of this order of priorities was the fact that the President broke precedent and failed to appoint a National Intelligence Officer for Russia. This omission sent a clear message that the country no longer counted for much. "They're organizing Russia down", former National Intelligence Officer for Russia Arnold Horelick rightly complained; the changes might be "bureaucratic and symbolic", but they certainly inflicted damage.[39] Not until the eve of Bush's re-election in 2004 was this omission remedied with the appointment of Thomas Graham.

At this time both the President and Rice were not of a mind to offer Putin any incentives that would offset Rumsfeld's belligerence. They were committed to further NATO expansion – into the Baltic – and focused on constructing "National Missile Defense" (NMD) in Eastern Europe, which meant abrogating the US-Soviet anti-ballistic missile treaty concluded under Nixon in 1972; a move that the Russians initially steadfastly opposed, but which Bush expected to pursue regardless. "Deployment of an NMD system is driven in the first instance by the threat posed by emerging powers", Congress was told. "It is appropriate to note the extant threat as well. Russia's ballistic missile forces are declining in size due to financial and production limitations. Nevertheless, the SS-27 ICBM Russia is deploying is a state-of-the-art system the Russians claim is explicitly designed to penetrate US missile defenses." [40] Indeed, even Tony Blair acknowledged that the Russians "in a sense understandably... saw [NMD] as aimed at them".[41] The infrastructure envisaged could be put to other uses.

What the administration did not tell Putin when they first met in June 2001 was just as important as what they did tell him. National Missile Defense was a goal for the long term. Topping the immediate agenda, and a key priority of the old guard in the administration, but which Bush had obviously not shared with the electorate, was his firm intention to overthrow Saddam Hussein, the dictator of Iraq, who had since 1991 been playing cat and mouse with UN inspectors looking at his ambitions to develop nuclear weapons. This was "unfinished business" – a term endlessly repeated – left over from Desert Storm, the first Gulf War, which Bush's father had waged on UN authority to drive the Iraqis out of Kuwait, occupied on 2 August 1990.

The US-led Operation Desert Storm, launched on 17 January 1991, had concluded with the evacuation of Kuwait and an armistice on 11 April. The elder Bush ('41), a cautious man, decided not to bring down the regime in Baghdad. At the Pentagon others had wanted more. But he was set on a second term and the country would not have taken kindly to such an expensive and open-ended commitment in a wilderness of sand that distracted from economic priorities at home. The aim of Bush ('43), ten years on, was not just to remove Saddam Hussein. The ultimate objective beloved of the neo-conservatives who campaigned for him encompassed the entire region of the Near East. This idea of a transformational crusade was a decade old. In 1991 Wesley Clark had a conversation with then Under Secretary for Policy at the Pentagon Paul Wolfowitz. The Iraq war had been won, and the Shia had risen up in rebellion while US forces stood by as passive observers. Wolfowitz not only felt that they should have disposed of Saddam but was enthralled by the idea that the Americans could go to war in the region without Soviet resistance and mused on the option of attacking Syria and Iran in like manner.[42]

Ten years later, early in 2001, on touring the Pentagon, Secretary of State Powell's chief of staff accidentally learned to his consternation that plans had indeed been drawn up to destroy other dictatorships in the region, including Iran and Syria. Apprised of Colonel (Larry) Wilkerson's informal intrusion, Rumsfeld had him promptly escorted off the premises.[43] In early November, a few weeks after 9/11, an officer at the Pentagon received a memorandum projecting an attack on seven countries in five years: Iraq, Syria, Lebanon, Libya, Somalia, Sudan and Iran. An extensive secret agenda had accidentally been uncovered. General Clark later described it as "a policy coup".[44]

On 10 January 2001 Iraq had taken first place on the agenda at a meeting Bush held with the Chiefs of Staff. It took up more than half the time at their disposal. Pressure for action came mainly from the office of the Vice President, backed by Rumsfeld. The leading option was not a military strike but covert action. Plans had advanced to a point in August when CIA officer Luis Rueda – chosen for his extensive experience, though not in the Arab world – was appointed chief of the agency's Iraq Operations Group. The initial idea was to train Iraqis to overthrow the dictatorship. Rueda was seeing Bush almost on a daily basis at the time when al-Qaeda struck New York's Twin Towers in September. Bush was "very engaged and very personable". Meanwhile, in Britain MI6 had been told ahead of time what was intended. Dearlove testified that Iraq "came on our agenda well before 9/11". The latter, it was always clear, was "not the trigger for a change in policy".[45]

At first Bush, still finding his feet and distracted by planning for the war on Iraq, was less than ready for his first summit with Putin. After their first meeting in Slovenia on 16 June, the President, at a loss for words (a family trait), assured the media around him that he "looked the man in the eye" and "found him very straightforward and trustworthy"; making the extravagant claim that he was "able to get a sense of his soul". The assembled journalists looked on incredulously, while Rice visibly stiffened. The Russianist John Beyrle – later ambassador to Moscow – was sitting with Daniel Fried, similarly trained, a foreign service officer who had under Clinton pushed for NATO expansion into Eastern Europe. They exchanged knowing glances: "Uh-oh!"[46]

The President had only himself to blame. His mind was elsewhere. He had foregone the appointment of a National Intelligence Officer on Russia who would have briefed him on what to expect from a former KGB officer trained to win people over. Bush later insisted that the notoriously inept comment about Putin was not his own and originated in notes written by Stephen Hadley, Rice's deputy; a most implausible assertion given Hadley's well attested professionalism, and an ungracious attribution that Hadley has since emphatically denied.[47] "We were never able to escape the perception that the president had naïvely trusted Putin…", Rice confessed in her memoirs.[48] She took it personally. The incident evidently continued to rankle years later.

At the summit, neither Bush nor Rice paid serious attention to unexpected warnings from Putin about Islamic fundamentalism – particularly in Afghanistan and Pakistan – that emerged out of secret intelligence from his war in Chechnya and unrest in Uzbekistan. "Putin suddenly raised the problem of Pakistan," Rice recalls. "He excoriated the Pervez Musharraf regime for its support of extremists and for the connections of the Pakistani army and intelligence services to the Taliban and al Qaeda. Those extremists were all being funded by Saudi Arabia, he said, and it was only a matter of time until it resulted in a major catastrophe…"[49] This was easily dismissed as sand thrown in their eyes. Only in retrospect did it make any sense in spite of the fact that over two years before, on 7 August 1998, having been thrown out of Sudan, and now based in Afghanistan, Islamic fundamentalists identifying as al-Qaeda had simultaneously blown up the American embassies in Nairobi (Kenya) and Dar-es-Salam (Tanzania). For his part Putin claimed to have "talked with the previous US [Clinton] Administration and alerted it to the bin Laden problem". He "was surprised by their reaction. They simply shrugged [their shoulders] helplessly and said, what can we do? The Taliban [in Afghanistan] refuse to turn him over." He remembered "being surprised".[50] Indeed, former operative – later Chief of the International Terrorism Group of the Counter Terrorism Center (CTC) – Ric Prado recalls with some bitterness that "Instead of beefing up our counterrorism capability, the Clinton administration cut the CTC's funding."[51] And, as Rice recalls, "When we liberated Mazar-i-Sharif, we found Chechens fighting there."[52]

Overwhelmed in his second term by impeachment over his seduction of the young intern Monica Lewinsky, Clinton had seriously underestimated the threat from Islamic fundamentalism. Contacts with the Russians on the subject had indeed been opened. In December 1999, with a second Russian war raging in Chechnya, the State Department noted that it was "aware of continuing cooperation between Bin Laden's al-Qaida organization and Chechen separatists including the terrorist Ibn Al-Khattab". Yet in talking points for an international terrorism workshop on 3 October 2000 other issues mattered more to the Americans. The team was instructed that in response to "Russian claims that Chechnya represents a case of international terrorism mission should note that we recognize a certain basis for that claim"; however, the concern for human rights should come first.[53]

On 19 February 2000 Talbott had hosted Defence Minister Sergei Ivanov, formerly head of analysis at foreign intelligence (SVR), deputy head of the FSB and subsequently chairman of Russia's Security Council. Ivanov spent a fascinating three days in Washington DC, which included a visit to CIA headquarters at Langley, Virginia. Here he assured Talbott that "Russia is willing to help the US bring Usama Bin Laden to justice, but it needs to know whether we [the Americans] consider Chechen Commanders [Al-]Khattab and [Shamil] Basayev 'Bandits or Freedom Fighters.'"[54] If there was one wish it was that the United States put counter-terrorism at the top of their agenda.

The Americans were never forthcoming, however. Evidently they suspected that the Russians were just grasping at an excuse to work together. Rice, though a more moderate member of the team, was not about to meet them halfway. She held to the view that the president should be "Tough on [the issue of] Chechnya believing that Putin's exploitation of it to stir up nationalism and strengthen the role of the military will inflict long term damage on Russia's political culture. She sees this as underlining the importance of protecting the vulnerable small states surrounding Russia, in whose independence the US has an interest…" More than that, she was also interested, as was the Blair team, in bolstering democratic forces within Russia. Rice emphasized "building ties with young Russians in the belief that the establishment of a civil society and market economy in Russia could take a generation…"[55]

9/11

Back in the spring CIA director George Tenet had tabled at the National Security Council a "Blue Sky Paper" initiated by Cofer Black, head of the Counter Terrorism Center, pressing for a covert agency and military campaign to destroy al-Qaeda. It involved "getting into the Afghan sanctuary, launching a paramilitary operation, creating a bridge with Uzbekistan". But Tenet was rebuffed and told that "we're not quite ready to consider this. We don't want the clock to start ticking." In early July head of CIA's al-Qaeda unit, Richard Blee, on the basis of multi-source information, reported "There will be significant terrorist attacks against the United States in the coming weeks or months. The attacks will be spectacular. They will be multiple. Al Qaeda's intention is the destruction of the United States." In answer to Rice, Black was blunt: "We need to go on a wartime footing now!" And at a CIA meeting towards the end of July, Blee looked at everyone and blurted out what he felt instinctively: "They're coming here."[56]

But not everyone was of that opinion. As the number three in the chain of command and pre-eminently an operations man, Prado recalls: "The Intel on al-Qaeda came in penny packets and pieces... The problem was, we simply did not have enough pieces of the puzzle in front of us."[57]

To say that the White House were unprepared is an understatement, and it was not merely because officers in the field (both CIA and FBI) were institutionally averse to comparing notes when Saudis arrived in the United States for flying lessons and instructors distinctly remembered at least two "as poor students who focused on learning to control the aircraft in flight but took no interest in takeoffs and landings".[58] The bottom line was that on the most important issues Rice, even had she taken it as seriously as the CTC, headed national security affairs effectively in name only; and those who dominated decisions, the leading hawks, viewed the warnings that came in as an annoying distraction from the main order of business: Iraq. On 4 September a Principals meeting on al-Qaeda finally convened, one which Richard Clarke, who coordinated counter-terrorism, had requested back in January. Here the issue was raised as a matter of urgency, but "Rumsfeld, who looked distracted throughout the session, took the Wolfowitz line that there were other terrorist concerns, like Iraq, and that whatever we did on this al Qaeda business, we had to deal with other sources of terrorism."[59] This was unfortunately the customary bureaucratic way of reshuffling the order of priorities.

Just one week later came the wake-up call. At 9.00 a.m. on a bright blue autumnal morning the United States was attacked live on television; the first direct attack against the homeland since Pearl Harbor in December 1941. Islamist terrorists from Saudi Arabia belonging to al-Qaeda seized civilian aircraft loaded with passengers and flew them into New York's Twin Towers, killing 2,997 people; they flew another at the Pentagon, and one more targeted Congress. This devastating act of war engineered by Osama Bin Laden from his lair in Afghanistan had a traumatic impact on the entire United States – it forged a sense of unity not seen for decades in American society – and, crucially, on Bush and Rice's state of mind. It also had an important, though lesser side effect. It temporarily relieved the tension in America's relations with Russia that had arisen with Bush's determination to pursue National Missile Defense in Europe alongside further enlargement of NATO into the Baltic states. In Moscow it was already late afternoon. Director of foreign intelligence (SVR) Sergei Naryshkin, a former classmate, phoned Putin with the news of the attacks. Putin, fascinated, switched on the television. An idea came to him. He promptly cancelled the meetings scheduled and "called in the heads of all the security and military agencies for a meeting".[60]

International relations have never been a matter of sentiment, for all the messages of sympathy that flooded in to Washington DC. Nonetheless Putin made sure that he was one of the first to call the White House and try to speak to Bush. But only Rice was available. Putin then rang Blair.[61] America's second Pearl Harbor had been seen instantly by Putin as a unique opportunity. Russia would hasten onto the world stage to offer help. What had been sought from Clinton and never even considered seriously might now, ironically, be obtainable from Bush: a bilateral special relationship that would ultimately free Russia from the recurring nightmare of further NATO expansion. Three days later Putin summoned the Russian Federation's Security Council. There he met "strong pressure on foreign policy on the part of the Ministry of Defence. And even the appointment of a political figure, Sergei Ivanov, in practice did not change the situation."[62] Formerly senior to Putin in the KGB, Ivanov had deputized for him when the latter briefly headed the FSB.

Antipathy to the Americans, deeply rooted since Kosovo, certainly made for fractious discussions at the Russian Security Council. "There are absolutely no grounds, even hypothetically, for allowing military operations by NATO in the Central Asian states of the former Soviet Union", Ivanov bluntly declared, somewhat prematurely, on behalf of the deep state. He explained later: "We were worried that once the Americans had a presence in the region, they would begin their 'promotion of democracy'. Some [at the meeting] said, if the Americans come our interests will suffer." But Putin pressed back, arguing forcefully that "the situation in the world is changing". They had to adjust to it.[63] Taking a serious risk, as he was out of step not only with Ivanov and his inner circle, but also powerful figures in the Duma, Putin overruled his security advisers and publicly offered Russia's full co-operation, even opening the intelligence files on Islamist activism to the Americans.[64]

Ivanov's misgivings were not groundless. When the policy of Russo-American co-operation against Islamic terrorism took effect, Senator Robert Torricelli of the Foreign Relations Committee argued that "It would be a serious mistake if we were to sacrifice our agenda for the promotion of democracy and human rights in exchange for security cooperation."[65] But the administration saw no need for sacrifice. Jack Crouch, the Assistant Secretary of Defense for International Security Policy, was reassuring: "because our actions are in their [Russian and Central Asian states'] security interest, this provides us more leverage, frankly, on the human rights side than we would have..."[66] Ivanov had, of course, been right. In 2000, during a joint training exercise, US troops were spotted by the Uzbek security service talking to known opponents of the regime. The US army's official history of the Afghan operation states: "The fact that the soldiers were Special Forces personnel resonated with Islam K. Karimov because those types of units often led forcible changes of Soviet-era satellite states."[67]

No more talk of human rights, however; the Americans now had other priorities. While all commercial flights to and from the United States were grounded, an array of Saudis were inexplicably and hastily flown back home. With Russian acquiescence, and after handing over half a billion dollars to the brutal Uzbek dictator Karimov, the Americans quickly set themselves up in

Karshi-Khanabad, a base area in south-eastern Uzbekistan next door to Tadzhikistan, in order to pursue more effective operations against the allies of the Islamic terrorists, the Taliban, in Afghanistan. When Karimov gave the go-ahead on 5 October, US transport planes across Europe immediately swarmed in and created a veritable traffic jam. It was an amazing sight. US military personnel mushroomed from 100 to over 2,000 within a week.[68] This was the first of several bases in Central Asia, where the Russians facilitated overflights and supplies for the war effort. Another key logistical hub was Manas in Kyrgyzstan. The decisions taken, Ivanov came to understand the importance of feeding his US counterparts with the secret intelligence they needed. "We knew where the training camps were in Afghanistan," he recalls. "We knew exactly the coordinates on the map. Those camps trained Chechen terrorists. We were counting on the Americans to liquidate those camps…" The bombing from Central Asia began on 10 October.[69]

Putin was reported to be "rather optimistic".[70] The former British ambassador to Russia Sir Roderick Lyne was singularly impressed with his response: "Putin put a huge effort in his first two or three years in power [2000–3] into developing close relations with the West. The support he gave to George Bush immediately after 9/11 and when the Americans went into Afghanistan was very important. It also caused the American attitude towards Putin to change: they, for example, turned in favour of Russia joining the G7 [the regular summit conferences of the leading economies]."[71] Britain's short-lived Defence Secretary Geoff Hoon testified at hearings in the House of Lords in October 2001 that "There is a sea change underway in Moscow. Some people would say that the catalyst of 11 September has moved things on faster than they were moving already…" Indeed, Hoon stated, "… actually the US engagement with Russia is moving more quickly at the present time than Europe's engagement is, and that there is a risk actually of Europe being left behind because of the meeting [between Bush and Putin] that is going to take place in two weeks' time in Crawford [Texas] where a number of enormously important strategic issues are on the table, and, certainly from my visit to Washington yesterday, a very considerable confidence that they are going to be resolved, and resolved in a way that will fundamentally change the strategic relationship with Russia and Europe and NATO and the United States."[72]

Putin had been very fortunate in his timing. Russia's petrodollar economy had turned around as the price of energy rose. Two-thirds of the country's exports came from that sector. As a result the Russians saw that they would be able to dispense with loans and advice from the West to modernize their economy. This gave them new-found confidence. From a low of $7 a barrel in 1999, the spot price of oil shot up to hit a peak of $147 in July 2008. It was this one fact that underwrote the first two terms of the Putin presidency. Not only was the financial pressure eased, but foreign debts could be met and at home there was largesse to distribute. A sovereign wealth fund was created.

Buoyed at the prospect of his forthcoming summit on 13–15 November 2001 at the Bush ranch in Crawford, Texas, Putin addressed the Western press in uncharacteristically enthusiastic terms about 9/11 sowing the seeds of a lasting alliance with "a qualitatively new level of trust". The relationship was now apparently securely anchored in common interests. "It is quite obvious to any objective observer", he said, "that we can find an effective response to these challenges only if we pool our efforts together." He was specific: "We would like our joint struggle against terrorism to lead to positive results, that terrorism not only in Afghanistan but the entire world be destroyed, uprooted, liquidated." On the other hand, he expressed continued objection to the Baltic states joining NATO, and in the course of his oration it began to look increasingly like an effort to forestall that prospect by re-engineering the alliance as something completely different. Russia, he insisted, had a great deal to offer. "I can tell you frankly that I have certain ideas of a general nature"; however, he added, "I can't elaborate them now, but they are very promising."[73] On

13 November Bush and Putin asked NATO to enhance relations with Russia to the level of "joint decision and coordinated/joint action".[74]

Yet Putin's grand gesture in relation to 9/11 was effectively wasted as it was badly misread in Washington DC. It appears to have been misinterpreted by the White House as a needy gesture on his part – a desperate bid for a powerful ally against a common foe – rather than a welcome concession from a former adversary and a potential partner. On the issue of fighting terrorism, Putin noted, "They agreed with us but, after a little time had passed, everything went back to normal."[75]

Rumsfeld Undercuts the Proposed NATO-Russia Council

Before that time had yet passed, Prime Minister Blair "even proposed (and got accepted at NATO) a new arrangement for cooperation with Russia, which gave them a far greater involvement in NATO decision-making".[76] The idea of a NATO-Russia Council was a body in which the Russians would have an equal role with what were then nineteen members of the alliance, operating in areas such as terrorism, arms proliferation, drug trafficking and peace keeping. The NATO Secretary-General Lord Robertson and Blair appeared to be at odds, however, as to whether that would hand the Russians a veto on any issue.[77] But certainly in November Blair favoured a much more inclusive role for Moscow only to be opposed by Rumsfeld "and some former Clinton administration officials on the grounds that there were not enough safeguards to protect NATO's freedom of action and military secrets".[78]

A fundamental change in Russia's standing with respect to NATO was thus blocked by Rumsfeld, now riding high in White House estimation as a result of the successful bombing campaign in Afghanistan (thanks not least to Putin). Rumsfeld weighed in, using his political muscle to tip over the apple cart. In Europe they knew nothing of this. There the new catchword in December was to be no longer NATO at nineteen (existing members) plus one (Russia), but NATO at twenty. It meant that instead of the NATO Council meeting and agreeing on policy beforehand separately from Russia, the Russians should instead be fully included in discussions and the decisions taken. This was an option that found favour with Chirac and the new German Chancellor, Gerhard Schröder of the SPD. The proposal was scheduled to appear in the forthcoming NATO communiqué. But Rumsfeld made a desperate eleventh hour bid to have "NATO at 20" removed entirely. He failed. His rival, Powell, always had good relations with the media and ensured that the rest of the world knew what was going on. "At one point on Wednesday [5th]", the *New York Times* reliably reported, "R. Nicholas Burns, the United States ambassador to NATO, told colleagues that he had conflicting guidance on how to proceed because Mr Rumsfeld's signed instructions were at odds with Secretary Powell's. Twelve hours passed before the deadlock was broken."[79]

Rumsfeld, however, was not to be underestimated. He may have lost a publicity skirmish. He had no ability to charm people in the manner of Powell or Rice, or to outmanoeuvre them like Cheney. But he was a natural at bare-knuckle bureaucratic in-fighting and could certainly intimidate his rivals with a sharp tongue and unnerve them with his notorious irascibility. Moreover, Rice carried the added burden that she had to struggle to establish her authority in the face of overt scepticism that verged on blatant hostility from Rumsfeld, not accidentally a former champion wrestler at Princeton University. Her natural charm was entirely wasted on him. In the words of Secretary of State Colin Powell, Rice "had a difficult path to walk because of Rumsfeld. Rumsfeld didn't get along with her." Deputy Secretary Armitage chimes in: "Not at all." Powell added: "From the beginning."[80] "She'd never served in a senior administrative position", Rumsfeld complained. "She'd been an academic. And, you know, a lot of academics like to have meetings. And they like to bridge differences and get people all to be happy", he snarled. It sounded a lot like plain jealousy: "Condi and the President – she is still his enabler and his best pal, buddy..."[81] Rice's closeness to Bush did, indeed, become a dependent personal relationship, visible from all sides. Her life was effectively her work, apart from evening concerts. Despite an image of cool unflappability, she was not averse to Russian charm, which Defence Minister and former KGB operative Ivanov had, among others, evidently spotted.[82] But it had no impact on her attitudes towards Russia.

At first it seemed like NATO at twenty would become a reality. On 18 December NATO's defence ministers met and the final communiqué welcomed the decision of foreign ministers meeting on 7 December:

> to give new impetus and substance to the partnership between NATO Allies and Russia with the goal of creating a new NATO-Russia Council to identify and pursue opportunities for joint action at 20. To that end, the North Atlantic Council in Permanent Session has been tasked to explore and develop, in the coming months, building on the Founding Act, new effective mechanisms for consultation, cooperation, joint decision, and coordinated/joint action. NATO's fundamental objectives remain as set out in the Washington Treaty under which provisions NATO will maintain its prerogative of independent decision and action at 19 on all issues consistent with its obligations and responsibilities. As Defence Ministers, we are determined to enhance the NATO-Russia partnership in the defence and military field.[83]

Rumsfeld, however, was determined to win the bureaucratic struggle by emptying "NATO at 20" of any substance and ensuring it would not be implemented. The problem for everyone else was that, faced with Rumsfeld, backed by Cheney, Bush as usual found himself adrift, at which point he became indecisive. There was no counter-balance to Rumsfeld-Cheney because Rice was instinctively deferential to the President. She simply did not have their sense of entitlement. And it was not in Powell's nature as a former Chairman of the Joint Chiefs of Staff to challenge the commander-in-chief. Rumsfeld, on the other hand, was no respecter either of persons or of office. He thought nothing, for example, of absenting himself from a top-level meeting with the British chaired by the President to stop a decision going through to which he objected.[84]

The open question was, of course, which issues would fall under the category of the twenty, including Russia, and which the nineteen. Because of Rumsfeld's objections NATO foreign ministers agreed to delay the NATO-Russia Council for six months while they thrashed out what exactly its functions would be.[85] During that time the US Defense Department set back any progress that had been made. And by the time the NATO-Russia Council was finalized on 28 May 2002 at the Rome summit, the proposed new structure was in practice an illusion, which was a serious problem because the Russians had insisted that "the new relationship has to have substance".[86] Bitterlich, Kohl's national security adviser, who had spent years trying to solve the puzzle of what to do about Russia, describes the Council as "stopping at less than half the distance…" He adds that "we did not manage to create pan-European structures in terms of security. The CSCE became the OSCE and began to fall into oblivion or a deep sleep." Russia's proposals were "not seriously examined by the Americans in NATO".[87]

Robert Hunter, the former US permanent representative to NATO who later participated in RAND's formulation of proposals for the establishment of the Council, did not hide his deep disenchantment: "the new NATO-Russia Council is surrounded by so-called safeguards that make it not much better than the old council [the Permanent Joint Council of 1997]. NATO allies have to agree before any item goes on the agenda; both NATO and Russia retain the right to act separately on any item; any NATO ally, on its own, can pull an item off the agenda." The alliance alone would determine membership and how it structured and operated military forces.[88] NATO at twenty was effectively dead. James Collins, the US ambassador to Moscow, wrote an epitaph with some regret: "the Bush Administration, for whatever reason, decided that they were not going to attach particular priority to relations with Russia, and that we had other major issues, and that Russia was not a major factor for us going forward, and I think we paid a price for that".[89]

It should have been evident to Russian officials that under American eyes the new Council was not going to lead to any more substantial involvement in NATO decision-making. But, a well-informed Russian analyst notes, "While those exceptions [participation in certain discussions and decisions] were clear to Moscow from the outset, it nevertheless had high initial expectations of its N[ATO]R[ussia]C[ouncil]membership, hoping that the status of an 'almost equal' NATO partner would give it additional leverage in bilateral discussions of collective defence and enlargement with key NATO nations."[90] The original idea of the Council was that meetings would take place without a pre-agreed agenda, treating Russia as an equal. But its implementation dispelled any illusions that anything substantial had changed in the NATO-Russia relationship. Kurt Volker covered Europe and Eurasia on the US National Security Council. His recollection is that the Americans arranged matters "so that we had a common NATO position" not least because "some allies... wanted to restrict topics on the agenda because they didn't want to discuss them with Russia" and there were "others [Germany] who did not want to pre-coordinate because they felt that it was not in the spirit of an open conversation..."[91] Thomas Graham, senior director for Russian affairs on the National Security Council, described it bluntly as "19 [members] +1 [Russia] all over again..."[92]

The Russians were thus completely cut out of all military discussions; indeed they felt keenly that they had less access than before. No sooner was the agreement signed than all informal contacts with the Russian delegation's military counterparts in NATO ground to an abrupt halt. In fact, the Russians were more isolated than they had ever been. Sergei Kislyak, sometimes described as "the diplomat's diplomat", was Russia's representative to NATO. He doubled as ambassador to Belgium and later became ambassador to the United States. He was personally mortified. All his hopes had gone up in smoke. The Russian half of the Partnership for Peace had effectively been hollowed out once the first recruits came in from Central and Eastern Europe, who would have rather not had Russia at the table at all.[93] Another disillusioned enthusiast was the current ambassador to Britain, Andrei Kelin. The son of a diplomat, he had chosen arms control as his specialism in the Foreign Ministry. He served under Kislyak. His recollections are just the same. All the talk about bringing the Russians in following their unilateral assistance with intelligence sharing after 9/11 had been squashed by Rumsfeld and Wolfowitz at the Pentagon. And it mattered a great deal. On his view this was a critical turning point in Putin's attitude to co-operation with the West.[94]

It had now become crystal clear to the Russians that they were, indeed, not welcome in Brussels. Blair had gone as far as he could and had obviously failed. This much was obvious before the Iraq war broke out in March 2003.[95]

The Second Gulf War

The overriding objective for the Bush White House was always the overthrow of Saddam Hussein. Rueda recalls that "there were elements who thought 9.11 was a speed bump in the efforts to do regime change in Iraq".[96] Cheney, for one, was anxious to get back to business. Months of sustained effort by Blair to forestall war by taking the issue of Iraqi intransigence on UN inspections for weapons of mass destruction back to the Security Council came to nothing. Finally, on 19 March 2003 Bush launched the invasion of Iraq, a country that for decades had been a close client state of the Soviet Union. The explicit purpose was regime change. And it was based on a transparently implausible cover story that was publicized by Powell at the United Nations – the argument that Saddam Hussein possessed weapons of mass destruction.[97] As a former MI6 officer later testified: "At the time I felt what we were doing was wrong... There was no new or credible intelligence or assessment which suggested that Iraq had restarted W[eapons of] M[ass] D[estruction] programmes and that they posed an imminent threat."[98]

The Russians were not informed in advance, let alone consulted.[99] At the United Nations Jeremy Greenstock, Britain's permanent representative, noted that "Moscow's determination to prevent unilateral action by the single remaining superpower had been hardened" by the 1999 Kosovo campaign.[100] Putin's default position was that "Saddam was a monster but he was not a direct threat."[101] As fixed US intentions became known, however, the Russians carefully backed away from outright opposition. The *New York Times* at the end of January signalled a new flexibility on the part of the Kremlin. Its commentary was revealing:

> It would not be the first time he had capitulated. Mr. Putin has often balked at American foreign policy thrusts – from the White House's abandonment of the cold-war era Antiballistic Missile Treaty to its support for expanding NATO into the former Soviet Union to a 2002 nuclear arms reduction treaty that many Russian experts criticized as weighted in favor of the United States. In the end, analysts and others say, he has shrugged and accepted each because his judgment is that close ties to the United States are a top priority if Russia is to rebuild its global role.

The question not asked was, how long could this last? The US administration was under the complacent impression that "Putin has always been much more protective of the relationship with the US, and especially with President Bush, than other people in his bureaucracy."[102] Certainly, it would have been hard to be less "protective" than Nikolai Patrushev, now chairman of the Security Council, and FSB director Aleksandr Bortnikov (who actually believed that those executed in the Great Terror really had been traitors), who became the holders of the keys to the deep state from 2008.

Putin could take some consolation at least from the obvious fact that Russia was certainly not alone in opposing the war. Although Blair could have refused to join the Americans, he chose to double down on the close relationship with Bush. Instead Putin found common ground with Germany and France. This was a gain for Moscow in the sense that NATO was now a house bitterly divided. In Berlin Chancellor Schröder was a veteran of the anti-American campaigns of his youth in the early 1980s and responded well to Putin's transparent overtures for a closer *Partnerschaft*. In Paris, Jacques Chirac, initially at least, "gave him [Putin] something of a cold-shoulder", Blair noted, adding for good measure: "Of course, in time all that changed and their relationship became very close as mine waned."[103] But this was chicken feed to Moscow, as no one questioned the sheer brute fact of American power. And the war gave the lie to the hope that the United States and Russia could be anything like equals.

Putin vented his frustration at the way in which the Americans hastened to dissolve the Iraqi army shortly after the invasion. "And what happened?' he later asked. 'Tens of thousands of soldiers and officers, former Baath party activists, thrown out onto the streets, are now packing the ranks of fighters. Perhaps it is this that, so to speak, accounts for the military capability of [the Islamist fundamentalist fighters] IGIL? They are very effective from a military point of view, real, professional people."[104] The only saving grace was that US unilateralism seemed to have reached its limits as the Americans were now bogged down not only in Afghanistan but also in Iraq. The hoped-for evidence of Saddam Hussein's links to al-Qaeda, which would convince the Russians that this rash gamble was a necessary part of the war on terror, never materialized. The war was a startling military success – a tribute to US firepower – but also a political disaster and, as a result, a major distraction from America's other interests overseas. Indeed, its reverberations drove another wave of terrorism in the Middle East, stoked by neighbouring Iran, further destabilizing an already precarious region. And it was that burgeoning instability that the Russians found so threatening.

Up to this point, Putin had a reputation for enormous self-control. But it had its limits as it became abundantly clear to everyone that Saddam Hussein did not have the weapons of mass destruction that were the purported grounds for the war. On 29 April 2003, Blair flew to Moscow in an urgent attempt to patch up relations with Russia. They had visibly deteriorated since his last visit in September 2002 under the strain of the Anglo-American attack on Iraq. Blair and Putin met outside Moscow at the palatial datcha of Novoe Ogaryovo for an unexpectedly lengthy six hours' discussion. Blair's spokesman Alastair Campbell was not present but keenly noted that at the press conference which followed that Putin had a "steely look in his eye" while Blair "was looking a bit on edge".[105] Sure enough, while the Prime Minister was doing his level best to look "unfazed", Putin proceeded to mock him openly about the ostensible cause of the war. And although Blair had agreed that measures for Iraqi reconstruction should be in the hands of the UN – they were actually in the utterly inept hands of the Pentagon – Putin said international inspectors should return to the country.

The coalition were unable to answer many questions, Putin said:

Where is Saddam? Where are the arsenals of weapons of mass destruction, if they existed? Perhaps Saddam is sitting somewhere in a secret bunker with weapons of mass destruction and is getting ready to blow it all up and jeopardise the lives of thousands of people? These questions have to be answered.[106]

For Blair this was an alarmingly unpleasant public humiliation for which he was utterly unprepared – only the second such encounter since he addressed the Women's Institute on 7 June 2000, where he was heckled and jeered for politicising an event traditionally non-partisan in tone and content. His cold-eyed onlooker, Campbell, unhesitatingly labelled it a "diplo-disaster".

They were then all invited into a smaller side-room. Blair could barely contain himself. Putin was coldly unapologetic, however. "He said the US had created this situation. In ignoring the UN they had created danger. They were saying there may be rules, but not for us. Time and again he made comparisons with the situation he faced in Georgia, used as a base for terrorists against Russia. 'What would you say if we took out Georgia or sent in the B-52 bombers to wipe out the terror camps?' And what are they planning next – is it Syria, Iran, Korea? 'I bet they haven't told you,' he added with a rather unpleasant curl of the lip. 'Also there is no consistency. Saudi and Pakistan are problems but for different reasons the Americans prop them up.' He said other parts of the world felt pressure to go for Israel. He said he didn't support that 'but these are dangerous games.' He said the Americans' enemy was anyone who didn't support them at the time. Anywhere from Algeria to Pakistan. Then what about the new powers like India and China, do their views matter or only America?" At dinner that evening the argument became even more heated.

It was not as though Blair had no understanding of the Russian position. His advisers made certain of that. But for him the United States was the pressing priority. Everything had to be filtered through the lens of relations with the White House. And because the Americans had become more difficult, they had to be won over. So why should not Putin likewise adjust to the new reality, however disagreeable it might be for him? "We have to help them [the Americans] to choose the multilateral route", Blair insisted. "But you have to understand that September 11 changed their psychology and it changed Bush's psychology personally. Before, anti-Americanism was just an irritant that they had to put up with. Now it became a threat." Putin, however, indicated that he found such special pleading "ridiculous". "I am a Russian", he said. "I cannot agree with the Americans on everything. My public won't let me for a start. I would not survive two years if I did that. We often have different interests." Putin's vehemence took Blair aback, as it did David Manning, his foreign policy adviser. "Fascinating, absolutely fascinating", Manning commented later, in the manner of the curious onlooker gripped by such an eye-opening occasion. There came a moment when Putin claimed that the whole US response to 9/11 was "designed to show off American greatness". They did not care what anyone else thought. When Blair began to reply, Putin cut him off: "Don't answer – there is no answer. That is the truth, Tony. You have to know it. There are bad people in the administration and you know it."[107] Unable to assault the organ-grinder, Putin had laid into the monkey.

Blair's attitude to Bush and Putin was not unlike that of a well-meaning priest, dutifully taking confession, working with the sinner in the hope of guiding him back onto the right path. And this is what Blair was also doing behind the scenes with the IRA to end terrorism in Northern Ireland. Encouraging Bush the unilateralist to become a multilateralist was no less intractable a challenge. In the Russian case Blair tried to counter Putin's Gaullist sense of inferiority by flattering his self-importance as a reward for good behaviour. He rarely lacked self-confidence. Indeed, at Camp David, he had the temerity to deliver a futile lecture to Cheney of all people that "he thought it was better to allow Putin a position on the top table and encourage Putin to reach for Western attitudes as well as for the Western economic model".[108] One does not have to stretch the imagination much to guess Cheney's reaction. Summing up, Thomas Graham, who joined the National Security Council as senior director for Russian affairs in 2004, comments that "in 2000, and 2001, when the United States was at the height of its power, I think we lacked the patience to play a longer game, to see whether it would have come out differently for the relationship between the United States and Russia".[109]

Meanwhile, matters were made worse by the fact that the Americans had no intention of giving up their ambitions for National Missile Defense, knowing that it would breach the 1972 Anti-Ballistic Missile treaty with the Soviet Union. Nor were they going to call a halt to NATO's eastward expansion, however much these objectives grated on Moscow. Graham recalls Putin seeking a quid pro quo in return for accepting the NMD programme, namely some kind of recognition of a Russian sphere of influence over the post-Soviet space.[110] Clearly this was to safeguard Russia's influence in Ukraine. In this respect William Burns, ambassador to Moscow, believes "Putin fundamentally misread American interests and politics. The Bush administration had no desire – and saw no reason – to trade anything for a Russian partnership against al-Qaeda. It had little inclination to concede much to a declining power."[111] This was not a lesson that the Russians were likely to forget: "the weakness, as they saw it, of the American efforts to construct a proper partnership", as Blair put it, an omission that he had good reason to regret.[112] The White House failed to foresee that were NATO expansion to proceed without some kind of Russo-American entente, then battle lines would sooner or later be drawn in Moscow.

The fact that the Baltic states were still scheduled for NATO entry in 2004 gave some urgency to Russian plans; Estonia was, after all, only 90 miles from St Petersburg. And although the creation of a NATO-Russia council nowhere stipulated an end to further NATO expansion, it is clear from an article Defence Minister Ivanov published in the *New York Times* that the Russian military, at least, held to the unrealistic expectation that "NATO at 19 [members] +1 [Russia]" should at the very least delay if not forestall Baltic accession. The common enemy of Islamist terrorism and the "war on terror" still bound Russia and the United States together. Relations had not yet completely unravelled. But, Ivanov wanted to know "why is an organization that was designed to oppose the Soviet Union and its allies in Eastern Europe still necessary in today's world?" He itemized elements of progress in the relationship with NATO since the creation of the Russia-NATO Council – including efforts against international terrorism, joint military exercises and progress on non-proliferation. However, he argued, Russia "would like the programs described in the Rome summit's declaration to receive higher priority". These included "the development of European missile defense". But, Ivanov insisted, "progress on these and other fronts" meant "settling differences through dialogue". "Such discussions", he suggested, "are jeopardized by the alliance's hurried expansion. Russia's military and political leadership has good reason to be concerned about the integration of Estonia, Latvia and Lithuania, particularly if NATO decides to create large military bases in those countries. The alliance is gaining greater ability to control and monitor Russian territory. We cannot turn a blind eye as NATO's air and military bases get much closer to cities and defense complexes in European Russia." In addition the Treaty on Conventional Armed Forces in Europe that had been concluded by the Soviet Union still needed updating to allow for the secession and independence of former republics. This made the Baltic a grey zone "that could allow the alliance to deploy any amount of heavy weaponry within them. Moreover, there has been little effort by the NATO leadership in Brussels or by the governments in those member states to ease Russia's concerns." Negotiations were required, and "our partners in the Russia-NATO Council must show that they take seriously our concerns about the alliance's approach to our borders".[113]

A further, unforeseen event within Russia highlighted the divergence of interests with the West. The brutal hostage taking by Chechen terrorists in Beslan, a town in the north Caucasus, on 1 September 2004 was about as ineptly handled by the Russian authorities as it could have been, with the adamant refusal even to consider negotiations. The absence of any experience in such situations and a resolute determination not to back down resulted in the horrendous massacre of 172 Russian schoolchildren when Russian forces stormed the building. The tragic event shone a harsh light on the fact that the West drew a distinction between moderate and extreme Chechen separatists, to the extent of funding the former, which, on the fundamentalist Russian view, was a distinction without a difference drawn by those whose populations were safely far distant from the battlefield.[114] Graham recalls: "Putin never believed that the United States gave Russia the type of unqualified support in dealing with what it saw as its primary terrorist problem, which was the Chechen rebellion, and certainly not to the same level as that Russia was prepared to support the United States in dealing with the United States' primary terrorist problem, which was al Qaeda."[115]

Further contention arose over the insistence of the United States on overstaying its conditional welcome in Central Asia. Indeed, according to the British ambassador, "contractors at the [Karshi-Khanabad] base were extending the design life of the buildings for ten to twenty-five years"[116] – until they were eventually thrown out of Uzbekistan after they sided with protestors shot by the dictator Islam Karimov. William Courtney had been US ambassador to both Kazakhstan and Georgia, as well as a senior adviser on the National Security Council. In the summer of 2002 the honeymoon with Moscow was still flourishing when he concluded complacently that "President Putin appears to have decided that Russia has a large stake in its relationship with the West". In this cosy atmosphere Courtney assured the Senate Foreign Relations Committee that the United States "has filled a security vacuum in southern Eurasia and Afghanistan" and that an "American pullout from southern Eurasia when events in Afghanistan allow it, would recreate a destabilizing vacuum".[117] It is hard to imagine any judgement more ignorant and complacently provocative to the Kremlin.

Part II

6

Regime Change

"It is time for a new Middle East. It is time to say to those who do not want a different kind of Middle East that we will prevail, they will not."

– Condoleezza Rice, 25 July 2006.[1]

The idea of regime change as a solution to the problems of the Middle East slipped out prematurely in the sweltering summer of 2002 during an interview in Washington DC held by Condoleezza Rice with the BBC correspondent Gordon Corera. As a result he was for a while shunned by the administration because he had unknowingly publicized sentiments rapidly disowned by the White House.[2] The comment from Rice was a premature declaration of neo-conservative intentions that had for the time being to be kept secret.

The American Republican Right had taken over and weaponized the ideals of President Woodrow Wilson, a Democrat, as an instrument for securing global supremacy. On the pattern of the Roman or British empires, it might have been expected that the dominant power would be satisfied defending the status quo, underwriting the existing international order and protecting it from predators. But the United States was a very different kind of state: a status quo power economically, it was nevertheless driven from within not just by overarching material self-interest but also by a political evangelism deemed essential to mobilize an American public otherwise prone to isolationism. This was a core lesson of the Cold War. The US national interest required other states to drop autocracy for democracy, however unrealistic a goal that would be in a less developed country with no such traditions. The crusade for democracy was intended to ensure that there would be another American Century.

Blair invariably latched onto a new idea. Régime change had become a leitmotif underlying US foreign policy from the end of the Cold War, vindicated by Gorbachev's retreat from Central Europe in 1989, followed by the collapse of communism within the Soviet Union and the destruction of Saddam Hussein's dictatorship in Iraq. Under the neo-conservative Republicans what American politicians saw as an altruistic strand in their foreign relations – firmly anchored in the Jeffersonian tradition – had transformed into the vigorous pursuit of US self-interest, backed by the unilateral use of force or "an alliance of the willing".

At the same time, and aside from American preferences, the demands for regime change had solid local foundations. The call for democracy arose spontaneously from the street when the repression unleashed by corrupt and autocratic governments and resistance to it finally led to a realization that change was possible. But that this could open the door to Islamic fundamentalism, as it had in Iran and Afghanistan, was entirely unacceptable to the Russians. The awkward question for the rulers of the United States was the issue of blatant inconsistency: why had they been content to live with autocratic allies, just as they had not long ago tolerated segregation at home, and adjust seamlessly to the despotism of, for example, Saudi Arabia, the original home of the most sectarian, medieval fundamentalism? To this the self-evident answer was that, at least prior to 9/11, and certainly after its commitment to the primacy of the US dollar in the oil trade, Saudi Arabia was essential to the security of the United States.

The Cold War had witnessed relentless efforts by the Western alliance to undermine the communist regimes installed in Eastern Europe by Moscow, which began seriously in the late 1940s, punctuated by open resistance in Hungary (1956) and Czechoslovakia (1968) and reinforced over four decades through the campaign for human rights launched after signature of the Helsinki Final Act in 1975. And now that communism was at an end in Europe, those instruments lost purpose, redundant unless they could be deployed beyond Europe's traditional boundaries. The danger was, however, exactly the same as it had been in Cold War Europe: legitimate democratic movements would be tarred with the brush of foreign meddling even when the role of the West was marginal to the indigenous roots of popular unrest. To avoid the insidious implication that financial and logistical assistance to democratic movements was provided by US intelligence, in 1983 the National Endowment for Democracy came into being, funded by Congress under the aegis of President Ronald Reagan.

Before 1990 the fear of Soviet military power constrained Western covert action within the countries of the Warsaw Pact. But now the collapse of the Soviet Union and the weakness of post-Soviet Russia effectively removed the remaining deterrents to US support for democratic subversion of autocracies beyond NATO's boundaries. Because US administrations saw the new Russia as weak, they gave little serious thought to the potential dangers of alienating it in pursuit of regime change elsewhere. The *siloviki* in Moscow, however, had reason to believe that such pressure would ultimately be applied to them. And the pursuit of universalist American values was indistinguishable from pursuit of the American national interest, as Bush ('41) had asserted. This was the case even though resurgent Islam had shown that there was widespread support for the wholesale rejection of American values in the Near East from the time of the Iranian revolution in 1979.

At first the United States had thought it could harness militant Islam as a wedge with which to dislodge the Soviet occupation of Afghanistan from December 1979, without any blowback that would damage America. The stratagem had certainly worked in hastening the fall of the Soviet regime. But it paid no attention to the dangers of militant Islam and the resolute determination of its most extreme followers to realize their ultimate goal: the creation of a grand caliphate. In the end what appeared to be a very convenient, malleable, tactical instrument of US foreign policy, put in place by Zbigniew Brzezinski, a Eurocentric national security adviser, turned out to have a life of its own well beyond the borders of Afghanistan.[3] Hence the attack on the American homeland on 11 September 2001.

Indigenous conditions had to ripen in any society before the Americans could make their efforts felt. The non-violent Rose Revolution – *vardebis revolutsia* – broke out in notoriously corrupt post-Soviet Georgia on 22 November 2003 after nearly three weeks of protest at the obviously fraudulent elections presided over by Eduard Shevardnadze, the former Soviet minister of foreign affairs. The floral theme recalled the revolution of the carnations in Portugal (25 April 1974) against a half-century of fascism. In Georgia an American educated populist, Mikheil Saakashvili, led a mob with roses in hand and entered parliament while the assembly was in session and seized government buildings on the following day. Mediation by the Russians then resulted in the resignation of Shevardnadze, bringing Saakashvili into power. The United States was the first to recognize the new regime before a delayed presidential election was held on 4 January 2004 and parliamentary elections on 28 March.

The *New York Times* summed up the situation as follows:

> Even before he was sworn in as president, Saakashvili pushed through constitutional changes that gave more power to the president at the expense of the legislature. During the next three years, democracy could be described as simply not a priority to the new government, which was intent on rooting out corruption, reforming the education system,

retraining police, reducing bureaucracy and strengthening the Georgian state. In concrete terms this meant that media freedom was reduced, an independent judiciary did not evolve, the government party sought to weaken opposition parties, and a one-party system (its fourth in less than 20 years) was solidified.[4]

But after the dreadful cost of turning Iraq into a democracy – estimated at some $815 billion – the American public had some difficulty identifying with the Bush administration's attempt during its second term of office to spread its own political values across the globe. Only 15 per cent of respondents in CBS/*New York Times* polls said yes to the question "Should the United States try to change a dictatorship to a democracy where it can, or should the United States stay out of other countries' affairs?"[5]

Whereas Georgia mattered to Russia rather more as a precedent than as a factor vital to its security, the "Orange Revolution" in neighbouring Ukraine that took place from 22 November 2004 was an entirely different matter. It changed everything for Putin. As described by the then senior director for Russian affairs on the National Security Council, "the United States makes an effort to remove a pro-Russian figure in favor of a pro-Western figure, then takes a number of steps to solidify its relationship with Ukraine, and if not directly, at least indirectly supports a Ukrainian government that wants to distance itself from Moscow".[6]

Seventeen days of protest broke out at the blatant attempt of Viktor Yanukovych – openly backed by the Russians – to steal the presidential election, with Putin publicly interfering by loudly voicing support for his favourite. Yanukovych's opponent, the reformist banker Viktor Yushchenko, had been mysteriously poisoned, his face disfigured by dioxin on 6 September and his supporters subjected to various forms of repression. Supporters from within Ukraine's security services (SBU) testified to widespread electoral fraud. The government's attempts at suppressing protests failed because of SBU resistance. And on 27 November parliament – *Verkhovna Rada* – declared the poll invalid, a resolution echoed by the supreme court on 3 December.

On 26 December a new ballot, which was heavily monitored by foreign observers, gave Yushchenko 52 per cent, and Yanukovych 44 per cent of votes cast. Support for Yanukovych came mostly from the east of the country, the heartland of Russian speakers in Ukraine. The US ambassador John Herbst shared the limelight with the victors, unabashed about defying diplomatic protocol. He had, he said, worked to "help ensure the conduct of a fair Ukrainian presidential election..."[7] It was a clear victory for Ukrainian nationalists, even though it still left the population badly divided given the regional disparities in support for the two rivals. It was also a victory for the Bush administration. After the White House weighed up policy alternatives, the Ukrainian issue had encouraged the president into adopting a position on Russia more consonant with neo-conservative values.[8] Greater activism seemed to be producing results. Organizations such as the US Agency for International Development (USAID) were seen as essential to such efforts, as they had been in Georgia.

Putin was, of course, furious. His vision of post-Soviet Russia – no different from that of Yeltsin before him – encompassed the inclusion of post-Soviet states within a new federation. In Georgia, an ethnic minority challenged the ruling majority – in Abkhazia – while Putin posed as the champion of its rights and prepared to afford military protection. Would this not also be an option in Eastern Ukraine? It is entirely possible that this now began to take shape in his mind as a potential option in the event that the course of politics in Kyiv took a decisive, one-way turn for the worse.

The US ambassador to Russia, Sandy Vershbow, had been a participant in the original decision on NATO expansion. He recalled the US immersion in Ukrainian electoral politics in 2004 as the "biggest watershed" in relations between the United States, NATO and Russia. "When I think Putin began to feel that all the West's talk of partnership was a smokescreen for a cynical plot to undermine Russia to deprive it of its rightful domination over its neighbors and even to bring about color revolutions all over the former Soviet space including in Russia itself and ultimately topple the Putin regime."[9] Yushchenko's victory had been catalytic in activating Ukrainian interest in joining the EU, if not NATO. But his presidency was cursed by disarray among politicians hostile to Russia and tainted by corruption. Thus the defeated Yanukovych managed to claw his way back into power as prime minister in the summer of 2006 while his successors fought over the spoils. Yet this was by no means the end of the story. The Americans failed to understand the aggravating impact of their activism on the overall state of relations with Russia. Here Rice was out of her depth: "we didn't see a contradiction between wanting to have good relations with the Russians and what was happening in the color revolutions. I think we might have – and maybe I'm the one who should have seen this – we might have been late to understand how Putin saw them."[10]

"Orange" revolutions began springing up elsewhere, notably across the Arab world. The United States found it impossible to resist the temptation of intervening on the side of those seeking to overturn dictatorships. On 25 July 2006 Rice enthusiastically declared that "It is time for a new Middle East. It is time to say to those who do not want a different kind of Middle East that we will prevail, they will not."[11] She was in fact hopelessly out to sea. "Apparently," Putin noted caustically in a swipe at Rice, who had also taken to repeating her protests against Russia's retreat from democracy, "those who constantly throw together new 'colour revolutions' consider themselves 'brilliant artists' and simply cannot stop."[12] Putin's creeping take-over of the Russian media, the assassination of journalists and raids on their premises, were already the object of growing alarm in the Western press. "Democracy In Retreat In Russia" was the title of hearings in the US Senate on 17 February 2005.[13] The United States and Russia appeared to be heading for a direct collision.

At a summit with Putin in St Petersburg during the summer

of 2006, "Bush drew attention to the challenges posed by democratic freedoms, especially freedom of the press, in Russia – and then noted that things had gotten much better in [occupied] Iraq. Putin immediately responded, 'Well, we really would not want the kind of democracy they have in Iraq.' The room filled with applause, and not everyone heard Bush's response, but Putin did: 'Just wait, it's coming.' What Bush appears to have had in mind was increased stability in Iraq. But it sounded more ominous: you'll see, democracy will be brought to you as well…"[14]

It is doubtful whether Putin realized the extent to which this was merely Bush's tin ear, or a Freudian slip blurted out in inappropriate company. Subsequent events suggest it was simply clumsiness. It touched a raw nerve. Bush and his advisers failed to understand that the simultaneous emergence of the Colour Revolutions in parallel with continued NATO expansion created a nightmare for Putin, alleviated – as with the Iraq war – only by the sight of NATO in disarray, which ultimately as usual turned out to be a mirage.

A message to Bush that in Russia the regime could act as it pleased, arrived on 7 October on Putin's 54th birthday. Anna Politkovskaya, perhaps Russia's best-known critic of the regime for its war against Chechen secession, was gunned down in her Moscow apartment by persons unknown. What had she dared to write two years before? "We are hurtling back into a Soviet abyss, into an information vacuum that spells death from our own ignorance", she wrote in her 2004 book *Putin's Russia*. "All we have left is the Internet, where information is still freely available. For the rest, if you want to go on working as a journalist, it's total servility to Putin. Otherwise, it can be death, the bullet, poison, or trial – whatever our special services, Putin's guard dogs, see fit."[15]

The Assassination of Litvinenko

When Putin felt personally threatened, he lashed out. He once confessed to the liberal Russian journalist Alexei Venediktov, owner of the fiercely independent radio station *Ekho Moskvy*, "Enemies are right in front of you, you are at war with them, then you make an armistice with them, and all is clear. A traitor must be destroyed, crushed."[16] Venediktov was lucky to be seen merely as an enemy, indeed at one time a potential recruit into the clan. Putin was always on the lookout for talent; a measure of dissent could always prove useful. The former FSB officer Alexandr Litvinenko was simply a traitor, however. Domestic intelligence, the FSB, under the ominous figure of Nikolai Patrushev, having proved itself against the Chechen rebellion in 2001 and which had poisoned Chechen leader Ibn al-Khattab, had obtained the formal right to operate abroad on its own account.

From his base in London, Litvinenko began looking into connections between the Tambov mafia that had long dominated St Petersburg and organized crime in Spain, which laundered its illicit proceeds. Litvinenko consulted for MI6 and had obtained recordings linking the Russian government to crime that backed up his findings. He had already met with a Spanish *Centro Nacional de Inteligencia* (CNI) representative and he was due in Madrid to brief them fully on his latest findings when he was poisoned with radioactive polonium, which a former colleague Andrei Lugovoi tipped into his tea at the Millennium Hotel bar in London on the morning of 1 November 2006.

The problem was that, since his early days in Petersburg, Putin had been co-operating with the Eurasian mafia, which had long since found shelter from the state.[17] It was one of the elements that enabled Putin to play off power factions within the state against one another. MI6 characterized the situation as "the very muddy nexus between business and corruption and state power in Russia." Similarly the British Government Communications Headquarters referred to the fact that "we've seen more evidence of ***serious and organised crime*** being connected at high levels of [the] Russian state and Russian intelligence" forming "a symbiotic relationship".[18] In 2010 an extensive briefing by the chief Spanish prosecutor, José Grinda, outlined for the Americans Litvinenko's thesis that the Russian intelligence services controlled organized crime in Russia. Grinda believed "the FSB is 'absorbing' them in two ways: by killing O[rganized] C[rime] leaders who do not do what the security services want them to do or by putting them behind bars to eliminate them as a competitor for influence".[19] Polonium from the Russian atomic agency, Rosatom, was used as the Russians wrongly thought it would never be identified because of its obscurity. The British (and Canadians), however, were among the few who knew anything about it. Yet, aside from trying and failing to extradite Lugovoi and his partner in crime from Russia, no substantial retribution was ever exacted for this blatant breach of British sovereignty. The allies looked the other way and carried on as though nothing had happened. Putin and the Russian intelligence services evidently took this to mean that they had a laissez-passer, which of course they made use of again. This was probably the worst combination NATO simultaneously presented: American assertiveness and West European (mainly German) timidity.

By the time of the annual European security conference that took place in Munich on 10 February 2007, Putin's mind had moved on to higher matters. Echoes of the Iraq war and the Orange Revolution in Ukraine resonated, though not explicitly, throughout what he had to say. Up to the moment Putin spoke, the atmosphere of the conference – in spite of Litvinenko's murder and the assassination of Politkovskaya – had, as usual, been congenial. That soon changed.

Up to the last moment, Putin was visibly nervous, fiddling with his papers, hurriedly rewriting parts of his speech. Although careful to underscore more than once his good personal relationship with President Bush, the brunt of his attack was targeted at the United States. It had placed itself in charge of the world where,

Putin insisted, more local and regional conflicts were occurring than ever before, with the result that more people had died; "no one any longer feels safe", he argued. Instead there should be "an architecture of global security". But instead of clarifying what exactly this was, Putin accelerated into a bitter invective. Russia, he said, confronted the expansion of NATO: "a provocative factor reducing the level of mutual trust. And we have a justifiable right to ask: against whom is this expansion [directed]? And what has become of those assurances given by [our] Western partners after the dissolution of the Warsaw Pact? Where are these assurances now? Nobody now even remembers them." Putin quoted former NATO secretary-general Wörner as having said: "The very fact that we are prepared not to deploy NATO forces beyond the territorial limits of the Federal Republic of Germany gives the Soviet Union firm guarantees of security." Some in the audience tittered.

The other issue that emerged out of a question from the floor was that of regime change, and the lesser charge of interfering in the domestic affairs of other states, in particular to further the spread of democracy through subsidies to those advocating radical change. "What worries us?" Putin asked. "I would say and I think that this is understandable to everyone: when these non-governmental organisations are essentially funded by foreign governments, then we see it as an instrument of a foreign state furthering its policy in relation to our country... What's the point of that?" he asked. "Is this normal democracy? It is hidden financial support, hidden from society. What's democratic about it? Can you tell me? No. You can't. And you'll never be able to say. Because this is not democracy, but simply the influence of one state on another."[20]

Stephen Hadley, a fervent conservative unilateralist, was close to Cheney. His current role was as deputy to Rice: "I think the problem really came with the color revolutions. We were in a dialog with Russia, a strategic dialog that was set up by the two presidents, that I actually ran at the working level as deputy national security adviser with the Russian counterpart, and we had developed a set of rules of the road of how United States and Russia were going to cooperate together in the near abroad; that is to say, those now independent states that used to be part of the Soviet Union... That progress all fell apart, really, under the pressure of the color revolutions, the revolutions in Georgia [November 2003] and Tajikistan and Ukraine and elsewhere."[21]

Medvedev Takes the Reins

It was confidently expected that the younger, apparently more Western-oriented prime minister Dmitrii Medvedev would succeed to the Russian presidency in May. It was in US interests to encourage a trend with which Medvedev could at least to some extent identify. This was certainly the British view. But the Americans eyed his accession instead as an ideal opportunity for attaining the unfulfilled objectives of the Bush presidency at the expense of a more liberal Russia. And these were also Rumsfeld's last months in office. As a result, and this was scarcely a surprise to those who understood the darker side of Russia, tension between Washington and Moscow rose to new heights. From Moscow in early February 2008 ambassador Burns warned of the "three potential trainwrecks" ahead that threatened to derail relations with Russia: Kosovo, the issue of Georgian and Ukrainian entry into NATO (under a Membership Action Plan) and National Missile Defense.

Burns had a constructive suggestion which the administration promptly dismissed:

> My view is that we can only manage one of these three trainwrecks without doing real damage to a relationship we don't have the luxury of ignoring. From my admittedly parochial perspective here, it's hard to see how we could get the key Europeans to support us on all three at the same time. I'd opt for ploughing ahead resolutely on Kosovo; deferring MAP

[Membership Action Plan] for Ukraine or Georgia until a stronger foundation is laid; and going to Putin directly while he's still in the Presidency to try to cut a deal on missile defense, as part of a broader security framework.

I fully understand how difficult a decision to hold off on MAP will be. But it's equally hard to overstate the strategic consequences of a premature MAP offer, especially to Ukraine.

Ukrainian entry into NATO is the brightest of all redlines for the Russian elite (not just Putin). In more than two and a half years of conversations with key Russian players, from knuckle-draggers in the dark recesses of the Kremlin to Putin's sharpest liberal critics, I have yet to find anyone who views Ukraine in NATO as anything other than a direct challenge to Russian interests. At this stage, a MAP offer would be seen not as a technical step along a long road toward membership, but as throwing down the strategic gauntlet. Today's Russia will respond... It will create fertile soil for Russian meddling in Crimea and eastern Ukraine.[22]

For good measure, Burns also predicted a conflict with Georgia. But his advice, which was spot on, was simply ignored. Later, Putin asked: "Who was it that in 2008, when things were just fine with no Crimean events in sight, suddenly said they wanted to join NATO, and NATO opened its doors to them, declaring at the summit in Bucharest that NATO's doors were open to Ukraine?"[23] This was a victory for Polish policy, that of Foreign Minister Sikorski, who got into a scrap with Germany's Foreign Minister Frank-Walter Steinmeier when the latter argued that "We can't take on countries that have frozen conflicts."[24] It was also the moment for Bush to cement his legacy, appearing on court in his last year with the feeling that he was entitled to nothing less than game, set and match. But Poland had not been closely coordinating its Russia policy with partners in the EU.

However much the Americans sympathized with the Poles, the Germans still played the key role.

On 17 February 2008 the Kosovan assembly declared unilateral independence. The Germans were its strongest backers. In unseemly haste the Americans, the French and the British quickly breached UN Security Council resolution 1244 by granting immediate diplomatic recognition to Kosovo. Given Russia's sensitivity on the subject of secession, and the fact that it was another blow to Serbia, this was a bitter pill to swallow. Putin warned of the consequences for international law and order.[25] And not a few in the West had misgivings about Kosovan war crimes and well documented involvement in the narcotics trade by Albanian Kosovar politicians. But where Germany asserted itself, no country other than the United States could effectively block it.

In a triumphalist mood, the Americans then unilaterally scheduled consideration of a Membership Action Plan for Georgia and Ukraine for a meeting of the NATO Council in Bucharest on 2–4 April 2008. The aim was to begin the process of incorporation at the NATO Foreign Ministers' meeting in December. Bush viewed the "new" Europe with a good deal more sympathy than the old, given the positions taken on the war in Iraq by France and Germany in contrast to the enthusiastic support from Poland. Moreover, the Americans saw Poland's Eastern policy was "an excellent complement to our own…" The Poles saw the Russians as a danger "in 10–15 years". They "pushed hard for Ukraine and Georgia's NATO accession, and called on NATO to make sure it can make good on Article V guarantees".[26]

But was Ukraine really interested? Yushchenko certainly was. He had spoken out in favour of inclusion at the NATO summit on 22 February 2005. However, in 2023 the US ambassador to Russia, Lynn Tracey, recalled the words of a predecessor, John Teft, who had been her senior in 2014. Teft had been reassigned to Moscow in July 2014 from Kyiv. On his view there had been Ukrainian interest in EU membership, "but for entry into NATO there was practically none".[27] The initiative from Washington DC none the less ran ahead and predictably met with vigorous opposition from German Chancellor and Christian Democrat Angela Merkel – in spite of her pro-Americanism – and, with more nuance, from the French.

The US embassy in Paris did not doubt the reasons behind French opposition. It reported that "French resistance to accept MAP for Ukraine stems, at least in part, from concerns over the likely Russian reaction to such a move."[28] President Nicolas Sarkozy took the view that "On the Russian question our interests are less aligned than one usually supposes."[29] And when in March Burns was invited to see Putin at his palatial retreat, Novoe Ogaryovo, it was explained to him politely but firmly that "no Russian could stand idly by in the face of steps toward NATO membership for Ukraine. That would be a hostile act toward Russia... We would do all in our power to prevent it." He then added: "If people want to limit and weaken Russia, why do they have to do it through NATO enlargement? Doesn't your government know that NATO is a very divisive issue there? Don't you know that Ukraine is not even a real country? Part of it is really East European, and part is really Russian. This would be another mistake in American diplomacy, and I know Germany and France are not ready anyway."[30] But Washington took no interest in what Burns had to say.

Merkel's resistance was crucial. And Bush did not escape her wrath.[31] The proposal reawakened dormant European suspicions from the mid-1990s during the Clinton administration. Quite apart from the Poles, the Americans appeared to be driven entirely by considerations that had little to do with the enhancement of European security or the interests of NATO as a whole. Moreover, Sarkozy took the view that "the Poles will never choose Europe against the United States. Their detestation of Russia, understandable of itself, will always be the dominant sentiment. But the whole of Europe cannot be held back or stop short by this visceral reaction in building relations between the European continent and the Russians."[32]

US representatives reported "a widespread suspicion among

German policymakers that our [the US] push for a MAP decision in December is not based on the merits, but really is about creating a legacy for the Bush Administration". German officials told their American counterparts of their "fear that, as soon as MAP is granted, the US will push immediately for offers of membership. The Germans therefore have moved the goal posts on what they think is required to join MAP." Thereafter Merkel had "shown little indication of backing down from her view that Georgia, because of a democratic deficit and separatist conflicts, and Ukraine, because of the uncertain public support for NATO membership, are simply not ready to join MAP and may not be for some time to come".

It was reported that the Chancellor's opposition came with "almost unanimous political support within Germany". Although the Germans had been emphatic that "non-NATO states, including Russia, cannot be given droit de regard over who can and cannot join the Alliance", Germany's foreign policy was "certainly predicated on building a strong working relationship with Moscow". And with regard to Georgia, the Germans suspected that "Tbilisi is interested in NATO only to achieve a resolution of other conflicts, not because Georgia shares NATO's values and strategic goals". Indeed, in Berlin there was "a fundamental lack of trust in Saakashvili and his commitment to democracy and a peaceful resolution of the separatist conflicts". Furthermore there existed "a widespread concern that Saakashvili, once in MAP or as a NATO member, could draw the Alliance into a conflict with Russia (in which as [Deputy Foreign and Security Advisor] Rolf Nikel put it, 'Tbilisi might not be totally blameless.')" Moreover Nikel said "that Ukraine is actually a far more difficult case for MAP given Ukraine's long and close association with Russia, dating back to Vladimir of Kyiv in 988. Nikel argued that many Russians still see Ukraine as inexorably intertwined with Russia, which obviously complicates the NATO question."[33]

At the NATO-Russia Council that convened on the final day, 4 April, and just as the Germans predicted, Putin in his last moments as president sounded a menacing note.[34] He "implicitly challenged the territorial integrity of Ukraine, suggesting that Ukraine was an artificial creation sewn together from [the] territory of Poland, Czechoslovakia, Romania, and especially Russia in the aftermath of the Second World War. He stated, 'the Crimea was simply given to Ukraine by a decision of the Politburo of the Soviet Communist Party Central Committee. There haven't even been any state procedures regarding [the] transfer of the territory, since we take a very calm and responsible approach to the problem.' Putin claimed that 90 percent of inhabitants of the Crimea are Russian, 17 out of 45 million Ukrainian citizens are Russian, and that Ukraine gained enormous amounts of its territory from the east and south at the expense of Russia. He added, 'if we add in the NATO question and other problems, the very existence of the State could find itself under threat.'"[35]

Back at home in Moscow commentator Dmitrii Trenin, ex-GRU, told Laurie Bristow, Minister-Counsellor at the British embassy: "this means war"; and he was not alone in saying so.[36] It was still weighing on Putin's mind nearly three years later at the world economic forum in Davos when he underlined the fact that the Budapest Memorandum of 1994 providing for the future security of Ukraine was never ratified by the Duma and he had never agreed with it.[37] In other words, as far as Russia was concerned there were no legitimate security guarantees for Ukraine. The West could not claim there had been no warning.

The former ambassador Sandy Vershbow recalled that by "pushing for that in 2008... just a few years after the Orange Revolution and the Rose Revolution in Georgia and failing to get the rest of the allies to support what we were trying to do, just arriving at the summit saying we want this and finding that the allies were just as opposed as Putin who was in attendance at the summit meeting in Bucharest, I think that was very counterproductive and it may have fueled Russian skepticism of not just of NATO but of partnership with the West."[38] Javier Solana had been Secretary General of NATO from 1995 to 1999 and was

High Representative for Foreign and Security Policy of the EU at the time. On the eve of Putin's invasion of Ukraine, Solana commented that "When they negotiated the historic agreement between Russia and the Alliance in 1997 it seemed that we were going to make progress, but a mistake was made at the NATO summit in April 2008, giving way to the temptation to speak as though Ukraine and Georgia were going to become members of the Atlantic Alliance... Russia came away with the talk about Ukraine being able to enter NATO and we are now in a manner of speaking living with the consequences."[39]

A world financial crisis began on 8 August 2008, as usual precipitated on Wall Street. It was also the eve of the Chinese Olympiad. And there was fighting across Georgia's frontier with Russia. Prematurely counting on American support and guided by President Saakashvili, the Georgian army finally began bombarding the breakaway republic of South Ossetia, which had increasingly come under Russian protection. Under Secretary Burns testified that this "short-sighted and ill-advised" action was taken "against our strong and repeated warnings".[40] The US ambassador to Russia, John Beyrle, also emphasized that fact.[41] Units of the 58th Russian army, however, were promptly sent in with air support to push the Georgian forces back. Fighting continued for several days until a ceasefire could be arranged. The conflict had evidently been sparked by NATO's controversial summit, though both sides had been spoiling for a fight for some time. The war in Georgia "revealed the continuing divisions within the alliance" concerning Georgia's membership in NATO. As was to be expected, Poland, the Czech Republic and the Baltic states were rather more inclined to side with Georgia while Germany in particular tended to show more sympathy for the position of Russia, even though all agreed that the air strikes crossed a red line.[42]

Since Schröder's chancellorship, Germany was seen as "the standard bearer for [the] pro-Russia camp", concerned at the likely effect on "NATO's long term relationship with Russia" of any punitive actions beyond a slap on the wrist. In this it was effectively backed by France.[43] The Danes, for example, recognized that the Georgians "had made mistakes", but they saw the Russians as responsible for escalating the conflict. A ceasefire had been agreed, yet Russia had "won a clear military victory that will not be undone by sanctions".[44] Only the fourth condition for ending the war that Russian Foreign Minister Sergei Lavrov was insistent upon – that Saakashvili leave office – was unacceptable to the Americans.[45]

Testifying to the Senate, Burns said this: "the Russian leadership has been deeply disturbed by a number of those steps [NATO enlargement and the proposals to line up Ukraine and Georgia for future entry], and that does create, notwithstanding our best efforts, the backdrop against which they shape some of their choices". "I think what it underscores for me", he added, "is not that we necessarily need to accept their concerns, or indulge them, we need to understand them." He cited the fact that they had gone through "a very rough period. Economic uncertainty, disorder – you know, for many Russians, a sense of lost dignity and national humiliation." Russia had experienced "a lot of anxiety, over the years, and particularly with regard to the question of Ukraine, which is, I think, in many ways, the brightest red line of all for many in the Russian political elite". What was evident in Russia at that time "is a Russia, in some ways, floating on high energy prices, that finds a fair amount of satisfaction in asserting itself". "There is," he stated, "across the Russian political elite, including within the Kremlin and in the government, I think, a pretty strong consensus on some of the issues that we've talked about today, whether we like it or not, with regard to the reassertion of Russian national interests and a willingness to be pretty aggressive in asserting those interests. There's a debate about tactics sometimes."[46]

Not surprisingly, events in Georgia were, as Kurt Volker, head of the US mission said, "coloring Allies' views of Ukraine and its membership prospects at NATO. Allies [were] divided on their perception of how the Bucharest Summit pledge of future membership to Georgia and Ukraine affected the current crisis. The German-led Allies argue that the Bucharest decision on eventual membership provoked the Russian aggression, while most others (including the new members and Canada) see it as we do: that Russia interpreted the denial of MAP as a green light for action against Georgia." Volker concluded that "For many Allies, the Georgia-Russia conflict provides new impetus to moving Ukraine into MAP and toward NATO membership, provided Ukraine continues to request it. Conversely if the Kremlin achieves all of its objectives in Georgia with few consequences and its international reputation intact – as Germany and others would have it – this may only embolden Russia to increase its bullying behavior towards Ukraine and others in the neighborhood."[47]

The expansion of NATO to include Georgia and Ukraine was not exactly a move that had met with unanimous approval in London either, certainly with respect to Ukraine. Before he moved back home, ambassador Lyne, a life-long Russianist and a onetime enthusiast single-minded in his belief that the relationship with Putin could be made to work, warned "that any push for Ukrainian membership in NATO was absolutely fissile material. It was clear to me all along, but I'm not sure all Western leaders really understood. I think there were people, particularly in America, in the neoconservative circles, the 'John Bolton Brigade', who simply didn't understand that because they actually had very little understanding of Russia."[48]

Having failed to mobilize NATO, and having armed the Georgians against the Russians, Poland's Foreign Minister Sikorski took the logical next step and turned towards the EU to build a coalition that would back the Polish policy of containment. His involvement in the NATO proposal, Poland's longstanding antipathy towards Russia and Polish proximity to the Bush administration made it critical to have the support of the Foreign Minister of Sweden, Carl Bildt. The two of them proposed a less provocative means of undermining Russia's attempt to hang on to former Soviet republics, Ukraine in particular. And since it meant expanding the influence of the EU, the Germans and French could scarcely object. This was the proposal for an Eastern Partnership, but as a secondary consideration while NATO membership still seemed a possibility.

The only American worry was lest Poland "get too far in front" not only in letting Georgia have "sensitive armaments" but also "by pushing through the sudden removal of most EU sanctions against Belarus". (These had been imposed in retaliation for electoral fraud and the crackdown on democratic rights.) The Partnership was designed "to deepen EU relations with Ukraine, Georgia, Moldova, Belarus, Armenia, and Azerbaijan." Its main aim, though unstated, was to "Counter Russia's influence in Eastern Europe", "to counter a resurgent Russia". US ambassador Victor Ashe reported: "Foreign Minister Sikorski told US officials the G[overnment] o[of] P[oland] used to think Russia would be a danger in 10–15 years, but after the Georgia crisis, it could be as little as 10–15 months. Polish analysts tell us having a pro-Western buffer zone in Ukraine and Belarus would keep Poland off the front line with an increasingly assertive Russia. By offering former Soviet republics the prospect of free trade and visa-free travel to the EU, the Eastern Partnership can spur the reforms needed for eventual EU membership and stem growing Russian influence." The Poles "called for a high-level strategic dialogue between Washington and Brussels – with Polish participation – on targeting assistance to eastern neighbors". Poland saw the Russian war with Georgia as vindicating their "warnings about Moscow's aggressive behavior. According to the 'Sikorski Doctrine', any further attempt by Russia to redraw borders by force or subversion should be regarded by Europe as a threat to its security, entailing a proportional response by the entire Euro-Atlantic community." Polish Ministry of Foreign Affairs officials expected the Russians to react sharply, "but they see a greater danger in doing nothing since they believe a resurgent, aggressive Russia is here to stay".[49]

Medvedev had taken over as President of Russia at the outset of the war with Georgia because his predecessor was not entitled to a consecutive term in office. Putin, however, was hardly idle as Prime Minister. From the US embassy Vershbow reported Moscow's mood of defiance.

> Having participated in Putin's convocation of editors in Sochi on August 29 [2008], both *Nezavisimaya Gazeta*'s Konstantin Remchukov and *Moskovskii Komsomolets*' Pavel Gusev separately told us [on] September 8 that they had seen Putin "at his toughest". Putin pushed aside the significance of any Western backlash to the Russian intervention in Georgia: on the Sochi Winter Olympics, scheduled for January 2014, "let them cancel it: we'll build one stadium instead of two;" on energy, "we'll sell Central Asian gas to those who want it, including Asia;" on estrangement from Europe, "don't worry, European leaders tell me that everything will be normal." If the West does not want Russia, Russia did not need the West, Putin repeated. "They cannot intimidate us." At the same time, Remchukov stressed that Putin did not advocate a preemptively punitive response and specifically demurred from pulling Russian investments from Fannie Mae and Freddie Mac (the publicly quoted US mortgage brokers) arguing that the markets needed more, not less, predictability. Putin maintained that Russia wanted to be like China – to "sit under the roots of the tree" and build its power quietly – but that immediate global responsibilities forced it to act. "When Russia is challenged, it must respond: we cannot just concede." Gusev, Vershbow explained, though "a prominent liberal and frequent critic of Putin, warned us that Russian actions were animated by a wave of patriotism and anti-American sentiment. 'Never have Russians been so united behind Putin and Medvedev'"[50]

Although Putin had taken a firm stance against Ukrainian entry into NATO, his attitude to the EU – which remained something of a black box to the Russians, as the EEC had once been for Kissinger – had initially appeared to be less confrontational when it remained a purely hypothetical issue. In his early days as President, on 10 December 2004, Putin told Spain's Prime Minister José Luis Zapatero that he was not opposed to Ukraine joining the EU as he expected that it would have a positive impact on Russia's economy. And seven years later – when Medvedev was president – the Russians appeared ready to link up with the Eastern Partnership and collaborate with the EU, at least according to Sikorski. "But", as he claims, "at some point in 2012, it seems that the Putin administration changed tactics."[51]

It was, however, much more than that: a complete change of outlook, of which Russia's attitude to the EU was but a part, and this took time to emerge. On 4 April 2009 at its Strasbourg summit, for instance, NATO reaffirmed entry for Ukraine and Georgia as an ultimate objective; it also committed itself "to improve the NATO-EU strategic partnership".[52] So the notion that the expansion of the EU to the East could in any sense be viewed independently of NATO enlargement was never credible. But while Medvedev was in office, the real impact of the events of 2008 was effectively delayed, though President Barack Obama got a taste of it on visiting Moscow a year later.

The strategy that evolved under Putin became one of undermining the primacy that the United States sought to sustain. "The ultimate realist," former US ambassador Burns noted, "Mr. Putin understands Russia's relative weakness, but regularly demonstrates that declining powers can be at least as disruptive as rising powers. He sees a target-rich environment all around him." Burns continued:

> If he can't easily build Russia up, he can take the United States down a few pegs, with his characteristic tactical agility and willingness to play rough and take risks. If he can't have a deferential government in Kiev, he can grab Crimea and try to engineer the next best thing, a dysfunctional Ukraine. If

he can't abide the risk of regime upheaval in Syria, he can flex Russia's military muscle, emasculate the West, and preserve Bashar al-Assad atop the rubble of Aleppo.[53]

Putin's indignation at Russia's failure to attain the much-valued status of equality with the United States had been a longstanding feature of Soviet policy that the Americans, whose own standing had been unchallenged since 1947, never grasped. On the second day of the one and only Moscow summit involving Bush's successor, Obama (6–8 July 2009), Putin, as prime minister, vented his feelings about the Bush administration for an entire hour, politely uninterrupted by his startled American guests. The diatribe, in reduced form, ran as follows:

> He liked President George W. Bush as a person, he told Obama, but loathed his administration. As Putin explained, he had reached out to Bush after September 11, believing that the United States and Russia should unite to fight terrorists as a common enemy. He had helped persuade leaders in Kyrgystan and Uzbekistan to allow the US to open air bases in their countries to help fight the war in Afghanistan. But in return, so he claimed, the Bush administration had snubbed him. Putin even suggested that Russia and the United States could have cooperated on Iraq had the Bush administration treated Russia as an equal partner. But it had not, and that's why US-Russia relations deteriorated so dramatically while Bush was president. The Bush team had supported color revolutions in Georgia and Ukraine – a blatant threat to Russia's national interests.[54]

"We've lost him", Bush later said of Putin. "You know, I don't know how, but we've lost him."[55] Such a statement inevitably gives rise to the thought: just how out of touch can a president be? But he was certainly not the exception.

7

Obama in Office

"On all these issues, but particularly missile defense, this, this can be solved, but it's important for him to give me space," Obama told Medvedev, referring to incoming Russian president Vladimir Putin.

"Yeah, I understand," Medvedev said. *"This is my last election. After my election, I have more flexibility,"* Obama added.

"I understand," Medvedev replied. *"I will transmit this information to Vladimir."*

– A stray microphone, 23 March 2012.[1]

Putin awoke to another false dawn in January 2009 when Obama took office. The President's strategic attention "seemed to be focused more on avoiding the kind of mistakes made by some of his predecessors, such as the disastrous war on Iraq, than on enunciating an overarching vision of his own". That, at least, was the sober conclusion of his third Secretary of Defense, Ashton Carter.[2] Faced with Republican sabre-rattling, Obama had, during the presidential debates, taken great care to reassure his opponents at home and abroad that the United States and Russia were not close to re-engaging in a Cold War.[3]

Unlikely as it may seem at first sight, Obama actually shared one crucial attitude to Russia with Bush. Former ambassador to Russia Vershbow recalls, "Obama repeated one mistake that was made during the Bush administration, particularly I mention Rumsfeld, and maybe Cheney bears the blame for this, which was in diminishing the importance of Russia – the argument that Russia didn't matter anymore, that we could basically solve most of our problems without Russia. If they want to help us – fine, we don't have to reward them for that. If they're acting in their own interests, such as helping us topple the Taliban in Afghanistan, then why pay them any compensation?"[4]

On 23 September Obama confidently addressed the United Nations in a more nuanced tone than his predecessor. He hinted that the US government had abandoned the crusade to expand democracy through regime change that marked the foreign policies of Clinton and Bush. "Democracy cannot be imposed on any nation from the outside", Obama reassured the world, in a statement of the obvious. "Each society must search for its own path, and no path is perfect. Each country will pursue a path rooted in the culture of its people and in its past traditions. And I admit that America has too often been selective in its promotion of democracy." This will have come as welcome news to the Russians. But then, harking back to the US Constitution of 1787, Obama went on to extol democracy as a "self-evident" truth and to reassert the extravagant claim – echoing his distant predecessor John Kennedy – that the United States "will never waver in our efforts to stand up for the right of people everywhere to determine their own destiny". At this point it must have been hard for anyone except true loyalists to draw a clear line of distinction between Obama and Bush.[5] The administration's subsequent response to events demonstrated that the more policy had changed, the more it appeared to remain the same. And, as Ashton Carter noted, one of Putin's core beliefs was "that the United States had made a mess of things by destabilizing countries and unhorsing their leaders, and would do the same to Russia and him if it could..."[6]

One of those fervently committed to human rights under Obama was Mike McFaul. He was new to the game as Special Assistant to the President and the Senior Director on the National Security Council for Russian and European Affairs. Blue-eyed, blonde-haired, Montana-born, he might easily have passed for a Mormon missionary in his high-minded youthful zeal. A Stanford professor new to diplomacy, he had just written *Advancing Democracy Abroad: Why We Should and How We Can* in collaboration with the fiercely anti-communist Hoover Institution, American capitalism's answer to the Institute of Marxism-Leninism in Moscow and once synonymous with the emigré community from Eastern Europe and the Soviet Union, though repopulated since the Cold War.[7]

As a Stanford professor, McFaul was in one sense a rank outsider, but he had spent eighteen months on the campaign trail. At the White House, chairing the inter-agency policy committee, McFaul rapidly found his feet and quickly locked arms with those sharing his vision. Throughout his stint in government, Vice-President Biden's national security adviser Tony Blinken was "both a friend and an ideological ally".[8] And the corollary to McFaul's doctrine – the rejection of any Kissinger-like deals with Russia except on arms control – was shared fully by Obama. The message soon found its way into Biden's high-minded speech to the Munich security conference on 7 February 2009, namely that "We will not recognize any nation having a sphere of influence."[9]

What had not entirely been thought through, however, was that if no one had a sphere of influence, everyone's business was America's business; even their internal affairs, let alone what went on in their own backyard. And it was not just Russia that found this objectionable. Obama, although foreswearing the extensive use of force applied by his predecessor, was unable to live up to his lofty promise. He upgraded the occupation of Afghanistan, unleashed a new offensive in Iraq, and killed numerous suspected terrorists (and sometimes their families as well) using drones remotely controlled from Afghanistan and the border region with Pakistan. These actions indicated that there was no complete about-turn from the Bush line.[10] It confirmed to the Russians that the underlying dynamics of US foreign policy were not susceptible to significant change merely through a presidential election.

Although McFaul recalls that for "many" on the team "promoting democracy inside Russia was not a priority",[11] at her nomination as Secretary of State Hillary Clinton made clear to the Committee on Foreign Relations that "the Helsinki Accords [1975] actually contributed to the eventual breakup of the Soviet Union" and "I think this work [pushing human rights as an issue] must continue".[12] The President was sympathetic and so too was "a critical ally in developing and getting approval for our new policy" in former ambassador Burns, now elevated to be Under Secretary of State for Political Affairs.[13]

A particular grievance that needled Putin and rattled his circle were Western subsidies to non-governmental organizations (NGOs) active in Russia. What brought the issue to the fore was less the activities of election monitors in Ukraine during the Orange Revolution, where Boris Berezovsky was also involved in their financing, than the discovery in December 2005 of an MI6 spy ring at the British embassy in Moscow, which used a fake rock containing a transmission device with which to communicate with Russian agents. Marc Doe, Christopher Pirt, Paul Crompton and Andy Fleming had been caught in flagrante delicto. Doe, as second secretary, unfortunately also happened to be responsible for distributing financial support to several NGOs as well as for recruiting Russian agents.[14]

With Obama now in office, the US administration increased "democracy assistance" for Russia to the tune of $3.5 million in 2010, shifting the emphasis to non-governmental organizations to exert "pressure" for change.[15] When McFaul tried to follow this up with the creation of a Russian-American civil society working group to highlight the issue for Russia, Medvedev's deputy chief of staff Vladislav Surkov was appointed to chair it. Certainly no friend of democracy, he had been the sponsor of the thugs, *Nashi*, who had harassed Britain's ambassador, Sir Tony Brenton, only a few years before, after Brenton, taking Blair's assurances of his close relations with Putin too seriously, had chosen to attend an oppositionist public meeting.[16] As usual, when Putin wanted to have a stab at the United States, he did so initially by jabbing its closest ally, the monkey rather than the organ-grinder.

A harsh light was soon focused on the contradiction in US foreign policy between sustaining domestic changes within Russia and simultaneously trying to improve relations with its government. Taking her cue from McFaul, Hillary Clinton had on 6 March 2009 at the United Nations made great show of the fact that Washington wished to "reset" relations along a more positive course. McFaul was well aware how under Bush "direct lines of communication between senior American and Russian officials had atrophied".[17] But the level of professionalism and knowledge of Russia in Washington DC that could easily be taken for granted under Horelick in the late 1970s or Ermarth in the 1980s had declined disastrously. It rapidly became apparent when Clinton ill-advisedly used the wrong Russian word in a theatrical exchange to which Foreign Minister Sergei Lavrov reacted graciously, not least because it put the Americans on the back foot. Instead of handing him a symbolic plastic device for "resetting" the course of relations between the two Powers, she inadvertently offered him one for "overloading" relations.[18] Clinton had unintentionally predicted the course relations were about to take.

The Arab Spring

From the turn of the millennium the Middle East gripped American attention while Russia remained a residual issue, confined to a peripheral line of vision. Moscow soon discovered that the rhetoric about resetting relations was just that; other issues, more vital to Obama, mattered more.[19] While Afghanistan and Iraq remained a perilous mess, soaking up yet more American blood and treasure, the Arab Spring burst into life in North Africa, first in Tunisia in January 2011 and then in neighbouring Libya and in Egypt. Whereas Obama had limited interest in foreign affairs and had some difficulty identifying with Europe, the Maghreb was a region that drew more readily on his sympathy and attention. Yet at the same time his administration was pursuing an understanding with its longtime enemy Iran – fiercely opposed by Israel – that was aimed at forestalling their early acquisition of a nuclear missile capability. To achieve a deal there he needed Russian help, which was given very grudgingly. Moscow never felt vulnerable to Tehran and did not understand why it should sacrifice any Iranian good will for the sake of American/Israeli interests.

The Russians, moreover, were emphatically against anyone democratizing the Arab world, least of all the Americans. In February 2011 the Gaddafi regime cracked down hard on popular protest that had spilt over the border from Tunisia's Jasmine revolution. Obama determined on the use of force to prevent further massacres. As matters came to a head, Medvedev decided on a crucial move in the direction of the United States. It was a gesture made behind strictly closed doors with Vice President Biden. Although opposed by the Russian Foreign Ministry, Medvedev had his way.[20] As a result, on 17 March 2011 Moscow abstained on a UN Security Council resolution authorizing a no-fly zone over Libya. The French had originally requested this, but it had been adroitly tossed aside in its original form – by the Americans – and instead augmented with "all necessary measures", ostensibly to protect the civilian population. One day later Obama launched the first air strikes in a major bombing campaign designed to destroy the regime.

On 21 March, while visiting a major missile plant in Votkinsk, Putin, apoplectic at Medvedev's naïveté, issued an impromptu statement to reporters gathered around him on the factory floor, criticizing the UN resolution as "defective and flawed". "It allows everything", he complained, adding for good measure a provocative jibe for the benefit of the Islamic world beyond: "It reminds me of a medieval crusade." Force was being resorted to instinctively, he added. "This is becoming a persistent tendency in US policy. During the Clinton era they bombed Belgrade, Bush sent forces into Afghanistan, then under an invented, false pretext they sent forces into Iraq, liquidated the entire Iraqi leadership – even children in Saddam Hussein's family died."[21] Putin thereby gracefully pirouetted as a concerned, humanitarian friend of the Arab world; at least, of its blood-stained absolute rulers and their offspring. Medvedev, infuriated at such blatant attention-seeking and public insubordination, could not let an unauthorized statement like that go unanswered. "In no way is it acceptable", he declared, the instant he heard Putin's remarks, "to use expressions that incite a clash of civilisations, such as 'crusades' and so on. It's unacceptable."[22]

In post-Soviet Russia the eruption of such deep differences at the top into the media was unprecedented. Attempting to reassure Medvedev, Obama called him on 23 March and "went out of his way to underscore that we [the USA] were not using this UN Security Council resolution to pursue regime change in Libya".[23] But in an undiplomatic volte face on 14 April, together with Prime Minister David Cameron and President Nicolas Sarkozy, Obama published an editorial in the *New York Times* stating that "It is impossible to imagine a future for Libya with Qaddafi in power... because he has lost the consent of his people any deal that leaves him in power would lead to further chaos and lawlessness... Qaddafi must go and go for good."[24] Targets on screen, F-111F fighter bombers flew from East Anglia in a circuitous route to Libya where they were joined by A-4 and A-6 strike aircraft from carriers of the US Sixth Fleet in the Mediterranean.

Taking his cue from Sarkozy, and looking to steal the new Arab wave, Obama deliberately chose to topple Gaddafi. Russia was of no account. Obama had what he wanted with UN resolution 1973 on 17 March in the guise of a blank cheque from Russia. Former Secretary of Defense Robert Gates admits that Moscow "had been persuaded to abstain at the UN on the grounds that the resolution provided for a humanitarian mission to prevent the slaughter of civilians. Yet as the list of bombing targets steadily grew, it became clear that very few targets were off-limits and that NATO was intent on getting rid of Qaddafi."[25] And this came from a president who had promised the smallest defence budget since the outbreak of the Second World War.[26] So there was a blatant contradiction at the heart of US security policy that worsened rather than improved throughout Obama's term because he lacked any real interest in and instinct for the conduct of international relations.

Russia analysts despaired. Once again the United States had acted as though its old rival counted for nothing in the international system. No attention at all had been given to the fact that the Americans had thereby hung Medvedev out to dry after assuring him that regime change in Libya was not on the agenda, and this when elections to the Duma were due in less than eight months' time and presidential elections within a year, and his rival Putin was itching to return to office and reset policy towards the West. What made matters worse for Medvedev was that Gaddafi, found cowering by a public drain, was murdered by the rebels on 20 October in conditions of complete anarchy, just as Putin had predicted. To the Russians, Libya began to look all too like Iraq, and Obama, very like Bush – but without the homespun, Texan charm. The Americans had unwittingly opened Pandora's Box in the Arab world. Libya proved a disaster that ended in the death of the US ambassador, intelligence and other officials in Benghazi at the hands of terrorists in September 2012 as a result of a deep-seated, self-righteous complacency that marked the conduct of foreign policy in the Obama administration.

Putin was not about to sit back and watch the Libyan experiment being repeated when Obama unveiled "A Moment of Opportunity" in the Middle East on 19 May: "It will be the policy of the United States to promote reform across the region, and to support transition to democracy." Putin retorted by bluntly castigating this as "missile-bombing democracy".[27] For his part Medvedev felt betrayed. The Americans seemed blindly driven entirely by the usual self-serving ideological motives. The prize of capturing the Arab world from below had been ostentatiously elevated above whatever potential remained for co-operating with Russia. Some years later, defending his annexation of Crimea, Putin alerted the world to the impact of all this: "You know it's not that it [the reset with the United States] has ended now over Crimea. I think it ended even earlier, right after the events in Libya."[28]

In these unpropitious circumstances, McFaul, branded by critics as the new Candide, made his début in Moscow on 10 January 2012. He succeeded the much more experienced John Beyrle as ambassador. Knowing no better, Secretary Hillary Clinton had ill-advisedly instructed McFaul "to find creative ways to get around government obstacles and communicate directly with the Russian people".[29] In this she was backed by Under Secretary Burns, whose good instincts on Russia had evidently given way to his ambition to succeed Clinton as Secretary of State. McFaul saw his mission as that of introducing a "dual-track" engagement with both the government and the opposition. It was obvious where this would lead, as the harassment of Britain's ambassador Sir Tony Brenton had shown until the moment he left in 2008. McFaul had no intention, however, of acting so provocatively on arrival. But he took up his post when some of the most vigorous manifestations of unrest in Russia for many years had burst out as a result of blatant fraud in the parliamentary elections the month before. Were these the early signs of an Arab Spring in Russia? Within days of McFaul's arrival, Burns turned up on a lightning visit when the ambassador had barely settled into Spaso House with his family. His host, McFaul, promptly found himself in a very awkward position. The ambassador had vainly hoped for a "slow, quiet start", but – thanks to Burns – an inept initiative precipitated a dramatic confrontation with the Russian authorities.[30]

On 16 January McFaul and Burns made the rounds. But the ambassador had yet to see Prime Minister Putin and, oblivious as to its likely impact upon him at a time of abnormal unrest, on the following day Burns entertained civil rights activists and opposition politicians in two separate meetings on embassy grounds.[31] Not the most diplomatic of beginnings for McFaul, it has to be said.

Only four days later there appeared an article in the Russian press written by a name unknown to readers. This was Veronika Krasheninnikova, who had ties with foreign intelligence – the SVR. Her skill in foreign languages enabled a meteoric rise from the Leningrad Institute for Shipbuilding. She gained a place at the prestigious *Sciences Po* – the *Institut d'études politiques* – in Paris, acted as a go-between for foreign businesses in Moscow, and was latterly posted to New York as chair of the Council on Trade and Economic Co-operation between the USA and the Commonwealth of Independent States. Now her position was that of General Director of the Institute for Foreign Policy Research and Initiative. She wrote:

> Plans for the liberalisation of Russia's political system, promulgated in a presidential address, is being implemented especially quickly and at the most inappropriate moment – on the eve of presidential elections, which some Washington circles together with the Russian 'opposition' are making use of in an attempt at 'regime change' in Russia.

> But before introducing free competition in the political field, one has to establish honest and fair conditions for this process. Today such rules are absent, because the majority of the socio-political space is occupied by Western NGOs [non-governmental organisations] and those cloned by them.

> The arrival to the post of US ambassador in Moscow of a

highly qualified specialist in subversion, who on his second
day of work held a meeting with 'Western dissidents'...
clearly indicate Washington's priorities in Russia. At the same
time the USA insists on complete freedom of action for its
subordinates.

Her argument was that since the United States had a Foreign
Agents Registration Act (FARA), Russia should have one too.
What she did not mention was that FARA was in fact a neglected
backwater of American law only potentially restricting the activity of foreigners seeking to influence US public opinion.[32]

Unsurprisingly, after McFaul's much publicized reception of
the opposition, Putin had the ambassador down as a marked man.
The mild-mannered Medvedev indecorously shuffled aside, Putin
was soon magically back in office to reassert himself as president
and make up for lost time. It came after a fraudulent election on
4 March in the face of an unprecedented wave of popular protests
from those aggrieved that their democratic rights had been suppressed. Meanwhile, the well-briefed journalist Mikhail Leont'ev
highlighted differences with the Americans by taking a scalpel to
McFaul's fair image on state-run Channel 1 television, where the
ambassador was caricatured – by the intelligence agencies – as
"not a specialist on Russia" but "a specialist on democracy promotion, pure and simple".[33] Democracy itself was now self-evidently
a direct threat to the regime and Putin himself. From being an
essentially geopolitical struggle, East-West relations had also
become an ideological war of a new kind.

Back in office (though his baggage had somehow never left the
hall), Putin was determined to show who was master in his own
house. By now Krasheninnikova's article had made its impact.
On 21 July, in a sequel to measures introduced in 2006, Putin
signed a law that went into effect on 20 November 2012 regulating non-profit organizations "carrying out the functions of a
foreign agent".[34] This covered any public body, including NGOs,
in receipt of foreign funding. At the Vladivostok summit of Asian

Pacific nations on 10 September, Lavrov warned Clinton that the Russians expected USAID to close its offices in Moscow.

It was scarcely a surprise. Putin had every reason to resent sustained American meddling in Russia's internal affairs. McFaul notes that "In the 1990s, USAID in Russia focused primarily on fostering economic reform and economic development, but shifted its shrinking resources over time to a greater focus on democracy-assistance programs. By the time I arrived in Moscow as ambassador, roughly half of its programs to Russia focused on civil society, rule of law, or other programs aimed at fostering democracy and human rights."[35] This was not exactly a finely tuned set of priorities likely to win enthusiasm from the Kremlin.

Putin's complementary move was to drop any attempt to build relations with the EU, which was seen as merely a junior partner to the United States. Instead he moved to create a Eurasian economic union, building on a customs union with Belarus and Kazakhstan created in 2010. And it was not long before he moved to force the incorporation of Ukraine into the mix.[36]

The Syrian Swamp

Meanwhile the Near East reared its head once again. Not unreasonably the Russians saw it as a region of "chronic instability".[37]

On this occasion it took the form of Iraq's immediate neighbour, Syria, which was ruled by another Arab strongman, Bashar al-Assad. His father had been a close client of the Soviet Union, and was regarded as a great statesman by Russian Arabists, though the world knew him as a notorious mass murderer.[38] The younger Assad, an eye specialist who hated the sight of blood, and initially viewed as a reformer, with a wife born and educated in Britain, now faced open rebellion blowing in with the Arab Spring. Until 2011 Syria's closest relationship had been with France, its protector against the United States. That ended somewhat abruptly. As early as July, four months after the Syrian uprising broke out, Secretary of State Clinton declared that al-Assad was "not indispensable, and we have absolutely nothing invested in him remaining in power".[39] If this did not signal his overthrow, it came very close. But, unlike Egypt or Tunisia, Assad's strength lay in his status as a part of the ruling Alawite minority backed by other minorities, which insulated the regime from public sentiment in that the security services and the armed forces were managed by men unconnected with and therefore not answerable to the majority of the population. It was at this point that the Russians stepped in.

The Syrian regime was also soon backed by neighbouring Iran, keen to repel Sunni Islamism. It ushered in the Lebanese Shiite terror group Hezbollah to provide military reinforcements. The Americans in turn began aiding the opposition.[40] From November 2012 in a clandestine military logistics operation the CIA increased airlifts of arms into Syria via Esenboga airport in Turkey.[41] Months before – in April – the White House also authorized a CIA programme to train the rebels at a base in Jordan.[42] Obama's national security adviser, Tom Donilon, came to see Putin in the company of McFaul not long after to discuss nuclear arms control issues. Scowling at the genial but now discomfited ambassador, who had clearly become Putin's particular *bête noire*, the president-elect bluntly demanded to know of McFaul "When... are you going to start bombing Syria?"[43]

Vitalii Churkin, an experienced Americanist from the Gorbachev era, was Russia's permanent representative on the UN Security Council. He recalls that "It was not possible to view the situation in Syria separately from the Libyan experience, when the demand for an immediate ceasefire turned into a wide-ranging civil war. The humanitarian, social, economic and military consequences of which splashed out well beyond the borders of Libya."[44] Assad's bombing of a Damascus suburb with Sarin gas on 21 August 2013, killing civilians including children, crossed a red line that Obama had publicly drawn. "Nearly everyone advocated for quick action", Derek Chollet, Assistant Secretary of Defense for International Security Affairs, remembered.[45] This included Susan Rice, now a low-profile Special Advisor to the President for National Security Affairs. On 29 August Obama brought together Biden, Philip Gordon, his special adviser on the region, Rice, Karen Donfried, his Europe adviser, and others. They agreed that, in spite of the refusal of the House of Commons to allow the Prime Minister to proceed, and British participation could normally be taken for granted, military action should nevertheless go ahead.[46] Air strikes were therefore prepared in the form of Tomahawk cruise missiles. But Obama all of a sudden recoiled, facing the imminent prospect of the St Petersburg summit of the G-20 on 5–6 September. At a fancy Italian restaurant with his wife in northern Virginia on 30 August the US Defense Secretary Chuck Hagel was startled to receive a call from the President telling him to stand down.[47]

Lurching between holding firm to high principle, allowing policy to emerge out of off-the-cuff statements and hamletic dithering, Obama was suddenly inspired to ask for Congressional permission to strike Syria. Hagel, wounded by White House caprice, recalls: "There's no question in my mind that it hurt the credibility of the president's word when this occurred." He added: "A president's word is a big thing, and when the president says things, that's a big deal."[48] Unfortunately for Hagel, he continued to be chided by foreign counterparts for what Obama had done many years later. At the Senate Foreign Relations Committee the new Secretary of State John Kerry, a strong advocate of military action, stepped up and underscored the message: "President Obama's policy is that Assad must go." Yet at the same time, as in the case of Libya, the administration – in the manner of Rumsfeld – "made crystal clear we have no intentions of assuming responsibility for Syria's civil war".[49] One could be forgiven for concluding that this would have been Iraq all over again. That is certainly what Putin had reason to believe.

Even before the Foreign Relations Committee convened, Putin had issued a threat that were the Americans to act, he too had plans for military intervention.[50] His statement made an immediate impact. On the second day of the summit in St Petersburg a way had been found out of the American dilemma that would save Obama's face. Putin would persuade Assad to relinquish his stock of chemical weapons in return for the United States backing down from air strikes.[51] Taking a leaf out of Medvedev's book, and in an astute move to exert further pressure on Obama, the Kremlin hired the public relations firm Ketchum to approach the *New York Times* for publication of an opinion piece signed by Putin, to which editor Andrew Rosenthal all too readily agreed.

The article mirrored liberal left sentiments to a tee. US military intervention had become "commonplace" and here the knock-on effects would be of deadly significance in the war against terrorism:

> The potential strike by the United States against Syria, despite strong opposition from many countries… will result in more innocent victims, and escalation, potentially spreading the conflict far beyond Syria's borders. A strike would… unleash a new wave of terrorism.

On his view, "Syria is not witnessing a battle for democracy, but an armed conflict between government and opposition in a multireligious country." And not far from the scene of battle lurked al-Qaeda, in the guise of the al-Nusra front. "Mercenaries from Arab countries fighting there, and hundreds of militants from Western countries and even Russia, are an issue of our deep concern. Might they not return to our countries with experience acquired in Syria? After all, after fighting in Libya extremists moved on to Mali. This threatens us all."[52] It was what Putin liked to call "the terrorist international".[53]

What clearly baffled the Russians was that a US coalition of the willing decapitated governments and destroyed the civilian infrastructure of a country by means of massed air power but, because it feared endangering the lives of its servicemen, it would unhesitatingly up sticks and leave societies whose economies had been dislocated to cope with the dire consequences. This was what Bush accomplished in Iraq, Obama did in Libya and, eventually, in despair, what the United States was to do in Afghanistan. And out of such chaos democracy was somehow miraculously to be born. In the brutal reality of the less developed Arab world, however, the mob, with or without élite democrats, was more likely to succeed in creating complete disorder, providing fertile soil for the growth and spread of Islamic fundamentalism.

In Iraq, for example, ISIS – the remnants of al-Qaeda – captured the key northern city of Mosul in June 2014 with a population of over one million. They were on their way to Baghdad and the Kurdish regions. Ashton Carter, coming in as Secretary of Defense in December that year, recalls that ISIS had also taken Tikrit "and wide swathes of northern Iraq, key oil and gas fields, the cities of Raqqa and Tabqa in Syria, and important border crossings that secured its ability to move forces, money, and matériel between Iraq and Syria freely. It had openly declared an Islamic caliphate in Iraq and Syria, and announced its intention to expand into Yemen, Saudi Arabia, Egypt, Algeria and Libya. Tens of thousands of foreign fighters had streamed into Iraq and Syria to bolster its ranks."[54] "ISIS' capability surprised us", confessed Derek Chollet, the Assistant Secretary of Defense for International Security. "The sense of urgency changed after Mosul", he recalls. "ISIS now had its hands on millions in cash from captured Iraqi banks, along with heavy armor and vehicles and tons of weapons from overrun Iraqi Army depots – most of which had been provided by the US after its army withdrew."[55]

To the Kremlin this was yet more evidence of high-handed US irresponsibility. Moreover, in their overriding concern for Russian security, Putin's people were utterly indifferent to the body count in the Middle East and beyond. Its extensive corps of Arabists had long been completely accustomed to the impact of the unforgiving desert landscape of the Bedouin and the marginal value of human life within it. Russia backed onto Asia. The hinterland of the Soviet Union, where they had fought for years against Turkmen and Basmachi tribesmen, had been no different. "Were there terrorists in Iraq?" Putin asked rhetorically. "There were no terrorists there until the country's state structures were destroyed. The same was true of Libya, where there were no terrorists at all. But as soon as this country's statehood was destroyed, who came along to fill the vacuum? Terrorists. The same is happening in Syria."[56] But here, Putin vowed, "It's not acceptable to allow anyone to attempt to play out the 'Libyan' scenario in Syria."[57] It was the spill-over into the Caucasus above all, and then through to Central Asia that worried him. The collective trauma of fighting Islamists in Afghanistan still clouded Russian consciousness.

Kerry inadvertently released the content of the Putin proposal to negotiate a solution, which, given that as Secretary of State he was deemed too important for Obama to rebuke, let alone dismiss, effectively meant that there was no way back. The mood across Capitol Hill did not favour intervention in Syria. Ever mindful of domestic opinion, Obama immediately sought to turn the situation tactically to his advantage and against his domestic rivals. It appeared that all the moralistic outrage at Assad's use of chemical weapons counted for little compared to Obama's loathing of the Republicans. His aversion towards them and their policy preferences governed his every decision in foreign policy. Obama's priorities were domestic and anything that discredited the Bush legacy was seen by him as a signal victory over the Republicans. "It will drive a stake through the heart of neoconservatism", he boasted. "Everyone will see they have no votes."[58]

The US Air Force stood down. The door stood ajar. This policy hardly squared with Obama's intentions when Putin returned to power. He had loftily instructed foreign policy staff that "the main challenge is to put him [Putin] in a box to stop [him] making mischief".[59] Instead Obama provided Russia with a unique opportunity for mischief-making and a clear path to preemptive action in the Near East, facilitating Russia's return as a force on the ground in a region neglected since the 1980s. In the meantime, and with Obama unawares, a renewed confrontation took shape over Ukraine.

8

Maidan

"And it turned out this way: we work with the highest élite, but those from the West work with the entire population. And this is the result. The élite bunked off, selling the pass on the interests of Ukraine, and the people were betrayed, their minds altered, with a new outlook oriented towards the West."

– Former FSB officer Igor Morozov, February 2023.[1]

On leaving office, the Bush team had effectively frozen relations with Russia, having had to abort the rapid entry of Ukraine and Georgia into NATO. They were dismayed at seeing Obama apologize for US misdeeds and his incoming team attempting to turn relations with Russia around.[2] Even so, everything that occurred thereafter seemed to confirm their belief that they were right about Russia. Continuity with the Bush era was reasserted once Hillary Clinton stepped down as Secretary of State in January 2013. She gave way to the former senator, Vietnam veteran John Kerry, characterized by high-minded naïveté and a single-minded stubborn persistence. But he did believe in delegating. His top priority – formulating a deal with Iran to delay its acquisition of nuclear weapons – became his sole priority. In May, with the appointment of Victoria Nuland as Assistant Secretary of State for European and Eurasian Affairs, a firm hand seized the wheel steering policy on Russia. As a career foreign service officer of Jewish East European descent, Nuland had held the post of US permanent representative to NATO in the previous administration. As Assistant Secretary, she had participated in the Interagency Policy Committee on Russia chaired by McFaul.

A formidable Russianist, she had for some bizarre reason once chosen to spend seven gruelling months on a Soviet trawler, where all she appears to have netted were some salty turns of phrase to add to her working Russian vocabulary. It mattered that Nuland was married to a prominent neo-conservative ideologue, historian Robert Kagan. She had also worked as deputy security adviser to Dick Cheney, the driving force behind the invasion of Iraq along with Secretary of Defense Rumsfeld, and she was very much a conduit for the idea that America should lead the war for democracy.[3] What did her husband Kagan have to say about the fate of Ukraine? "Might not the successful liberalization of Ukraine, urged and supported by the Western democracies, be but the prelude to the incorporation of that nation into NATO and the European Union – in short, the expansion of Western liberal hegemony?"[4]

Yanukovych Spurns the EU

Ukraine thus became the focal point of confrontation between Moscow and Washington (and the EU), accentuated by the fact that one-third of the country's population, in the east and to the south, were in the main Russian-speaking regions. President Yanukovych, whose election in 2010 met with no great enthusiasm in the Kremlin, found himself under siege from the opposition for reneging on a firm commitment to sign an association agreement with the European Union and instead accepting a massive loan from the Russian government.

At this point there was no great enthusiasm for NATO membership at all. Indeed, the Pew Research Center, which has had a sound reputation for probity, found that 51 per cent of Ukrainians opposed entry into the alliance; only 28 per cent were in favour. Membership of the European Union was, on the other hand, a not implausible possibility.[5] Yet an association agreement with the EU was only an initial step towards possible membership; membership itself lay much further away (Turkey has been waiting since 1963). It did, however, offer free trade to Ukraine but only if it were to follow stringent requirements entailing the eradication of widespread corruption and a rebalancing of the books, entailing higher taxation. Ukraine in principle already had free trade with Russia and the rest of the Commonwealth of Independent States. Were it to sign up with the EU, Putin's Eurasian Economic Union would be dead in the water. What also concerned the Russians were the larger political consequences of Ukraine's absorption into the EU trading area.

Henry Kissinger, eager still for influence, had assiduously kept in regular contact with Putin, both in person and by telephone, in German. He had not welcomed the neo-conservative pursuit of regime change. Instead he saw Russia's relations with the West entirely in geopolitical terms. In retrospect his judgement was not entirely wrong: "The situation that arose", he noted, "… evolved over a period of months, in which I think that the Western side did not fully understand the implications of what was brewing, and did not use the opportunities that might have been available to talk about the fundamental problem, which is the long term relationship of Russia to the West".[6] Putin, indeed, recalled telling "our partners, both American and European partners, that hurried negotiations behind the scenes on Ukraine's association with the EU were possibly fraught with serious risks – we did not even say anything about politics, we spoke only about economics – serious risks for the economy; that such steps taken without prior notice which impinged upon the interests of many third parties, including Russia as Ukraine's main trading partner, required a wide ranging discussion of the issues". After all, he pointed out, negotiations for Russia joining the World Trade Organization took nineteen years. But in this instance Russia was not consulted. "No one wanted to listen and no one wanted to have a discussion, we were simply told: this is none of your business; that's all; that was the entire discussion... Everyone washed their hands of the matter: that's what happened."[7]

Catherine Ashton was at that time the High Representative of the EU for Foreign Affairs and Security Policy. The officials handling the association agreement with Ukraine were entirely taken up in finalizing terms without much thought given to the politics of it all. Meanwhile those handling political matters under Ashton, including her deputy, former German diplomat Helga Schmid, had not done their homework. They were consumed by the complexities of the proposed nuclear agreement with Iran along with Russia and the United States and complacently assumed that the thorny issue of Ukraine was unproblematic. Ashton disarmingly confesses in her memoir, "we should have looked harder for trouble and examined more closely the politics as well as the economics".[8]

Meanwhile, Putin's close adviser Vladislav Surkov, never notably modest, gives us some idea of what was not happening in the Kremlin. Surkov is a Chechen with a Russian mother, and something of a political chameleon, having run public relations for the ruthless oligarch Khodorkovsky and having subsequently worked with the more liberal Medvedev as president. "I hit upon [the issue of] Ukraine", he recalled. "Just intuitively. No one mentioned it to me and I knew nothing about it, and in truth no one knew anything about it. I simply felt, more precisely intuited, that it would become an important matter. It was a guess, even before anything had begun to happen, that this would be a real battle with the West. Serious. With victims and sanctions. Because the West would stop at nothing. In fact I had a feeling. I am now amazed that I foresaw this in the summer of 2013. At that time with nothing going on. And it all turned out that way."⁹ Indeed, what is so striking is just how thin Russian press coverage of Ukraine was at the time – it was invariably an indicator of Kremlin concerns – until it came to a head in the autumn of 2013. This in itself goes some way to explain complacency on the matter in Brussels and Washington DC.

One could usually count on the fact that an EU process would trudge along at a snail's pace, but not this thorny issue. In the past Romano Prodi, the Italian High Commissioner until 2004, believed that he had "good personal relations" with Putin. And Prodi had been keen to split the difference with Russia on matters of trade,to forestall rivalry between Russia's Eurasian customs union and the EU. He had the illusion that Ukraine could bridge East and West.[10] But Prodi's successor, the right-wing Portuguese politician José Manuel Barroso, was entirely dismissive of the Russians. He had no interest at all in an accommodation. Moreover, the High Commission was under prolonged Polish pressure to hasten Ukraine's membership.

In February 2012, just as Putin's state of mind had begun to shift to the EU's disadvantage, Sikorski boasted that Poland "did everything possible to ensure that an association and free trade agreement was signed with the EU". Ukraine was too important a country to remain isolated, he insisted, adding that "Ukraine could move much faster along the path to European integration and become a member of the EU."[11] In March Ukraine did, indeed, initial an association agreement. And Poland, evidently aware that Russia was retreating back into its armoured shell, was pressing that it be signed as soon as possible. The popular Polish tabloid *Fakt* reminded its readers at the end of the year that "Poland has been trying to convince EU countries to sign the Association Agreement [with Ukraine] for a long time…"[12] The EU, however, appeared to be in no particular hurry.

A gulf separated the Polish attitude to Ukraine and that of its partners in Western Europe. It was well expressed by the EU ambassador to Kyiv, not by accident a Pole. Jan Tombiński did not mince words: "Ukraine is a part of Europe. Unless the European Union reaches out to this part of Europe, Europe will not understand its own history, because this part of Europe is also a part of European history. In Western Europe, there is a big gap in the understanding of what happened in the Eastern part of Europe. It even reflects now in our political approach to Ukraine. Often, people do not realise that Ukraine is something different from Russia..."[13]

The Germans and the French had acted decisively to block American pressure for Ukraine's potential entry into NATO in 2008 for fear of Russian retaliation. Merkel and her chief adviser Christoph Heusgen did not want another confrontation over the association agreement. They thereafter pressed for some kind of accommodation on trade between Russia and the bloc. But, as Heusgen complained, "the arrogance of the bureaucrats" prevailed. The Commission's attitude on trade was that of "take it or leave it".[14] For their part, the Ukrainians themselves had certain misgivings about the economic reform programme they were being asked to undertake as a precondition for the association agreement, which looked all too similar to the severe austerity plan that the IMF proposed at US insistence. This amounted to "(i) increased exchange rate flexibility combined with policies to strengthen the financial sector; (ii) ambitious fiscal consolidation; (iii) increases in domestic energy tariffs, and (iv) comprehensive structural reforms to improve the business climate and support growth".[15]

Suddenly alert to the possibility of a direct collision with Ukraine that lay not far ahead, and evidently apprised of what was happening by his adviser Surkov, Putin visited Kyiv in July to express his disquiet at the direction events were taking, and began selectively exerting economic pressure. At a meeting of the Valdai Club – a forum to which sympathetic opinion makers from the West and jobbing journalists were invited – in Novgorod he repeated the warning he had already given that if Ukraine became part of a free market with the EU, then it could undercut the Russian economy with which it already had tariff-free trade. Moscow would thus be forced to retaliate.[16] Putin caught up with the Ukrainian president Viktor Yanukovych in Sochi that October to follow through on his position. He bluntly threatened economic sanctions (Ukraine was dependent upon Russia for its gas supply) and made tempting offers of money – $15 billion in credits – to forestall the agreement that was shortly due for signature.[17]

In 2004, the Americans had, as we have seen, taken the lead on Ukraine during the Orange Revolution. Four years later they had abruptly called for Ukraine's entry into NATO but failed to secure an immediate commitment from their allies. Yet they had most certainly not given up. The commitment to Ukraine was self-evident. From 1991 through to early February 2014 the United States had spent as much as $5 billion on Ukraine to further its integration into Europe "and other goals".[18] Between financial years 2008 and 2013 alone it is estimated to have spent the colossal sum of $1.09 billion on the country, led by USAID at $373 million.[19]

Now the Americans began again to stir themselves into more direct action. In Washington DC the National Endowment for Democracy (NED), which had been created by Reagan in 1983 as an arm's length propaganda outfit divorced from CIA operations, sprang into action. (Walter Raymond, a propaganda specialist from the agency, had put the organization on its feet.)[20] The NED had funded a great deal of activism in Ukraine – more than sixty-five projects – over the previous decade.

Its president, Carl Gershman, suddenly appeared in the *Washington Post* on 26 September 2013 with an editorial call to arms: "Former Soviet states stand up to Russia. Will the US?" This was, of course, a rhetorical question. Echoing Brzezinski, he forcefully argued that "the restoration of Russia's imperial greatness… would be inconceivable if Ukraine joined Europe". Gershman added a prediction that for the Kremlin it was not just a working assumption but an alarming consequence of the US pursuit of regime change. "Putin", he wrote, "may find himself on the losing end not just in the near abroad but within Russia itself."

The bureaucrats in Brussels, however, appeared oblivious to the larger political ramifications of the association agreement with Ukraine, even on the eve of the EU-Ukrainian summit in Vilnius on 28 November 2013. And the British initially did not even think it important enough to merit Prime Minister Cameron's attendance, though he did eventually decide to come.[21] Clearly infuriated, Putin's threats to Yanukovych finally made an impact. Contrary to expectations, on his arrival in Lithuania Ukraine's president immediately informed an astonished Chancellor Merkel that he would not sign the agreement. Everyone present was baffled and affronted. Instead of the grand celebration they were looking forward to, the occasion turned into a wake. Those present were so exasperated that they were disinclined to listen to anything else Yanukovych might have to say, even while he was pleading for tripartite negotiations with the Russians. Some of his hosts thought that he was artfully engaged in raising the stakes. They utterly underestimated the degree of Russian determination and showed themselves unexpectedly eager to oblige by digging deeper into their pockets for extra subsidies for Kyiv to offset Putin's blandishments. But Yanukovych, entirely out of character, appeared resolute.

The Reaction

The news exploded back home in Ukraine under conditions already primed by the Endowment for Democracy. Protests had begun on 21 November, even before the Vilnius summit. After news came in, demonstrators began pouring onto Maidan Nezalezhnosti, the main square in Kyiv, even while the rest of the city went about its daily routine in manifest indifference. Moscow was caught unawares. "At the outset", one Russian observer recalled, "I did not take what was taking place as something serious. Nonetheless, we had at our disposal certain information that on the part of the Western countries something bigger was being prepared, capable of changing radically the situation in the country."[22] Miraculously three new television stations suddenly appeared out of nowhere on the air waves: Spilno TV (21 November), Hromadske TV (23 November) and Espreso TV (24 November). The second, at least, was partly funded by the US embassy and George Soros' International Renaissance Foundation.[23] The Russians noticed late on 30 November how few demonstrators there were until the television cameras arrived at 4.00 a.m. the following morning. Word rapidly spread far and wide, however, just as the Endowment for Democracy intended. Very soon tens of thousands of demonstrators were gathered at Maidan. The first wake-up call was news of training camps in Poland, Lithuania and Western Ukraine. Then the West began taking sanctions against pro-Russian politicians. It was also reported that two Lockheed C-130 Hercules aircraft requested the right to land, carrying the US diplomatic post. The Prime Minister, Mykola Azarov, demanded to know of Yanukovych: what sort of post is that? The planes were met by a US embassy vehicle and armoured cars.[24] The arrival of Brian Fink, heading USAID in Ukraine, in early December was noted by a journalist loyal to the government. Party of the Regions deputy Oleg Tsarev also learned that three specialists each from the United States, Germany, Britain and Serbia had arrived to guide the demonstrations into open violent confrontation, with the forceful seizure of government buildings. At their disposal were powerful young males in considerable numbers. They wanted casualties, he warned in Putin's favourite paper, *Komsomol'skaya pravda*.[25]

The regime panicked. The Berkut special police reinforced by paramilitary volunteers attacked everyone in sight within the vicinity of the square. A Polish journalist was assaulted by Berkut and about eighty protestors ended up in hospital. Thereafter, along with Congressmen flying in uninvited to show solidarity, including Senator John McCain, Assistant Secretary of State Nuland could be seen handing out snacks in the icy cold to the protestors in full view of the cameras on 11 December. She was responding directly to the brutal crackdown on demonstrators by riot police the night before. That same day she scolded Yanukovych for his actions, which had, in her words, been "absolutely impermissible".[26] The president dithered. As the confrontation worsened, on 21 January at a government meeting Prime Minister Azarov said all the red lines had been crossed. It was time to act to protect the constitutional order. But Yanukovych refused to call a halt to negotiations with the opposition. "Russia many times warned Ukraine's representatives how all this would end", Azarov bitterly recalls.[27]

It must have been apparent to the Russians from the stark difference between the hectoring of Nuland and the more conciliatory tone of Ashton that they did not face an entirely united front. Indeed, the Americans and the Europeans appeared to be at odds as to how the crisis should be resolved. Ashton had hitherto been trying to broker a deal with the opposition that would leave Yanukovych in power. After a lull from mid-January, demonstrators faced increasing violence from the forces of "order". For the previous two months US Vice President Biden had regularly been phoning Yanukovich urging him to come to terms with the opposition, but to no avail.[28] Meanwhile, with the demonstrators still out in force, and with the EU unable to change the situation, Nuland assumed the mantle of Proconsul. On an open line on or around 25 January she held a detailed discussion with a very nervous Geoffrey Pyatt, the US ambassador, about her preference in respect of the alternatives to Yanukovych.[29] Pyatt then cautioned her that the EU were not ready for this. Her response was characteristically direct: "Fu*k the EU."[30] A knowing onlooker, Robert Hunter, concluded, "Nuland and Pyatt – whether acting on their own or on instructions from top-level US officials – were clearly seeking to draw Ukraine firmly into the US orbit."[31]

Ashton's deputy, secretary-general for political questions, Helga Schmid, was irritated at a further leaked intercept, in which she had told EU ambassador Jan Tombiński: "It's very annoying that the Americans are going around criticizing the EU and saying we're too soft."[32] "But Helga," Tombiński, a subtle and experienced Polish diplomat with an outstanding record, retorted, "we must above all be clear that we are not in a race to see who is stronger; we have other means [at our disposal]."[33] Tombiński, however, shared Brussels' longstanding delusion that the solution to every problem was the power of the purse. Although a Pole accustomed to Moscow's ruthlessness, he had not, however, on this occasion reckoned on Russian determination.

Ashton turned up in Kyiv on 28 January, defying the foul weather to show solidarity with the protestors. She had tried to talk Yanukovych into conceding a compromise – which Nuland had not even bothered to attempt as she had given up on him.[34] Meanwhile Putin had personally warned Ashton in Brussels, just before she left, against joining the demonstrators. He was as usual brutally frank: "I can only imagine what the reaction [in the European Union] would be if in the heat of the crisis in Greece or Cyprus, our foreign minister came to an anti-European rally and began urging people to do something."[35] This entire episode had become an entirely unexpected and alarmingly high stakes game played out in full view of the media. Russia's First Deputy Prime Minister Igor Shuvalev, an arch realist, who invariably knew which way the wind was blowing, commented dryly: "We will win, because we care more."[36] Clearly the Russians had no intention of backing away.

Assistant Secretary Nuland was infuriated at the slow pace of EU decision-making – and she was not alone in this respect. Nuland felt strongly that the time for negotiation had long passed.[37] ABC News reported: "Dmitry Loskutov, an aide to Russian Deputy Prime Minister Dmitry Rogozin, was among the first on Twitter to link to the video, which surfaced Tuesday. Along with the video link, Loskutov tweeted, 'Sort of controversial judgment from Assistant Secretary of State Victoria Nuland speaking about the EU'."[38] The Kremlin was impatient. It had picked up news that Yanukovych, his family and other oligarchs had been threatened with the sequestration of their investments by the Americans. The Russians also asserted that the Americans were funding the protests to the tune of $20 million a week, including weaponry. On 6 February Putin's adviser on Ukraine, Sergei Glaz'ev, went public with this news in *Kommersant'*, along with his conviction that "The Ukrainian authorities are making a mistake delaying a resolution of the crisis through force; and in the event that Maidan does not disperse of its own accord a crackdown of the protests by force will be inevitable…"[39] In breaking standard practice on the release of secret intelligence, Putin was surely making it apparent to the West that he was at the limits of his tolerance.

Tension eventually peaked on 20 February 2014, however, when snipers again opened fire, two days after key government buildings had been seized by the rebels. More than fifty were killed. Former ambassador to Moscow McFaul, in his memoirs, plainly states that "We do not know for sure who shot first"; and he had access to the traffic.[40]

This was not a mass uprising. The cameras showed only the main square of Kyiv. On arrival the Italian journalist Giorgio Bianche was amazed to discover how misleading prevailing news coverage had been, and that most inhabitants of the city carried on as usual. Meanwhile, television coverage focused on protestors dressed in normal civilian attire. While "in reality there were groups of paramilitary of the extreme right, well trained, who knew how to operate in the field, who knew how to build a barricade, who knew how to attack the police, how to retreat throwing Molotov cocktails, in some cases also shot at the police". And he was shocked when he tried to photograph a policeman who had been shot, with blood streaming over his visor, one of the demonstrators waving a truncheon stood right in front of him to stop him filming.[41]

Was there not, indeed, shooting from both sides? One Republican senator, Dana Rohrabacher, known for his Russian sympathies, pressed Nuland on this point at the Senate Foreign

Relations Committee hearings on 8 May. It was an awkward moment. Nuland equivocated unconvincingly twice, after which Rohrabacher finally summed up: "So the answer is – the answer is yes then."[42] A telephone conversation had taken place between Ashton and the Estonian Foreign Minister Urmas Paet in which the latter reported information deemed reliable from the head of the team of doctors, Olha Bohomolets: "what was quite disturbing", he told Ashton, "all the evidence shows that people were killed by snipers from both sides among policemen and people from the streets".[43] Gabriel Gatehouse, the BBC correspondent, talked to at least one Maidan sniper from the opposition who was supplied with a box of high velocity ammunition and to a lawyer who found it impossible to get a proper investigation of some of the killings.[44] Witnesses interviewed by German television (ARD) testified to snipers firing from buildings held by the protestors, in particular the eighth and ninth floors of the Ukraine hotel. Doctors also found that both police and protestors had been hit by the same type of bullets.[45]

The Italian photo-journalist Bianche asked: "who paid the bill for all this, because… managing a situation of this kind requires organisational costs, the disbursement of considerable sums…?"[46] Nuland readily acknowledged that a great deal of US government money had played a role over a number of years up to the overthrow of Yanukovych.[47] And there were Maidan militants who were certainly being paid by the Soros Foundation; indeed, in private the organizers actually boasted about it.[48] "One of the things that many people recognized about you was that you, during the revolutions of 1989, funded a lot of dissident activities, civil society groups in Eastern Europe and Poland, the Czech Republic," Fareed Zakaria said in interviewing Soros a few months later. "Are you doing similar things in Ukraine?" Soros replied: "Well, I set up a foundation in Ukraine before Ukraine became independent of Russia. And the foundation has been functioning ever since. And it played a – an important part in events now."[49]

And the reluctance of subsequent administrations to make a

thoroughly transparent investigation of the massacre, calling to account those responsible for the shooting and prosecuting them, meant that the full truth of what took place will probably never be known. The investigation that was carried out by the Maidan victors who seized power could not escape the perception of a blatant conflict of interest.[50]

Ashton's reference to Ukraine as part of "our neighbourhood" was an unmistakeable sign that the EU was not of a mind to back away.[51] It effectively meant that Ukraine was passing into the Western sphere of influence. On the night of 20 February Biden, positioned as Obama's quarter-back for Ukraine, phoned Yanukovych. The Vice President insisted that Putin could do nothing to help him. "I was telling him it was over; time for him to call off his gunmen and walk away…"[52]

EU foreign ministers Sikorski (for Poland), Steinmeier (for Germany) and Laurent Fabius (for France) held their noses and flew in to press the leaders of Maidan into a compromise with Yanukovych the following day. The extreme right of the opposition swore they would continue fighting, but, under direct threat from Sikorski, caught on camera, they gave way. The resulting agreement conceded constitutional reform and the holding of new elections. Worryingly, at the last moment Putin had second thoughts and Russia's representative Vladimir Lukin – the former ambassador to the United States whom Yanukovych had requested – was unexpectedly instructed not to sign. It looks like it was too late, however, as his signature unaccountably appears on the document.[53] None the less Putin had sent up a flare. But, not for the first time, in the face of the widespread elation, no one paid sufficient attention.

Meanwhile that evening, having signed up to the compromise, Yanukovych phoned Putin to tell him, somewhat implausibly, that he was off to a meeting in Kharkiv, Ukraine's second city close to the Russian border. His ostensible purpose was to attend a Party of the Regions conference. Putin had no particular liking for Yanukovych – the Russians saw him as hopelessly weak – but this was not exactly good news. Putin explicitly warned that, whatever Yanukovych did, he should on no account withdraw the military and the police from the capital.[54] But Yanukovych ignored his advice, drove back to his massive, ornate mansion, packed a very large hold-all and, while his motorcade drove on without him, flew by helicopter along with his dog to Kharkiv, and arrived several days later in Moscow via Crimea as a not entirely welcome guest. It was his initial resort to deadly force and his cowardice in escaping the consequences that made a coup d'état inevitable. A day later, the majority of the *Verkhovna Rada* breached article 111 of the constitution and voted to remove Yanukovych from office on the illegitimate grounds that the president had deserted his post.[55]

Coup d'état?

The involvement of the United States and the EU in events that led to the overthrow of an elected president became known to the entire world when the telephone conversation between Nuland and the US ambassador to Ukraine, which is quoted above, mysteriously appeared in the media. The *New York Times*, mouthpiece of the Democratic Party in power, had to resort to equivocal assertions that "it appears much of the protests in Kiev were organic"; implying that a good deal were not, but, as Putin also maintained, "fomented and sponsored by the West".[56] The Rada immediately took action to enforce use of the Ukrainian language at the expense of Russian throughout the regions.

The only authoritative, cool voice of reason was from the pen of Brzezinski, which was all the more impressive given that he had been among the first in authority at the end of the Cold War to call for the perpetuation of "America's own dominant position for at least a generation and preferably longer still…"[57] He was evidently uneasy at the current thrust of US policy in Ukraine and the direction it had taken. What Brzezinski – in his new guise as Cassandra – published in the *Financial Times* on 23 February 2014 was the following warning:

> Russia can still plunge Ukraine into a destructive and internationally dangerous civil war. It can prompt and then support the secession of Crimea and some of the independent eastern portions of the country.

He had a solution to hand:

> The US could and should convey clearly to Mr. Putin that it is prepared to use its influence to make certain a truly independent and territorially undivided Ukraine will pursue policies toward Russia similar to those so effectively practised by Finland; mutually respectful neighbours with wide-ranging economic relations with Russia and the EU; no participation in any military alliance viewed by Moscow as directed at itself but expanding its European connectivity... The US and the EU, hopefully with Russia's constructive co-operation, should continue to press the dominant democratic forces in Kiev to adopt a stance not of revenge and retribution but of national unification and political moderation.

But he was one day too late. On 22 February the *Wall Street Journal* reported the Kremlin's reaction to events. "'This is a major defeat,' said a senior Kremlin adviser, adding that the events of the last 24 hours bitterly remind Russian officials of the 2004 Orange Revolution, when Mr. Yanukovych saw his fraud-tainted election victory overturned after massive street protests brought a pro-Western government to power. 'We made the same mistakes again this time,' said the Kremlin adviser, who spoke on condition of anonymity... 'For us, the conclusion is that the West succeeded in engineering a coup d'état.' Many in the Kremlin continue to believe the West is seeking to engineer the same kind of revolution in Russia, advisers say. 'This is just the start of a major battle in the post-Soviet space,' said one, referring to the latest events in Kiev."[58]

The Kremlin's portrayal of events, captured later in the newspaper of the military-industrial complex, *Voenno-promyshlennyi kur'er*, on 17 March inevitably gave no quarter:

> Ukraine has experienced a revolution. The situation here from the first developed exactly according to the scenario of 'the Arab spring.' The activities of the leaders of the West combined with precisely coordinated events and actions of the leaders of Maidan allows one to say with confidence that the disorders in Ukraine were prepared and initiated above all by the USA and its closest allies.

But to what end? Here Moscow had no doubt. The whole purpose of the coup was to fasten Ukraine's élite to the West by means of its integration with the EU, evidently followed by its eventual inclusion within NATO. "Ultimately," the argument ran, and here it highlighted Putin's ultimate concern, "Ukraine would evidently be used as a means of transposing the revolution to Russia."[59] Putin's rage at the former US ambassador McFaul could be heard clearly in the dread fears of contagion from uncontrolled democracy roaming the streets of Russia and overwhelming the *siloviki*. This was undoubtedly the final straw. Years later, a new US ambassador handed over her credentials on 5 April 2023. By that time war was blazing in Ukraine. Putin made a point of condemning "the use by the United States of America in its foreign policy of such instruments as support for the so-called coloured revolutions, linked to this the support for the coup d'état in Kyiv in 2014 in the end led to today's Ukrainian crisis..."[60]

Ukraine might have found a place in "our neighbourhood" – in Ashton's innocuous words – but it also appeared to be on its way into an American sphere of influence. It certainly appeared that the United States had been pushed back on one front – Syria

– only to advance on another: Ukraine, which was of vital interest to Russia on its south-western flank. Putin was therefore having none of it. He had pointed out at the NATO-Russia Council in 2008 that Ukraine's possession of Crimea was a bone of contention with Russia. Pro-Russian separatism on the peninsula had gathered pace in 1994–5, and in the two years following the Orange Revolution Moscow had fuelled communal tensions directed at Crimean Tatars recently returned from deportation as well as ethnic Ukrainians living on the peninsula.[61]

Russia Lashes Out

In Moscow a meeting was summoned late at night on 22 February 2014 that ran through to 7.00 a.m. on the following morning. Putin's Minister and Deputy Minister of Defence, Sergei Shoigu and Valerii Gerasimov, along with the director of foreign intelligence, Sergei Naryshkin, argued that the military operation Putin was proposing was too great a risk.[62] It does not appear that Lavrov or any of his deputies was even consulted. The decision to proceed was nonetheless taken and, with the assistance of experienced veterans, plans were laid to seize Crimea by deploying special units of the GRU (military intelligence), marine commandos and paratroops, stripped of all insignia identifying them as Russian. This allowed Putin to claim publicly when they were discovered that they were not members of Russia's armed forces; though by the same token it did carry the risk that they could be – in extreme necessity – disavowed by the Kremlin, attacked and removed by NATO special forces on behalf of Ukraine without formally confronting Moscow. There was no such danger, however. The Americans gave explicit instructions to the Ukrainians not to act. The take-over was under way by 27 February 2014, beginning with seizure of the seat of local government and the two local airports on the following day. A referendum to join Russia was hurriedly arranged for 16 March that, given military occupation and control over the ballot stations, unsurprisingly claimed 95 per cent in favour of reunion; though Putin later forgot the number and spoke somewhat more plausibly of 75 per cent support.[63] The bill passed by the Duma two days later was merely a formality.

Sweden's Foreign Minister Carl Bildt summed it up: "What we have learned about Mr. Putin is that he is unpredictable. We have learned that he is fairly opportunistic in his policies. If he sees a weakness, if he sees an opportunity to move, he can be tempted to move. That was clear in the case with Crimea."[64] Having firmly made his point, in late April Putin gave a specious explanation for the events at a party belatedly celebrating former Chancellor Schröder's birthday at the Yusupov palace in St Petersburg – the site of Rasputin's murder. Towards the end of the proceedings the President made a surprise appearance, to the horror of the German ambassador, Rüdiger von Fritsch, who had a very good idea that the press would take it as an official endorsement of Russian policy.

Putin claimed that once the West had "organised" Maidan, the Russians had to take action. But, as the epitome of sweet reason, what he indignantly claimed not to understand was, "Why had they not waited for the elections in the spring? It would have been impossible for Yanukovych to win them! And then we would have had a government, it would have been well disposed, and we would have given 15 million dollars to Ukraine and a gas price that was far too low."[65] Behind all this, however, he hinted at the bigger picture that more accurately explained his determination to resort to force. There was "an underlying reason", Putin said, and here he did not stray far from the truth. "The crisis itself in Ukraine is the product of the imbalance [of power] in international relations."[66]

Putin delivered his formal defence before Duma deputies, the Federation Council, leaders from the regions and others packed into the Kremlin on 18 March, at which they enthused at the recovery of Crimea. And for a simple reason: Putin had not just rapped NATO and the EU over the knuckles, he had also wiped clean years of humiliation and raised his standing in the eyes of the Russian public, its new élite in particular. He explained his task as that of readjusting the balance with the West by the most expedient and symbolic means at his disposal. Russia had been hemmed in for centuries.

> But everything has its limits. And in the case of Ukraine our Western partners have crossed the line, behaved in an uncivilised manner, irresponsibly and unprofessionally.
>
> They well knew that millions of Russians live in Ukraine and Crimea. How far does one have to go to lose one's political instincts and sense of proportion for them not to foresee all the consequences of their actions? Russia has reached its limits, from which it can no longer retreat. If a spring is coiled tight, it will at some point burst open. One should always remember that.

He added that NATO itself was apparently acceptable. But "we are opposed to it as a military organisation setting up house right next to our fence, right next to our home or on territory that has historically been ours... We are obviously coming into collision with opposition from abroad, but we must decide for ourselves whether we are going to stand by our national interests consistently or whether we are to give way forever, retreating into the unknown."

For Putin, quite apart from the arguments about historical possession, the fate of the historic naval base at Sevastopol – leased from Ukraine in 1997 and renewed in 2010 – and issues of ethnicity, the seizure of Crimea was a tit for tat. As far as he was concerned, "time and again they have deceived us, taking decisions behind our back, confronting us with *faits accomplis*". He cited the example of NATO expansion, the relocation of its military infrastructure to the Russian border, the construction of bases for national missile defence. "Despite all our fears, the machine works, it moves forward." And the other side always responded by saying "Well, none of this need concern you." Annexing Crimea was one answer to this. He cited "the well known Kosovo precedent, a precedent that our Western partners themselves established... in a situation that was precisely analogous to Crimea, they recognized the removal of Kosovo from Serbia as legitimate, demonstrating to everyone that there is no need for the consent of the central authorities of a country for a unilateral declaration of independence".[67]

The Americans and Allies Hold Back

Having contributed to the crisis, Obama was loath to take resolute retaliatory action in response to Russian aggression. Ukrainian forces were told to stand down. It is clear that Putin, in Bildt's words, saw "weakness" in Obama. No one seriously proposed taking out the "little green men" who had landed in Crimea, even though Putin had been scrupulously careful to give himself plausible deniability by denying that they were Russian forces. Obama was simply not interested. Even the head of the Crimean Tartars was to his amazement told by the Americans to hold back from resistance.[68] The US President's reaction to Putin's actions in violating the UN charter, the 1994 Budapest memorandum and the 1997 Ukraine-Russia treaty was thus scarcely robust. Obama went so far as to claim implausibly years later that "there was not an armed invasion of Crimea".[69] In that case Russian tourists came exceedingly well equipped. At the time Obama tried instead to negotiate a Russian retreat. As he excused it later with greater understanding than he had shown at the time: "Putin acted in Ukraine in response to a client state that was about to slip out of his grasp." And in answer to the question why he had not done more, he said that Ukraine "is going to be vulnerable to military domination by Russia no matter what we do".[70] The problem was that for someone who had gone out of his way to deny that states should have spheres of influence, it has to be said that acknowledging Ukraine to be "a client state" of Russia sounded decidedly feeble.

Speaking nearly a decade later, as though referring to someone else in office at the time, Obama reflected on "democracies that had gotten flabby and confused and feckless around the stakes of things we tended to take for granted". He added that "part of our complacency grew out of the notion that once the Berlin Wall fell and Nelson Mandela was released and the world was flat and you had McDonald's everywhere, and now suddenly that was it—we were done."[71] It would, however, have been more honest as well as more accurate to substitute the first-person singular for the first-person plural in both statements given that he overruled stronger action proposed by those who served under him.

The most experienced Russia watcher in the administration was Deputy Secretary of State Burns. In his eyes Putin's strike "was not a surprise at all… The way in which he went about it, the 'little green men' and hybrid warfare and everything else, was kind of interesting to watch as well because it was very cleverly done."[72] Everyone else, it seems, had been taken completely unawares. "We were obviously surprised", a senior Defense official admitted. It was a daring move predicated on the US President's inner timidity.

One Obama adviser had it right. Putin had now "recognized that President Obama was reluctant to engage in military conflicts". And Blinken, Biden's dithering national security adviser, had to accept that they had "misjudged" Putin. Ian Kelly, the US ambassador to Georgia, recalls: "Obama didn't want to sell lethal weapons, Obama didn't want to escalate, Obama didn't react with much in 2014".[73] "The day after Russia invaded Crimea in early March 2014", Chollet recalled, "Obama told his national security team that it needed to 'right size our response to actual interests, rather than be side tracked by the chattering classes.'"[74] In other words, the "chattering classes", whom Obama looked down upon, were agitating for direct action. Senior Director for European

Affairs on the National Security Council Charles Kupchan recalls Obama as "cautious to a fault".[75] To the president US interests were simply not at stake. On 26 March in Brussels he told his European allies: "This is not another cold war that we're entering into. The United States and Nato do not seek any conflict with Russia. Now is not the time for bluster... There are no easy answers, no military solution."[76] But he had no answers. Clear exceptions to the state of indecision were the bold Deputy Assistant Secretary of Defense Emily Farkas, who – in the spirit of Albright and Nuland – pressed for the despatch of Javelin anti-tank missiles to be sent to Ukraine, backed by Vice President Biden, only to be summarily overruled from above. "We were very concerned not to pour fuel on the fire", recalled the much more easily intimidated Kupchan.[77]

The EU as a whole was certainly no more robust, having precipitated the problem in the first place, even though Merkel had been the first to call for sanctions. At a summit on 6 March Britain made an effort to press for such punitive economic measures while Germany, on further reflection, and Italy, instinctively, held back. The follow-my-leader French President François Hollande invariably deferred to Merkel as to what should be done next. This meant that nothing was immediately decided upon because the Chancellor, in spite of strong personal feelings, was herself captive to her predecessor Schröder's Russian policy and that of her SPD Foreign Minister, Steinmeier. The détente era veterans in the party – Helmut Schmidt, Egon Bahr, Erhard Eppler, and Klaus von Dohnanyi – all opposed the very idea of sanctions. And policy towards Russia was ultimately captive to Germany's massive export machine, upon which the entire economy floated. The biggest German companies – BASF, Siemens, Volkswagen, Adidas and Deutsche Bank – all expressed their opposition. For her part, Merkel "always kept in mind what was tolerable to Russia", her chief adviser on foreign and security policy, Christoph Heusgen recalls. On his view, the pursuit of Nordstream II – a second Baltic oil pipeline from Russia to Germany – was a mistake. But this was seen by the Chancellor as an economic matter beyond his competence.[78] Although Heusgen advised her, it is hard to credit the fact that there existed no national security council where all the dimensions of foreign policy were considered as an integrated whole. It was symptomatic of the fact that Germany was above all a *Handelsstaat* rather than a traditional Great Power, a situation reminiscent of General Motors in the early 1950s, whose president Charles Wilson "thought what was good for our country was good for General Motors, and vice versa. The difference did not exist."[79] In its foreign relations the German state at times certainly gave every appearance of being subservient to business interests. And conflict with Russia was definitely bad for business.

Obama, who had been almost indifferent, characteristically passed the buck. He accused America's European allies of avoiding sanctions against Russia: "I often had to drag them kicking and screaming to respond in ways that we would have wanted to see from those who describe themselves as Western democracies."[80] The allusion is, of course, primarily to Germany, France, along with Britain and Italy. They were undeniably reluctant to cut their ties to Russia but, arguably, no less so than the Americans. Everyone in NATO seemed to be searching for a convenient alibi, and someone else to blame. The absence of leadership was deeply depressing. The British diplomat Dame Alison Leslie, at the time Britain's permanent representative to NATO, was not the only diplomat disenchanted by this collective hesitancy. She bitterly recalled: "There was still, even when I left in 2014, denial about how serious things were becoming with Russia, even after they grabbed Crimea... There was a lot of denial because it was inconvenient."[81]

Russia then sought further leverage against Ukraine by sending forces into the Donbas heavy industrial region, where the population was in its majority Russian-speaking, though not necessarily in favour of Putin. In early April Moscow was vociferous about defending its brethren in south-eastern Ukraine: "Russia does not intend to view in silence what is going on in Little Russia [the traditional Tsarist term for Ukraine]", the hard-line newspaper *Vzglyad* intoned, and ominously talked of reforming Ukraine into a "federation". Claiming that "a single united Ukraine also no longer exists," it added menacingly: "No one intends to join Donetsk and Lugansk to Russia," at least "while there is a chance of maintaining, or more accurately, founding a Ukrainian federation." In the meantime the people of the south-east were looking for assistance. "There is no doubt that it will receive it."[82]

By inciting and arming separatists who claimed self-government for Donetsk and Luhansk, Moscow could ensure that Ukraine would never be at peace. And if Ukraine's borders remained in dispute, admission to NATO would become an intractable problem because no one wanted a new ally already locked into conflict. Russian claims in turn acted as a catalyst to extreme Ukrainian nationalists who identified themselves with the independence movement of Stefan Bandera, which was adopted by the Nazis in the 1930s and taken over by the Allies in the late 1940s. These dubious associations played into the hands of the cyber warfare campaign run by an old Putin friend, the ex-criminal Yevgeny Prigozhin, at his Internet Research Agency operating from 55 Savushkina Street, St Petersburg, blackening Ukraine's leaders as neo-Nazi.[83]

Shootdown

In the resulting mayhem a Buk missile launcher driven into the Donbas by Russian troops for the purposes of air defence on 17 July shot down the Malaysian airliner MH-17, which was overflying the region, killing 298 innocent people. Not unlike the shooting down of the Korean airliner KAL 007 in September 1983, which had apparently inadvertently strayed into Soviet airspace, it revealed a baleful lack of training and the manifest incompetence of those charged with such a deadly weapons system. Three Russians and one Ukrainian, the former associated variously with the FSB and Russian military intelligence (RU), were subsequently indicted for multiple homicide by the Dutch authorities.[84] Finally, the resistance to sanctions was brought abruptly to a halt by Dutch Foreign Minister Frans Timmermans, who would tolerate no more special pleading from fellow ministers.[85] He was entitled to serious respect not least because the Netherlands lost 193 of its citizens in the disaster. And there could be no doubt that, were the Russians not deterred, they would continue annexing Ukrainian territory. On 24 August ten armed Russian paratroops were detained in the Donetsk region, the first contingent of many. They were identified as serving in Russia's 331st Regiment in the 98th Sverskii Division of airborne forces.[86]

Predictably, the minimal sanctions imposed from the West had no decisive impact, and encouraged import substitution in Russia, certainly in the field of agriculture, where the Russians actually retaliated by banning EU produce. Nor was there any interruption in Russia's vital supplies of oil and gas to Germany or in plans under way for the construction of the new gas pipeline through the Baltic – Nordstream II, which went ahead as planned, with former Chancellor Gerhard Schröder in the chair. The assertion that Germany would lose nearly 1 per cent of its GNP were harsher sanctions adopted said it all.

Attempts by the leading states of the EU to mediate between the government in Kyiv and the rebel strongholds in the Donbas resulted in the Minsk Protocols of 2014–15 (which were "reinforced" in 2017) that provided for a ceasefire; the legitimacy of these protocols was never in practice recognized by either party, as the failed ceasefires and over 20,000 dead showed all too clearly.[87] The first protocol was agreed on 5 September 2014. The United States stood by. It did not explicitly insist on Minsk, so the Ukrainian government, very much a dependent, was not likely to take its implementation seriously; neither did the neighbouring Polish government, which was aiding the Ukrainian resistance to the Russian take-over of eastern Ukraine. As the leading specialist on Ukraine at the Foreign and Commonwealth Office subsequently noted, the agreement and its sequel, signed on 12 February 2015, "are mistakenly predicated on compromise" when in fact there is "an unresolvable contradiction – what could be called the 'Minsk conundrum': is Ukraine sovereign, as Ukrainians insist, or should its sovereignty be limited, as Russia's leaders demand?"[88]

The US government behaved towards Ukraine as though it were some kind of protectorate because it provided so much in the form of financial support, while simultaneously pressing for action against rampant corruption and the reorganization of the gas sector. It was not just Nuland's actions in 2014 that indicated the dominance of US influence but also the fact that in December 2015 Vice President Biden held hostage $1 billion in aid until the government sacked Ukraine's chief prosecutor, Viktor Shokin, and subsequently boasted of it in front of the television cameras.[89] Meanwhile Biden's son was milking the opportunities available to him by virtue of his father's office through the company Burisma and the reorganization of the gas sector.[90]

After 2014 the two regions, Donetsk and Luhansk, both claiming the right to independence from Ukraine, were not recognized as such by Moscow, in spite of sustained pressure from the Duma. Sporadic fighting between Russian irregulars and Ukrainian forces continued for the next eight years, monitored at every stage by the Organization for Security and Co-operation in Europe. Putin embarked upon the construction of a mammoth twelve-mile bridge connecting Crimea to the Kerch peninsula, which was finally completed in 2018. This would appear to suggest that, for the time being at least, Putin saw the breakaway regions of Donetsk and Luhansk in a different category from Crimea, as pawns in a future negotiation aimed at a larger prize rather than as major pieces determining the outcome of this deadly confrontation. The question that lingered, however, was how long the status quo could be sustained.

Meanwhile every effort was being made to prevent further NATO expansion.

9

The Road to Damascus

> "You [Americans] declare war on terrorists
> and simultaneously try to use some of them to arrange
> the figures on the Middle East board in your own interests,
> as you may think."
>
> – Putin, 2015.[1]

The outlook from the Kremlin was grimly pessimistic. Putin continued to indict the West for limitless expansion into Russia's sphere of influence: "although the contours of 'new' relations with NATO have not finally been drawn," he pointed out, "the alliance is already creating 'facts on the ground.'"[2] Even little Montenegro, a Balkan state with a population of only 650,000, moved to join NATO only for the Russians to over-react, using covert action to forestall it, in spite of the fact that their highest priority was Ukraine, followed by Serbia, which of course reliably regarded NATO as unalterably hostile after the loss of Kosovo.[3]

Russian military intelligence was tasked with mobilizing unrest in Macedonia. But, as the *Wall Street Journal* later reported with respect to the secretary of the Russian Security Council Nikolai Patrushev: "One of the few public glimpses into his activities was in 2016 when he went to clean up a mess left after the failure of a political interference operation in the tiny Balkan nation of Montenegro. Russia's military intelligence had tried to cause unrest to prevent it from joining NATO." It added: "The operation, run from neighboring Serbia, failed, and the Russian agents were publicly exposed, causing fallout for Moscow's allies in the region. Patrushev traveled to Serbia to reassure the government and brought the operatives home. Montenegro joined NATO a year later [on 5 June 2017]."4

Until its Crimean adventure Russia had seemed fated by weakness always to be on the back foot. A new security architecture encompassing both Russia and the Atlantic alliance had been talked about by the Europeans but never actually implemented because the Americans were not interested and the effort seemed to be too much trouble. Putin had long been waiting for some opportunity to emerge, in the absence of which he was steadily rearming. He was now determined to seize the initiative and force his foreign "partners" to adjust to Russian priorities for a change.5 A unique opportunity at last appeared when Obama took fright and hesitated to strike in the Near East as Syria rapidly disintegrated.

By March 2014 there were some 23,000 extremists, including 7,000 al-Qaeda affiliated fighters in the Nusra Front and Islamic State of Iraq and Levant (ISIS; IGIL in Russian) embattled against the Syrian regime. And the alarm bells were going off in Moscow. Even in Washington DC the outspoken Senator Bob Corker (Tennessee), soon to be Chairman of the Committee on Foreign Relations, was surely not far off the truth when he described the administration's restraint as nothing short of "delusional".6 Putin was no less damning, indeed sardonic, in his contempt for Obama's policy: "I consider that it's an absolutely utopian, unprofessional policy with no basis in reality. The civilised democratic opposition in Syria had to be supported; so they were supported by arming them. And the next day half of the fighters went off and joined IGIL. Would it not have been possible to have thought about this just a little earlier?"7

The retrospective Russian assessment was that the Assad regime, in a desperate plight, held barely one-sixth of the country and IGIL/ISIS up to one-half, which might have been mostly empty space, but the towns they held had become "intellectual centres for radical Islam" and oil gave them an income.[8] Speaking at the UN General Assembly for the first time in a decade, on 27 September 2015, Putin condemned the United States for creating chaos across the region. "It is now obvious that the power vacuum created in some countries of the Middle East and North Africa led to the creation of anarchic areas which immediately started to be filled with extremists and terrorists", he said. Putin called on the Security Council to coordinate action against IGIL/ISIS in Iraq and Syria, arguing that only Assad was actually fighting them. By then the Russians were already unofficially embedded in Syria, with "military advisers" on the ground and combat aircraft flying in and out of their air base near Latakia.[9] "Keeping air force and naval bases in the Mediterranean is a strategic move", former ambassador Aleksandr Aksenenok emphasized, "meaning that Russia does not have any 'withdrawal scenarios'."[10]

The Syrian Intervention

The Russian landings in Syria resembled US forays in the Third World; though the Russians did not, of course, say so. It was just how the powerful were expected to behave. Putin's ideal model, certainly in relation to the Near East, was actually Israel. "Look at Israel's example", he told the Valdai conference in 2016. "Israel never steps back but always fights to the end, and this is how it survives. There is no alternative. We need to fight. If we keep retreating, we will always lose."[11] The fact that as a result Israel was in a perpetual state of siege at enormous economic and human cost – let alone peace of mind – evidently did not occur to him, or, if it did, certainly did not bother him. On 30 September 2015 Russian forces at last officially committed to the defence of the Syrian regime. Foreign minister Lavrov was as usual not even informed. *Nezavisimaya gazeta*, with its weary war correspondents haunted by the disastrous Soviet intervention in Afghanistan, caught the general scepticism with the headline "Russia Has Begun Its Near Eastern War".

The newspaper went on to describe the formalities with which military action was hurriedly decided upon, unanimously, "in closed session" by the upper house after merely "ten minutes" of debate, which did not even mention Syria as the target of the military intervention. Head of the Kremlin administration, former defence minister Sergei Ivanov, agreed to brief the press. He took care to underline Putin's assurance that only air power would be used. Ground forces were ruled out. Thousands of volunteers from the Commonwealth of Independent States had joined IGIL/ISIS and were fighting in Syria. It was expedient not to wait until "they turn up at our home". Background briefings did not rule out the use of special forces in the operation.[12] For the details, however, one had to turn to the *New York Times*, as usual briefed by US intelligence. Meeting Rüdiger von Fritsch, the German ambassador, a leading Russian officer boasted: "They threatened us, and we have solved the problem in place in Syria. Totally."[13]

A few days later another German (unnamed), who was visiting Moscow, pointed out that Iran was not so pleased at the intervention. To which Putin retorted with obvious pride, inadvertently revealing the true scope of the Russian operation: "I can tell you why. We were not there just with our air force. With our advisers we have led the entire Syrian army and taken charge of the entire operation."[14] The ground troops sent in came from Prigozhin's mercenaries, the Wagner Group, whose ferocity was soon well established as was its focus on recapturing oil and gas facilities in return for a sizeable chunk of the profits, amounting to no less than 25 per cent of production. Much of the revenue went to the Russian state.[15] Putin thereby eventually succeeded in keeping the Baathist regime afloat through massive military aid – more than handsomely repaid by hundreds of millions of dollars – and ruthlessly bombing targets, including hospitals, without regard to the laws of war. When the major city of Idlib near the Turkish border came within range of Russian guns in 2017, for example, Fritsch expressed the futile hope that this would not turn into another Aleppo, the second largest city in Syria, and the oldest, by then reduced to a pile of rubble. The destruction of Aleppo was described by the UN as "a complete meltdown of humanity". Fritsch received a blunt rebuff from his Russian colleague: "How do you intend to solve the problem of terrorists there, other than through air strikes?"[16]

As far as Putin was concerned, it was quite simple: everyone they liquidated was by definition a terrorist. The tactics were not much different from US bombing campaigns in the Vietnam war, when the commanding officer in Ben Tre is notoriously reputed to have said that they had to destroy the city in order to save it. The Russians had little hope of solving the Syrian regime's underlying problems on their own, any more than the Americans had in Vietnam or, indeed, more recently in Iraq. But they knew that. None the less, Russian diplomats did work tirelessly to bring about an eventual political settlement through "the Geneva process". These were peace negotiations between the Syrian government and the opposition. But they had to contend with the intransigence of Assad. "The Syrian people are known to hold different views of the country's situation and of Russia's role in Syria's affairs", the Arabist Aksenenok has stressed. "Part of civil society is currently outside Syria, and they are by no means terrorists or Russophobes. Consequently, as it supports Bashar al-Assad, Russia emphasizes an intra-Syrian agreement on a model of Syria's future state that would ensure the country against bloody civil wars." And Aksenenok has been emphatic in warning Syria that for the Russians it will not always be top priority: "At the level of government and opposition forces," he commented, "the Syrian people should take into account the fact that Russia has its own global interests that do not always coincide with those of the Middle East. Russia–Syria relations cannot be equated with relations with influential regional actors, which are based on different considerations."[17]

The bloodbath continued with chemical weapons used again before long, recrossing Obama's red line more than once. This made the US President's dependence on Moscow to secure a peace settlement between government and opposition in Syria look feeble; indeed, manifestly hypocritical. Syria was a crowded international battlefield with the Russians on the front line. The only plus for the Americans was that it meant that Russia would be held equally to account for Assad's atrocities, but with the unforeseen consequence that their allies in Turkey and Western Europe faced a flood of unwelcome refugees. Moreover, when Assad's air force yet again used chemical weapons on civilians in Idlib province in early April 2017 – headlined by the *New York Times* as the "Worst Chemical Attack in Years in Syria" – the new administration under Donald Trump was, on this issue at least, forced to backtrack on the pro-Russian stance with which it entered office three months before.[18]

Syria was effectively about Russia's return to reclaim its status as a Great Power in the Near East. Whatever the final outcome might be, Putin's supporters at home congratulated themselves on the fact that the empire had finally struck back. The *New York Times* commented: "What is true… is that in the shortest possible time Moscow has become one of the most influential players in the region, where the interests of several power centres interconnect: the United States, the EU, Turkey, Israel, Iran and the oil producing Arab monarchies. All of them one way or another have been obliged to come to terms with Moscow." Moreover, the EU and the United States had bowed out of the area and Turkey had proved unable to expand its territory at Syria's expense. "By intervening in the Syrian conflict, Moscow has broken with the wanton practice of liquidating its positions in those countries where they still existed, that they inherited from the Soviet era." And what had the West hitherto been doing in the Middle East? "It doesn't matter what exactly we are talking about – markets for sales, the development of [oil] fields or [the construction of] military bases – the scenario was repeated over and over again. Western countries helped to topple a regime with which Russia successfully co-operated, and welcomed in the establishment of a new government that nullified Russian positions on the principle of 'I'm not repaying any debts, so don't expect me to. And nothing personal – just business.'" This was the case in Iraq, and partly the case in Libya, "but in Syria this model failed as Russia decided to use the methods of its geopolitical adversaries". The process of reuniting Syria would be "long, complicated and tedious" but "at least it has started, and the mission no longer seems impossible".[19]

Syria was taken as a "clear example of an achievement in Russian foreign policy", that Russia had progressed from being "marginal" to "one of the most influential forces" in the region; indeed, the "most influential." Adviser Andrei Kortunov's only misgiving – shared with former ambassador Aksenenok – was lest Assad take the Russians for granted. To secure the future through extensive reconstruction, he would have to look beyond Russia, which possessed only "modest means", to others with "deeper pockets". And here Kortunov had a history lesson to offer Putin. In the more distant past Russia had liberated the Balkans from the Turks, for example, only to see a major gain – Bulgaria – fall into Germany's sphere of influence because the latter had the stronger economy. It might win the war but lose the peace.[20]

10

Trump Fails

"The previous president [Trump] simply did not have the space for the 'deals' so dear to him (including with Russia) as a result of resistance from the Washington élite."

– Russian commentator Stanislav Borzyakov, 17 June 2021.[1]

From May 2014 a Russian covert intelligence operation called Project Lakhta evolved to spread disinformation and cause disruption in the electoral politics of the West by undermining confidence in democratic institutions.[2] The base of operations was the so-called Internet Research Agency. As the US presidential elections loomed on the horizon, its attention focused on the United States. A long-time friend of Putin in the St Petersburg days, former criminal Yevgeny Prigozhin modestly claimed that "I was never just the financier of the Internet Research Agency. I thought it up, I created it, I managed it for a long time".[3] The messages it propagated chimed in with ill-considered statements from populist businessman and media icon Donald Trump. He was touring the United States in a febrile campaign for the presidency and exploiting social media to that end in an unprecedented manner.

The Hillary Clinton campaign, which husband Bill derided

as being incapable of selling "p-y on a troop train", found itself on a back foot.[4] It was severely embarrassed by the much publicized revelation that she had jeopardized national security by relying upon a private server to send and receive tens of thousands of documents when she had been Secretary of State, 2,115 of which were later deemed classified.[5] In the absence of anything of substance with which to counter Trump, the Democrat National Committee with the assistance of the mainstream media came up with the claim that he had been compromised by Russian secret intelligence. By the time they had finished, however, it began to look as though the shoe could be on the other foot.

The Conspiracy Against Trump

On 26 July 2016, at the high point of the campaign, Obama was briefed by CIA Director John Brennan about an "alleged approval by Hillary Clinton of a proposal from one of her foreign policy advisers to vilify Donald Trump by stirring up a scandal claiming interference by Russian security services". What should have worried Obama and his staff was that this information came from "Intelligence agencies" who had "obtained insight into Russian intelligence analysis". But at this stage they had no idea just how accurate it was.[6] Belatedly, on 7 September "intelligence officials forwarded an investigative referral to FBI Director James Comey and Deputy Assistant Director of Counterintelligence Peter Strzok regarding "Presidential candidate Hillary Clinton's approval of a plan concerning Presidential candidate Donald Trump and Russian hackers hampering elections as a means of distracting the public from her use of a private mail server."[7]

The Clinton campaign's resort to underhand methods was a backhanded compliment to the unanticipated breadth of popular support for Trump's whirlwind populism. The smear involved the Democrats commissioning an incriminating dossier of files collated by a former MI6 officer, Christopher Steele, who had once served undercover as second secretary at the British embassy in Moscow. Composed of hearsay evidence from sources in Washington DC and marred by elementary errors any Russianist could spot, most of the dossier was actually assembled by an informant of Russian extraction living in the United States, Igor Danchenko. He was knowingly misdescribed as "Russian-based" – evidently to add false credibility to the fake dossier – when he was in fact a US resident.[8] The most libellous claims appear to have been introduced by a sub-source, an American public relations consultant who had high-level contacts with the Russian embassy in Washington DC, Charles Dolan. Dolan had "meetings with the Kremlin" in June 2016. He also backed the Clinton campaign and came to have his own suspicions about where Danchenko's true loyalties lay: "when I first met him he knew more about me than I did".[9] Moreover, US counter-intelligence knew Danchenko had "had previous contact with the Russian Embassy and known Russian intelligence officers". He had tried to solicit classified material from more than one American with security clearance, as a result of which he had been under investigation since 2009. Unbelievably, the FBI had then lost him when he left the country on a brief visit to London but he had found his way back onto American soil without USCIS (the immigration service) primed to report that fact.[10]

Nonetheless, both Danchenko (with the FBI left in ignorance) and Dolan were encouraged to work together against Trump. On 15 June 2016, Dolan emailed from Moscow: "I'm in Russia making plans to be adopted in the event this mad man [Trump] gets elected." Danchenko was with Dolan in Moscow, and flew into London and met Steele on 18 June. Two days later part of the Steele dossier was produced with the most salacious allegations about Trump's stay at the Ritz Carlton three years before.[11] Danchenko always denied that this least credible section of the dossier was his own product and disowned its authenticity.[12] It was an assertion deliberately concealed when the FBI and the Department of

Justice testified to the Foreign Intelligence Surveillance Court and to Congress that the dossier was genuine, but on the basis of no intelligence corroboration whatsoever; as was their mendacious assertion that Steele was a "Crown Source" (MI6).[13] Indeed, in January 2017 the British government thought it necessary to disavow the claim that Steele was a "Crown Source" and worked for them.[14] Furthermore, none of the claims against Trump were ever corroborated.[15] The suspicion lingers that Russian intelligence had every reason to take a direct interest in furthering the alleged conspiracy for its potentially disruptive effect on the US elections and thereafter.

The impact on American public opinion was all the greater because the dossier appeared at a time when, under Project Lakhta, the Russians "conducted social media operations targeted at large audiences with the goal of sowing discord in the political system". The Mueller Report later found no evidence at all of collusion by Trump.[16] Indeed, the Steele dossier, compiled entirely for partisan purposes, lacked the slightest credibility. And those Democrat protégés led by Brennan, who shut out CIA's experienced Russian analysts to claim in a hurriedly published finding that Moscow sought Trump's victory in the election, allowed political prejudice to overrule professional judgement.[17]

The Clinton campaign conspirators had more than one helping hand from the FBI, whose New York office paid retired CIA officer Stefan Halper – Confidential Human Source 1 in the Durham Report – to gather whatever information he could on Lt General Michael Flynn, as he had on others, from his location in Cambridge, England.[18] Flynn had, after Trump's election, imprudently made contact by telephone with Sergei Kislyak, the Russian ambassador to the United States, an enthusiast for good relations with his hosts who – as already noted – had in the past represented his country at NATO and had been personally bruised by the alienating experience. It is at around this time that the Obama White House also took a direct hand in hobbling the incoming administration by undermining trust in Flynn. His phone calls were intercepted by the National Security Agency on what were extremely dubious grounds.[19]

Presidential Uncertainty

On 8 November 2016 Trump was elected president. And, as anticipated, on 17 November it was announced that Flynn would be the next Special Advisor to the President on National Security Affairs. The Russians were relieved, just the establishment *New York Times* was appalled. In Moscow the headline in the hardline newspaper *Vzglyad* ran "The appointment of a general in the White House foreshadows a rapprochement with the Kremlin". It went on to explain why. Flynn, a former director of military intelligence, had "called for fighting in Syria shoulder to shoulder with the Russians against the common enemy". The Russians did not, however, believe this would come without a price, it was only the beginning of negotiations, since Trump was "a businessman to the root of his being". They also reported that Flynn, a Democrat, had fallen out with Obama's Secretary of Defense Ashton Carter because Flynn had opposed the military support given to Islamic fundamentalists fighting the Syrian regime and that, in toppling Gaddafi in Libya, they had inadvertently opened another front for Islamists in North Africa.[20]

Nixon's former advisor on national security, of long experience in foreign affairs, Henry Kissinger had not planned to vote for Trump; his wife was in favour, however. Only a long conversation with his driver-cum-bodyguard persuaded Kissinger to do so. An appointment with the Trump transition team was scheduled, but then delayed because his wife had had a fall. But on the afternoon of 19 December the meeting went ahead. Kissinger's world view, reinforced by occasional telephone conversations in German with Putin, whom he had first met when Putin was deputy mayor of St Petersburg, favoured some kind of grand geopolitical compromise with Russia that would meet its core security needs.[21] But the meeting proved a disaster because the Trump team took particular objection to Kissinger's stance in favour of sustaining, if not enhancing, co-operation with China. Kissinger believed, for example, that Beijing was entitled to build island fortresses in the South China Sea as it was "theirs". Kissinger came away feeling humiliated. The encounter dashed all his hopes of one last throw in the game and left him with a very bad taste in the mouth at having his legacy trashed with such unaccustomed disdain. So much so that he later gloomily confided to Reagan's Secretary of State George Shultz, then at Stanford University in California, that he was throwing in the towel and might like to move out West.[22]

On 5 January, the day of Trump's inauguration and before he had actually entered the White House, a meeting took place in the Oval Office chaired by Obama, which included Vice President Biden, Deputy Attorney General Sally Yates, FBI Director James Comey and the Special Advisor to the President for National Security Affairs Susan Rice. Comey, who had been directly involved in the attempts to compromise Trump during the campaign, suggested that there was something suspicious about Flynn's meetings with the Russian ambassador and that he could be "sharing sensitive information".[23] The FBI then secured Flynn's removal by entrapping him into denying that he had discussed with Kislyak the possibility of relieving Russia of the sanctions that Obama had imposed after the seizure of Crimea.

The Trump administration, like most incoming teams, was in disarray. But it was made far worse by Flynn's dismissal, as he was the only one who had a coherent and plausible stance on foreign policy – whatever one thought of it. Those whom Trump subsequently appointed, including General H. R. McMaster as his Special Advisor on National Security Affairs, simply did not have a sophisticated view on foreign policy matters. Moreover, as the Russians now sensibly assumed, US national interests were not fundamentally altered by the elections. Trump, despite what they called his well-meaning public rhetoric, had suggested nothing definite about how he would go about improving relations. The new presidency offered no certainty of anything beneficial to Russia. The champagne remained corked while they watched and waited. All initiatives were checked.

Rex Tillerson, the new Secretary of State, was seen as having had "a positive experience in co-operating with Moscow" because he had headed the corporate oil giant Exxon, which had multiple contacts with its Russian competitors. Whereas his counterpart as Secretary of Defense, James ("mad dog") Mattis, a former Marine Corps General, was seen as a typical hawk of Cold War vintage.[24] The two effectively appeared to cancel one another out by meeting somewhere in the middle before presenting a joint position. And there was no one present with Kissinger's vision of a grand strategy that would both engage Russia and simultaneously protect US interests. That option had been carelessly cast aside weeks before the inauguration.

For the first year, instead, "the common pattern was that Mattis would hold forth, Tillerson would agree, everyone else would fold without significant comment, thereby ending the meeting".[25] Mattis was of course a retired four-star general and not used to being contradicted. McMaster was merely a serving three-star lieutenant general. A cautious man, McMaster deferred to the combined advice of Tillerson and Mattis until, in utter frustration at the lack of progress, he finally moved into action only to find that he had little to contribute. McMaster had turned down secretary of the Russian national Security Council Nikolai Patrushev's suggestion of meeting when he first joined the White House. He retrieved it a year later only when he realised that what he politely called Tillerson's "valiant efforts to find areas of cooperation with Russia had foundered".[26]

Trump was, however, an eccentric president, and not an easy man to serve. He was obviously not part of the Washington élite and he wished to remain so. And this meant that, like Obama, another outsider, he did not necessarily share its core assumptions. His business background was local to New York. It meant that his horizon was not much more elevated than that of a corner shop window. Trump argued that the United States should leave NATO if other members continued to be subsidized by the American taxpayer by not paying their full dues. It was a perspective he shared with his electorate – whom his rival, Hillary Clinton, herself no blue blood, notoriously dismissed as "deplorables", those whose wages had not risen in real terms since the mid-1970s, and whose jobs had been at the mercy of private capital as it expanded across the globe with the end of the Soviet Union and the birth of Chinese state capitalism. Their situation had been made infinitely worse by the economic crisis of 2008. Obama had self-evidently failed to meet their needs by deferring to the demands of the influential banking establishment – the likes of Goldman Sachs and J. P. Morgan. He did not let them go to the wall in 2008 even though they were the ones who had caused the crisis in the first place by placing sequential bets on derivatives of derivatives. They were free to carry on making money. The taxpayer covered the commercial damage. The "deplorables" lost their jobs.

The sequence of wars fought by Trump's predecessors had also enriched the military-industrial complex and enhanced the standing of others, including those Obama stigmatized as the "chattering classes". On Trump's view, as was originally the case with Obama, the policies that led to this situation had to be shut down; standing conflicts over issues that had no immediate bearing on core American interests, such as Afghanistan and Iraq, ended, and those ostracized by previous administrations because they did not share the values of liberal internationalism – except for Iran and ISIS – should be accepted as valid negotiating partners.

Trump Disappoints Putin

The Kremlin, however, had never known what would emerge from an American election, any more than anyone else. Putin was resigned to wait and see, and with low expectations. He told *Le Figaro* on 29 May 2017 "I have already spoken to three US Presidents. They come and go, but politics stay the same at all times. Do you know why? Because of the powerful bureaucracy. When a person is elected, they may have some ideas. Then people with briefcases arrive, well dressed, wearing dark suits, just like mine, except for the red tie, since they wear black or dark blue ones. These people start explaining how things are done. And instantly, everything changes. This is what happens with every administration."[27]

In these circumstances no grand geopolitical offer was ever put forward by Putin. Meanwhile, the Syrian crisis completely disrupted the still hazy plans of the Trump team for turning the tide in relations with Russia, and any lingering hope in Moscow that a genuine "re-set" was possible. On 7 April, fifty-nine US Tomahawk cruise missiles launched from warships in the Eastern Mediterranean hit the Sharyat airbase from which the Syrian regime had launched yet another chemical weapons attack. To avert a direct military confrontation, the Russians were notified in advance. To some in Moscow this nevertheless came as an unpleasant surprise.

But not to all. From the vantage point of the intelligence services, Veronika Krasheninnikova was as usual quick to react. "The mask has been cast aside." In sharp contrast to Bush and Obama, who waited months before acting, Trump had moved in the matter of hours. "The real Trump stands in front of us. This is the way, by means of surprise military and political blows, that Trump is determined 'to make America great again'... It was with their help that he has got the message out." She continued, "Trump talked about a 'deal' with Russia. But what did he have in mind? In his political half ignorance and megalomania, self-love and machismo, Trump was certain: he would come to terms with Putin so that Russia would drop Syria, Iran and China and generally follow Trump." "Until the elections", Putin was for him "an exemplar of sorts: Trump evidently secretly hungered after becoming – so he thought – the same kind of authoritarian dictator. That he would also be 'loved'. But now that Trump is president, victory over Putin, in reality his strongest opponent, is a matter of honour for his clinically ill, gigantic ego."[28] What Russia potentially faced was even more dramatic than the Syrian air strikes. They had no idea that an opportunity had also arisen to assassinate Assad, but that Mattis had refused to go along with Trump's suggestion that they do so.[29]

Medvedev, whose own presidency had been undercut by Obama's air assault on Libya and for whom the United States was a bitter disappointment, hastened to condemn Trump's attack on Syria on Facebook the very day of the assault. "That's it", he wrote. "The remains of the pre-electoral fog have lifted. Instead of the widely canvassed thesis about a joint struggle against the common enemy – IGIL [ISIS] – the Trump administration has demonstrated that it will lead a struggle against the lawful government of Syria out of blind rage." Medvedev claimed that, once Trump was elected, he personally had waited to see how long it would take before "the existing machinery of power breaks Trump's pre-electoral stance". Trump himself was having none of it, however: "I really think there's going to be a lot of pressure on Russia to make sure that peace happens," he said, "because frankly, if Russia didn't go in and back this animal [Assad], we wouldn't have a problem right now."[30] A further move by Trump only confirmed Medvedev in his sense of foreboding. In early August 2017 Secretary of Defense Mattis visited Ukraine and recommended the despatch of $50 million worth of Javelin anti-tank missiles to secure Eastern Ukraine, a proposal notoriously rejected by Obama in 2015 because he feared that it would escalate the conflict. On 1 March 2018 Trump finally decided to break with Obama and supply Ukraine with 37 missile stations for 210 Javelins.

Trump's disturbing unpredictability in his willingness to attack Syria had now unexpectedly become a problem for Russia. Putin, however, was not at all as warm-blooded as Medvedev. Those who conducted negotiations with Putin that proved abortive noticed no visible change in his demeanour, only a tell-tale narrowing of the eyes. The sole outward impact, other than a refusal to meet Tillerson when he came calling, was – after a decent interval to establish that the two events were apparently unconnected – to begin the cautious process of pulling out of Syria. This culminated on 6 December 2017 when Putin arrived at the Russian air base – and against the evidence – prematurely declared victory (rather as Bush had in Iraq) and announced that his forces were leaving.[31]

For those in the West who sought to save face and meet him on his own terms, Putin could formally claim to have met them a part of the way. Clearly he did not wish to go so far as to burn his bridges with Trump over Syria, where his commitment to Assad could be sustained through other, unofficial means, including Prigozhin's Wagner Group, and with the help of Iran. Trump's dramatic mishandling of NATO Europe – see below – was far more important and not something to be ignored, and there the lesson was to sit back and enjoy Western disarray. Three years on, Moscow did express some regrets about Syria, however. The Russians had to acknowledge that "Yes, not everything went smoothly: there were mistakes, losses; there were potentially dangerous crises and grave disagreements with the forces of our main ally, the President of Syria."[32]

US-Russian Relations at Stalemate

Businessmen rarely make good politicians. Negotiating with other companies, even so-called "multinationals", in no way qualifies one to negotiate with entire states, whose national interests are not infrequently enmeshed in age-old irrational prejudices. Rex Tillerson had been a successful leader of a global oil conglomerate. However, as Secretary of State he tended to undervalue the professional expertise to hand and failed to make the kind of senior appointments that normally forestall the ship of state drifting out to sea. In particular, he made the elementary mistake of seeing Sergei Lavrov, his Russian counterpart, as in some sense, by virtue of office, the man in charge; an assumption for which there had never been any evidence whatever, under any Russian regime. McMaster, perhaps better advised by his senior director for Russia and Europe on the National Security Council, Fiona Hill, more appropriately turned to Patrushev instead. However, although invited to do so a year earlier, McMaster delayed meeting him until 16 February 2018 and, even then, only on neutral ground in Geneva at the US consulate.

The message deliberately sent was that McMaster did not think the meeting a priority. Not surprisingly it was a flop. After the events of April 2017, no traces remained of Flynn's priority of joint Russian-American action against ISIS, which, in any case, had by then been overtaken by events – ISIS was on the run in Iraq, and it had lost both Mosul and Raqqa. What the Russian had to say had all been said four years before and, indeed, was to be reiterated regularly for the next four years. No one could say that Putin was anything other than consistent. Patrushev, echoing his master's voice, argued that Russia's moves into Crimea and Eastern Ukraine were a defensive reaction to the coup in Kyiv; that NATO expansion and the rotation of alliance forces through what had been Soviet-held territories were threatening to Russia; and that US military intervention in Afghanistan, Iraq and Libya had increased terrorism in the region.[33] From Patrushev's exposition one clear conclusion could be drawn. Nothing that the United States had done since 2014, including sanctions and attempted co-operation to delay Iran's acquisition of a nuclear capability, had changed the course of Russian foreign policy one iota.

Although McMaster complained that Russian actions in Syria indirectly encouraged terrorism, he offered nothing that might tempt Putin to desist. The brunt of his complaints were directed instead at Russian election meddling, for which Obama, when in office, had signally failed to call the Kremlin to account. And to anyone who had closely observed US-Russian relations since 1991, it was an underlying symptom rather than an originating cause of tension between the two Powers. The Americans had themselves been interfering in foreign elections for decades, certainly since 1948 in Italy, throughout Latin America and most recently in Israel.[34] As to the idea of reorganizing the security architecture between both sides on the Kissinger model, not a word was spoken, not one idea suggested. Imaginative statesmanship was nowhere apparent, from either side. Certainly in foreign policy Patrushev was, after all, merely the messenger; McMaster was no different. In both cases the locus of decision lay elsewhere.

This was as much a problem for liberals in Russia as it was for Americans. The leading analyst of foreign policy at *Kommersant*, Elena Chernenko, could be described as a liberal-leaning realist. She had most unusually been invited to write for an opinion piece for the *New York Times*, where her trenchant commentary, however, made little visible impact on American thinking, Democrat or Republican, because it was not what they wished to hear. And what Chernenko wrote in the spring of 2018 was a wake-up call: "Even the [Russian] president's opponents admit that he is so popular that he could win even without manipulating the results at the ballot box. And Russia's foreign policy in recent years is a significant contributor to that popularity." She also offered a penetrating intuition about Putin: "As he eyes the eventual exit, he may be looking to leave a more august legacy, one that includes real and durable achievements. The problem is that in recent years, what Russia sees as victory too often means a loss for someone else."[35]

McMaster did gain something from his time with Patrushev, however: direct insight into his Russian counterpart's state of mind that should have made him think more deeply about relations with Moscow. On meeting him McMaster noted that "the combination of fear and injured pride was palpable".[36] This was also something Chernenko had consistently pinpointed, connecting Russian public opinion to Putin's adventurous foreign policy.

Yet throughout his reflections on the recent past, McMaster never showed the slightest awareness that the United States might have borne even a shred of responsibility for what had gone so badly wrong in the relationship under other presidents prior to the election of his *bête noire*, Obama.

Moreover, most of those working for Trump, including McMaster, found his unpredictable improvisations no less hard to accommodate than those of his predecessor, albeit for different reasons. As the NATO Brussels summit drew near (11–12 July 2018), the President's hostile intentions towards the alliance that the United States had once created were scarcely a state secret. Railing against his allies within the walls of the White House was one thing; going public on the worldwide web and in front of the cameras in order to cause maximum embarrassment to them was quite another. It cost the United States enormous, perhaps irreparable reputational damage.

NATO Cast into Chaos

In a deal hastily concluded at the NATO summit in Cardiff on 4–5 September 2014 after Putin's seizure of Crimea, the allies had been pressed into agreeing to raise their defence expenditure to 2 per cent of GNP. The East Europeans, led by the Poles, who were consistently hostile to Russia, characteristically wanted to raise the bar even higher. During the election campaign Trump had declared that NATO was "obsolete". This was manifestly bluff. At his first summit in April 2017 he insisted that all members meet their budgetary obligations. How could at one and the same time NATO be obsolete and then require a greater degree of commitment from its European members? This demand, less strident perhaps, was in fact nothing new to the alliance; it was a standing American complaint going back to its inception. Unlike almost every president, including General Eisenhower, however, Trump did not just take it on the chin, content merely to moan about it. It had become an *idée fixe*. He was particularly angered at Germany, the richest of all, paying only 1.2 per cent of GNP. Trump threatened to reduce US payments to the German level if a satisfactory answer were not found. What enraged him most was, as he revealed to the world via Twitter before a further summit in July 2018: "On top of this [low defence spending] the European Union has a trade surplus of $151 million [billion]… with big Trade Barriers on goods. No!"[37] Having signed into law the possibility of imposing sanctions on companies engaged in the construction of the Nordstream II gas pipeline to Russia – whose CEO, Matthias Warnig, had been an officer in the East German secret police and was a friend of Putin – for good measure Trump accused Germany of being a Russian "hostage".[38] Putin could not but notice where the shoe pinched.

For all his threats of pulling out of NATO, what Trump appeared not to know – and no one appears to have told him – was that George Bush ('41) and his successor Bill Clinton feared that the United States would be jettisoned from Europe if it did not remain, sustain and expand the alliance. Stalin had once told the British ambassador to Moscow that he who dominates Europe, dominates the world.[39] Europe was not Africa. If the United States were not a permanent presence in Europe, how could it claim to be a global Power? As a consequence the Americans had since the early 1990s consistently sabotaged any practicable and meaningful exclusively "European defence initiative" for fear it could begin the process of supplanting the existing alliance. European leaders, certainly in Britain, France and Germany, did realize this. But they were too polite to say so, at least in public. Who, exactly, needed whom? The Russians understood, and were therefore not expecting to see the Americans fold their tents and quit the field before long. The best coverage appeared on 6 July in the hardline newspaper *Vzglyad*, a trusted voice of the Russian deep state, under the headline "Trump Wants to Break Up the European Union".

The president was going to rough up his European allies at the forthcoming summit, the diehard conservative and firm Putin supporter Petr Akopov predicted. Akopov did not, however, credit "leaks of the most mindless variety – that US forces would leave Germany". This was "basically" just "blackmail". What he found entirely plausible, however, was that "Trump wants to weaken Europe, which he sees not as a satellite or younger partner, but a dangerous competitor – and is prepared to achieve this by the widest variety of means. One that he favours most is the demand that the Europeans increase defence expenditure to the level already promised, by 2 per cent of GNP." Trump also wanted the $600 billion European market open to US goods. And Germany was not only the most resistant to paying up, it sold its cars to the United States while blocking American vehicles from the European market. Trump also wanted the allies to pay for US military bases. "As though America draws no special advantages from a military presence across the entire globe in contrast to those countries that it protects with its own forces."

Akopov did not find the threats altogether credible. And here he hit upon the crucial reasoning in the White House at the end of the Cold War:

> Why should the USA deprive itself of a key element of its global leadership, military control over Europe? Perhaps, the dollar will then lose its status as a reserve currency, Hollywood would close down, along with all the American bases across the world? His point of departure is that the European Union, like the USA, is a part of what we know as the West, which is an Atlantic supranational project in which there is no full sovereignty. And Trump wants to return national sovereignty to the USA – breaking the unity of the West to obtain it.

Sustaining US economic hegemony required that Europe – Germany – had to be the weaker partner. Merkel was thus the focal point of attack. "The USA was pressing on Germany from every direction. Only the Germans have learned how to extricate themselves on the Russian front as it is suggested they suffer on the Iranian [front]. And what lies ahead? Sanctions for working with China?" Akopov suggested that "Trump is getting a taste of Germany's patience – and here it begins to get interesting." And here the commentator took off into the realm of fantasy. Even though American influence on the country had weakened after reunification and European integration, which strengthened Germany, "took place under the gaze of the Atlantic élite", it became more difficult for "the Anglo-Saxons" to exert influence on the management of Europe. Akopov predicted that this process would continue and Germany would eventually become "not the object but a subject in world politics – with all the potential that flowed from it. The main being the possibility of independently choosing the direction of travel, the formulation of alliances and blocs. As an example: Berlin-Moscow-Beijing."[40]

Under President Trump the United States had re-emerged after years of economic stagnation. Though well disposed towards Putin, indeed to other dictators, too, Trump was unpredictable and, not unlike Ronald Reagan with the slogan Make America Great Again, he prided himself on enhancing American military power and cautiously consolidating it for future necessity. Thus, although determined to cut his losses in Afghanistan and in Iraq where the Pentagon had predictably failed, no negotiation would be concluded at the expense of his own self-esteem or of the military budget. At home, the damage wrought by Prigozhin's cyber warfare during the presidential elections exacerbated fissures that the Obama administration had expanded into an all-out effort to nullify the neo-conservative agenda. Repeated impeachment of Trump by Obama's erstwhile supporters on the specious grounds that he was some kind of Russian puppet not only distracted the White House from focusing on a deal with Putin, it also inhibited the formation of a coherent foreign policy focused on interests rather than responding to domestic political pressure on the Hill.

Although an unpredictable president was the stuff of

nightmares to his more genteel counterparts, the disturbing habit President Trump demonstrated of reasserting US military prowess did not give the Russians an easy ride either. And it was not just with respect to pushing for Assad's assassination, bombing Syria or blocking the Russo-German oil pipeline. On 20 October 2018, for instance, in answer to a correspondent's question Trump unexpectedly announced his intention to withdraw from the intermediate range forces treaty signed in 1987. This had simultaneously removed theatre nuclear missiles from both sides of divided Europe. The Russians knew full well that they were themselves in breach of the agreement: they had been deploying missiles in the Baltic fortress of Kaliningrad because NATO refused to adjust limits on conventional weapons in response to reductions in Soviet-era forces. But the allies, who were also well aware of that fact, became agitated and Merkel forced a delay in a process that was already anything other than immediate because the treaty allowed for a generous timeline for abrogation. Once again she acted to ease Kremlin anxieties.

Supporters and allies alike found Trump's instinctive aversion to condemning Putin, Xi Jinping or Kim Jong Un of North Korea equally annoying. Just as Truman had seen Stalin from a forgiving mid-Western perspective as a typical authoritarian and corrupt party boss like his erstwhile patron in Missouri, Tom Pendergast, so too did Trump's career negotiating with corrupt construction unions in New York inspire the delusion that making deals with foreign dictators was merely a matter of reasoned bargaining reinforced by unusual strength of character. McMaster's successor, John Bolton, was more worldly, though no mean ego himself, and understood human frailty better than most. He explained Trump's habits and psychology, though not with approval: "Trump seemed to think that criticizing the policies and actions of foreign governments made it harder for him to have good personal relations with their leaders. This was a reflection of his difficulty in separating personal from official relations."[41]

The problem for the deep state in Washington DC, and not

only them, was that this rule of thumb applied only to adversaries. To Trump, allies were not partners but competitors (in trade) or clients (in defence). Germany was an exceptional economic success as a nation proudly reunited but in defence essentially a client state with no nuclear capability. For allies like Merkel, his jibes were insultingly personal. But how was it that Germany found itself in the direct line of fire? There were underlying reasons that had nothing to do with the person of Trump, as will be explained below.

Moscow was unimpressed. On 11 September 2020, former ambassador Aleksandr Aksenenok, a finely tuned diplomat and expert on Europe as well as the Arab world, summed it up in what almost reads like an American deep state indictment of Trump:

> Having failed to adapt to a world in which it has lost its global dominance, the United States under Obama and particularly under Trump chose to neglect traditional diplomacy, which involves finding ways to align with possibly diverging allied interests. With regard to Europe, this policy was encapsulated in withdrawal from multilateral trade partnership agreements, the use of NATO to exert pressure on allies, the introduction of sanctions, and the employment of other methods of gaining unilateral economic and political advantages… the Trump administration approaches the 2020 presidential elections with an unprecedented burden of problems in its relations with its North Atlantic allies, in almost complete isolation owing to its illegal actions in the UN Security Council concerning the lifting of the Iranian sanctions, and having generally lost its moral and political prestige.[42]

11

Paying the Gas Bill

A Russian commentator wrote that "as history reveals, economic ties are the stronger. If a project is advantageous to business, a political decision will be found."

– A. Kuznetsov, 10 September 2021.[1]

Angela Merkel was Trump's bugbear. And, as the de facto head of the EU, she held some of the best cards in NATO's pack. Yet payment of the growing bill for Russian gas came at a political price. Germany was also very important to Russia, not least for economic reasons. So the Chancellor did have leverage had she been determined to exercise it. But Merkel resolutely refrained from doing so. The Russian economy – its entrepreneurial spirit stifled by corruption and repression – drifted in the doldrums. Punished for his unanticipated annexation of Crimea, Putin publicly belittled the modesty of NATO's retaliation; he was conscious of the fact that economic sanctions had been resorted to only because the Americans refused to consider full-scale military aid to Ukraine. Placing the blame on the United States was a wedge to drive into NATO. "Sanctions – what are they? They are the continuation of the same policy of imposing their own [American] values", Putin, with one eye to the Germans, insisted to those attending the Eastern economic forum in Vladivostok on 7 September 2017.[2] Whatever he said, however, sanctions had unquestionably damaged trade, tipping the Russian economy into recession, and prompted significant capital flight. Only a few months after Putin's boast Alexei Kudrin, the economist who worked directly under him as Minister of Finance from 2000 to 2011, warned that it would take fifteen years for Russia to escape from the economic rut and that this would require a cut in consumption of some 30 per cent. Between 1991 and 2015 the accumulated material losses amounted to no less than those suffered in the Second World War. It would, he said, take 27–28 trillion roubles to put this right.[3]

However, the only actions against Russia that could have delivered anything close to a death blow to its declining economy would have been to cut off its European export market for natural gas and oil. Gas had been contributing a weighty 20 per cent to the national budget and a refusal to buy Russian oil as well could have deprived it of even more. But this would have been a decision that severely damaged the German economy, and also one with serious Europe-wide repercussions for Germany's best customers. To the Russians, while the United States was tantalisingly always out of reach, Germany was inevitably seen as a soft touch.

The two Nordstream gas pipelines that ran through the Baltic Sea – the second still not yet complete in 2020 – underpinned trade relations with Germany. Germany was Russia's main partner in this venture, with the Netherlands and France following in its wake. The Germans blinded themselves to the obvious. After Putin annexed Crimea in 2014, NATO Secretary General Anders Fogh Rasmussen warned Merkel against making Germany more dependent on Russia. For the Russians, he said, the projected Nordstream II pipeline "had nothing to do with business or the economy—it was a geopolitical weapon". She did not listen, even though Putin, in anger at sanctions, is reported to have threatened Merkel at the time "that he wanted to destroy the European Union".[4] Thereafter Russia, despite the ups and downs in their relationship, appears to have been confident that Germany would ultimately remain pliable, at least while Merkel was in office and remained hostage to the pro-Russian SPD, which continued to hold the balance in the coalition government.

Russian commentator Dmitrii Bavyrin summed up just how good relations were between Germany and Russia in the Merkel era despite the storm over Crimea and the Donbas: "Even at the most heated moments of the Ukrainian crisis [in 2014] the illusion prevailed of complex but at the same time special relations between Moscow and Berlin. Thus both brought in a lot of money, we built north streams [gas pipelines] together and we almost spoke the same language: President Vladimir Putin, as you know, speaks German, and Chancellor Merkel – Russian."[5] The rigidity of Merkel's stance inevitably encouraged Putin to believe that he could damage US-German relations at low cost. Trump drove home the obvious fact that German commercial self-interest consistently clashed with Merkel's pro-American instincts.

Gas in Russia is a state monopoly, though publicly quoted. "Gazprom is a key element in the state's system of energy security, its export potential", Putin declared. "And no less importantly, a powerful factor in the economic and political influence of Russia in the world."[6] On paper a private company, the *Financial Times* insisted that Gazprom "remains an arm of the government. All the key decisions are taken in the Kremlin. Both psychologically and practically Gazprom is not a commercial enterprise. It is the single most important part of the resurgent Russian state."[7]

The gas supply to Europe could be cut off at an instant and switched back on at a whim, as Lithuania had discovered in 1990 (under Gorbachev) and Ukraine in 2006 and 2009. Yet the Germans signed up for the first Baltic pipeline, Nordstream, in 2011, knowing what had been inflicted on these countries, presumably deluded by the notion of German exceptionalism, an economistic view of international relations embedded among the élite since victory in the Cold War. The problem was that this was not an assumption shared in Moscow, where domination of world commodity markets was seen as the best means of rescuing Russia as an effective Great Power. The graduate thesis Putin submitted to the St Petersburg Institute of Mining – bidding for attention as a future strategist – highlighted Russia's natural resources as the most promising means of furthering the country's foreign policy as well as its commercial interests.[8] The research may well have been plagiarized, as has been asserted, but Putin made the conclusions his own.[9]

Nearly one-half of Russia's foreign exchange income came from the sale of oil and gas by 2021. And the EU was its best customer.[10] At that time the Europeans were already receiving one-third of their natural gas from Russia. And the Commissioner responsible for energy, Miguel Arias, did not want dependency to grow.[11] Nordstream I had come into operation as recently as 2011, the same year that the explosion of the Fukushima plant in Japan prompted the planned abandonment of nuclear energy in Germany. The idea of a parallel pipeline therefore seemed all the more tempting to some as an alternative over the long term.

Arias cautioned that the proposed Nordstream II pipeline from Russia to Germany "is a project that has huge political consequences."[12] His nickname, however, was "the caterpillar", an unattractive insect that in Spain is synonymous with having the patience to await transformation into a beautiful butterfly. Not too much was to be expected from him in the immediate future. Echoing the concerns expressed by many, the CDU Chairman of the Bundestag's Foreign Affairs Committee Norbert Röttgen denied that Nordstream II could be accepted as a purely commercial matter. This was "clearly wrong", he stated, "because everyone knows that energy always is political".[13] But here again logic did not lead to action, and for good reason. Röttgen was deeply entangled in the politics of coalition with the SPD, which was congenitally pro-Russian. Furthermore, he had also been the Federal Minister for the Environment, Nature Conservation and Nuclear Safety who, after Fukushima, summarily cancelled Germany's nuclear programme. So even though he recognized the political nature of Nordstream II, he had himself cut Germany off from the only realistic long-term alternative. In this sense Röttgen personally epitomized the German dilemma in relations with Russia, which proved politically insoluble.

It was obviously much easier for the Americans to object to Nordstream II than for the Europeans themselves to do so. The prospect of a collision on this matter was foreseeable, especially after Putin had annexed Crimea and was fighting for a secure foothold in Eastern Ukraine. Berlin's commitment to Nordstream II inevitably became a bone of contention. Amos Hochstein, US Special Envoy and Coordinator for International Energy Affairs, warned that "This is a project that will serve the Russian narrative completely from all aspects… and it creates just the chasm [the Russians] want in the middle of Europe." He added that "Nobody spends money building pipelines in a low-oil environment when you already have a pipeline that works just fine. That's not a commercial deal. That's a political deal – and a bad one." The US ambassador to Germany stated that "We continue to push our concerns about Nord Stream both at the EU level and with Germany."[14] They did, indeed, and for a while they thought that there was a chance of succeeding. Victoria Nuland, the hardline Assistant Secretary of State for European and Eurasian Affairs, later acknowledged that "we were, in 2016, on our way to stopping the pipeline".[15] But they were blocked by Merkel, and Obama was simply not prepared to put up a fight. Two years later, with Trump as President, Secretary of Defense Mattis complained that "the European Union has embraced Putin". His evidence for this – and we know that the US National Security Agency was listening in[16] – was the fact that Merkel "talks to Putin two times a week, for one or two hours at a time".[17] A commentator in Russia's nationalist newspaper *Vzglyad* did not seriously take issue with the idea. Although the "Frau Chancellor" took a robustly critical view of Putin's treatment of the opposition, he wrote, there were political forces in Germany – the Free Democrats, the Greens, CDU bigwig Friedrich Mertz and her presumptive heir apparent

Annegret Kramp-Karrenbauer – in comparison with whom Merkel seemed "quite moderate". And it was "mostly thanks to Merkel that economic co-operation between the two countries – albeit at a reduced level – is preserved".[18]

Merkel later defended her consistent stance over the preceding decade: "my policy on Russia and Ukraine... was an attempt to prevent this war. The fact that this attempt failed does not mean that the attempts were wrong."[19] What she did not understand was that appeasing Putin was almost certainly the wrong way of going about it. She had claimed that it had not been the job of her government to approve the construction of Nordstream II and that, if she had legislated to prevent it, this would have "dangerously worsened the climate with Russia".[20] Arguably, however, a worsening of relations might have sobered up the Russian president from thinking that his wedge-driving and adventurism would work. And Merkel's problem was that she did not have any fixed beliefs or even a policy to call her own. She inhabited a plastic and pragmatic matrix of shifting interests, political and commercial, that led her simply to follow her coalition partners along the line of least resistance to Moscow. This, by default, left Putin with the initiative, if not the whip hand. And it mattered a great deal because, to the Russians, leverage over Germany, at the core of NATO, was necessary and convenient compensation for leverage over the United States. Trump's inconsequential ranting at NATO Europe about defence expenditure had predictably met with manifest indifference on the part of Germany.

A coalition builder and as such a consummate pragmatist, Merkel had in fact several reasons for adopting this attitude, not least to avoid confronting her SPD partners in office. Until 2017 the party was headed by Schröder's volatile protégé, Vice Chancellor Sigmar Gabriel. He also ran a key ministry that dovetailed economic affairs and energy, while Schröder's other protégé, Steinmeier, held the Ministry of Foreign Affairs. Gabriel's understanding of international relations had a lot in common with Obama in the belief that the world was "a global community" rather than an arena of conflict.[21] In contrast to Merkel the events in Ukraine made little impact upon him. And for her, as *Frankfurter Allgemeine Zeitung* journalists Bingener and Wehner point out, "a kind of deal existed with the Social Democrats: in return for the SPD sharing the burden of unpopular sanctions against Russia, Merkel took no action against the comrades' favourite project, the gas pipeline. The German energy industry was also for the construction of the pipeline; likewise Merkel did not think it advisable to come into conflict with them."[22]

The momentum therefore lay incontestably with pipeline enthusiasts led by the formidable ex-chancellor Gerhard Schröder, whom Putin had in his pocket. On 9 December 2005, after leaving office, Schröder received a call from Putin offering chairmanship of the committee of Nordstream, reportedly at one-quarter of a million dollars a year. He went on to head the supervisory board of Nordstream II.[23] The pipeline beneficiaries – primarily E.ON and BASF/Wintershall from Germany – succeeded in neutralizing EU-wide resistance by linking up with Royal Dutch Shell, Engie of France and OMV from Austria.

On 23 August 2019 in the Kleiner Tiergarten of Berlin, Zelimkhan 'Tornike' Khangoshvili, a Georgian who had fought in the second Chechen war, was shot at close range by Vadim Krasikov of the FSB's special unit Vympel. He was caught and gaoled for life.[24] Merkel's response was minimal. The embassy in Moscow scarcely reacted.[25] Just two Russian diplomats were expelled from Germany.

By the time Trump faced re-election, tension in US relations with Germany had reached a peak. The Russian business newspaper *Kommersant* appeared in June with the headline: "One Bad Friend Deserves Another: How Germany Has Become the USA's Main Enemy in Europe". Observing the latest tit-for-tat in the ongoing dispute over defence commitments to NATO, Elena Chernenko highlighted Trump's threat to reduce American troops in Germany from 34,500 to 25,000.[26] On 16 June 2021, she wrote an opinion column for the *New York Times* in which she brutally punctured the bloated and conceited notion that the United States any longer had real influence over Russian opinion:

> Even among Russians who actively support democracy, the rule of law and human rights, Mr. Biden won't find much support. Over the past decades, many Russian liberals have become disillusioned with the West, especially the United States. For some, America's image started to crack with the bombing of Yugoslavia and the war in Iraq. For others, it was the revelations of WikiLeaks and Edward Snowden, which brought to light a host of America's covert operations and dirty dealings, that soured feelings of admiration.
>
> And for many, the presidency of Donald Trump – during which Washington abandoned international agreements, treated allies as clients, badly mismanaged the pandemic and, most important, exacerbated political polarization and social dysfunction – definitively stripped America of its authority. With this legacy, no American president would have a substantial audience in Russia.
>
> Secure internally and with little to lose, Vladimir Putin is ready for President Biden. As for his image in the United States and the rest of the West, it's fair to assume – after years as their arch-villain and evil mastermind – that Mr. Putin couldn't care less.[27]

With that, Chernenko concluded her post-mortem on American illusions.

Conclusion

The War of the Russian Succession?

"Ukraine is part of the effort to destabilise Russia."

– Putin, 13 June 2023.[1]

Russia's political system during Putin's last decade in power has been an autocracy in all but name. But the damage inflicted on Russia's image in the West, which Moscow has spent considerable sums of money to sustain, has been immense. Putin's foreign policy advisers console themselves that it has afforded Russia opportunities denied the democracies. What they euphemistically call the "special" Russian system has, they assert, enabled Moscow to react more quickly to events and to mobilize resources more efficiently to serve foreign policy objectives, as political opposition can be ignored, along with public opinion as a whole.[2]

It can, however, be argued that what Putin has gained in power at home has been more than squandered in influence abroad. The price paid within Russia but not openly acknowledged has been that he is unsure of his footing, forever in doubt about the true extent of his support, and therefore vulnerable to unexpected surprises from within. Thus he even found it necessary on the eve of the presidential election in March 2024 to have Alexei Navalny removed from a prison in European Russia to one within the Arctic Circle, where he died, ostensibly from "natural causes" after brutal ill treatment. Putin's major problem has been that a democratic alternative still exists within living memory, however imperfect it may have been under Yeltsin, and it remains the norm across the face of Europe and beyond.

Democratic resistance has long been a vital factor making Putin insecure, though one that Putin has so far succeeded in suppressing. The people remain entirely under his thumb while he retains a monopoly of force and a patriotic domestic consensus, sustained by censorship, that he knows how to manipulate. This – despite the late Yevgeny Prigozhin's short-lived mutiny in June 2023 followed by his assassination in a fatal air crash on 23 August – has yet to break down even under the growing strains of a manifestly bungled war. Yet what makes it potentially so dangerous for him is the fact that it is intimately linked – certainly in his own mind – to the other key element that has significantly grown in magnitude, and which lies well beyond his reach: NATO expansion up to Russia's doorstep.

Putin undoubtedly deluded himself about Ukraine's vulnerability in his fateful decision to go to war. This did not mean that he had changed fundamentally from the hard-nosed young KGB officer unexpectedly marooned in Germany on the collapse of the Berlin Wall in 1989. But his patience had worn thin and he had become increasingly isolated from those who could offer alternative advice on foreign affairs during the pandemic. The bottom line was that in keeping his own counsel he simply blundered. That this was a costly miscalculation rather than some wild delusion matters, as it stemmed from strategic assessments based on the behaviour of the other Powers, which bear responsibility for their own actions and, indeed, just as importantly, their craven inaction. Putin is, as he always was, a "rational" actor. Indeed, only three months before invading Ukraine, on 21 December 2021 he offered an unusually cool, "realist" assessment of East-West relations. This stands in striking contrast to his more baroque outbursts, which have received more than their share of publicity in the Western media, such as the extraordinary essay published under his name: "On the Historical Unity of the Russians and the Ukrainians" on 12 July 2021, and, nearly a year later, the bizarre comparison he drew between himself and Peter the Great.[3] Those theatrical outbursts suggest another hand at work – that of the extreme nationalist, former culture minister Vladimir Medinskii, who has gained a reputation for Russian historical fantasy and has overseen the publishing of patriotic textbooks for schoolchildren stuffed with propaganda.[4]

Putin's colourful forays into historical fiction played to the gallery and attracted great attention. But the statement below has generally passed unnoticed as it is utterly in the raw, devoid of gothic theatricality. It is wholly rational in form and in substance:

> Take the recent past: in the late 1980s and early 1990s, when we were told that our concerns about NATO's potential expansion eastwards were absolutely groundless. And then we saw five waves in the bloc's eastward expansion. Do you remember how it happened? All of you are adults. It happened at a time when Russia's relations with the United States and main member states of NATO were cloudless, if not completely aligned... Sometimes I wonder: why did they do all this in those conditions? This is unclear. I think the reason lies in the euphoria from the victory in the so-called Cold War or the so-called victory in the Cold War. This was due to their incorrect assessment of the situation at that time, due to their unprofessional, mistaken analysis of probable scenarios. There are simply no other reasons.[5]

These were the words of a trenchant realist, certainly not the dreamy fantasist that some imagine him to be. Putin was too well-informed to attribute to the United States a malign long-term objective. On the contrary, he gave it the benefit of the doubt and suggested that policy emerged largely from hubris. This certainly fits the known facts. It did not, of course, make him more forgiving, however. Actions have consequences independently of intention, particularly in the conduct of international relations, where their impact is especially hazardous to predict. And Putin as a statesman has characteristically been less concerned with motives than with consequences; not least in framing his country's defence posture. It is obvious that for Russia the expansion of NATO has represented and continues to represent an alarming shift in the European balance of power, which Putin concluded was ultimately going to destabilize Russia from within. And when the Russians persistently warned what might come of NATO enlargement, the Americans carried on regardless, accustomed as they were to regarding the Russians as weak and powerless to stop the process.

In this respect the United States recognised no real difference between Yeltsin's Russia and Putin's Russia, the one being the result of the other. After all, the White House reasoned, what could Russia do: go to war? The allies in Western Europe, however, were never so confident that this process would end well. They repeatedly voiced serious objections to the trajectory of US policy because they read the runes. They knew their history; but, for fear of alienating the Americans, they went along with them, as they had always done; even pro-Russian German social democrats who consistently consoled themselves that in the end trade made for peace. This touching faith was expressed two millennia ago by the Roman Florus the Epitomist "Take away commerce and you break the bond that ties mankind together".[6] Opposition to US objectives would just cause trouble and achieve nothing, or so they rationalized. A formidable German defence posture was thus reduced to servicing what critics liked to call foreign policy as social work in places like Afghanistan. Moreover, resisting American demands could fracture NATO, which, after endless chatter and grandstanding behind the scenes, the allies never seriously considered supplanting. The force lay with the United

States, and everyone knew that it alone could call a halt to the process of enlargement.

In respect of the military balance, Putin specifically objected to "the deployment of B[allistic] M[issile] D[efence] systems in Poland and Romania, and the launchers that have been stationed there, the Mk 41, can be used to launch Tomahawk missiles and other offensive systems. This creates a threat to us – it's an obvious fact. What's happened in response to all our appeals and requests not to do this? You can see it now. As a result, we had to – I want to stress this – we had to reciprocate by launching the creation of hypersonic weapons. This was our response. But we were not the first to start all this – it all began when our partners withdrew from the ABM Treaty and later from the INF treaty."[7] Both sides, however, have sufficient experience and expertise in arms control – not least at the Russian embassy in London (Andrei Kelin) and in Washington DC (Anatoly Antonov) – to sort this out through compromise if the will were there. And this much is still obvious to both.

The fault here lies with the United States. Of all the countries that the Americans encouraged to join NATO, from the very first Ukraine elicited the fiercest objections on the part of the Russians. This was not least by virtue of its position: what at the time of Napoleon they used to call *landkartnoe davlenie* – literally "land map pressure", or, in today's parlance, geopolitics. To the Russians after the fall of the Soviet Union in 1992, the fate and status of Ukraine were never fixed. It floated in a geostrategic void. Brzezinski had correctly argued that without Ukraine Russia could never re-emerge as an empire, which Russia had invariably been. Entirely unknown to the Russians, as far back as 1994 the Clinton administration had against the best advice secretly provided for Ukraine's eventual entry into NATO. The Budapest memorandum signed by Russia and the United States at the end of that year, which denuclearized Ukraine and recognized Ukrainian sovereignty within existing borders, was never ratified by the Russian Duma. This very fact should have set the alarm bells ringing. But a deep-rooted complacency was everywhere apparent.

Instead, the Duma's objections were buried under a mound of Panglossian assumptions, piled high alongside muted West European criticism of NATO enlargement, mostly confined to the dignity of diplomatic reception rooms. The Americans were thus simultaneously and fatally at liberty to be both provocative and complacently naïve; the worst possible combination for the conduct of foreign policy, surprising even from amateurs, particularly in dealing with a hard-nosed Power like Russia. The abrupt, unanticipated attempt by the United States in 2008, driven by mindless triumphalism, to launch the process of admitting Ukraine into NATO was brought to a screeching halt only by vociferous German and French defiance for fear of its negative impact on Russia. And then, to cap it all, the diplomatic correspondence between the NATO states appeared in *WikiLeaks*. At this point Putin in person left no doubt that Ukraine's admission would cross "a red line". If this were not clear enough, in January 2011, and with another Democrat administration under Obama in the making, Putin repeated such warnings in conversation with ex-president Clinton.[8]

At a video conference given by Putin more than a decade later on 30 November 2021, investors primed with questions pressed him about Russia's red line. "You have asked about Ukraine and where the red lines run", Putin responded. "They are, above all, the threats to us that can come from that territory. If the enlargement, the [NATO military] infrastructure continues to expand – I have said this publicly, but you are business people and may not have the time to follow this – I will repeat this once again that the issue concerns the possible deployment on the territory of Ukraine of [first] strike systems with a flight time of 7–10 minutes to Moscow, or 5 minutes in the case of hypersonic systems. Just imagine that… The flight time to Moscow is 5 minutes."[9] Similarly, at a news conference on 13 July 2023, Putin referred to "Ukraine's membership of NATO, we have spoken of this more than once – it will create a threat to the security of Russia, obviously. And, as a matter of fact, the reason for the special military operation [the war], one of the reasons – is the threat of Ukraine's entry into NATO."[10]

As already indicated, the real question was not just armaments or NATO as an adversarial alliance, though these issues were inevitably thrust to the fore for the purpose of highlighting differences. And, because it was about much more than that, all the technical expertise in the world could not square this circle. For Putin himself, the entire issue of Ukraine was further complicated by a larger, existential menace. Even were Russia a democracy, the fate of Ukraine would certainly still matter, just as the fate of Canada or Mexico in the nineteenth century, or the arrival of Soviet missiles in Cuba in the twentieth century, mattered deeply to the United States. And they were taken as grounds for war. Geopolitics has of necessity played a critical part in Putin's thinking. But the fact that Russian pluralism and democracy were systematically dismantled piece by piece to establish what has effectively been a mafia state run by billionaire *siloviki* inevitably made Ukraine a potential Trojan horse; just as in 1968 Czechoslovakia's Prague Spring – democratizing communism – by its very existence threatened the core of Soviet hegemony.

In this context the chance of an opening between East and West when Putin came to power in 2000, which was scotched by Secretary of Defense Rumsfeld in 2002, remains one of history's tantalizing lost opportunities. In retrospect, Blair's foreign policy adviser at the time, Sir David Manning, has expressed serious "doubt whether real cooperation would ever have been a long-term prospect once the ex-KGB colonel and his gang established themselves. The gulf in values and interests was too great." He has suggested instead that "If there was a chance for a different outcome in relations with Russia, it was in the early nineties."[11] And we have seen how that possibility was discarded. Of course, had Putin been admitted inside the tent at the outset in 2000–1, those differences would have been less likely to fester in the way that they did, as it was the relentless expansion of NATO in the face of continued Russian resistance and increasing isolation that corroded any possibility of trust between East and West.

The mingling of geopolitical factors and the confrontation of values was further complicated by the undoubted fact that the cultures of Russia and Ukraine are too close, the population too intermingled, the dangers of a pluralist, democratic infection, however imperfect, too great to make complete separation practicable: not unlike the reasons that Canada and the United States share the same telephone system, their defence planning inseparable. Given firmly rooted Russian suspicions of the West, exacerbated by American self-interest and ineptitude, friction was inevitable, and collision surely a matter of time. But had the United States not extended the idea of regime change in 2004 under the younger Bush to what Putin regarded as his rightful sphere of influence, the issue might never have come to a head so sharply four years later with plans for Ukraine's admission into NATO. And then, of course, there were the Maidan protests.

Here the prospects for NATO expansion intersected with a newly, unanticipated, enhanced threat to Putin's supremacy. Up to 2004, the Kremlin appeared unperturbed by the prospect of Ukraine entering the EU, although the latter's centralizing tendencies and empire building were already much in evidence. The process of absorbing Ukraine was slow, the country's body politic riddled with corruption – which in turn later infected Americans like the Bidens, who came into direct contact with it. Its oligarchic political system was porous in the face of determined Russian penetration, as Moscow still held out the possibility of a rapprochement with Europe and some form of economic embrace over the longer term. But once Obama, Sarkozy and Cameron took advantage of Russia's abstention at the UN Security Council to remove Gaddafi in 2011 by force, blatantly reneging on explicit assurances against regime change, Putin completely recast the Russian regime's state of mind to one of determined retaliation and proactive, hostile penetration of Ukraine.

This was also a direct consequence of the fact that Russia was roiled by popular unrest unprecedented since 1993, with vociferous protests against fraudulent elections to the Duma. Back in office, Putin began applying pressure against Ukraine's entry into the EU; offering instead the mirage of a protectionist Eurasian economic union. In 2014 the effective overthrow of Yanukovych, the elected President of Ukraine, who had on Putin's instructions blocked the signature of an EU association agreement, prompted Putin to begin brutally dismembering Ukraine as a unitary state, with the seizure of Crimea and an undeclared war in the Donetsk basin to assure Russia of a land bridge and water supply to the Crimean peninsula. This effectively crippled hopes of Ukrainian entry into NATO. Before long it prompted the Americans into aiding Kyiv's effort to contain Russian-inspired insurrection in the east. Yet ultimately it resolved nothing.

Were Russia destined to give up Ukraine, Putin had determined by 2014 that he would not lose it entirely. Indeed, Ukraine would pay a heavy penalty by ceasing to be a unitary state. Making a hastily improvised argument for Russian territorial expansion, Putin – no doubt courtesy of his former culture minister and aide Medinskii – later suggested a bizarre parallel with Russia's historic expansion into the Baltic under Peter the Great, who fought the Great Northern War against Sweden and took the Ladoga region, where he founded St Petersburg in 1703.[12] A severe breakdown in Putin's health during the pandemic and too much time spent brooding in luxurious isolation appear to have accelerated plans for solving once and for all the issue of Ukraine. If Putin were to go down in history as the man who reconstructed the territorial landmass of what had been the Soviet Union – certainly the southern boundaries conquered by Catherine the Great – which he promised before his election in 2000, at the very least he could be expected to aggrandize Russia at the expense of Ukraine.

Putin succeeded in consolidating his primacy at home through constitutional changes pushed through the Supreme Court that ensured the possibility of him retaining the presidency for life. He then persistently tried to dispose of his most fearsome opponent, the charismatic populist Alexei Navalny, through assassination and, failing that, neutralize him by indefinite incarceration in conditions that would lead inevitably to his demise. Putin soon mopped up most of the mass media, expanding the intimidation of investigative journalists and liquidating their sources within business if they failed to pay sufficient attention to the precariousness of their situation.

But before risking war, Putin had specifically to assess the capacity and will of Ukraine to resist. Second, he had to be certain that the United States lacked the will to come to the aid of Ukraine directly. Third, he needed to know that Germany, at the head of Europe, was unlikely to follow through resolutely on serious sanctions against the Russian economy.

The Fifth Service of the FSB for Operational Information and International Information under Sergei Beseda was primarily responsible for secret intelligence within the former Soviet Union as a whole, which meant the Near Abroad.[13] Its Ukraine unit grew from 30 agents in 2019 to 160 in 2021.[14] But quantity certainly did not mean quality. In respect of Ukraine the faulty assessment that emerged was that a small minority of extreme nationalists dominated the scene and that a reservoir of support for their liberation by Russia could be counted upon even within Kyiv, inside the government. It was yet one more demonstration that secret intelligence can be suborned when sufficient pressure is exerted from above, a weakness apparent not only in authoritarian states.

Given Putin's assumption that the United States did not embark on NATO expansion in order to attack Russia, but was none the less more than content to reduce the scope of Russia's reach without the direct application of force, Putin could safely assume that the Americans under Biden would not respond to his invasion of Ukraine by resorting to arms. The disastrously executed and humiliating abandonment of Afghanistan by the United States in 2021 revealed two conflicting aspects of the administration: first, the president's unreasoning stubbornness when committed to a policy, a stance undoubtedly enhanced by reduced mental capacity, and a known side effect of it; second, the complete and embarrassing disarray demonstrated to the world by the departments of State and Defense at Biden's direction to cut and run from longstanding commitments in Central/South Asia and its crucial communications centre monitoring China's nuclear facilities at Bagram air force base.[15]

The President's stubbornness also showed itself in the abortive negotiations with the Russians led by Deputy Foreign Minister Sergei Ryabkov and US Deputy Secretary of State Wendy Sherman on 10–13 January 2022. The Russians had presented their terms a month before on 17 December 2021, reinforced by Putin at a press conference four days later. It was transparently inflated, with a view to reduction in the course of extensive negotiation. The terms included no movement eastward by NATO and an end to continued NATO military activity in Eastern Europe, the Transcaucasus and Central Asia. Everything had to be on paper and legally binding. Ryabkov said "There is no other option, since a characteristic feature of the current stage of relations between Russia and the collective West is a complete lack of trust." No additional deployment of troops and weapons from the original NATO states were to be made without prior consent. And there was to be a ban on the deployment of short- or medium-range missiles. Prior notification of military exercises was deemed essential.[16]

The *Wall Street Journal* reported:

> NATO and Biden administration officials have criticized Russia for publicizing the two proposed agreements, instead of trying to resolve its concerns behind closed doors. A reversal of Russia's military buildup near Ukraine, they said, would establish a more conducive atmosphere for progress at the negotiating table. As for Ukraine's future security arrangements, Mr. Biden has said it should be up to NATO

and Ukraine to decide if the country should formally be admitted into NATO.

Mr. Ryabkov rejected those points. Moscow went public with its demands on NATO because years of quiet diplomacy had been 'brushed off,' he said, while the US and its allies continued to train Ukrainian forces, conduct exercises with Ukraine and conduct military flights over Ukrainian territory.

"In that sense, Ukraine de facto is already a NATO member", Ryabkov claimed.[17] If it were, however, there would have been world war when Russia invaded.

The irreducible essence of the Russian position was laid bare after the invasion had begun and stalled unexpectedly on the soon to be abandoned march to Kyiv. The only disinterested intermediary willing and equally acceptable to both parties was the Israeli Prime Minister Naftali Bennett. He came to Sochi to meet Putin for the first time in January 2022. They spent half a dozen hours together. Putin evidently admired Bennett as the former leader of a commando raid into the Lebanon for his ruthless handling of Hezbollah – resulting in the Qana massacre of April 1996. Zelensky had asked Bennett to arrange a summit with Putin, but when the subject was finally broached in their conversations Putin turned sour. It was nonetheless evident that he liked and trusted Bennett. The invasion was thus inevitable. But once it had occurred, and within a week, it was obvious that Putin's ambitious plans had fallen badly short; Bennett resumed his role as intermediary after consultations with the NATO leaders. The latter were divided, the Germans (Olaf Scholz) and French (Emmanuel Macron) favoured compromise, the Americans under Joe Biden were less than helpful, and the British under Boris Johnson were totally opposed. On 6 February, Bennett flew secretly to Moscow with only his interpreter, Ze'ev Elkin. Here he succeeded in obtaining two "huge concessions", as he described them: first, Putin agreed not to assassinate Zelensky, thus implicitly dropping the demand for "denazification"; and, second, he agreed to abandon the insistence on Ukrainian disarmament. In return, Zelensky would have to renounce NATO membership. Bennett telephoned Zelensky with the news en route to the airport.[18] Meanwhile the formal negotiations that originated in Minsk at the end of February finally caught up with what Bennett had negotiated when they were translated to Istanbul. But at this delicate point the Americans stepped in. "They blocked it", Bennett recalls. The bad news was delivered to Zelensky in Kyiv on 9 April by Prime Minister Johnson.

Talks were chaired by President Recep Erdogan in Istanbul. They had originated in Minsk on 27 February, but no progress was reported. The leader of the Ukrainian team was Davyd Arakhamia, a Russian-born aide to Zelensky and an admirer of the hardline Chinese regime; on the Russian side Vladimir Medinskii, an aide to Putin and his nationalist mouthpiece, whom we have already encountered. Roman Abramovich, the Russian billionaire, played some kind of shadowy role behind the scenes, as he had personal contact with Putin. In the words of Ukrainian negotiators, "We cleaned up all the nonsense about 'denazification', 'demilitarisation', the Russian language and so on. We noted there that Ukraine was not ready to join NATO in exchange for tough and clear security guarantees. A framework for the agreement was prepared... But then the delegations simply could not move further. We say, guys, the issue of Crimea and Donbas is about territorial status. No one here is authorised to even talk about it. Let the presidents meet and decide where to go. We need a meeting between the leaders", said one of the sources in Zelensky's office.

Two obstacles, however, promptly overshadowed the chances of further advance: first the news of the barbaric massacres inflicted on the villagers of Bucha, Borodianka and Mariupol by Russian forces. And, second, on 9 April the untimely arrival in Kyiv of British Prime Minister Boris Johnson, puffed up with characteristic bravado. "Johnson brought two simple messages to Kyiv. The first is that Putin is a war criminal; he should be pressured, not negotiated with. And the second is that even if Ukraine is ready to sign some agreements on guarantees with Putin, they are not. We can sign [an agreement] with you [Ukraine], but not with him. Anyway, he will screw everyone over", is how one of Zelensky's close associates summed up the essence of Johnson's visit.[19]

Having succeeded in blocking the Ukrainian tank counter-offensive that opened on 3 June and which was aiming fifty or so miles to the sea, Putin returned again to the abortive negotiations at his press conference on 13 July 2023: "By the way, the draft document that I have mentioned many times, namely the draft agreement between Russia and Ukraine, which was prepared in Istanbul and which was then thrown into the bin by the Ukrainian regime, set out in great detail the issue of ensuring Ukraine's security. We still had to think about whether we agreed with everything that was stated there, but on the whole I think that this document was acceptable."[20]

The eagerness to talk stemmed directly from the failure of an invasion that had stunned the Russians. An authoritative commentator in the heart of Moscow, Andrei Kortunov, has pointed out what was most strikingly at variance with Putin's cherished assumptions when he decided to invade: "The resilience of Ukrainian society and the Ukrainian political system, the resilience of the Ukrainian armed forces were quite spectacular."[21] In the face of this, whether or not Putin continues to remain in office, given the humiliating collapse of his strategy, is impossible to predict. His hold on those around him is formidable, the St Petersburg mafia forming its core, retained through thick and thin in spite of crass ineptitude from some and wobbling commitment from others. But military stalemate means that ultimately there have to be negotiations as a slow, deadly war of attrition achieves no purpose for either party, given that war is the continuation of policy by other means. The Russian war has demonstrably failed in its objectives. Russian diplomats and commentators are utterly lost, and the more farsighted could be forgiven for fishing haphazardly for a way out. Even in the worst circumstances, it was a tactic much used under Stalin by Commissar for Foreign Affairs Maxim Litvinov to work on foreign statesmen to elicit proposals that might prompt a Russian response. Thus what appears to emerge from China, Turkey or Saudi Arabia could well have roots elsewhere, closer to home.

Russian analyst Kortunov, who is normally enough of a realist to accept the fact of Ukrainian resilience, adopted an absurd line of reasoning that reads as if it were inserted by another hand. "It's about the nature of the political regime in Ukraine", he argues. "If this regime is not changed, we will see an emphatically anti-Russian revanche seeking irredentist leadership, which will look for opportunities to start it all over again. The only way to avoid it is to make sure that some political changes will turn Ukraine into a country that is not as hostile to Russia as it is right now and where the Western influence will not be as significant as it is today. The Russian position might turn out to be tougher and more rigid, but it is probably too early to talk about the final settlement."[22]

Invading a country and seizing its territory, as Russia has twice done to Ukraine, is bound to lead to irredentism. That is a fact of life, the price to be paid. And when one fails, concessions to the adversary are inevitable. Given that Ukraine has not lost, taking up "the other narrative" about changing Ukraine to suit Russian convenience is pie-in-the-sky politics. It is equally true, however, that the nature of the regime in Russia is also not up for negotiation in any peace deal. Yet both sides have to be realistic in a way that Boris Johnson self-evidently was not.

Russia is at a dead point. The benefits of peace, however limited in scope, are obviously enormous. To get there the country has to face up to a fundamental blunder in reuniting its former Western "partners" as adversaries, precipitating harsh sanctions and thereby inflicting long-lasting damage on its own failing economy. Dependence on its neighbouring economic giant, China, has only grown. To the Chinese Russia looks like

Typhoid Mary, once the healthy carrier of a deadly disease, and they have responded by withholding anything near full support. As the Japanese expression goes, they share the same bed, but they dream different dreams. Meanwhile, Russia's neighbours in the Near Abroad, from Kazakhstan down to the Caucasus, were making easy money as way stations for Western exports forbidden direct entry into Russia.

Russia's moral stature is at a new low. The economy is bleeding talent with a brain drain at over a million emigrants in all directions, except towards Belarus; a new diaspora of the highly educated, magnifying the impact of the massive losses on the field of battle. A coming commodity boom on the back of a major slump in the global economy may yet give considerable relief, just as Putin had argued back in the late 1990s. But here timing is everything and prediction all too fallacious. The dream of a Sino-American conflict is no more than wishful thinking. And China is potentially a hegemonic Power threatening to dominate its more backward neighbour well into the future. Further afield, talking to the Taliban in Kabul and having friends in New Delhi are not much compensation. Nor is the exploitation of Third World resentment at the dominance of the dollar, through aligning with the leading countries that make up BRICS (Brazil, Russia, India, China and South Africa) likely to lead anywhere in the short to medium term. What divides them – not least India and China – remains far greater than what unites them. The Eurodollar is still too convenient for those in business around the world to discard. In the meantime Russia's youth has to live with the appalling prospect of death on the battlefield – and we know what impact the Vietnam war had on young Americans and what impact that unnecessary war had in dividing society – while those at home in the western regions from Pskov to Belgorod or, indeed, Moscow now watch the skies anxiously for drone attacks emanating from Ukraine even if economic shortages are insufficient to sow doubt.

Through hasty resort to war, Putin could in the end bring about what he was determined to forestall: the collapse of his regime and the fall of all who serve in it. This is exactly what happened to Nicholas II, who ultimately chose war to save the autocracy. This too could prove to be an unintended war of the Russian succession. If so, we will all sooner or later have to come to terms with a new regime, democracy or dictatorship. And as former president of France Nicolas Sarkozy notes: "Countries do not change their address."[23] But are we in any way prepared for this? Have we learned anything?

Sources

Declassified Documents, Official Releases, Presidential Statements, Congressional Testimony, Official History

Germany. *Akten zur Auswärtigen Politik der Bundesrepublik Deutschland, 1991* (Oldenbourg: De Gruyter, 2022).

Great Britain. House of Lords, Session 2001–02, 11th Report, Select Committee on the European Union, *The European Policy on Security and Defence*, Vol. II: Evidence (London: HMSO, 2002).

Great Britain. Intelligence and Security Committee of Parliament, *Russia*, HC 632, 21 July 2020.

Great Britain. National Archives. Premier Papers.

Italy. Istituto Luigi Sturzo, *Archivio Giulio Andreotti*, NATO Series, Box 176, Subseries 1, Folder 11.

Italy. Camera dei Deputati. Senato della Repubblica. XVI Legislatura. Doc XXIII. N6. *Commissione Parlamentare di Inchiesta Sull'Affare Telekom-Serbia* (istituita con legge 21 maggio 2002, n.99).

Switzerland. *Diplomatische Dokumente der Schweitz*, 1991, ed. S. Zala et al. (Bern: Dodis, 2022).

United Nations, *International Tribunal for the Prosecution of Persons Responsible for Serious Violations of International*

Humanitarian Law Committed in the Territory of the former Yugoslavia since 1991. Bosnia Judgement, 24 March 2016.
- USA. CNBC TV Live: House Intelligence Committee holds a hearing on worldwide threats to the US – 8 March 2022.
- USA. *The 9/11 Commission Report. Final Report of the National Commission on Terrorist Attacks Upon the United States* (Washington DC: USGPO, 2004).
- USA. R. Mueller, *Report on the Investigation Into Russian Interference in the 2016 Presidential Election* (US Department of Justice: Washington DC March 2019).
- USA. The United States vs Igor Danchenko Indictment: www.justice.gov/sco/press-release/file/1446386/download
- USA. Special Counsel John Durham, *Report on Matters Related to Intelligence Activities and Investigations Arising Out of the 2016 Presidential Campaigns* (Washington DC, 12 May 2023).
- USA. *Hearings before the Committee on Foreign Relations*, US Senate, 113th Congress, 2nd Session.
- USA. US Defense Intelligence Agency, *Russia Military Power. Building a Military to Support Great Power Aspirations*: www.dia.mil/Portals/110/Images/News/Military_Powers_Publications/Russia_Military_Power_Report_2017.pdf
- USA. *Hearings Before the Subcommittee on European Affairs of the Committee on Foreign Relations*, US Senate, 104th Congress, 1st Session, April 27 and May 3 1995.
- USA. *Hearing before the Subcommittee on Central Asia and South Caucasus of the Committee on Foreign Relations*, US Senate, 107th Congress, Second Session, 27 June 2002.
- USA. *Hearings before the Committee on Foreign Relations*, US Senate. 110th Congress, 2nd Session, 17 September 2008.
- USA. *Hearings before the Committee on Foreign Relations*, US Senate, 113th Congress, 1st Session, 3 September 2013.
- USA. *Hearings before the Committee of the House of Representatives*, 113th Congress, 2nd Session, 8 May 2014.
- USA. Dale Vesser, "Defense Planning Guidance, FY 94-99":

nsarchive.gwu.ed/document/1825-national-security-archive-doc-07-fy-94-98

USA. E. Degen and M. Reardon, *Modern War in an Ancient Land. The United States Army in Afghanistan 2001-2014*, Vol. 1 (Washington DC: Center of Military History, United States Army, 2021).

USA. *House Republican Interim Report*, "A 'Strategic Failure:' Assessing the Administration's Afghanistan Withdrawal": https://foreignaffairs.house.gov/wp-content/uploads/2022/08/HFAC-Republican-Interim-Report-A-22Strategic-Failure22-Assessing-the-Administrations-Afghanistan-Withdrawal.pdf

US Department of State, *After Action Review on Afghanistan January 2020-August 2021* (Washington DC: March 2022).

IMF. "Russian Federation: Recent Economic Developments". IMF Staff Country Report No. 99/100, 22 September 1999: www.imf.org/en/Publications/CR/Issues/2016/12/30/Russia-Recent-Economic-Developments-3212

Craigmurray.org.uk/documents/

Wikileaks: Public Library of US Diplomacy. https://wikileaks.org/plusd/cables

https://bush41library.archives.gov

https://clinton.presidentiallibraries.us/

https://georgewbush-whitehouse.archives.gov/infocus/bushrecord

Memories and Diaries

A. Adamishin, *V raznye gody. Vneshnepoliticheskie ocherki* (Moscow: Ves' mir, 2016).

A. Adamishin, *Angliiskii divertisment* (Moscow: Khudozhestvennaya literatura, 2018).

M. Albright. www. millercenter.org/the-presidency/presidential-oral-histories/madeleine-k-albright-oral-history

C. Ashton, *And Then What* (London: Elliott and Thompson, 2023).

J. Attali, *Verbatim*, Vol. 3, Chronique des années 1988-1991 (Paris: Fayard, 1995).

P. Aven and A. Kokh, *Gaidar's Revolution: The Inside Act of the Economic Transformation of Russia* (London: Taurus, 2005).

Lt. General Barmyantsev interview, "Prishtinskii marsh-brosok rossiiskikh VDV", *Armeiskii vestnik*, 12 June 2019M.

M. Bell, *In Harm's Way. Bosnia: A War Reporter's Story* (London: Icon Books, 2012).

E. Bergbusch, "NATO Enlargement: Should Canada Leave NATO?", *International Journal*, Winter, 1997/1998, Vol. 53, No 1, Winter, 1997/1998.

Samuel Berger. Presidential Oral Histories, Miller Center, University of Virginia: https://millercenter.org/the-presidency/presidential-oral-histories/samuel-r-berger-oral-history

J. Biden, *Promise Me, Dad. A Year of Hope, Hardship, and Purpose* (London: Pan, 2018).

J. Bitterlich, "Reflections on 'The End of the Cold War?'", *Exiting the Cold War, Entering a New World*, ed. D. Hamilton and K. Spohr (Washington DC: Brookings, 2019).

J. Bitterlich, *Grenzgänger: Deutsche Interessen und Verantwortung in und für Europa: Erinnerungen eines Zeitzeugen* (Ibidem, 2021: Kindle edition).

J. Bolton, *The Room Where It Happened* (New York: Simon and Schuster, 2020).

J. Borgor, "We knew in 2011 Putin would attack Ukraine, says Bill Clinton", *Guardian*, 5 May 2023.

R. Braithwaite, "Hope Deferred: Russia from 1991 to 2021", *Survival*, Vol. 64, No 1, February 2022.

W. Burns, "How we Fool Ourselves on Russia", *New York Times*, 7 January 2017.

W. Burns, "How the US Russian Relationship Went Bad", *The Atlantic*, April 2019.

Burns, 14 June 2017: *PBS* Frontline Interviews: "Putin and the Presidents".

W. Burns, *The Back Channel. American Diplomacy in a Disordered World* (London: Hurst, 2021).

A. Campbell, *The Blair Years: Extracts from the Alastair Campbell Diaries* (London: Hutchinson, 2007).

A. Carter, *Inside the Five-Sided Box. Lessons From a Lifetime of Leadership in the Pentagon* (New York: Dutton, 2020).

A. Carter and W. Perry, *Preventive Defense. A New Security Strategy for America* (Washington DC: Brookings, 1999).

D. Chollet, *The Long Game. How Obama Defied Washington and Redefined America's Role in the World* (New York: Public Affairs, 2016).

W. Christopher. "Warren Christopher and Strobe Talbott Oral History Transcript", 15 April 2002 and 16 April 2002. University of Virginia, Miller Center. Personal Histories.

J. Cirincione. "Rumsfeld's Russian Assault", *Carnegie Endowment for International Peace* (21 February 2021): https://carnegieendowment.org/2001/02/21/rumsfeld-s-russian-assault-pub-628

R. Clarke, *Against All Enemies. Inside America's War on Terror* (New York: Free Press, 2004).

D. Fried, 21 June 2017: PBS Frontline Interviews: "Putin and the Presidents".

The Ambassadorial Series: Deans of US-Russia Diplomacy Transcript of the Ambassador James Collins.

H. Clinton, *Hard Choices* (New York: Simon and Schuster, 2014).

"Bill Clinton: I Tried to Put Russia on Another Path", Institute for Geopolitics, Economy and Security, *The Atlantic*, 10 April 2022.

W. Collins, www.nsarchive.gwu.edu/sites/default/files/pdf/ambassadorial_series_transcripts_-_collins.pdf

V. Dashichev, *Ot Stalina do Putina. Vospominaniya i razmyshleniya o proshlom, nastoyashchem i budushchem* (Moscow: Novyi khronograf, 2015).

(R. Dearlove) "MI6 regrets helping Vladimir Putin to win power, says ex-spy chief", *The Times*, 1 October 2018.

A. Demurenko, "Menya muchili somneniya", in E. Gus'kova, ed., *Nashi mirotvortsy na Balkanakh* (Moscow: Indrik, 2007).

C. Doyle, *Witness to War Crimes. The Memoirs of an Irish Peacekeeper in Bosnia* (Newbridge: Merrion, 2018).

R. Dumas, interview, *Tribune Libre*, 15 March 2022.

E. Edelman. Oral History, Miller Center, University of Virginia: https://millercenter.org/the-presidency/presidential-oral-histories/eric-edelman-oral-history

R. von Fritsch, *Russlands Weg als Botschafter in Moskau* (Berlin: Aufbau, 2022).

R. Gates, *Duty. Memoirs of a Secretary at War* (London: W. H. Allen, 2015).

J. Greenstock, *Iraq: The Costs of War* (London: Heinemann, 2016).

Interview, Goldberg and Welch, Department of Defense, 18 October 2004: httpss//history.defense. gov>Portals>oral_history

T. Graham interview: Ivan Grek: "US-Russian Relations under Bush and Putin", Collective Memory Project, Center for Presidential History, Southern Methodist University.

Hadley, *Frontline* interview, 27 July 2017: www.pbs.org/wgbh/frontline/interview/stephen-hadley/

"Hagel: The White House Tried To Destroy me", interview with *Foreign Policy*, 18 December 2015.

(Hall) Diplomatic Oral History Program, Churchill College, Cambridge:
https://archives.chu.cam.ac.uk/wp-content/uploads/sites/2/2022/01/Hall.pdf

(Heusgen) Interview with Merkel's Foreign Policy Adviser. "I Have Eliminated 'the West' From My Vocabulary." *Der Spiegel*, dated 23 September 2021.

Heusgen interview, "Ich wolte etwas Idealistisches machen", *Rheinische Post* online, 6 December 2020.

A. Kozyrev, *Firebird. The Elusive Fate of Russian Democracy* (Pittsburgh: University of Pittsburgh, 2019).

"Kudrin rasskazal o druzhbe s Putinym", *Lenta.ru*, 12 October 2020.

"Kudrin rasskazal o pereezde s Putinym v Moskvu v 1990-kh", *Lenta.ru*, 18 July 2021.

J. le Carré, *The Pigeon Tunnel. Stories from My Life* (London: Viking, 2016).

Dame A. Leslie. *British Diplomatic Oral History Project*, Churchill College archives.

Sir D. Logan. *British Diplomatic Oral History Project*, p. 62: https://archives.chu.cam.ac.uk/wp-content/uploads/sites/2/2022/01/Logan_David.pdf

"Interview with Fyodor Lukyanov", Ivan Grek: "US-Russian Relations under Bush and Putin", Collective Memory Project, Center for Presidential History, Southern Methodist University.

Sir Roderic Lyne, Britain's ambassador to Moscow: https://uc.web.ox.ac.uk/article/the-uc-interview-series-sir-roderic-lyne

M. McFaul, *From Cold War to Hot Peace. The Inside Story of Russia and America* (London: Penguin, 2019).

H. McMaster, *Battlegrounds. The Fight to Defend the Free World* (London: HarperCollins, 2020).

"Sir John Major Oral History", Miller Center, University of Virginia: https://millercenter.org/the-presidency/presidential-oral-histories/sir-john-major-oral-history

Meyer interview with *Diplomacy and Commerce*, 10 July 2019.

The Ambassadorial Series: Deans of U.S.-Russia Diplomacy Transcript of the Ambassador Thomas Pickering.

B. Perry, "From Hope to Hostility: US Relations with Putin's Russia", *At the Brink*: atthebrink.org/podcast/from-hope-to-hostility-us-relations-with-putin's-russia/

T. Pickering, www.nsarchive.gwu.edu/sites/default/files/pdf/ambassadorial_series_transcripts_-_pickering.pdf

C. L. Powell and Richard L. Armitage. Presidential Oral Histories. Miller Center, University of Virginia: https://millercenter.org/the-presidency/presidential-oral-histories/colin-l-powell-and-richard-l-armitage-oral-history

R. Prado, *Black Ops. The Life of a CIA Shadow Warrior* (New York: St Martin's Press, 2022).

E. Primakov, *Politik, Diplomat, Uchenyi. Evgenii Primakov* (Moscow: 'Vest-Konsalting', 2019).

E. Primakov, *Mirnoe pole politiki* (Moscow: Molodaya Gvardiya, 2006).

B. Rhodes, *The World As It Is. Inside the Obama White House* (London: Vintage, 2019).

C. Rice interview: Ivan Grek: "US-Russian Relations under Bush and Putin", Collective Memory Project, Center for Presidential History, Southern Methodist University.

C. Rice, *No Higher Honor: A Memoir of My Years in Washington* (New York: Simon and Schuster, 2011).

Karl Rove. Presidential Oral Histories. University of Virginia, Miller Center, Presidential Histories:
https://millercenter.org/the-presidency/
presidential-oral-histories/karl-rove-oral-history-part-ii

Rühe, "Opening NATO's Door", in *Open Door. NATO and Euro-Atlantic Security After the Cold War*, ed. D. Hamilton and K. Spohr (Washington DC: SAIS/Brookings) p. 218.
https://transatlanticrelations.org/wp-content/
uploads/2019/04/10-Ruhe.pdf

Rumsfeld television interview, 14 February 2001.

Rumsfeld interview, *CBS News*, 7 February 2011.

N. Sarkozy, *Le temps des combats* (Kindle, 2023).

D. Scheffer, *The Sit Room. In the Theater of War and Peace* (Oxford: Oxford University Press, 2019).

John Shalikashvili, Presidential Oral Histories, Bill Clinton, Miller Center, University of Virginia:
https://millercenter.org/the-presidency/
presidential-oral-histories/john-shalikashvili-oral-history

R. Sikorski, *Mission to Kyiv* (Warsaw: Znak, 2018).

W. Slocombe, *A Crisis of Opportunity. The Clinton Administration and Russia* (Ithaca: Cornell University Press, 2017).

J. Solana interview, 20 February 2022: www.epe.es/es/
politica/20220220/javier-solana-ucrania-otan-13263095

J. Steinberg, Presidential Oral Histories, Miller Center, University of

Virginia: https://millercenter.org/the-presidency/presidential-oral-histories/james-steinberg-oral-history

A. Torkunov, "Akademik ob akademike", in *Politik, Diplomat, Uchenyi Evgenii Primakov* (Moscow: 'Vest-Konsalting', 2019).

L. Tracey interview: *Kommersant*, 27 April 2023.

The Ambassador Series: Deans of US-Russian Diplomacy. Transcript of Alexander Vershbow Interview. National Security Archive. gwu.edu/media/23521/ocr

A. Vershbow, "Present at the Transformation: An Insider's Reflection on NATO Enlargement, NATO-Russia Relations, and Where We Go From Here": https://transatlanticrelations.org/wp-content/uploads/2019/04/18-Vershbow.pdf

Vershbow interview: Ivan Grek: "US-Russian Relations under Bush and Putin", Collective Memory Project, Center for Presidential History, Southern Methodist University.

K. Volker interview: Ivan Grek: "US-Russian Relations under Bush and Putin", Collective Memory Project, Center for Presidential History, Southern Methodist University.

J. Walker, "Enlarging NATO: The Initial Clinton Years": transatlanticrelations.org/wp-content/uploads/2019/04/12-Walker.pdf

Secondary Sources

V. Akopov, "Tramp reshil razvalit' Evrosoyuz", *Vzglyad.ru*, 6 July 2018.

A. Aksenenok, "Rossiya i Siriya: nyuansy soyuznicheskikh otnoshenii", 11 September 2020:
https://russiancouncil.ru/analytics-and-comments/analytics/rossiya-i-siriya-nyuansy-soyuznicheskikh-otnosheniy/

D. Allan, "The Minsk Conundrum: Western Policy and Russia's War in Eastern Ukraine", May 2020, Research Paper, Ukraine Forum, Chatham House, 2.

C. Altermatt, "The Stockholm Meeting of the CSCE Council", _journals_hels_4_1_article-p5_2preview (7).pdf

"Analiticheskaya zapiska 'Garantii nerasshireniya NATO. Pryamaya rech'", *fond razvitiiya grazhdanskogo obshchestva*, 19 January 2022.

R. Asmus, *Opening NATO's Door. How the Alliance Remade Itself for a New Era* (New York: Columbia University Press, 2002).

"Backstage at the NATO Summit", *Harper's Magazine*, December 1997.

T. Balmforth, "New US Ambassador to Russia Gets Frosty Reception", *RFE/RFL*, 18 January 2012.

J. Barnes, "The President and Foreign Affairs": https://ropercenter.cornell.edu/sites/default/files/2018-07/45015.pdf

L. Bassets, *Javier Solana. Revindicación de la política: veinte años de relaciones internacionales* (Madrid: Debate, 2010).

R. Benko, "Chuck Hegel Propels Barack Obama Into History", *Forbes*, 3 March 2014.

A. Bezrukov, O. Rebro and A. Sushentsov, *Donal'd Tramp: professional'nyi profil' novogo presidenta SShA* (Valdai, Moscow: January 2017).

R. Bingener and M. Wehner, *Die Moskau Connection. Das Schröder-Netzwerk und Deutschlands Weg in die Abhängigkeit* (Munich: Beck, 2023) pp. 203–204

R. Bonner, "War Crimes Panel Finds Croat Troops 'Cleansed' the Serbs", *New York Times*, 21 March 1999.

S. Borzyakov, "Rossiiskie voennye v Sirii reshili pyat' glavnykh zadach", *Vzglyad ru*, 30 September 2020.

J. Bransten, "Middle East: Rice Calls for a 'New Middle East'", *Radio Free Europe/Radio Liberty*, 25 July 2006.

D. Brinkley, "Democratic Enlargement: The Clinton Doctrine", *Foreign Policy*, 106, Spring 1997.

"British cabinet at odds over Nato pact with Russia", *Guardian*, 10 December 2001.

"Brosok v Prishtinu: kak general Kvashnin zastavil Zapad schitat'tsya s Rossiei", *Vesti.ru*, 9 January 2022.

"Zbigniew Brzezinski on the End of the Cold War", *New Atlanticist*, 4 November 2009.

D. Catsam, "Wilson and Bush: Unready Internationalists", *Origins: Current Events in Historical Perspective*, September, 2005.

E. Chernenko, "What Makes Putin So Popular At Home? His Reputation Abroad", *New York Times*, 16 March 2018.

E. Chernenko and G. Dudina, "Drug platezhom krasen: Kak Germaniya stala glavnym opponentom SShA v Evrope", *Kommersant*, 17 June 2020.

E. Chernenko, "Sorry Mr. Biden. Putin Honestly Could Not Care Less", *New York Times*, 16 June 2021.

C. Chivers and E. Schmitt, "Arms Airlift to Syrian Rebels Expands, with Aid from C.I.A.", *New York Times*, 24 March 2013.

C. Clarke, *Understanding the Baltic States. Estonia, Latvia and Lithuania Since 1991* (London: Hurst, 2023).

"Clinton, Lavrov push wrong re-set button on ties", *Reuters*, 6 March 2009.

Conradi, *Who Lost Russia? From the Collapse of the USSSR to Putin's War on Ukraine* (London: Oneworld, 2022).

M. Dobbs, "Enthusiasm for Wider Alliance Marked by Contradictions", *Washington Post*, 7 July 1995.

S. Erlanger, "NATO Offers Russia New Relationship but Without Any Veto", *New York Times*, 26 February 2002.

"Ex-NATO head says Putin wanted to join alliance early on in his rule", *Guardian*, 4 November 2021.

"A Fateful Error", *New York Times*, 5 February 1997.

"The Final Insult in the Bush-Cheney Marriage", *New York Times*, 10 October 2013.

"Five things you need to know about Russian Intelligence failures ahead of the invasion of Ukraine", *Washington Post*, 20 August 2022.

T. Friedman, "Clinton Keeping Foreign Policy on a Back Burner", *New York Times*, 8 February 1993.

"Gazprom at 15: Russia's gas monopoly remains an instrument of the state", *Financial Times*, 13 February 2008.

"Glava RSMD Andrei Kortunov vystupil protiv voennoi operatsii Rossii", *Krasnaya vesna*, 26 February 2022.

"Sergei Glaz'ev: federalizatsiya – uzhe ne ideya, a ochevidnaya neobkhodimost'", *Kommersant*, 6 February 2014.

M. Glenny, "Here We Go Again", *London Review of Books*, 9 March 1995.

"Agreement on the Settlement of Crisis in Ukraine - full text", *Guardian* (21 February 2014): www.theguardian.com/world/2014/feb/21/agreement-on-the-settlement-of-crisis-in-ukraine-full-text

J. Goldgeier, *Not Whether But When. The US Decision to Enlarge NATO* (Washington DC: Brookings, 1999).

J. Goldgeier, "Not when but who", *NATO Review*, 1 March 2002.

J. Goldgeier and M. McFaul, *Power and Purpose: US Policy Toward Russia After the Cold War* (Washington DC: Brookings, 2003).

A. Gurzu and J. Schatz, "Great Northern Gas War", *Politico*, 10 February 2016.

J. Guyer, "What Biden learned the last time Putin invaded Ukraine", *Vox*, 7 February 2022.

J. Haslam, "A Pipeline Runs Through It", *National Interest*, No 92, Nov–Dec. 2007, pp. 18–24.

J. Haslam, *Russia's Cold War. From the October Revolution to the Fall of the Wall* (New Haven: Yale, 2011).

J. Haslam, *Near and Distant Neighbours* (Oxford: Oxford University Press, 2015).

J. Haslam, "There Really Was an Afghan Trap", *H-Diplo*, 30 May 2022.

"President Václav Havel Interviewed by Jacques Rupnik", *Perspectives*, Summer 1994, No 3.

P. Healy, "Mindful of the Past [Hillary] Clinton Cultivates the Military", *New York Times*, 27 March 2007.

M. Hemingway, "The Curious Case of Stefan Halper, Longtime 'Zelig' Scandals Who Crossfired Trump", *RealClearInvestigations*, 8 March 2022.

D. Herszenhorn, "In Crimea, Russia Moved to Throw Off the Cloak of Defeat", *New York Times*, 24 March 2014.

G. Hewitt, "Some thoughts on Ronald Asmus' 'Little War that

Shook the World: Georgia, Russia and the Future of the West' (Palgrave, 2010)", *European Security*, Vol. 21, 2021, No 1.

R. Hunter, "The Ukraine Crisis: Why and What Now?", *Survival*, Vol. 64, No. 1, February 2022.

R. Hunter and S. Rogov, "NATO, Russia Can Get Far with Small Steps", *The RAND Blog*, 22 May 2002.

IMF, "A Project in Every Port", FINANCE & DEVELOPMENT, December 2012, Vol. 49, No. 4: www.imf.org/external/pubs/ft/fandd/2012/12/people.htm

"In Spat on NATO and Russia, Powell Fends off Rumsfeld", *New York Times*, 8 December 2001.

S. Ivanov, "As NATO Grows, So Do Russia's Worries", *New York Times*, 7 April 2004.

R. Kagan, "League of Dictators?", *Washington Post*, 30 April 2006.

R. Kaiser, "Don't Let This Russian Spook You", *Washington Post*, 25 February 2001.

I. Katchanovski, "The 'Snipers' Massacre' on the Maidan in Ukraine": https://papers.ssrn.com/sol3/papers.cfm?abstract_id=2658245

A. Kelin, "O rasshirenie NATO i interesakh bezopasnosti Rossii", *Evropeiskaya bezopasnost': sobytiya, otsenki, prognozy*, No. 12, June 2004.

M. Kennard, *Declassified UK*, 25 March 2022.

I. Klimin, *Rosiya i Ukraina: trudnyi put' k vzaimoponimaniyu (1990-2009)* (St Petersburg: Nestor, 2009).

D. Klion, "The Loud American", *The Baffler*, 11 June 2018.

"Kogda vse zastaivaemsya, zovut liberalov", *Kommersant*, 17 February 2021.

V. Krasheninnikova, "Rossii nuzhen Zakon o registratsii iinostrannykh agentov – kak v SShA", *Regnum*, 20 January 2020.

Krasheninnikova, "Tramp snimaet masku", *Literaturnaya gazeta*, No. 14 (6593), 12 April 2017.

S. La Franiere, "Russia's Putin Calls the Iraq War 'A Mistake,'" *Washington Post*, 18 March 2003.

S. Lamby, *Ernstfall – Regieren in Zeiten des Krieges* (Kindle, 2023).

D. Levin, *Meddling in the Ballot Box: The Causes and Effects of Partisan Electoral Interventions* (Oxford: Oxford University Press, 2020).

A. Little, "Moral Combat – NATO at War", *Panorama Special*, 12 March 2000; www.david-morrison.org.uk/kosovo/kosovo-lhto.pdf

"Libya's Pathway to Peace", *New York Times*, 14 April 2011.

J. Lloyd, "The Logic of Vladimir Putin", *New York Times* magazine, 19 March 2000.

"Naznachenie generala v Belyi dom predveshchaet sblizhenie s Kremlem", *Vzglyad.ru*, 18 November 2016.

"Obama: I Underestimated the Threat of Disinformation", *The Atlantic*, 7 April 2022.

"Oni sovsem strakh poteryali?", Patrushev interviewed in *Rossiiskya gazeta*, 27 March 2023.

"Putin ob''yavil 'spetsoperatsiyu' v Ukraine. Armiya Rossii podtverdila, chto nanosit udary po voennym ob''ektam v Ukraine", *Novaya gazeta*, 24 February 2022.

F. Lucas, "Exclusive: Documents Reveal Rush to Target Trump's National Security Pick in Obama's Waning Days as President", *The Daily Signal*, 7 July 2023.

F. Lukyanov, "What Russia Learned from the Iraq War", *Al-Monitor*, 18 March 2013.

M. Marginedas, "San Petersburgo y la mafia Tambov, los primeros tratos de Putin con el crimen organizado", *el Periódico de España*, 30 July 2022.

M. Mazzetti, "C.I.A. Study of Covert Aid Fueled Skepticism About Helping Syrian Rebels", *New York Times*, 14 October 2014.

P. Mellgard, "Kissinger: Putin is Not Stalin", *HuffPost*, 5 November 2014.

L. Mitchell, "Viewing Georgia, Without the Rose-Colored Glasses", *New York Times*, 15 September 2008.

V. Mukhin and I. Rodin, "Rossiya nachala svoyu blizhnevostochnuyu voinu", *Nezavisimaya gazeta*, 1 October 2015.

"NATO Enlargement and Russia: A Military Perspective", *Open*

Door. NATO and Euro-Atlantic Security After the Cold War, ed. D. Hamilton and K. Spohr (Washington DC: SAIS/Brookings).

M. Nizza, "Bush on Why Georgia Matters to Americans", *New York Times*, 15 August 2008.

J. O'Loughlin, G. Ó Tuathail and V. Kolossov, "'A Risky Westward Turn'? Putin's 9-11 Script and Ordinary Russians," *Europe-Asia Studies*, Vol. 56, No 1, (January 2004).

"Obrashchenie Prezidenta Rossiiskoi Federatsii", 24 February 2022: *kremlin.ru*.

"Opravdano li rasshirenie NATO (Osoboe mnenie Sluzhby vneshnei radzvedki Rossii)?", *Nezavisimaya gazeta*, 26 November 1993.

P. Ostellino, "Responsabilità politiche e mani sporche", *Corriere della Sera*, 6 September 2003.

A. Ostrovsky, "Dinner with the FT: Father of the Oligarchs", *Financial Times*, 23 November 2004.

"Other people's wars", *The Economist*, Vol. 352, No. 8130, 31 July 1999.

R. Parry, "A Shadow US Foreign Policy", *Consortiumnews*, 27 February 2014.

B. Pancevski, "Did Merkel Pave the Way for the War in Ukraine?", *Wall Street Journal*, 26 May 2023.

"Pravi zashchitit' svoikh", *Vzglyad*, 9 April 2014.

"The Premature Partnership", *Foreign Affairs*, March/April 1994.

"Pryamaya Linaya. 'Allo, "Komsomolka"? Srochno soedinite s Putinym!'", *Komsomol'skaya pravda*, 10 February 2000.

V. Putin interview with *Bild*, 18 September 2001.

Putin Speech, 18 March 2014: http://kremlin.ru/events/president/news/20603

Putin, "Rossiya i menyayushchii mir", *Moskovskie novosti*, 27 February 2012.

Putin, "A Plea for Caution from Russia", *New York Times*, 11 September 2013.

"'Putina v Kremle priglasil ya'. Byvshii glava upravdelami prezidenta Pavel Borodin o svoei rabote v 90-ee gody", *Lenta.ru*, 8 December 2015.

C. Rice, "Promoting the National Interest", *Foreign Affairs*, Vol. 79, No. 1 (January/February 2000).

P. Richter, "Russia Policy Under Review", *Los Angeles Times*, 12 December 2004.

"Rossiya i menyayushchii mir", *Moskovskie novosti*, 27 February 2012.

J. Risen, "Bosnia Reportedly Told Iran of US Spy", *Los Angeles Times*, 15 January 1997.

R. Romaniuk, "From Zelensky's 'surrender' to Putin's surrender: how the negotiations with Russia are going", *Ukrainskaya pravda*, 5 May 2022.

S. Rosenfeld, "A Timely Warning. The CIA Predicts a Blowup in Yugoslavia", *Washington Post*, 30 November 1990.

"Rossiya i menyayushchii mir", *Moskovskie novosti*, 27 February 2012E.

E. Rumer, *Russia and the Security of Europe*, (Washington DC: Carnegie Endowment for International Peace, 2016).

D. Ryurikov, *Vremena zverya. Novyi mirovoi poryadok. Arkhitektory raschelovechivaniya* (Moscow: Knizhnyi Mir, 2018).

G. Saratov. "Byvshii pomoshchnik Yeltsina ob"yasnil pochemu tot vybral Putina svoim preemnikom", "Shkola grazhdanskogo prosveshchenie', YouTube, 10 February 2021; also news.ru, 5 January 2022.

J. Scahill, "The Assassination Complex. Secret Military Documents Expose the Inner Workings of Obama's Drone Wars", *Intercept*, 15 October 2015.

M. Schwirtz, "NATO Signals Support for Ukraine in Face of Threat from Russia", *New York Times*, 16 December 2014.

E. Sciolino, "Albright's Audition", *New York Times* magazine, 22 September 1996.

E. Sciolino and T. Purdum, "Al Gore, One Vice President Who Is Eluding the Shadows", *New York Times*, 19 February 1995.

S. Sengupta and N. McFarquhar, "Vladimir Putin of Russia Calls for Coalition to Fight ISIS", *New York Times*, 27 September 2015.

J. Shifrinson, "Deal or No Deal? The End of the Cold War and the US Offer to Limit NATO Expansion", *International Security*, Vol. 40, No. 4, 2016.

P. Short, *Putin. His Life and Times* (London: Bodley Head, 2022).

"Sikorski: Stovarzyszenie UE-Ukraina warukowo możliwe v 2013 roku", *Fakt*, 10 December 2012.

K. Sivkov, "Ukraina: period poluraspada", *Voenno-promyshlennyi kur'er*, 17 March 2014.

G. Snodgrass, *Holding the Line. Inside Trump's Pentagon with Secretary Mattis* (New York: Sentinel, 2019).

V. Solov'ev, "Al'yans vnutri Al'yansa", *Nezavisimaya gazeta*, 15 March 2002.

Editorial, "Sovsem ne konets istorii. O fatal'nykh proschyota politiki SShA posle kholodnoi voiny", *Nezavisimaya gazeta*, 19 July 2022.

P. Sperry, "Secret Report: How CIA's John Brennan Overruled Dissenting Analysts Who Concluded Russia Favored Hillary", *RealClearInvestigations*, 24 September 2020.

P. Sperry, "FBI Chief Comey Misled Congress's 'Gang of 8' Over Russiagate, Lisa Page Memo Reveals': *RealClearInvestigations*, 9 June 2022.

"Surkov dal pervoe posle otstavki interv'yu. Chto on skazal i chto eto znachit?", BBC News, 26 February 2020: www.bbc.com/russian/news-51640715

"Todesschüsse in Kiew. Wer is für das Blutbad vom Maidanverantwortlich", "Monitor" No. 660 on *ARD*, 10 April 2014.

M. Trachtenberg, "The United States and the NATO Non-extension Assurances of 1990: New Light on an Old Problem?" *International Security*, 45:3 (2021) 162–203.

M. Troitsky, "Negotiating Russia's Status in Post-Soviet Eurasia", M. Troitsky and F. Hampson, *Tug of War: Negotiating Security in Eurasia*, (Waterloo, Canada: Centre for International Governance Innovation, 2017).

V. Trukhachev, "Merkel razveyala illyuzii Rossii naschet Germanii", *Vzglyad.ru*, 20.

T. Walker and A. Laverty, CIA Aided Kosovo Army All Along, *Sunday Times*, 12 March 2000A.

von Westphalen, "Nato-Osterweiterung: 'Das ist eine brillante Idee! Ein Geniestreich!'", 16 May 2018: *Telepolis* – www.heise.de/tp/features/Nato-Osterweiterung-Das-ist-eine-brillante-Idee-Ein-Geniestreich-4009027.html?seite=all

"Ukraina mogla by dvigat'sya putem evrointegratsii bystree – Sikorskii", *Obozrevatel*, 10 February 2012.

C. Whipple, "What the CIA knew before 9/11: New details", *Politico*, 13 November 2015.

C. Wiebes, *Intelligence and the War in Bosnia 1992–1995* (Münster-Hamberg-London: Lit Verlag, 2003).

M. Wines, "Threats and Responses: The Kremlin; Russia Softens Opposition to Military Action in Iraq", *New York Times*, 31 January 2003.

"Yeltsin Says NATO Is Trying to Split the Continent Again", *New York Times*, 6 December 1994.

Media

Armeiskii vestnik
Bellingcat
Economist
Financial Times
Forbes
Guardian
Independent
Komsomol'skaya pravda
Krasnaya vesna
Moscow News
Moskovskie novosti
Natsional'naya oborona
New York Times
Nezavisimaya gazeta
Novaya gazeta
Politico
Regnum
Repubblica
Reuters
Rossiiskaya gazeta
Twitter
Vzglyad
Wall Street Journal
Washington Post
YouTube

Documentaries

BBC TV: *Putin versus the West*, 1:1, "My Backyard".
BBC Radio 4: Gordon Corera, 1. "The Decision". *Shock and War: Iraq 20 Years on.*
BBC TV: *Putin, Russia and the West*, Season 1, Episode 1.

Additional information from interviews/corrections from

Dr Duncan Allan
Baroness Ashton
Joachim Bitterlich
Sir Tony Blair
Sir Rodric Braithwaite
Sir Tony Brenton
Sir Laurie Bristow
The Hon. Charles Clarke
Andrei Kelin
Bridget Kendall
Sir David Logan
Professor Mike McFaul
Lord Macdonald
Sir David Manning
Łukasz Pawłowski
Jonathan Powell
Professor Jeffrey Sachs
Sir John Sawers
Professor Marc Trachtenberg

Endnotes

1. Pax Americana

1. "Remarks on United States Foreign Policy", *U.S. Department of State* (8 August 2010): https://2009-2017.state.gov/secretary/20092013clinton/rm/2010/09/146917.htm
2. "Putin ob"yavil 'spetsoperatsiyu' v Ukraine. Armiya Rossii podtverdila, chto nanosit udary po voennym ob"ektam v Ukraine", *Novaya gazeta*, 24 February 2022.
3. CNBC TV Live: House Intelligence Committee holds a hearing on worldwide threats to the US – 8 March 2022. CIA said two days. Operational instructions found by Ukrainians, however, later suggested three: "At first we did not know the exact plans of the Russian Federation. But when we seized the staff documents from dead Russian commanders near Kyiv, we understood everything. It was all noted there – when and where the particular group should be, and elite paratroopers had to clear the government quarter in Kyiv within 72 hours. The same 72 hours that all our partners had told us about", one of Zelenskyy's top "security officers" explained in a conversation with Ukrainska Pravda: www.pravda.com.ua/eng/articles/2022/05/5/7344096/
4. Retrospective Western intelligence assessments: "Five things you need to know about Russian Intelligence failures ahead of the invasion of Ukraine", *Washington Post*, 20 August 2022.
5. Interview with David Ignatius, *Washington Post*, 23 February 2023.
6. Personal information.
7. R. Sikorski, "How did we get here and what do we do know?", *DGAP*, 11 October 2022: https://dgap.org/sites/default/files/dgap_lecture_radek_sikorski_oct_11_2022.pdf

8   E. Rumer, *Russia and the Security of Europe* (Washington DC: Carnegie Endowment for International Peace, 2016) p. 3.

9   Testimony from Fritz Ermarth, the Helsinki Commission, 27 July 2006: www.csce.gov/sites/helsinkicommission.house.gov/files/Ermarth%20Testimony.pdf; J. Haslam, *Near and Distant Neighbours* (Oxford: Oxford University Press, 2015) p. 271.

10 "Obrashchenie Prezidenta Rossiiskoi Federatsii", 24 February 2022: *kremlin.ru*

11 R. Gates, *Duty. Memoirs of a Secretary at War* (London: W.H. Allen, 2015) p. 157.

12 Speech, 18 March 2014: http://kremlin.ru/events/president/news/20603

13 Remarks at Texas AM University in College Station, Texas, 15 December 1992: https://bush41library.tamu.edu/archives/public-papers/5117

14 Memorandum for the President, "Thickening Our Defense Relationship with Russia's Armed Forces", 31 March 1993, Clinton Presidential Library: https://clinton.presidentiallibraries.us/items/show/57249

15 PBS, Frontline interview, 27 July 2017: www.pbs.org/wgbh/frontline/interview/stephen-hadley/

16 Editorial, "Sovsem ne konets istorii. O fatal'nykh proschyota politiki SShA posle kholodnoi voiny", *Nezavisimaya gazeta*, 19 July 2022.

17 W. Perry, "From Hope to Hostility: US Relations with Putin's Russia", *At the Brink*: atthebrink.org/podcast/from-hope-to-hostility-us-relations-with-putin's-russia/ Perry had vast cumulative experience since the Cuban missile crisis in 1962, reaching a high point as Under Secretary to Secretary of Defense Harold Brown in the Carter administration.

18 Quoted in Haslam, *No Virtue Like Necessity. Realist Thought in International Relations Since Machiavelli* (New Haven and London: Yale University Press, 2002) p. 31.

19 They would not certainly have been among the more junior diplomats, either, given Kortunov's elevated status: "Glava RSMD Andrei Kortunov vystupil protiv voennoi operatsii Rossii", *Krasnaya vesna*, 26 February 2022. As late as mid-February, he had been closeted at the British embassy with unofficial emissaries, including the former head of station in Moscow, later head of MI6, John Scarlett, desperately trying to avert disaster.

20 "Bill Clinton: I Tried to Put Russia on Another Path", Institute for Geopolitics, Economy and Security, *The Atlantic*, 10 April 2022.

21 W. Christopher: "Warren Christopher and Strobe Talbott Oral History Transcript", 15 April 2002 and 16 April 2002. University of Virginia, Miller Center. Personal Histories.

22 Ibid.

23 22 July 2022: *Fox News*, 23 July 2022.

24 R. Dumas, interview, *Tribune Libre*, 15 March 2022.

25 "A Fateful Error", *New York Times*, 5 February 1997.

26 "Opposition to NATO Expansion", *Arms Control Association*: www.armscontrol.org/act/1997-06/arms-control-today/opposition-nato-expansion

27 Memorandum to the President for the Vancouver Summit, 3–4 April 1993: Clinton Presidential Archive: https://clinton.presidentiallibraries.us/items/show/101269

28 "Zbigniew Brzezinski on the End of the Cold War", *New Atlanticist*, 4 November 2009.

29 M. Trachtenberg, "The United States and the NATO Non-extension Assurances of 1990: New Light on an Old Problem?" *International Security*, 45:3 (2021) 162–203. This is an exhaustive study of the documentation in German and in English. For the evidence from the Russian documents, available in translation: https://nsarchive.gwu.edu/briefing-book/russia-programs/2017-12-12/nato-expansion-what-gorbachev-heard-western-leaders-early

30 "Analiticheskaya zapiska 'Garantii nerasshireniya NATO. Pryamaya rech'", *fond razvitiiya grazhdanskogo obshchestva*, 19 January 2022.

31 J. Shifrinson, "Deal or no Deal? The End of the Cold War and the US Offer to Limit NATO Expansion", *International Security*, Vol. 40, No 4, 2016, pp. 22–23.

32 Quoted from Russian archives: E. Primakov, *Mirnoe pole politiki* (Moscow: Molodaya Gvardiya, 2006) p. 68.

33 Quoted in Shifrinson, "Deal or No Deal?...", p. 20.

34 Memcon, Meeting with Foreign Minister Primakov, 23 January 1997: US State Department Virtual Archive – *Talbott Papers* F2107-13804.

35 A. von Westphalen, "Nato-Osterweiterung: 'Das ist eine brillante Idee! Ein Geniestreich!'", 16 May 2018: *Telepolis* – www.heise.de/tp/features/Nato-Osterweiterung-Das-ist-eine-brillante-Idee-Ein-Geniestreich-4009027.html?seite=all

36 "Gespräch des Bundesministers Genscher mit dem amerikanischen Aussenminister Baker in Washington", *kten zur Auswärtigen Politik*

der Bundesrepublik Deutschland 1991 (Oldenbourg: De Gruyter, 2022) doc. 78.

37 "Drahtbericht des Botschafters von Ploetz, z.Z. Prag", 26 April 1991: ibid.

38 "Deutsch-französische Botschaftkonferenze in Weimar", 16/17 May 1991: ibid. docs. 165 and 166.

39 See H. Seton-Watson, *Eastern Europe Between the Wars 1918–1941* (Cambridge: Cambridge University Press, 1945).

40 "Gespräch des Bundeskanzlers Kohl mit dem sowjetischen Aussenminister Bessmertnych", 12 June 1991: ibid., doc. 197.

41 R. von Fritsch, *Russlands Weg als Botschafter in Moskau* (Berlin: Aufbau, 2022) p. 339.

42 Distinguished Voices Series with Robert B. Zoellick, Council on Foreign Relations, 10 September 2020.

43 "NATO Expansion: What Gorbachev Heard": https://nsarchive.gwu.edu/briefing-book/russia-programs/2017-12-12/nato-expansion-what-gorbachev-heard-western-leaders-early

44 *Diplomatische Dokumente der Schweitz*, 1991, ed. S. Zala et al. (Bern: Dodis, 2022) doc. 16.

45 Created in 1815 by the reactionary monarchies of Austria, Russia and Prussia, to hold the line by policing the European states system against dangers to the established order from republicanism.

46 R. Dumas interview, *Tribune Libre*, 15 March 2022.

47 Memcon, Mitterrand and Bush, 5 July 1992: George H. W. Bush Presidential Library – https://bush41library.tamu.edu/archives/memcons-telcons

48 "Defense Planning Guidance, FY 1994–1999", 18 February 1992: nsarchive.gwu.ed/document/18215-national-security-archive-doc-07-fy-94-98 [sic]

49 8 March 1990: J. Attali, *Verbatim*, Vol. 3, *Chronique des années 1988–1991* (Paris: Fayard, 1995) p. 440.

50 "Interview with The Honorable Robert E. Hunter , 2011": https://tile.loc.gov/storage-services/service/mss/mfdip/2011/2011hun01/2011hun01.pdf, p. 179

51 M. Dobbs, "Enthusiasm for Wider Alliance Marked by Contradictions", *Washington Post*, 7 July 1995.

52 Attali, *Verbatim*, p. 441.

53 W. Christopher: "Warren Christopher and Strobe Talbott Oral History Transcript", 15 April 2002 and 16 April 2002. University of Virginia, Miller Center. Personal Histories.

54 W. Slocombe, *A Crisis of Opportunity. The Clinton Administration and Russia* (Ithaca: Cornell University Press, 2017) p. 80.
55 Acknowledged in retrospect by Yevgeny Primakov, once head of foreign intelligence, later foreign minister: Primakov, *Minoe pole politiki*, p. 170.
56 "Drahtbericht des Botschafters Blech, Moskau", 14 February 1991: *Akten zur Auswärtigen Politik der Bundesrepublik Deutschland, 1991* (Oldenbourg: De Gruyter, 2022) doc. 56. See also Haslam, "Attaining Baltic Independence: In Search of a Helping Hand", in C. Clarke, *Understanding the Baltic States. Estonia, Latvia and Lithuania Since 1991* (London: Hurst, 2023) pp. 49–60.
57 "Vorlage des Ministerialdirektors Chrobog für Bundesminister Genscher", 9 April 1991: *Akten zur Auswärtigen Politik der Bundesrepublik Deutschland 1991*, doc. 123.
58 "President Václav Havel Interviewed by Jacques Rupnik", *Perspectives*, Summer 1994, No 3, p. 5.
59 Memcon, 22 October 1991: *George Bush Presidential Library*.
60 Former Foreign Minister Jan Kavan, 20 November 2021: www.transform-network.net/en/blog/article/jan-kavan-not-giving-in-to-pressure-from-the-powerful-inspires-respect-giving-unwanted-lessons-mak/ [sic]
61 C. Altermatt, "The Stockholm Meeting of the CSCE Council", _journals_hels_4_1_article-p5_2preview (7).pdf. I have taken the liberty of making the English sound less stilted.
62 Remarks made at Texas AM University in College Station, Texas, 15 December 1992: www. bush41library.tamu.edu/archives/public-papers/5117
63 Eric Edelman Oral History, Miller Center, University of Virginia: https://millercenter.org/the-presidency/presidential-oral-histories/eric-edelman-oral-history
64 Presidential Review Directive/NSC-36: US Policy Toward Central and Eastern Europe", 6 December 1993: www. clinton.presidentiallibraries.us/items/show/12774. The story behind the drafting is to be found In D. Brinkley, "Democratic Enlargement: The Clinton Doctrine", *Foreign Policy*, 106, Spring 1997, pp. 110–127.
65 L. Panetta, "Interview with L. Panetta", *Frontline Nightline*: www.pbs.org/wgbh/pages/frontline/shows/clinton/interviews/panetta2.html
66 Lake memorandum: "Meeting with President Yeltsin", 3–4 April 1993, Vancouver" – Clinton Presidential Archive: https://clinton.presidentiallibraries.us/items/show/101269

67 Slocombe, *A Crisis of Opportunity*, p. 78.
68 Quoted in J. Barnes, "The President and Foreign Affairs": https://ropercenter.cornell.edu/sites/default/files/2018-07/45015.pdf
69 T. Friedman, "Clinton Keeping Foreign Policy on a Back Burner", *New York Times*, 8 February 1993.
70 Interview with Jeffrey Sachs, 3 April 2023, *passim*. Sachs had previously worked sorting out the Bolivian national debt on behalf of Jim Baker, US Secretary of State, whose family, it turned out, owned much of it. Also IMF, "A Project in Every Port", FINANCE & DEVELOPMENT, December 2012, Vol. 49, No. 4: www.imf.org/external/pubs/ft/fandd/2012/12/people.htm
71 *Nezavisimaya gazeta*, 16 December 1992.
72 A. Kozyrev, *Firebird. The Elusive Fate of Russian Democracy* (University of Pittsburgh Press, 2019) p. 191.
73 Ibid., p. 194.
74 Ibid., p. 195.
75 Memorandum to the President from Lake, "Meeting with President Yeltsin, 3–4 April 1993, Vancouver: Clinton Presidential Library: https://clinton.presidentiallibraries.us/items/show/101269
76 Kozyrev, *Firebird*, p. 195.
77 Ibid., pp. 193–194.
78 Talbott, Oral Histories, Clinton Presidency, Miller Center, University of Virginia: https://millercenter.org/the-presidency/presidential-oral-histories/strobe-talbott-oral-history-2010.
79 Warren Christopher: "Warren Christopher and Strobe Talbott Oral History Transcript", 15 April 2002 and 16 April 2002. University of Virginia, Miller Center. Personal Histories.
80 Ibid.
81 G. Stephanopoulos, "Interview with George Stephanopoulos", *Frontline Nightline*: www.pbs.org/wgbh/pages/frontline/shows/clinton/interviews/stephanopoulos.html
82 According to *Institutional Investor* (13 January 2006), "after years of litigation, Harvard, Shleifer and others agreed to pay at least $31 million to settle a lawsuit brought by the US government. Harvard had been charged with breach of contract, Shleifer and an associate, Jonathan Hay, with conspiracy to defraud the US government".
83 W. Burns, *The Back Channel. American Diplomacy in a Disordered World* (London: Hurst, 2021) p. 238. Burns witnessed this as US ambassador to Russia.

84 Editorial, "Sovsem ne konets istorii. O fatal'nykh proschyota politiki SShA posle kholodnoi voiny", *Nezavisimaya gazeta*, 19 July 2022.
85 IMF, "A Project in Every Port", FINANCE & DEVELOPMENT, December 2012, Vol. 49, No. 4: https://www.imf.org/external/pubs/ft/fandd/2012/12/people.htm
86 *Financial Times*, 24 July 2018.

2. Russia Elbowed Out

1 Here Genscher is outlining his government's position: "Gespräch des Bundesministers Genscher mit dem französischen Aussenminister Dumas und dem spanischen Aussenminister Fernández Ordóñez in Paris", 11 October 1991: *Akten zur Auswärtigen Politik der Bundesrepublik Deutschland 1991* (Oldenbourg: De Gruyter, 2022) doc. 343.
2 *NATO's Future: Problems, Threats, and US Interests. Hearings before the Subcommittee on European Affairs of the Committee on Foreign Relations*, US Senate, 104th Congress, 1st Session, p. 2.
3 J. Bitterlich, "Reflections on 'The End of the Cold War?'", p. 489.
4 E. Bergbusch, "NATO Enlargement: Should Canada Leave NATO?", *International Journal*, Winter, 1997/1998, Vol. 53, No 1, Winter, 1997/1998, p. 9.
5 "Interview with The Honorable Robert E. Hunter, 2011": https://tile.loc.gov/storage-services/service/mss/mfdip/2011/2011hun01/2011hun01.pdf, p. 175.
6 V. Rühe, "Opening NATO's Door", in *Open Door. NATO and Euro-Atlantic Security After the Cold War*, ed. D. Hamilton and K. Spohr (Washington DC: SAIS/Brookings) p. 218. https://transatlanticrelations.org/wp-content/uploads/2019/04/10-Ruhe.pdf
7 Ibid., p. 222.
8 Clinton Presidential records, NSC Cables, September 1993.
9 Rühe, "Opening NATO's Door", in *Open Door*.
10 D. Waller, "Infighting Over NATO Expansion", *Time*, 14 July, 1997.
11 Quoted in J. Anderson, "The Tarnoff Affair", *AJR*, March 1994: https://ajrarchive.org/Article.asp?id=1255&id=1255
12 M.R. Gordon, "Christopher, in Unusual Cable, Defends State Dept.", *New York Times* (16 June 1993): www.nytimes.com/1993/06/16/world/christopher-in-unusual-cable-defends-state-dept.html. For William Safire's brutal accusation of monumental incompetence on

Christopher's part: *Chicago Tribune*, 4 June 1993: www.chicagotribune.com/news/ct-xpm-1993-06-04-9306040032-story.html

13 Quoted in R. Asmus, *Opening NATO's Door. How the Alliance Remade Itself for a New Era* (New York: Columbia University Press, 2002) p. 29.

14 Presidential Oral Histories, Clinton Administration, Miller Center, University of Virginia: https://millercenter.org/the-presidency/presidential-oral-histories/james-steinberg-oral-history

15 For an authoritative study of NATO's unique status: R. Osgood, *NATO. The Entangling Alliance* (Chicago: Chicago University Press, 1962).

16 Director of Central Intelligence, NIE 15-90, *Yugoslavia Transformed*, 18 October 1990: www.cia.gov/readingroom/docs/DOC_0000254259.pdf

17 S. Rosenfeld, "A Timely Warning. The CIA Predicts a Blowup in Yugoslavia", *Washington Post*, 30 November 1990.

18 Sir Peter Hall. *Diplomatic Oral History Program*, Churchill College, Cambridge: https://archives.chu.cam.ac.uk/wp-content/uploads/sites/2/2022/01/Hall.pdf

19 Numbers cited by Kohl: "Gespräch des Bundeskanzlers Kohl mit dem französische Staatspresidenten Mitterrand", 18 September 1991: *Akten zur Auswärtigen Politik der Bundesrepublik Deutschland 1991*, doc. 315.

20 J. Bitterlich, *Grenzgänger: Deutsche Interessen und Verantwortung in und für Europa: Erinnerungen eines Zeitzeugen* (Ibidem, 2021: Kindle edition) 2652–2653.

21 Gespräch des Bundeskanzlers Kohl mit dem amerikanischen Präsidenten Bush in Washington", 16 September 1991: *Akten zur Auswärtigen Politik der Bundesrepublik Deutschland 1991*, doc. 309.

22 "Gespräch des Bundeskanzlers Kohl mit dem französische Staatspräsidenten Mitterrand", 18 September 1991: *Akten zur Auswärtigen Politik der Bundesrepublik Deutschland 1991*, doc. 315.

23 UN Archives, Yugoslavia, Series S-1086, Box 105, File 3: https://search.archives.un.org/uploads/r/united-nations archives/2/9/e/29 e15ee9aba4dc34f845511205f02b2681efa44e021bddf2ac8ea5ed3a43a31 d/S-1086-0105-03-00003.pdf

24 Gespräch des Bundesminister Genscher mit dem amerikanischen Aussenminister Baker in Moskau", 11 September 1991: *Akten zur Auswärtigen Politik der Bundesrepublik Deutschland 1991*, doc. 301.

25 UN Archives. Yugoslavia, Series S-1086, Box 105, File 3: https://search.archives.un.org/uploads/r/united-nations archives/2/9/e/29

e15ee9aba4dc34f845511205f02b2681efa44e021bddf2ac8ea5ed3a43a31 d/S-1086-0105-03-00003.pdf

26 M. Bell, *In Harm's Way. Bosnia: A War Reporter's Story* (London: Icon Books, 2012) p. 49.

27 Ibid., p. 3. This is a commonplace among British diplomats who served in Europe; also M. Glenny, "Here We Go Again", *London Review of Books*, 9 March 1995. The demands of the social chapter were seen as economically burdensome. Tony Blair, however, heading the Labour Party, later accepted it since it neutralised trades union resentment at his otherwise pro-capitalist policies. So the price was not worth paying anyway.

28 B. Boutros-Ghali, *Mes années à la maison de verre* (Paris: Fayard, 1999) p. 65.

29 Presidential Oral Histories: www. millercenter.org/the-presidency/presidential-oral-histories/madeleine-k-albright-oral-history

30 UN, *International Tribunal for the Prosecution of Persons Responsible for Serious Violations of International Humanitarian Law Committed in the Territory of the former Yugoslavia since 1991. Bosnia Judgement*, 24 March 2016, pp. 1079–1080

31 C. Doyle, *Witness to War Crimes. The Memoirs of an Irish Peacekeeper in Bosnia* (Newbridge: Merrion, 2018) p. 124.

32 Meyer interview with *Diplomacy and Commerce*, 10 July 2019.

33 Interview, Goldberg and Welch, Department of Defense, 18 October 2004: httpss//history.defense. gov>Portals>oral_history

34 https://vk.com/wall-177432219_75755?lang=en

35 Interview, "Prishtinskii marsh-brosok rossiiskikh VDV", *Armeiskii vestnik*, 12 June 2019.

36 L. Bassets, *Javier Solana. Revindicación de la política: veinte años de relaciones internacionales* (Madrid: Debate, 2010).

37 A. Adamishin, *V raznye gody. Vneshnepoliticheskie ocherki* (Moscow: Ves' mir, 2016) p. 240.

38 Adamishin (London) to Yeltsin (Moscow), 17 September 1995: A. Adamishin, *Angliiskii divertisment* (Moscow: Khudozhestvennaya literatura, 2018) p. 112.

39 Kozyrev, *Firebird. The Elusive Fate of Russian Democracy*, pp. 158–159.

40 For the lack of secret intelligence and its consequences: C. Wiebes, *Intelligence and the War in Bosnia 1992–1995* (Münster-Hamberg-London: Lit Verlag, 2003).

41 M. Albright. www. millercenter.org/the-presidency/presidential-oral-histories/madeleine-k-albright-oral-history. She was not wrong. The

Europeans "should not expect that the United Nations divert its indispensable resources to intervene in a conflict in Europe at the expense of other conflicts in Africa, in Asia, or in Latin America": Boutros-Ghali, *Les années*, p. 74. But, of course, none of these countries was a permanent member of the Security Council.

42 Boutros-Ghali, *Les années*, p. 76.
43 Ibid., p. 78.
44 E. Sciolino and T. Purdum, "Al Gore, One Vice President Who Is Eluding the Shadows", *New York Times*, 19 February 1995.
45 The most vivid and detailed account can be found in D. Scheffer, *The Sit Room. In the Theater of War and Peace* (Oxford: Oxford University Press, 2019). Scheffer was Senior Adviser and Counsel to the US Permanent Representative to the United Nations, Madeleine Albright, the leading proponent of direct action using force.
46 Boutros-Ghali, *Les années*, p. 157. The administration via the *New York Times*, blamed it on the UN: ibid., p.160.
47 Ibid., p. 180.
48 H. Jackson, *Guardian*, 19 March 2011.
49 Boutros-Ghali, *Les années*, p. 109.
50 J. Risen, "Bosnia Reportedly Told Iran of US Spy", *Los Angeles Times*, 15 January 1997.
51 R. Bonner, "War Crimes Panel Finds Croat Troops 'Cleansed' the Serbs", *New York Times*, 21 March 1999.
52 *Wilson Center*. https://digitalarchive.wilsoncenter.org/assets/media_files/000/027/073/27073.pdf
53 NSC, "Russia, NATO and the Two January Summits", 29 September 1993: https://clinton.presidentiallibraries.us/items/show/118449
54 "Retranslation of Yeltsin letter on NATO expansion", *National Security Archive* (15 September 1993): https://nsarchive.gwu.edu/document/16376-document-04-retranslation-yeltsin-letter
55 In November 1993, according to head of Russian foreign intelligence, the SVR, Yevgeny Primakov, "We had absolutely reliable evidence that strategic military planning at NATO headquarters includes the 'worst case' with the use of nuclear weapons…" – Primakov, *Minnoe pole politiki* pp. 164–165.
56 Lunch with Mitterrand, 8 March 1990: Attali, *Verbatim*, p.443.
57 Attali, *Verbatim*, Vol. 3.
58 J. Bitterlich, "Reflections on 'The End of the Cold War?'", *Exiting the Cold War, Entering a New World*, ed. D. Hamilton and K. Spohr (Washington DC: Brookings, 2019) pp. 484–485.

59 "Your January Trip to Europe", Christopher to Clinton, 22 December 1993: https://clinton.presidentiallibraries.us/items/show/101271
60 Talbott to Peter Tarnoff, 18 February 1993: *Talbott Papers* – F2017-13804.
61 Talbott to Summers, 26 February 1993: ibid., F2017-13804.
62 A. Carter and W. Perry, *Preventive Defense. A New Security Strategy for America* (Washington DC: Brookings, 1999) p. 24.
63 John Shalikashvili, Presidential Oral Histories, Bill Clinton, Miller Center, University of Virginia: https://millercenter.org/the-presidency/presidential-oral-histories/john-shalikashvili-oral-history.
64 A. Carter, *Harvard Crimson*, 3 March 2022.
65 S. Jacobs, "For Ashton Carter, a perennial search for balance", *Boston Globe* (4 February 2015): www.bostonglobe.com/news/nation/2015/02/04/ashton-carter-savvy-tactician-independent-thinker/zKndB5RZVF38mq8Foe1B7I/story.html
66 In conversation with Conquest not long after the trip. But no one could tell it like he did.
67 "NATO Enlargement and Russia: A Military Perspective", *Open Door. NATO and Euro-Atlantic Security After the Cold War*, ed. D. Hamilton and K. Spohr (Washington DC: SAIS/Brookings), p. 554; https://transatlanticrelations.org/wp-content/uploads/2019/04/Open-Door_full.pdf
68 His position as ambassador in Canada became extremely uncomfortable after Russia seized Crimea, not least because of the size of the Ukrainian diaspora in his host country. In response Mamedov continued to insist that "normally the more tense the situation becomes the more active discussion becomes". 21 June 2014: https://torontovka.com/news/canada/18991230/19767.html
69 Clinton Presidential Records, NSC Cables, 3 September 1993.
70 National Security Archive: https://nsarchive.gwu.edu/document/16144-document-30-memorandum-boris-yeltsin
71 National Security Archive: https://nsarchive.gwu.edu/briefing-book/russia-programs/2018-03-16/nato-expansion-what-yeltsin-heard, doc. 8.
72 "Secretary Christopher's meeting with President Yeltsin, 10/22/93", Moscow National Security Archive: https://nsarchive.gwu.edu/document/16380-document-08-secretary-christopher-s-meeting
73 *Politik, Diplomat, Uchenyi. Evgenii Primakov* (Moscow: 'Vest-Konsalting', 2019) pp 267–268.

74 Primakov, *Minnoe pole politiki*, pp. 164–165.
75 "Opravdano li rasshirenie NATO (Osoboe mnenie Sluzhby vneshnei radzvedki Rossii)?", *Nezavisimaya gazeta*, 26 November 1993.
76 Primakov, *Minnoe pole politiki*, p. 165.
77 "The Brussels Summit Declaration": www.nato.int/cps/en/natohq/official_texts_24470.htm
78 J. Deparle, *New York Times* magazine, 20 August 1995.
79 "PFP and Central and Eastern Europe", 26 January 1994: Memorandum for the President, the Vice President and Lake – https://clinton.presidentiallibraries.us/items/show/57563. Although later written for the record, she will have impressed her opinions on the president in person during the Prague visit.
80 J. Goldgeier, "Not when but who", *NATO Review*, 1 March 2002.
81 Memcon, The President's Meeting with Czech leaders, 11 January 1994: https://nsarchive.gwu.edu/document/16383-document-11-president-s-meeting-czech
82 R. Asmus, *Opening NATO's Door. How the Alliance Remade Itself for a New Era* (New York: Columbia University Press, 2002) p. 66.
83 J. Walker, "Enlarging NATO: The Initial Clinton Years": transatlanticrelations.org/wp-content/uploads/2019/04/12-Walker.pdf
84 Ibid., p. 10.
85 Warren Christopher: "Warren Christopher and Strobe Talbott Oral History Transcript", 15 April 2002 and 16 April 2002. University of Virginia, Miller Center. Personal Histories.
86 Samuel Berger, Presidential Oral Histories, Miller Center, University of Virginia: https://millercenter.org/the-presidency/presidential-oral-histories/samuel-r-berger-oral-history
87 James Steinberg, Presidential Oral Histories, Miller Center, University of Virginia: https://millercenter.org/the-presidency/presidential-oral-histories/james-steinberg-oral-history
88 Warren Christopher: "Warren Christopher and Strobe Talbott Oral History Transcript", 15 April 2002 and 16 April 2002. University of Virginia, Miller Center. Personal Histories.
89 Walker, "Enlarging NATO: The Initial Clinton Years", p. 9.
90 James Steinberg, Presidential Oral History, Miller Center, University of Virginia: https://millercenter.org/the-presidency/presidential-oral-histories/james-steinberg-oral-history
91 A. Vershbow, "Present at the Transformation: An Insider's Reflection on NATO Enlargement, NATO-Russia Relations, and Where We

Go From Here": https://transatlanticrelations.org/wp-content/uploads/2019/04/18-Vershbow.pdf, p. 430.

92 Warren Christopher: "Warren Christopher and Strobe Talbott Oral History Transcript", 15 April 2002 and 16 April 2002. University of Virginia, Miller Center. Personal Histories.

93 Walker, "Enlarging NATO: The Initial Clinton Years", p. 7.

94 Goldgeier, "Not when but who", *NATO Review*, 1 March 2002.

95 Primakov to Talbott, Memcon, 6 March 1997: *Talbott Papers* – F2017-13804.

96 P. Healy, "Mindful of the Past [Hillary] Clinton Cultivates the Military", *New York Times*, 27 March 2007.

97 For French opposition: ibid.

98 The Ambassadorial Series: Deans of US-Russia Diplomacy Transcript of the Ambassador Thomas Pickering: www. nsarchive.gwu.edu/sites/default/files/pdf/ambassadorial_series_transcripts_-_pickering.pdf

99 Telegram dated 9 December 1994: W. Burns, *The Back Channel. American Diplomacy in a Disordered World* (London: Hurst, 2021) pp. 91–92.

100 D. Logan, *British Diplomatic Oral History Project*, p. 62: https://archives.chu.cam.ac.uk/wp-content/uploads/sites/2/2022/01/Logan_David.pdf

101 Francis Richards, *British Diplomatic Oral History Project*, p. 22: https://archives.chu.cam.ac.uk/wp-content/uploads/sites/2/2022/01/Richards.pdf

102 Bitterlich, *Grenzgänger*, p. 3092.

103 Ibid., p. 3104.

104 Bitterlich, *Reflections*, p. 488.

105 Bitterlich, *Grenzgänge*, p. 3105.

106 Ibid., p. 3116.

107 Ibid., p. 3147.

108 James Steinberg, Presidential Oral History, Miller Center, University of Virginia: https://millercenter.org/the-presidency/presidential-oral-histories/james-steinberg-oral-history

109 Ibid.

110 Record of the meeting, 19 October 1994: *Talbott Papers* – F2017-13804.

111 Record of the meeting, 20 October 1994: ibid.

112 "Yeltsin Says NATO Is Trying to Split the Continent Again", *New York Times*, 6 December 1994.

113 "Gore-Yeltsin Discussions", no date: *Talbott Papers* - F 2017-13804.

114 "Declassified Documents Concerning NATO", *Clinton Digital Library*, Expansion: https://clinton.presidentiallibraries.us/items/show/57563

115 Quoted in I. Klimin, *Rossiya i Ukraina: trudnyi put' k vzaimoponimaniyu (1990–2009)* (St Petersburg: Nestor, 2009) pp. 11–12.

116 *Nezavisimaya gazeta*, 3 February 2000.

117 These formed part of the much feared forward based systems that so worried Soviet military planners: Haslam, *The Soviet Union and the Politics of Nuclear Weapons in Europe, 1969–87* (Ithaca: Cornell University Press, 1990).

118 *Rossiya-Ukraina 1990-2000. Dokumenty i materialy*. Vol. 2 1996-2000 (Moscow: Mezhdunarodnye otnosheniya, 2001) docs. 192–196.

119 *Pravda Ukrainy*, 21 July 1994.

120 A. Wilson, *The Ukrainians: Unexpected Nation* (New Haven and London: Yale, 2022).

121 Memorandum to the Secretary, 11 December 1994: *Talbott Papers*: F-2017-13804.

122 "From Hope to Hostility: US Relations with Putin's Russia", *At the Brink*: atthebrink.org/podcast/from-hope-to-hostility-us-relations-with-putin's-russia/

123 J. Goldgeier, *Not Whether But When. The US Decision to Enlarge NATO* (Washington DC: Brookings, 1999) pp. 75–76.

124 "From Hope to Hostility: US Relations with Putin's Russia", *At the Brink*: atthebrink.org/podcast/from-hope-to-hostility-us-relations-with-putin's-russia/

125 *NATO's Future: Problems, Threats, and US Interests*. Hearings Before the Subcommittee on European Affairs of the Committee on Foreign Relations, US Senate, 104th Congress, 1st Session, April 27 and May 3 1995, pp. 11–16.

126 "Clinton-Kuchma Summit", 2 December 1994: *Talbott Papers* – F2107-13804.

127 *NATO's Future: Problems, Threats, and US Interests*. Hearings Before the Subcommittee on European Affairs of the Committee on Foreign Relations, US Senate, 104th Congress, 1st Session, April 27 and May 3 1995, pp. 11–16.

3. Western Europe Caves In

1 NATO EXPANSION: PLANS UNDERWAY. Eur A/S Holbrooke, Budapest, 25 February 1995. Clinton Presidential Library.

2 J. le Carré, *The Pigeon Tunnel. Stories from My Life* (London: Viking, 2016) p. 149.

3   Primakov, *Minnoe pole politiki*, p. 165.
4   Memcon, Yeltsin-Clinton meeting, 21 March 1997: *Talbott Papers* – F-2017-13804.
5   Karl Rove interview: University of Virginia, Miller Center, Presidential Histories: https://millercenter.org/the-presidency/presidential-oral-histories/karl-rove-oral-history-part-ii
6   A. Kelin, "O rasshirenie NATO i interesakh bezopasnosti Rossii", *Evropeiskaya bezopasnost': sobytiya, otsenki, prognozy*, No. 12, June 2004, p. 5.
7   *Los Angeles Times*, 1 March 2009. The information appeared in the Dutch report on the Srebrenica massacre: *Guardian*, 22 April 2002.
8   The detailed investigation by the Russian deputy commander of UNPROFOR in Sarajevo threw doubt on the assumption that this was a Serb attack. He went public with his findings, which resulted in his brisk repatriation. It was not what everyone wanted to hear: A. Demurenko, "Menya muchili somneniya", in E. Gus'kova, ed., *Nashi mirotvortsy na Balkanakh* (Moscow: Indrik, 2007) pp. 61–65. But Akashi, responsible for UN operations in Bosnia, reported as much to Boutros-Ghali, who in turn briefed Christopher: Boutros-Ghali, *Les années*, p. 216.
9   Talbott to Secretary of State, 15 September 1995: *Talbott Papers* – F2017-13804.
10 Mid-September 1995: Adamishin, *Angliiskii divertisment*, pp. 113–114.
11 Ibid., p. 112.
12 Adamishin, *V raznye gody. Vneshnepoliticheskie ocherki*, pp. 415–417.
13 The term used by Adamishin: ibid., p. 115.
14 Telegram, 14 April 1995: Istituto Luigi Sturzo, *Archivio Giulio Andreotti*, NATO Series, Box 176, Subseries 1, Folder 11.
15 Burns, *The Back Channel*, p. 98.
16 Meeting with Rifkind, London, 13 January 1997: *Talbott Papers* – F-2017-13804.
17 Memcon with Chirac, 14 January 1997: *Talbott Papers* – F-2017-13804.
18 Memcon with Kohl, 15 January 1997: ibid.
19 The Secretary's Meeting with John Major, 19 February 1997: ibid.
20 Adamishin, *Angliiskii divertisment*, p. 170.
21 Memcon with Primakov, 6 March 1997: *Talbott Papers* – F2017-13804.
22 Memcon: Morning Meeting with Russian President Yeltsin, 21 March 1997: Clinton Presidential Library.
23 "Sir John Major Oral History", Miller Center, University of Virginia:

    https://millercenter.org/the-presidency/presidential-oral-histories/sir-john-major-oral-history
24 A. Ostrovsky, "Dinner with the FT: Father of the Oligarchs", *Financial Times*, 23 November 2004.
25 https://economics.rabobank.com/publications/2013/september/the-russian-crisis-1998/
26 G. Saratov. "Byvshii pomoshchnik Yeltsina ob"yasnil pochemu tot vybral Putina svoim preemnikom", "Shkola grazhdanskogo prosveshchenie', YouTube, 10 February 2021; also news.ru, 5 January 2022.
27 The Ambassadorial Series: Deans of US-Russia Diplomacy Transcript of the Ambassador James Collins: www.nsarchive.gwu.edu/sites/default/files/pdf/ambassadorial_series_transcripts_-_collins.pdf
28 *Vechernyaya Moskva*, 25 June 2014.

4. NATO Goes to War

1 Clinton-Yeltsin Memcon, 20 June 1999: https://clinton.presidentiallibraries.us/items/show/101606
2 Camera dei Deputati. Senato della Repubblica. XVI Legislatura. Doc XX111. N6. *Commissione Parlamentare di Inchiesta Sull'Affare Telekom-Serbia* (istituita con legge 21 maggio 2002, n.99), footnote, p. 75.
3 "Serbs question Hurd's role in helping the regime", *Guardian*, 2 July 2001.
4 Testimony from Stefano Sannino, then head of the secretariat of under-secretary for foreign affairs Piero Farsino: Camera dei Deputati…*Commissione Parlamentare*, p. 545. Also, P. Ostellino, "Responsabilità politiche e mani sporche", *Corriere della Sera*, 6 September 2003.
5 T. Walker and A. Laverty, CIA Aided Kosovo Army All Along, *Sunday Times*, 12 March 2000; Allan Little, "Moral Combat – NATO at War", *Panorama Special*, 12 March 2000; www.david-morrison.org.uk/kosovo/kosovo-lhto.pdf
6 Albright's words: E. Sciolino, "Albright's Audition", *New York Times* magazine, 22 September 1996.
7 Albright (Washington DC) to US embassy (Moscow), 26 January 1999: Talbott Papers - F-2017-13804.
8 J. Greenstock, *Iraq: The Costs of War* (London: Heinemann, 2016) p. 65.
9 R. Hunter, "The Ukraine Crisis: Why and What Now?", *Survival*, Vol. 64, No1, February 2022.

10 Bitterlich, *Grenzgänger*, p. 2732.
11 Sandy Berger, Presidential Oral Histories, Clinton Presidency, Miller Center, University of Virginia: www. millercenter.org/the-presidency/presidential-oral-histories/samuel-r-berger-oral-history
12 "Other people's wars", *The Economist*, Vol. 352, No. 8130, 31 July 1999.
13 During the onslaught the Americans targeted a building in the Chinese embassy where personnel were aiding and abetting the Serbs: www.theguardian.com/theobserver/1999/nov/28/focus.news1. According to an unpublished memoir, Jiang Zemin, former president of China, acknowledged that the building sheltered Serbian military intelligence units: https://wikileaks.org/gifiles/docs/26/2602908_china-serbia-nato-kosovo-chinese-embassy-in-belgrade-hid.html
14 Primakov, *Minnoe pole politiki*, pp. 294–297.
15 Clinton-Yeltsin Telcon, 19 April 1999: *Clinton Presidential Library* – https://clinton.presidentiallibraries.us/items/show/101600
16 Briefing by Talbott.
17 "Brosok v Prishtinu: kak general Kvashnin zastavil Zapad schitat'tsya s Rossiei", *Vesti.ru*, 9 January 2022; and interview with Barmyantsev, "Prishtinskii marsh-brosok rossiiskikh VDV", *Armeiskii vestnik*, 12 June 2019.
18 "Pristina An Airport Too Far", 13 April 2018: https://medium.com/lapsed-historian/pristina-an-airport-too-far-42e010e19f12; "1999 god. Kak Rossiiskii batal'on zakhvatil aerodrom v stolitse Kosovo Prishtine...": www.youtube.com/watch?v=wJeI3E1NK0Y
19 The Ambassadorial Series: Deans of US-Russia Diplomacy Transcript of the Ambassador James Collins: www.nsarchive.gwu.edu/sites/default/files/pdf/ambassadorial_series_transcripts_-_collins.pdf
20 V. Dashichev, *Ot Stalina do Putina. Vospominaniya i razmyshleniya o proshlom, nastoyashchem i budushchem* (Moscow: Novyi khronograf, 2015) p. 339. Dashichev was formerly a colonel in military intelligence. For his role in the abandonment of East Germany and my connection to him: J. Haslam, *Russia's Cold War* (Yale: Yale University Press, 2011).
21 "Russian Federation: Recent Economic Developments". IMF Staff Country Report No. 99/100, 22 September 1999: www.imf.org/en/Publications/CR/Issues/2016/12/30/Russia-Recent-Economic-Developments-3212
22 This was recorded by CBC cameraman Brian Kelly: "Backstage at the NATO Summit", *Harper's Magazine*; *Washington Post*, 11 July 1997 and *New York Times*, 11 July 1997.
23 Secretary's Meeting with Chernomyrdin, 20 February 1997.

24 Memcon. President Yeltsin's meeting with President Clinton, 19 November 1999: Clinton Presidential Library: https://clinton.presidentiallibraries.us/items/show/57569

25 P. Aven and A. Kokh, *Gaidar's Revolution: The Inside Act of the Economic Transformation of Russia* (London: Taurus, 2005) p. 67.

26 *Jamestown Foundation Monitor*, Vol. 7, No 115, 27 August 2000; and personal information. The British knew all of this courtesy of its consul, Barbara Fry. She was consul when Putin was still there, in 1992. She was sent back after he became president to fill in the details and did so with considerable aplomb: interview with Sir David Manning, 6 September 2022.

27 Her archive is online at Miami University, Ohio, thanks to the late Karen Dawisha, who pioneered studies of Russian corruption: www.miamioh.edu/cas/academics/centers/havighurst/additional-resources/putins-russia/salye-commission-landing/index.html. Her study of the subject was rejected for publication by Cambridge University Press, fearing a legal barrage from those named and shamed: obituary, *Guardian*, 20 April 2018.

28 "Kudrin rasskazal o druzhbe s Putinym", *Lenta.ru*, 12 October 2020 and "Kudrin rasskazal o pereezde s Putinym v Moskvu v 1990-kh", ibid., 18 July 2021.

29 " 'Putina v Kremle priglasil ya'. Byvshii glava upravdelami prezidenta Pavel Borodin o svoei rabote v 90-ee gody", *Lenta.ru*, 8 Decembeer 2015. The account by K. Smirnov and A. Bagrov, appears to be inaccurate regarding Chubais ("Tridtsad' tri putinskikh bogatyrya", *Kommersant vlast'*, 13 November 2001).

30 More of Kudrin's recollections: "Kogda vse zastaivaemsya, zovut liberalov", *Kommersant*, 17 February 2021.

31 https://agentura.co.uk/profile/federalnaja-sluzhba-bezopasnosti-rossii-fsb/departament-kontrrazvedyvatelnyh-operacij-dkro/. An incoming British diplomat moved into his apartment – protected by several security front doors, including one of steel. He and his wife arranged a small party. They left to buy something they needed and when, on return, he opened the freezer to hand out the ice cream, he found it had been melted in the microwave. Every so often someone would gain entry and rearrange books on the shelves. In the end, before asking for his removal, in an act of blatant intimidation they drove a car behind theirs, bumper to bumper through the streets of Moscow.

32 J. Lloyd, "The Logic of Vladimir Putin", *New York Times* magazine,

19 March 2000. Much has now been superseded, but this is the best summary of the time.
33 Memcon. President Yeltsin's meeting with President Clinton, 19 November 1999: Clinton Presidential Library.

5. Face to Face with Putin

1 "Why it took the UK a long time to become a Russia hawk", *Financial Times*, 24 April 2022. For more detail: Intelligence and Security Committee of Parliament, *Russia*, HC 362, 21 July 2020 – https://isc.independent.gov.uk/wp-content/uploads/2021/01/20200721_HC632_CCS001_CCS1019402408-001_ISC_Russia_Report_Web_Accessible.pdf
2 D. Catsam, "Wilson and Bush: Unready Internationalists", *Origins: Current Events in Historical Perspective*, September, 2005: https://origins.osu.edu/history-news/wilson-and-bush-unready-internationalists?language_content_entity=en
3 "Pryamaya Linaya. 'Allo, "Komsomolka"? Srochno soedinite s Putinym!", *Komsomol'skaya pravda*, 10 February 2000.
4 Stenographic transcript in *Komsomol'skaya pravda*, 11 February 2000.
5 V. Chudowsky and T. Kuzio, "Does public opinion matter in Ukraine? The case of foreign policy", *Communist and Post-Communist Studies*, Vol. 36, No. 3, pp. 273–290.
6 Dale Vesser, "Defense Planning Guidance, FY 94-99": nsarchive.gwu.ed/document/1825-national-security-archive-doc-07-fy-94-98.
7 "The Premature Partnership", *Foreign Affairs*, March/April 1994, p. 80.
8 Much later quoted by SVR director Sergei Naryshkin in interview with former KGB officer Nikolai Dolgopolov, deputy editor, *Rossiiskaya gazeta*, 19 June 2023: http://svr.gov.ru/smi/2023/06/razvedka-znaet-tochno.htm
9 "Putin preduprezhdal Ukrainu ob ugroze NATO v 2000", *Vzglyad.ru*, 18 April 2023.
10 Interview, 15 November 2022.
11 Also, "MI6 regrets helping Vladimir Putin to win power, says ex-spy chief", *The Times*, 1 October 2018.
12 Intelligence and Security Committee of Parliament, *Russia*, HC 632, 21 July 2020, p. 21.
13 Personal information. Also, in 2006 Marc Doe, Christopher Pirt, Paul Crompton and Andy Fleming, all under diplomatic cover, were all caught in flagrante delicto with a fake brick containing a communications device that looked like it was inspired by an American

B movie: O. Dmitrieva, "Shpionskii kamen'", *Vzglyad.ru*, 23 January 2006.
14. Telcon with British Prime Minister Blair, 13 October 1999: *Clinton Papers*.
15. Interview, 22 August 2022.
16. Blair, *A Journey*, Kindle edition, 2011, 5120.
17. Comment from adviser Andrei Kortunov: www.youtube.com/watch?v=uPyflrCehYM
18. *Kommersant*, 20 January 2022.
19. "Ex-NATO head says Putin wanted to join alliance early on in his rule", *Guardian*, 4 November 2021.
20. BBC Radio 4, "Breakfast with Frost", 5 March 2000.
21. "Putin's Progress", Briefing notes for John Sawers, the Prime Minister's diplomatic adviser, prior to his visit to Washington DC: UK National Archives, *Prem49/2352*.
22. M. Kennard, *Declassified UK*, 25 March 2022.
23. Karl Rove interview: University of Virginia, Miller Center, Presidential Histories: https://millercenter.org/the-presidency/presidential-oral-histories/karl-rove-oral-history-part-ii
24. Colin L. Powell and Richard L. Armitage Oral History: Miller Center, University of Virginia - https://miller-center.org/the-presidency/presidential-oral-histories/colin-l-powell-and-richard-l-armitage-oral-history.
25. "US Politics: Bush Cabinet", 4 January 2001, Notes for Sawer: ibid.
26. "The Final Insult in the Bush-Cheney Marriage", *New York Times*, 10 October 2013.
27. Audio diary, quoted by biographer Jon Meacham: www.latimes.com/nation/politics/la-na-elder-bush-criticizes-cheney-rumsfeld-in-new-biography-20151105-story.html For the biography, J. Meacham, *Destiny and Power; the American Odyssey of George Herbert Walker Bush* (2015, Kindle).
28. This was Phil Petersen. His chief source, Vyacheslav Dashichev, was also my own: Haslam, *Russia's Cold War*, pp. 381–382.
29. Chief of Staff at No. 10 Jonathan Powell (Washington DC) to Blair (London), 16 January 2001: *Prem49/2352*.
30. Cowper-Coles, "Contact Group Dinner", 11 January 2001: ibid.
31. Personal information obtained at the time.
32. Television interview, 14 February 2001: https://carnegieendowment.org/2001/02/21/rumsfeld-s-russian-assault-pub-628

33. J. Darby, "Briefing for John Sawers' Visit to Washington", 12 January 2001: *Prem49/2352*.
34. S. La Franiere, "Russia's Putin Calls the Iraq War 'A Mistake'," *Washington Post*, 18 March 2003.
35. Manning (Brussels) to Jones Parry (London) 19 January 2001: *Prem49/2352*.
36. R. Hunter, The Ukraine Crisis: Why and What Now?", *Survival*, 64, No 1, February 2022, p. 13.
37. C. Rice, "Promoting the National Interest", *Foreign Affairs*, Vol. 79, No 1 (January/February 2000), pp. 57 and 59.
38. Goldgeier, "Not who but when", *NATO Review*, 1 March 2002.
39. R. Kaiser, "Don't Let This Russian Spook You", *Washington Post*, 25 February 2001.
40. S. Cambone, director of research, Institute for National Strategic Studies, National Defense University. Testimony to the House Armed Services Committee, 28 June 2000: *Prem49/2352*.
41. Blair, *A Journey*, 5153.
42. Clark's address to the Commonwealth Club in San Francisco, 3 October 2007.
43. Gordon Corera, 1. "The Decision". BBC, Radio 4, "Shock and War: Iraq 20 Years on".
44. Address to the Commonwealth Club in San Francisco, 3 October 2007.
45. Rueda interview: Corera, 1. "The Decision". BBC, Radio 4, "Shock and War: Iraq 20 Years on".
46. Interview with Daniel Fried, 21 June 2017: PBS Frontline Interviews: "Putin and the Presidents".
47. *Frontline* interview, 27 July 2017.
48. C. Rice, *No Higher Honor: A Memoir of My Years in Washington* (New York: Simon and Schuster, 2011) p. xxx.
49. Rice, *No Higher Honor*, p. 62.
50. Putin interview with *Bild*, 18 September 2001.
51. R. Prado, *Black Ops. The Life of a CIA Shadow Warrior* (New York: St Martin's Press, 2022) p. 232.
52. Interview, 14 April 2022: Ivan Grek: "US-Russian Relations under Bush and Putin", Collective Memory Project, Center for Presidential History, Southern Methodist University.
53. "NATO-Russia: Talking Points for Workshop on International Terrorism", 3 October 2000: *Talbott Papers*.
54. 19 February 2000: *Talbott Papers*.

55 "Background. US Policy on Russia". Briefing notes for Sawer's talks with the incoming administration: *Prem49/2352*.
56 C. Whipple, "What the CIA knew before 9/11: New details", *Politico*, 13 November 2015.
57 Prado, *Black Ops. The Life of a CIA Shadow Warrior*, pp. 292–293.
58 *The 9/11 Commission Report. Final Report of the National Commission on Terrorist Attacks Upon the United States* (Washington DC: USGPO, 2004) p. 222.
59 R. Clarke, *Against All Enemies. Inside America's War on Terror* (New York: Free Press, 2004) pp. 237–238.
60 Putin's interview with *Bild*, 18 September 2001.
61 Testimony of Jonathan Powell, adviser to Prime Minister Blair, 6 September 2022.
62 V. Solov'ev, "Al'yans vnutri Al'yansa", *Nezavisimaya gazeta*, 15 March 2002.
63 Documentary, *Putin, Russia and the West*, Season 1, Episode 1.
64 J. O'Loughlin, G. Ó Tuathail and V. Kolossov, "'A Risky Westward Turn'? Putin's 9-11 Script and Ordinary Russians," *Europe-Asia Studies*, Vol. 56, No 1, (January 2004) 3–34.
65 "Balancing Military Assistance and Support for Human Rights in Central Asia", *Hearing before the Subcommittee on Central Asia and South Caucasus of the Committee on Foreign Relations, United States Senate, 107th Congress, Second Session*, 27 June 2002.
66 Ibid.
67 How "often" is not disclosed, but it is not impossible that they included such events as Vilnius in 1991. For Karimov: E. Degen and M. Reardon, Modern War in an Ancient Land. The United States Army in Afghanistan 2001-2014, Vol. 1 (Washington DC: Center of Military History, United States Army, 2021) p 55, footnote 101.
68 Ibid., p. 75.
69 Documentary, *Putin, Russia and the West*. For the half billion: Craig Murray (Tashkent) to FCO (London), 18 March 2003: Craigmurray.org.uk/documents/
70 Interview with *ARD* in Vladivostok, 17 November 2014.
71 Testimony, Sir Roderic Lyne, Britain's ambassador to Moscow: https://uc.web.ox.ac.uk/article/the-uc-interview-series-sir-roderic-lyne
72 Testimony, 31 October 2001: House of Lords, Session 2001-02, 11th Report, Select Committee on the European Union, *The European*

Policy on Security and Defence, Vol. II: Evidence (London: HMSO, 2002) p. 83.
73 *New York Times*, 11 November 2001.
74 Ibid., 8 December 2001.
75 11th Valdai meeting, 24 October 2014: www.kremlin.ru/events/president/news/46860
76 Blair, *A Journey*, p. 5153.
77 *New York Times*, 24 November 2001.
78 S. Erlanger, "NATO Offers Russia New Relationship but Without Any Veto", *New York Times*, 26 February 2002.
79 "In Spat on NATO and Russia, Powell Fends off Rumsfeld", *New York Times*, 8 December 2001.
80 Ibid.
81 Rumsfeld interview, *CBS News*, 7 February 2011.
82 At a performance of *The Nutcracker* during the Bush visit, Rice and Ivanov slipped away at Ivanov's suggestion to attend a modern dance performance. Their presence was captured on film and can be seen online: www.bbc.co.uk/iplayer/episode/b01b3hkm/putin-russia-and-the-west-1-taking control. It prompted humourous gossip among British diplomats.
83 Final Communiqué. Meeting of the North Atlantic Council, 18 December 2001: www.nato.int/docu/pr/2001/p01-171e.htm
84 Testimony from Jonathan Powell, 6 September 2022. He witnessed one such awkward occasion.
85 "British cabinet at odds over Nato pact with Russia", *Guardian*, 10 December 2001.
86 Erlanger, "NATO Offers Russia New Relationship but Without Any Veto", *New York Times*, 26 February 2002.
87 Bitterlich, *Grenzgänger*, p. 3192.
88 R. Hunter and S. Rogov, "NATO, Russia Can Get Far with Small Steps", *The RAND Blog*, 22 May 2002.
89 The Ambassadorial Series: Deans of US-Russia Diplomacy Transcript of the Ambassador James Collins: https://nsarchive.gwu.edu/sites/default/files/pdf/ambassadorial_series_transcripts_-_collins.pdf
90 M. Troitsky, "Negotiating Russia's Status in Post-Soviet Eurasia", M. Troitsky and F. Hampson, *Tug of War: Negotiating Security in Eurasia*, (Waterloo, Canada: Centre for International Governance Innovation, 2017) p. 20.
91 Interview, 19 July 2021: Ivan Grek: "US-Russian Relations under

Bush and Putin", Collective Memory Project, Center for Presidential History, Southern Methodist University.

92 Interview, 19 March 2021: ibid.
93 Testimony of the Russian ambassador in London, Andrei Kelin, 2 June 2022. He was Russia's Deputy Permanent Representative to NATO from 1998 to 2003 under Sergei Kislyak, having headed the Department of Overall European Co-operation at the Foreign Ministry in Moscow.
94 Kelin interview, 2 June 2022.
95 Jonathan Powell interview, 6 September 2022. This is also the recollection of others involved.
96 Gordon Corera, 1. "The Decision". BBC, Radio 4, "Shock and War: Iraq 20 Years on". BBC Radio 4: www.bbc.co.uk/programmes/m001kocg
97 Ibid.
98 Ibid.; also, G. Corera, "How the search for Iraq's secret weapons fell apart": www.bbc.co.uk/news/world-64914542
99 https://nsarchive2.gwu.edu/NSAEBB/NSAEBB129/index.htm. This also contains the original NIE and the US Senate, Select Committee on Intelligence, *Report of the US Intelligence Community's Prewar Intelligence Assessments on Iraq*, 108th Congress. For the Russian reaction: CRSR Report, "Russia and the War in Iraq", April 14, 2003 RS21462; and Ambrosio, "The Russo-American Dispute over the Invasion of Iraq". For the lie, inter alia, see the memoirs of Britain's permanent representative to the United Nations, Jeremy Greenstock, cited below, who asserted on his own knowledge that both the British and American Governments knew full well that Saddam Hussein had no weapons of mass destruction and whose book was therefore held up from publication by Whitehall for several years.
100 J. Greenstock, *Iraq: the Cost of War* (London: Heinemann, 2016) pp. 127–128.
101 A. Campbell, *The Blair Years: Extracts from the Alastair Campbell Diaries* (London: Hutchinson, 2007) p. 694. Campbell paraphrasing Putin.
102 M. Wines, "Threats and Responses: The Kremlin; Russia Softens Opposition to Military Action in Iraq", *New York Times*, 31 January 2003.
103 Blair, *A Journey*, pp. 5131–5142.
104 11th Valdai Meeting: www.kremlin.ru/events/president/news/46860
105 Campbell, *The Blair Years*, p. 293.

106 *Lenta.ru*, 30 April 2003.
107 Campbell, *The Blair Years*, pp. 694–695; also, Sir David Manning interview: 6 September 2022.
108 *Sky News*, 30 December 2022.
109 Interview, 19 March 2021: Ivan Grek: "US-Russian Relations under Bush and Putin", Collective Memory Project, Center for Presidential History, Southern Methodist University.
110 Graham interviewed on 19 June 2007: PBS Frontline Interviews – Putin and the Presidents".
111 W. Burns, "How the US Russian Relationship Went Bad", *The Atlantic*, April 2019.
112 Blair, *A Journey*, p. 5153.
113 S. Ivanov, "As NATO Grows, So Do Russia's Worries", *New York Times*, 7 April 2004.
114 Burns, "How the US Russian Relationship Went Bad", *The Atlantic*, April 2019.
115 Interview, 19 March 2021: Ivan Grek: "US-Russian Relations under Bush and Putin", Collective Memory Project, Center for Presidential History, Southern Methodist University.
116 Craig Murray (Tashkent) to FCO (London), 18 March 2003: Craigmurray.org.uk/documents/
117 "Balancing Military Assistance and Support for Human Rights in Central Asia", *Hearing before the Subcommittee on Central Asia and South Caucasus of the Committee on Foreign Relations, United States Senate, 107th Congress, Second Session, 27 June 2002*.

6. Régime Change

1 J. Bransten, "Middle East: Rice Calls for a 'New Middle East'", *Radio Free Europe/Radio Liberty*: www.rferl.org/a/1070088.html
2 Gordon Corera: 1. "The Decision". BBC, Radio 4, "Shock and War: Iraq 20 Years on". Transmission was delayed. In the meantime Bush had on further advice decided to withhold the message.
3 J. Haslam, "There Really Was an Afghan Trap", *H-Diplo*, 30 May 2022: https://networks.h-net.org/group/28443/search?search=%22There%20Really%20Was%20an%20Afghan%20Trap%22%2C%20%20
4 L. Mitchell, "Viewing Georgia, Without the Rose-Colored Glasses", *New York Times*, 15 September 2008.
5 M. Nizza, "Bush on Why Georgia Matters to Americans", *New York Times*, 15 August 2008.

6   Interview, 19 March 2021: Ivan Grek: "US-Russian Relations under Bush and Putin", Collective Memory Project, Center for Presidential History, Southern Methodist University.

7   "John Herbst", *US–Ukraine Business Council*: www.usubc.org/site/biographies/john-herbst

8   P. Richter, "Russia Policy Under Review", *Los Angeles Times*, 12 December 2004.

9   The Ambassadorial Series: Deans of US-Russia Diplomacy. Transcript of the Alexander Vershbow interview: https://nsarchive.gwu.edu/briefing-book/russia-programs/2021-06-16/us-ambassadors-to-russia-interviewed

10 Interview with Rice, 14 April 2022 – Ivan Grek: "US-Russian Relations under Bush and Putin", Collective Memory Project, Center for Presidential History, Southern Methodist University.

11 J. Bransten, "Middle East: Rice Calls for a 'New Middle East'", *Radio Free Europe/Radio Liberty*, 25 July 2006: https://www.rferl.org/a/1070088.html

12 Speech, Valdai conference, 24 October 2013.

13 *Democracy In Retreat In Russia, Hearings before the Committee on Foreign Relations, United States Senate, 109th Congress, First Session, February 17, 2005* (Washington DC: USGPO, 2005).

14 F. Lukyanov, "What Russia Learned from the Iraq War", *Al-Monitor*, 18 March 2013.

15 R. Coalson, "Fifteen Years After Her Murder, Journalists Say Politkovskaya's Fears Have Been Realized", *Radio Free Europe/Radio Liberty*, 6 October 2021.

16 Quoted by D. Remnik, "Echo in the Dark", *New Yorker*, 15 September 2008.

17 M. Marginedas, "San Petersburgo y la mafia Tambov, los primeros tratos de Putin con el crimen organizado", *el Periódico de España*, 30 July 2022.

18 Testimony to the Intelligence and Security Committee of Parliament during the Russia enquiry in February 2019: Intelligence and Security Committee of Parliament, *Russia*, HC 632, 21 July 2020, p. 12.

19 "Spain details its strategy to combat the Russian mafia": Telegram from the US embassy in Madrid to various officials in Washington DC and the Justice Department representative in Moscow, 8 February 2010: www.theguardian.com/world/us-embassy-cables-documents/247712

20. Kremlin trasnscripts: http://kremlin.ru/events/president/transcripts/24034
21. [S.] Hadley, *Frontline* interview, 27 July 2017: www.pbs.org/wgbh/frontline/interview/stephen-hadley/
22. Burns, *The Back Channel*, p. 233.
23. Putin, "Meeting with war correspondents", 13 June 2023: http://en.kremlin.ru/events/president/news/71391
24. Interview with Rice, 14 April 2022: Ivan Grek: "US-Russian Relations under Bush and Putin", Collective Memory Project, Center for Presidential History, Southern Methodist University.
25. Kremlin press conference, 14 February 2008: *Pravda.ru*.
26. Ashe (Warsaw) to European Political Collective and Secretary of State, 12 December 2008: https://wikileaks.org/plusd/cables/08WARSAW1409_a.html
27. Lynn Tracey interview: *Kommersant*, 27 April 2023.
28. US embassy, France, to NATO, 26 February 2008: https://wikileaks.org/plusd/cables/08PARIS338_a.html
29. N. Sarkozy, *Les temps des combats* (Kindle, August 2023) p. 54.
30. Burns, *Back Channel*, pp. 237–238.
31. Witnessed by Simon Macdonald, foreign policy adviser to Prime Minister Gordon Brown.
32. Sarkozy, *Les temps des combats*, p. 55.
33. US representatives in Berlin to JCS, DIA, Secretary of State, et al., 5 June 2008: https://wikileaks.org/plusd/cables/08BERLIN744_a.html. For an objective assessment of the Georgian war from the Abkhazian side, see G. Hewitt, "Some thoughts on Ronald Asmus' 'Little War that Shook the World: Georgia, Russia and the Future of the West' (Palgrave, 2010)", *European Security*, Vol. 21, 2021, No 1, pp. 128–137. If Wikileaks were reading this, so were the Russians.
34. Volker (NATO) to CIA et al., 14 August 2008: https://wikileaks.org/plusd/cables/08USNATO290_a.html
35. Volker (NATO) to CIA et al., 14 August 2008: ibid.
36. Interview: Sir Laurie Bristow, 20 July 2023.
37. In conversation with Bill Clinton. J. Borger reporting from Washington DC: *Guardian*, 5 May 2023.
38. *The Ambassador Series: Deans of US-Russian Diplomacy*. Transcript of Alexander Vershbow Interview. National Security Archive. gwu.edu/media/23521/ocr

39 J. Solana interview, 20 February 2022: www.epe.es/es/politica/20220220/javier-solana-ucrania-otan-13263095
40 *Russia's Aggression Against Georgia: Consequences and Responses*. Hearings before the Committee on Foreign Relations, US Senate. 110th Congress, 2nd Session, 17 September 2008.
41 http://moscow.usembassy.gov/beyrleint082508.html
42 NATO to CIA et al., 8 August 2008: https://wikileaks.org/plusd/cables/08USNATO276_a.html; and NATO to CIA et al., 11 August 2008: https://wikileaks.org/plusd/cables/08USNATO281_a.html
43 NATO to CIA et al., 13 August 2008: https://wikileaks.org/plusd/cables/08USNATO287_a.html
44 Denmark Copenhagen to NATO, 14 August 2008: https://wikileaks.org/plusd/cables/08COPENHAGEN436_a.html
45 Interview with Stephen Hadley: *Frontline* interview, 27 July 2017: www.pbs.org/wgbh/frontline/interview/stephen-hadley/
46 *Russia's Aggression Against Georgia*.
47 Volker (NATO) to CIA et al., 14 August 2008: https://wikileaks.org/plusd/cables/08USNATO290_a.html
48 https://uc.web.ox.ac.uk/article/the-uc-interview-series-sir-roderic-lyne
49 Ashe (Warsaw) to European Political Collective and Secretary of State, 12 December 2008: https://wikileaks.org/plusd/cables/08WARSAW1409_a.html
50 Moscow to Secretary of State et al, 9 September 2008: https://wikileaks.org/plusd/cables/08MOSCOW2701_a.html
51 Ibid., p. 42.
52 "Strasbourg / Kehl Summit Declaration", *North Atlantic Treaty Organization* (4 April 2009): www.nato.int/cps/en/natolive/news_52837.htm
53 W. Burns, "How we Fool Ourselves on Russia", *New York Times*, 7 January 2017.
54 M. McFaul, *From Cold War to Hot Peace. The Inside Story of Russia and America* (London: Penguin, 2019) pp. 130–131.
55 Thomas Graham, Director of Russian Affairs and then Senior Director, National Security Council, interview 19 June, 2017: PBS Frontline Interviews: "Putin and the Presidents". Graham never indicated the date of the comment.

7. Obama in Office

1 Reuters, "Obama tells Russia's Medvedev more flexibility after

election", *Reuters* (26 March 2012): www.reuters.com/article/us-nuclear-summit-obama-medvedev-idUSBRE82P0JI20120326

2 A. Carter, *Inside the Five-Sided Box. Lessons From a Lifetime of Leadership in the Pentagon* (New York: Dutton, 2020) p. 268.
3 M. Moorhead, "Obama: Romney called Russia our top geopolitical threat", *Politifact* (23 October 2012): www.politifact.com/factchecks/2012/oct/22/barack-obama/obama-romney-called-russia-our-top-geopolitical-fo/
4 Interview, 12 August 20021: Ivan Grek: "US-Russian Relations under Bush and Putin", Collective Memory Project, Center for Presidential History, Southern Methodist University.
5 The White House, Office of the Press Secretary, "Remarks by the President to the United Nations General Assembly", *The White House, President Barack Obama* (23 September 2009), https://obamawhitehouse.archives.gov/the-press-office/remarks-president-united-nations-general-assembly
6 Carter, *Inside the Five-Sided Box. Lessons From a Lifetime of Leadership in the Pentagon*, pp. 272–273.
7 Published by Rowman and Littlefield, 2009.
8 McFaul, *From Cold War to Hot Peace*, p. 96.
9 Ibid., p. 97.
10 J. Scahill, "The Assassination Complex. Secret Military Documents Expose the Inner Workings of Obama's Drone Wars", *Intercept*, 15 October 2015.
11 McFaul, *From Cold War to Hot Peace*, p. 94.
12 *Nomination of Hillary R. Clinton to be Secretary of State*. Hearings before the Committee on Foreign Relations, 111th Congress, 1st Session, 13 January 2009.
13 McFaul, *From Cold War to Hot Peace*, p. 95.
14 O. Dmitrieva, "Shpionskii kamen'", *Vzglyad.ru*, 23 January 2006.
15 Ibid., pp. 117–118.
16 Ibid., p. 122.
17 Ibid., *From Cold War to Hot Peace*, p. 121.
18 "Clinton, Lavrov push wrong re-set button on ties", *Reuters*, 6 March 2009: www.reuters.com/article/idUSN06402140; for McFaul: D. Klion, "The Loud American", *The Baffler*, 11 June 2018.
19 "Measures for the Further Reduction and Limitation of Strategic Offensive Arms" were agreed on 8 April 2010 came into effect on 5 February 2011.

20 "Interview with Fyodor Lukyanov", Ivan Grek: "US-Russian Relations under Bush and Putin", Collective Memory Project, Center for Presidential History, Southern Methodist University.
21 Reuters, "Putin likens U.N. Libya resolution to crusades", *Reuters* (21 March 2011): www.reuters.com/article/us-libya-russia-idUSTRE72K3JR20110321
22 *Financial Times*, 21 March 2011.
23 McFaul, *From Cold War to Hot Peace*, p. 225.
24 "Libya's Pathway to Peace", *New York Times*, 14 April 2011.
25 R. Gates, *Duty. Memoirs of a Secretary at War* (London: W. H. Allen, 2015) p. 530.
26 For a misplaced eulogy: R. Benko, "Chuck Hegel Propels Barack Obama Into History", *Forbes*, 3 March 2014.
27 "Rossiya i menyayushchii mir", *Moskovskie novosti*, 27 February 2012.
28 McFaul, *From Cold War to Hot Peace*, p. 227.
29 H. Clinton, *Hard Choices* (New York: Simon and Schuster, 2014) p. 460.
30 McFaul, *From Cold War to Hot Peace*, pp. 248–249.
31 *Moscow News*, 17 January 2012.
32 V. Krasheninnikova, "Rossii nuzhen Zakon o registratsii iinostrannykh agentov - kak v SShA", *Regnum*, 20 January 2020: https://regnum.ru/article/1490137; also https://www.invissin.ru/structure/
33 T. Balmforth, "New US Ambassador to Russia Gets Frosty Reception", *RFE/RFL*, 18 January 2012.
34 http://kremlin.ru/acts/bank/35748
35 McFaul, *From Cold War to Hot Peace*, p. 362.
36 *Izvestiya*, 4 October 2011: http://archive.government.ru/docs/16622/
37 A. Aksenenok, "Rossiya i Siriya: nyuansy soyuznicheskikh otnoshenii", 11 September 2020: https://russiancouncil.ru/analytics-and-comments/analytics/rossiya-i-siriya-nyuansy-soyuznicheskikh-otnosheniy/
38 Ibid. In 1982 he razed the city of Hama to the ground.
39 Quoted by Andrew Tabler: www.washingtoninstitute.org/policy-analysis/sea-change-washingtons-policy-toward-syria
40 McFaul, *From Cold War to Hot Peace*, p. 258.
41 C. Chivers and E. Schmitt, "Arms Airlift to Syrian Rebels Expands, with Aid from C.I.A.", *New York Times*, 24 March 2013.
42 M. Mazzetti, "C.I.A. Study of Covert Aid Fueled Skepticism About Helping Syrian Rebels", *New York Times*, 14 October 2014.

43 McFaul, *From Cold War to Hot Peace*, p. 261.
44 Churkin, *Trudnosti perevoda*, p. 314.
45 Quoted, but his post is mistakenly identified in McFaul, *From Cold War to Hot Peace*, p. 351.
46 P. Gordon, *Losing the Long Game. The False Promise of Regime Change in the Middle East* (New York: St Martin's Press, 2020) p. 228–229.
47 "Hagel: The White House Tried To Destroy me", interview with *Foreign Policy*, 18 December 2015.
48 Ibid.
49 "The Authorisation of the Use of Force in Syria", *Hearings before the Committee on Foreign Relations*, US Senate, 113th Congress, 1st Session, 3 September 2013.
50 *Guardian*, 4 September 2013.
51 McFaul, *From Cold War to Hot Peace*, pp. 354-355.
52 V. Putin, "A Plea for Caution from Russia", *New York Times*, 11 September 2013.
53 Valdai: www.en.kremlin.ru/events/president/news/61719
54 Carter, *Inside the Five-Sided Box. Lessons From a Lifetime of Leadership in the Pentagon*, p. 228.
55 D. Chollet, *The Long Game. How Obama Defied Washington and Redefined America's Role in the World* (New York: Public Affairs, 2016) p.148.
56 Valdai, 27 October 2016: http://en.kremlin.ru/events/president/news/53151
57 "Rossiya i menyayushchii mir", *Moskovskie novosti*, 27 February 2012.
58 B. Rhodes, *The World As It Is. Inside the Obama White House* (London: Vintage, 2019) p. 240.
59 Chollet, *The Long Game*. p. 163.

8. Maidan
1 T. Chugaenko, "I. Morozov: Okazalos', chto global'nyi mir - ne delya vsekh", *Ukraina.ru*, 5 February 2023.
2 Hadley, *Frontline*, 27 July 2017: www.pbs.org/wgbh/frontline/interview/stephen-hadley/
3 Letter to the *Financial Times* from Harland Ullman, leader of the Shock and Awe Study Group of which Cheney was an ad hoc member, 6 July 2021.
4 R. Kagan, "League of Dictators?", *Washington Post*, 30 April 2006.
5 Pew Research Center Report, 29 March 2010.

6   P. Mellgard, "Kissinger: Putin is Not Stalin", *HuffPost*, 5 November 2014: www.huffpost.com/entry/kissinger-putin-not-stalin_b_6108426
7   11th session of Valdai, 24 October 2014: www.kremlin.ru/events/president/news/46860
8   C. Ashton, *And Then What* (London: Elliott and Thompson, 2023) p. 182; interview with Baroness Ashton, 23 January 2023.
9   "Surkov dal pervoe posle otstavki interv'yu. Chto on skazal i chto eto znachit?", BBC News, 26 February 2020: www.bbc.com/russian/news-51640715
10 The tenor of his comments delivered at Valdai in September 2013: http://kremlin.ru/events/president/news/19243
11 "Ukraina mogla by dvigat'sya putem evrointegratsii bystree - Sikorskii", *Obozrevatel*, 10 February 2012.
12 "Sikorski: Stovarzyszenie UE-Ukraina warukowo możliwe v 2013 roku', *Fakt*, 10 December 2012.
13 https://voxukraine.org/en/jan-tombinski-europe-needs-ukraine-to-understand-its-own-destiny
14 Quoted in P. Short, *Putin. His Life and Times* (London: Bodley Head, 2022), p. 570.
15 Press Release: Statement by IMF Mission to Ukraine, 31 October 2013: https://www.imf.org/en/News/Articles/2015/09/14/01/49/pr13419
16 http://kremlin.ru/events/president/news/19243
17 D. Herszenhorn, "In Crimea, Russia Moved to Throw Off the Cloak of Defeat", *New York Times*, 24 March 2014.
18 Speech delivered to the US-Ukraine Foundation by Assistant Secretary of State Victoria Nuland in Washington DC, 13 December 2013: www.youtube.com/watch?v=U2fYcHLouXY
19 "Za predelami voennoi pomoshchi: na chto eshche SShA potratilis' na Ukraine posle 'maidana'", *RT*, 21 November 2023. The numbers were compiled from US Government sources.
20 R. Parry, "A Shadow US Foreign Policy", *Consortiumnews*, 27 February 2014.
21 *Putin versus the West*, BBC documentary, 1:1, "My Backyard".
22 E. Pozdnyakov, Rafael' Fakhrutdinov and Anastasia Kulikova, *Vzglyad*, 21 November 2023.
23 The record of payment was shown on Oliver Stone's documentary *Ukraine on Fire*.
24 "Nikolai Azarov. Tsel'yu Maidana bylo vtravit' Ukrainu v voinu s Rossiei", *Vzglyad*, 21 November 2023.
25 Facebook and ForPost. *Novosti Sevastopolya*, 7 December 2013;

supplemented by "Deputat Verkhovnoi Rady Oleg Tsarev – 'KP': Amerikantsy khotyat zhertv!", *Komsomol'skaya pravda*, 10 December 2013. Fink, born 24 March 1983, arrived in Borispol' on a flight from Paris to Kiev. His diplomatic passport number was cited as 910104001. He received a distinguished honour award in 2015: https://pdf.usaid.gov/pdf_docs/PBAAC279R.pdf

26 Speech delivered to the US-Ukraine Foundation by Assistant Secretary of State Victoria Nuland in Washington DC, 13 December 2013: www.youtube.com/watch?v=U2fYcHLouXY

27 "Nikolai Azarov. Tsel'yu Maidana bylo vtravit' Ukrainu v voinu s Rossiei", *Vzglyad*, 21 November 2023.

28 Information from within the White House: NBC News sourcing Associated Press, 25 February 2014.

29 https://rus.azattyq.org/a/25257410.html

30 V. Nuland, G. Pyatt and J. Marcus, "Ukraine Crisis: Transcript of Leaked Nuland-Pyatt Call. 'F**k the EU'", *Mark Taliano* (20 March 2022), https://marktaliano.net/ukraine-crisis-transcript-of-leaked-nuland-pyatt-call-fk-the-eu/. The audio clip was posted on Twitter by Dmitrii Loskutov, aide to Russia's Deputy Prime Minister Dmitrii Rogozin: www.reuters.com/article/us-usa-ukraine-tape-idUSBREA1601G20140207

31 Hunter, "The Ukraine Crisis: Why and What Now?", *Survival*, 64, No. 1, February 2022, p. 17.

32 D. Chiacu and A. Mohammed, "Leaked audio reveals embarrassing U.S. exchange on Ukraine, EU", *Reuters* (7 February 2014): www.reuters.com/article/us-usa-ukraine-tape-idUSBREA1601G20140207

33 www.welt.de/print/die_welt/politik/article124647118/und-wissen-Sie-scheiss-auf-die-EU.html

34 Interview with Baroness Ashton, 23 January 2023.

35 *Putin versus the West*, 1:1, "My Backyard"; also, quoted in A. Gardner, "Ashton Joins Ukraine Leaders for Crisis Talks", *Politico*, 29 January 2014.

36 Interview with McFaul, 17 August 2023.

37 YouTube, 6 February 2014. Ashton had arrived back in Kyiv on 4 February.

38 Broadcast, 6 February 2014.

39 "Sergei Glaz'ev: federalizatsiya - uzhe ne ideya, a ochevidnaya neobkhodimost'", *Kommersant*, 6 February 2014.

40 McFaul, *From Cold War to Hot Peace*, p. 397.

41 "Ucraina. Uno scomodo testimone - Eugenio Miccoli

intervista Giorgio Bianche", 3 April 2018: www.youtube.com/watch?v=WDCMnsZpK+M

42 "Russia's Destabilization of Ukraine", Hearings before the Committee of the House of Representatives, 113th Congress, 2nd Session, 8 May 2014.

43 YouTube, 5 March 2014.

44 "Ukraine: The Untold Story of the Maidan Killings", BBC (15 February 2015): www.bbc.co.uk/programmes/p02jcrf3

45 "Todesschüsse in Kiew. Wer is für das Blutbad vom Maidanverantwortlich", "Monitor" No. 660 on *ARD*, 10 April 2014; G. Stack, "Kyiv Blog: What triggered the Maidan massacre?", 13 February 2015: https://bne.eu/kyiv-blog-what-triggered-the-maidan-massacre-500444157/?archive=bne

46 "Ucraina. Uno scomodo testimone - Eugenio Miccoli intervista Giorgio Bianche", 3 April 2018: www.youtube.com/watch?v=WDCMnsZpK+M

47 "Victoria Nuland's Admits Washington Has Spent $5 Billion to 'Subvert Ukraine'", YouTube (9 February 2014): www.youtube.com/watch?v=U2fYcHLouXY

48 Personal information. Soros himself has publicly not admitted as much.

49 Interviewed by F. Zakaria, 25 May 2014 on CNN: www.youtube.com/watch?v=kPGMPIEHLTA

50 I. Katchanovski, "The 'Snipers' Massacre' on the Maidan in Ukraine": https://papers.ssrn.com/sol3/papers.cfm?abstract_id=2658245. Excerpts from videos taken at the time underscore the text. And for a rebuttal of attacks upon his work: www.dailysceptic.org/2022/08/12/ivan-katchanovski-responds-to-ian-ron

51 Stated at 3.40 p.m.: www.theguardian.com/world/2014/feb/21/ukraine-crisis-president-claims-deal-with-opposition-after-77-killed-in-kiev?view=desktop#block-5307624ae4b0b08ea9f4a437

52 J. Biden, *Promise Me, Dad. A Year of Hope, Hardship, and Purpose* (London: Pan, 2018) p. 98.

53 "Agreement on the Settlement of Crisis in Ukraine – full text", *Guardian* (21 February 2014): www.theguardian.com/world/2014/feb/21/agreement-on-the-settlement-of-crisis-in-ukraine-full-text

54 11th Meeting of Valdai, 24 October 2014: www.kremlin.ru/events/president/news/46860

55 The four conditions required were: resignation; incapacity by reasons of health; impeachment or death.

56 Herszenhorn, "In Crimea, Russia Moved to Throw Off the Cloak of Defeat", *New York Times*, 24 March 2014.
57 Z. Brzezinski, *The Grand Chessboard. American Primacy and its Geostrategic Imperatives* (New York: Basic Books, 1997) p. 214.
58 G. White, "Russia Stung By Ally Yanukovych's Defeat in Ukraine", *Wall Street Journal*, 22 February 2014.
59 K. Sivkov, "Ukraina: period poluraspada", *Voenno-promyshlennyi kur'er*, 17 March 2014.
60 http://kremlin.ru/events/president/news/70868
61 For detail: US embassy in Kyiv to NATO, Secretary of State, 7 December 2006: https://wikileaks.org/plusd/cables/06KYIV4489_a.html
62 *Wall Street Journal*, 23 December 2022.
63 Documentary on Rossiyya-1, "Krym. Vozrashchenie Rodinu", 8 March 2015. The full transcript was published in *Lenta.ru*, 15 March 2015.
64 Interview, *Politico*, 1 May 2017.
65 von Fritsch, *Russlands Weg als Botschafter in Moskau*, pp. 116–117.
66 11th session of Valldai, 24 October 2014: www.kremlin.ru/events/president/news/46860
67 http://kremlin.ru/events/president/news/20603
68 Personal information.
69 23 June 2023: https://transcripts.cnn.com/show/ampr/date/2023-06-23/segment/01
70 J. Goldberg, "The Obama Doctrine", *The Atlantic*, April 2016.
71 "Obama: I Underestimated the Threat of Disinformation", *The Atlantic*, 7 April 2022.
72 [W.] Burns, 14 June 2017: *PBS* Frontline Interviews: "Putin and the Presidents".
73 J. Guyer, "What Biden learned the last time Putin invaded Ukraine", *Vox*, 7 February 2022.
74 Chollet, *The Long Game*, p. 163.
75 *Daily Caller*, 3 April 2017.
76 "Full Transcript: President Obama Gives Speech Addressing Europe, Russia on March 26", *Washington Post* (26 March 2014): www.washingtonpost.com/world/transcript-president-obama-gives-speech-addressing-europe-russia-on-march-26/2014/03/26/07ae80ae-b503-11e3-b899-20667de76985_story.html
77 *Putin versus the West*, 1:1, "My Backyard".
78 Interview with Merkel's Foreign Policy Adviser. "I Have Eliminated

'the West' From My Vocabulary." *Der Spiegel*, dated 23 September 2021. "Yes, in hindsight it was a mistake", he told *Welt am Sonntag* in December 2022: *Merkur de*, 31 December 2022. For his moralism: Heusgen interview, "Ich wolte etwas Idealistisches machen", *Rheinische Post* online, 6 December 2020.

79 *Hearings before the Committee on Armed Services, United States Senate, 83rd Congress, 1st Session on Nominee Designates*, 15–16 January 1953 (Washington DC: USGPO, 1953) p. 26.

80 "Obama: I Underestimated the Threat of Disinformation", *The Atlantic*, 7 April 2022.

81 Dame Alison Leslie interview: *British Diplomatic Oral History Project*, Churchill College archives: http://archives.chu.cam.ac.uk/wp-content/uploads/sites/2/2022/01/Leslie.pdf

82 "Pravi zashchitit' svoikh", *Vzglyad*, 9 April 2014.

83 P. Conradi, *Who Lost Russia? From the Collapse of the USSSR to Putin's War on Ukraine* (London: Oneworld, 2022) chapter 21; also, www.gov.uk/government/news/uk-exposes-sick-russian-troll-factory-plaguing-social-media-with-kremlin-propaganda. For Prigozhin's indictment on 6 October 1981 by the Leningrad city court for various acts of theft and burglary: https://meduza.io/en/feature/2021/06/29/prigozhin-s-criminal-past-straight-from-the-source

84 *Government of Netherlands*: www.government.nl/topics/mh17-incident.

85 *Putin versus the West*, 1:1, "My Backyard".

86 https://ru.krymr.com/a/sem-dokazatelstv-prisutstviya-voyennih-rossii-nadonbasse/29568097.html

87 "Protocol on the results of consultations of the Trilateral Contact Group (Minsk Agreement)", *United Nations Peacemaker* (5 September 2014): https://peacemaker.un.org/ua-ceasefire-2014

88 D. Allan, "The Minsk Conundrum: Western Policy and Russia's War in Eastern Ukraine", May 2020, Research Paper, Ukraine Forum, Chatham House, 2.

89 Biden boasted of this on 6 October 2019 at the Council of Foreign Relations: www.youtube.com/watch?v=rnIPw_Who7E

90 D. Morgan, "Family ties were big part of Hunter Biden brand, former Burisma official says", *Reuters*, 3 August 2023.

9. The Road to Damascus

1 http://en.kremlin.ru/events/president/news/50548

2 Putin, "Rossiya i menyayushchii mir", *Moskovskie novosti*, 27

February 2012; A.Q. [al Qaeda] is on our side in Syria" – Jake Sullivan to Hillary Clinton, Spot Report, 12 February 2012: wikileaks.org/Clinton - emails/23225

3 For the clearest statement of priorities: S. Borzyakov, "Rasshirenie NATO za schet Balkan predstavlyaetsya neizbezhnym", *Vzglyad*, 19 July 2017.

4 T. Grove et al., "How Putin's Right-Hand Man Took. Out Prigozhin", *Wall Street Journal*, 22 December 2023.

5 For the Pentagon's unclassified assessment of Russian capabilities and intentions: US Defense Intelligence Agency, *Russia Military Power. Building a Military to Support Great Power Aspirations*: www.dia.mil/Portals/110/Images/News/Military_Powers_Publications/Russia_Military_Power_Report_2017.pdf

6 "Syria After Geneva: Next Steps for US Policy", *Hearings before the Committee on Foreign Relations*, US Senate, 113th Congress, 2nd Session, 26 March 2014.

7 11th session of Valdai, 24 October 2014: www.kremlin.ru/events/president/news/46860

8 Borzyakov, "Rossiiskie voennye v Sirii reshili pyat' glavnykh zadach", *Vzglyad.ru*, 30 September 2020.

9 S. Sengupta and N. McFarquhar, "Vladimir Putin of Russia Calls for Coalition to Fight ISIS", *New York Times*, 27 September 2015.

10 Aksenenok, "Rossiya i Siriya: nyuansy soyuznicheskikh otnoshenii", 11 September 2020: https://russiancouncil.ru/analytics-and-comments/analytics/rossiya-i-siriya-nyuansy-soyuznicheskikh-otnosheniy/

11 13th session of Valdai, 27 October 2016: http://en.kremlin.ru/events/president/news/53151

12 V. Mukhin and I. Rodin, "Rossiya nachala svoyu blizhnevostochnuyu voinu", *Nezavisimaya gazeta*, 1 October 2015.

13 von Fritsch, *Russlands Weg als Botschafter in Moskau*, p. 165.

14 Reported to the German ambassador in Moscow: von Fritsch, *Russlands Weg als Botschafter in Moskau*, p. 162.

15 Video, *Wall Street Journal*, "Shadow Men: Inside Wagner, Russia's Secret War Company", 9 June 2023: www.wsj.com/video/series/shadow-men/shadow-men-inside-wagner-russias-secret-war-company/29735C37-0B4E-4E70-8E8C-C46FB711370C?mod=hp_lead_pos8 – In particular, note testimony from the director of the US Treasury's sanctions agency, John Smith.

16 Ibid., pp. 166–167.

17 Aksenenok, "Rossiya i Siriya: nyuansy soyuznicheskikh otnoshenii", 11

September 2020: https://russiancouncil.ru/analytics-and-comments/analytics/rossiya-i-siriya-nyuansy-soyuznicheskikh-otnosheniy/
18. *New York Times*, 4 April 2017.
19. Ibid.
20. Andrei Kortunov, Director of the Russian Institute of International Affairs: www.youtube.com/watch?v=uPyflrCehYM

10. Trump Fails

1. S. Borzyakov, "Vstrecha s Putynim pokazala chem Baiden luchshe Trampa", *Vzglyad.ru*, 17 June 2021.
2. https://home.treasury.gov/news/press-releases/sm577; www.justice.gov/opa/pr/russian-project-lakhta-member-charged-wire-fraud-conspiracy
3. *Reuters*, 14 February 2023.
4. *New York Post*, 12 December 2023.
5. "Final Batch of Hillary Clinton's Emails Released", *Wall Street Journal*, 1 March 2016.
6. Special Counsel John Durham, *Report on Matters Related to Intelligence Activities and Investigations Arising Out of the 2016 Presidential Campaigns* (Washington DC, 12 May 2023) p. 81.
7. Ibid., p. 82.
8. Ibid. p. 126.
9. Ibid., pp. 143–148.
10. Ibid., p. 14.
11. Ibid., pp. 143–148. Dolan was never interviewed subsequently by the FBI evidently because of his connection with the Clintons.
12. See also The United States vs Igor Danchenko Indictment: www.justice.gov/sco/press-release/file/1446386/download
13. P. Sperry, "FBI Chief Comey Misled Congress's 'Gang of 8' Over Russiagate, Lisa Page Memo Reveals': *RealClearInvestigations*, 9 June 2022. The FISA court is the Foreign Intelligence Surveillance Court whose job it is to sanction the interception of communications (and search) for foreign counter-intelligence purposes even from US citizens if they are shown to be connected to those under scrutiny.
14. This information was delivered by hand to General Flynn's team: https://justthenews.com/accountability/political-ethics/fbis-russia-collusion-case-fell-apart-first-month-trump-presidency
15. Special Counsel John Durham, *Report on Matters Related to Intelligence Activities and Investigations Arising Out of the 2016 Presidential Campaigns*, p. 236.

16. R. Mueller, *Report on the Investigation Into Russian Interference in the 2016 Presidential Election* (US Department of Justice: Washington DC March 2019) pp. 174–175.
17. P. Sperry, "Secret Report: How CIA's John Brennan Overruled Dissenting Analysts Who Concluded Russia Favored Hillary", *RealClearInvestigations*, 24 September 2020. The National Security Agency that monitors secret communications did not contribute to the report.
18. M. Hemingway, "The Curious Case of Stefan Halper, Longtime 'Zelig' Scandals Who Crossfired Trump", *RealClearInvestigations*, 8 March 2022. Halper is easily identified as "CHS-1" in the Durham Report.
19. F. Lucas, "Exclusive: Documents Reveal Rush to Target Trump's National Security Pick in Obama's Waning Days as President", *The Daily Signal*, 7 July 2023.
20. "Naznachenie generala v Belyi dom predveshchaet sblizhenie s Kremlem", *Vzglyad.ru*, 18 November 2016.
21. Personal information: Kissinger and I had met at the Century Club in the spring. He gave me lunch at the Brook Club on Park Avenue, we engaged in a tour d'horizon for nearly two hours, just before his meeting with the Trump team.
22. Personal information from Stanford that reached me a week later. This was what is known as an "Oxford secret".
23. The Hill Staff, "READ: Susan Rice's email discussing Michael Flynn and Russia", *The Hill* (19 May 2020): https://thehill.com/policy/national-security/498593-read-susan-rices-email-discussing-michael-flynn-and-russia/
24. A. Bezrukov, O. Rebro and A. Sushentsov, *Donal'd Tramp: professional'nyi profil' novogo presidenta SShA* (Valdai, Moscow: January 2017) p. 4.
25. J. Bolton, *The Room Where It Happened* (New York: Simon and Schuster, 2020) p. 177. Bolton was forewarned of this pattern of behaviour when he arrived to take over from McMaster.
26. H. McMaster, *Battlegrounds. The Fight to Defend the Free World* (London: HarperCollins, 2020) p. 28.
27. http://en.kremlin.ru/events/president/news/54638
28. V. Krasheninnikova, "Tramp snimaet masku", *Literaturnaya gazeta*, No 14 (6593), 12 April 2017.
29. A. Shaw, "Trump says he had 'a shot' to take out Syria's Assad, but ex-Defense chief Mattis opposed it", *Fox News* (15 September 2020): www.foxnews.com/politics/trump-syrias-assad-defense-mattis

30 *New York Times*, 12 April 2017.
31 *Vzglyad.ru*, 11 December 2017.
32 Borzyakov, "Rossiiskie voennye v Sirii reshili pyat' glavnykh zadach", *Vzglyad.ru*, 30 September 2020.
33 McMaster, *Battlegrounds*, pp. 31–32.
34 B. Shaw, "Obama's shocking interference into Israel's election process", *Jerusalem Post*, 3 February 2015. For a recent and wide-ranging history of this: D. Levin, *Meddling in the Ballot Box: The Causes and Effects of Partisan Electoral Interventions* (Oxford: Oxford University Press, 2020).
35 E. Chernenko, "What Makes Putin So Popular At Home? His Reputation Abroad", *New York Times*, 16 March 2018.
36 McMaster, *Battlegrounds*, p. 64.
37 Bolton, *The Room Where It Happened*, pp. 135–138.
38 *Nezavisimaya gazeta*, 11 July 2018.
39 Quoted in Haslam, *Russia's Cold War*, p. 33.
40 V. Akopov, "Tramp reshil razvalit' Evrosoyuz", *Vzglyad.ru*, 6 July 2018.
41 Bolton, *The Room Where It Happened*, p. 181.
42 "Rossiya i Siriya: nyuansy soyuznikcheskikh otnoshenii", 11 September 2020: https://russiancouncil.ru/analytics-and-comments/analytics/rossiya-i-siriya-nyuansy-soyuznicheskikh-otnosheniy/

11. Paying the Gas Bill

1 "Proekt 'Bol'shaya Evrazia': chto eto takoe i kak eto budiet razvivat'sya. Vo Vladivostoke obsudili krupnogo mezhdunarodnogo proekta", *Komsomol'skaya pravda*, 10 September 2021.
2 "Putin's Speech", YouTube (9 July 2017): www.youtube.com/watch?v=OQ1fKpRZFt0
3 O. Solov'eva, "Dlya vykhoda iz krizisa Rossii potrebuetsya 15 let", *Nezavisimaya gazeta*, 13 February 2018.
4 B. Pancevski, "Did Merkel Pave the Way for the War in Ukraine?", *Wall Street Journal*, 26 May 2023.
5 D. Bavyrin, "Konets epokhi Merkel' ne sulit Rossii nichego khoroshego", *Vzglyad.ru*, 30 December 2020.
6 14 February 2003: http://kremlin.ru/events/president/transcripts/21873. See also, "Gazprom at 15: Russia's gas monopoly remains an instrument of the state", *Financial Times*, 13 February 2008.
7 "Gazprom at 15", *Financial Times*, 13 February 2008.

8   "Strategicheskoe planirovanie vozproizvodstva mineral'no-syrevoi bazy regiona v usloviya formirovaniya rynochnykh otnoshenii (Sankt-Peterburg i Leningradskaya Oblast')."

9   According to Olga Litvinenko, the daughter of the rector of the Mining Institute that gave Putin his degree, her father wrote the thesis in 1994 examined in 1997. He soon became a multimillionaire: *Novaya gazeta*, 6 March 2018. For implementation of his recommendations: J. Haslam, "A Pipeline Runs Through It", *National Interest*, No. 92, Nov–Dec. 2007, pp. 18–24. It is worth noting that the Royal Institute of International Affairs journal, *International Affairs*, to its shame rejected the article without comment. The in-house team, the editor included, were wrong about Putin.

10 Russia's Central Bank: www.reuters.com/markets/europe/russias-oil-gas-revenue-windfall-2022-01-21/

11 The answer given on behalf of the EU Commission, 7 September 2015: www.europarl.europa.eu/doceo/document/E-8-2015-011252-ASW_EN.pdf

12 A. Gurzu and J. Schatz, "Great Northern Gas War", *Politico*, 10 February 2016.

13 Ibid.

14 Ibid.

15 Testifying during her nomination in 2021: youtube.com/watch?v=5pFd1RoV5WE. But her words were subsequently struck from the written record, presumably at her request.

16 The NSA made use of Danish cables for that purpose: *Reuters*, 31 May 2021: www.reuters.com/world/europe/us-security-agency-spied-merkel-other-top-european-officials-through-danish-2021-05-30/

17 G. Snodgrass, *Holding the Line. Inside Trump's Pentagon with Secretary Mattis* (New York: Sentinel, 2019) p. 230.

18 V. Trukhachev, "Merkel razveyala illyuzii Rossii naschet Germanii", *Vzglyad.ru*, 20 August 2021.

19 *Novaya gazeta*, 9 December 2022.

20 R. Taha, "Merkel defends decisions on Russian energy", *DW* (12 July 2022): www.dw.com/en/merkel-defends-decisions-on-russian-energy/a-64018499

21 *The Independent*, 6 December 2017.

22 R. Bingener and M. Wehner, *Die Moskau Connection. Das Schröder-Netzwerk und Deutschlands Weg in die Abhängigkeit* (Munich: Beck, 2023) pp. 203–204.

23 K. Bennhold, "The Former Chancellor Who Became Putin's Man in Germany", *New York Times*, 23 April 2022.
24 "Bellingcat Statement on Verdict of Berlin Kammergericht (Tiergarten Murder)", *Bellingcat* (15 December 2021): www.bellingcat.com/bellingcat-statement-on-verdict-of-berlin-kammergericht-tiergarten-murder/
25 Testimony from the British embassy.
26 E. Chernenko and G. Dudina, "Drug platezhom krasen: Kak Germaniya stala glavnym opponentom SShA v Evrope", *Kommersant*, 17 June 2020.
27 E. Chernenko, "Sorry Mr. Biden. Putin Honestly Could Not Care Less", *New York Times*, 16 June 2021.

Conclusions The War of the Russian Succession?
1 http://en.kremlin.ru/events/president/news/71391
2 www.youtube.com/watch?v=uPyflrCehYM
3 http://en.kremlin.ru/events/president/news/66181; and A. Troianovski, "Putin the Great? Russia's President Likens Himself to Famous Czar", *New York Times*, 9 June 2022.
4 "Leading Russian Academics Criticize Government Handling Of Minister's Plagiarism Case", *Radio Free Europe/Radio Liberty* (28 October 2016): www.rferl.org/a/russia-culture-minister-medinsky-protest-plagiarism/28080045.html
5 "Soveshchanie s postoyannymi chlenami Soveta Bezopasnosti": http://kremlin.ru/events/president/news/by-date/21.12.2021
6 Quoted in Haslam, *No Virtue Like Necessity*, p. 133.
7 "Soveshchanie…"
8 J. Borger, "We knew in 2011 Putin would attack Ukraine, says Bill Clinton", *Guardian* (5 May 2023): www.theguardian.com/world/2023/may/05/we-knew-putin-would-attack-ukraine-back-in-2011-says-bill-clinton
9 "Investitsionnyi forum 'Rossiya Zovet!': http://kremlin.ru/events/president/news/67241
10 http://kremlin.ru/events/president/news/71667
11 Manning to Haslam, 7 September 2022.
12 https://rg.ru/2022/06/09/putin-petr-i-v-severnuiu-vojnu-vozvrashchal-zemli-a-ne-ottorgal.html
13 Strobel and Gordon, "Reported Detention of Russian Spy Boss Shows Tension Over Stalled Ukraine Invasion, US Officials Say", *Wall Street Journal*, 19 March 2022.

14 Miller and Belton, "Russia's spies misread Ukraine and misled Kremlin as war loomed", *Washington Post*, 19 August 2022.
15 US Department of State, *After Action Review on Afghanistan January 2020-August 2021* (Washington DC: March 2022). This long-awaited report was bowdlerised to save the face of the administration. For a stark contrast: Congressman Michael McCaul, *House Republican Interim Report, "A 'Strategic Failure:' Assessing the Administration's Afghanistan Withdrawal:* https://foreignaffairs.house.gov/wp-content/uploads/2022/08/HFAC-Republican-Interim-Report-A-22Strategic-Failure22-Assessing-the-Administrations-Afghanistan-Withdrawal.pdf
16 *Wall Street Journal*, 17 December 2021.
17 *Wall Street Journal*, 6 January 2022.
18 Bennett interview: www.youtube.com/watch?v=qK9tLDeWBzs
19 R. Romaniuk, "From Zelensky's 'surrender' to Putin's surrender: how the negotiations with Russia are going", *Ukrainskaya pravda*, 5 May 2022. Interestingly no alternative account has subsequently emerged.
20 http://kremlin.ru/events/president/news/71667
21 A. Kortunov, Director of the semi-official International Affairs Council, "Who Blinks First – the Conflict in Europe", 7 July 2023: https://russiancouncil.ru/en/analytics-and-comments/analytics/who-blinks-first-the-conflict-in-europe/
22 Ibid.
23 Sarkozy, *Le temps des combats*, p. 55.

Acknowledgements

With thanks to Neil Belton (Head of Zeus), Robert Dudley (Literary Agent), Professor Emeritus Georges Soutou (University of Paris, Sorbonne), and Professor Vladimir Zubok (London School of Economics).

Index

Abramovich, Roman 266
Adamishin, Anatoly 50, 86–8
Afghanistan 129–30, 131, 141, 147, 152, 153–4, 174, 191, 223, 257
    the Taliban 126, 127, 132, 176, 269
    US occupation of 177, 190, 234, 238, 243, 263–4
Africa 51
    Organisation of African Unity 49
Akropov, Petr 242–3
Aksenenok, Aleksandr 222, 224, 226, 245
al-Qaeda 189, 190
    9/11 15, 121, 125, 128–34, 143–4, 145, 147
    and Syria 221
Albright, Madeleine 46, 64, 109, 116, 121, 215
    and the Kosovo war 100–1, 101–2
Algeria 190
Antonov, Anatoly 258
Arab Spring 179–83
    and Syria 186–92
Arakhamia, Davyd 266
Argentina 8
Arias, Miguel 249
Armenia 171
Armitage, Dick 120, 135

Ashe, Victor 171
Ashton, Catherine 196, 202, 203, 205, 206
Åslund, Anders 35
Aspin, Les 10, 39, 69
Assad, Bashar al- 174, 186–7, 188, 189, 191, 222, 224, 225, 226, 236, 237, 244
Atlantic Alliance 56
Austria 43, 71
Azarov, Mykola 201, 202
Azerbaijan 171

Badinter, Robert 44
Baggett, Joan 29
Bahr, Egon 59, 215
Baker, James 16, 18, 20, 25, 44
Balkans *see* Yugoslavia
Baltic states 24, 26, 107
    and Georgia 168
    and NATO enlargement 54, 68, 73, 74, 91, 93, 108, 133, 145, 146
Bandera, Stefan 217
banks
    and the financial crisis 234
Barmyantsev, Lt General 104, 105, 106
Barroso, José Manuel 197

Bavyrin, Dmitrii 248
Belarus 171, 186, 269
Bennett, Naftali 265–6
Berezovsky, Boris 89, 115, 178
Bergbusch, Eric 38
Berger, Samuel ("Sandy") 66, 100, 102
Berlin Wall 214, 255
Beseda, Sergei 263
Bessmertnykh, Alexander 19
Beyrle, John 126, 168, 183
Bianche, Giorgio 205
Biden, Hunter 219
Biden, Joe 4, 253, 263, 264–5
    as vice-president 177, 180, 188, 202, 206, 215, 219, 232
Bildt, Carl 170–1, 211, 213
Bin Laden, Osama 127, 129–30
Bitterlich, Joachim 37–8, 39, 43, 55–6, 71, 72, 102, 137
Black, Cofer 128
Blair, Tony
    government 116–20, 124
    and the Iraq war 139, 141, 142, 142–4, 143
    and the NATO-Russia Council idea 134
    and Putin 116–20, 121–2, 128, 142–4
    and régime change 152
Blanche, Giorgio 204
Blech, Klaus 19
Blee, Richard 128
Blinken, Anthony 4, 177, 214
Bohomolets, Olha 205
Bolton, John 69, 244
Borodin, Pavel Pavlovich 112
Bortnikov, Aleksandr 141
Borzyakov, Stanislav 227
Bosnia Herzegovina 26, 29, 44, 45–7, 51, 53, 67, 68, 84–9, 101, 102
Bosnian Serbs 46–7, 85–7

Boutros-Ghali, Boutros 45–6, 51, 52, 53
Bowie, Bob 16
Brennan, John 228, 230
Brenton, Sir Tony 179, 183
BRIC countries (Brazil, Russia, India, China and South Africa) 269
Bristow, Laurie 167
Britain xviii, 8
    Blair government 116–20
    bombing of Libya 181
    GCHQ 117
    and Iraq 125
    and NATO expansion 17, 23, 70–1, 72–3, 78, 91–2
    and Russia 178–9, 183
        the Litvinenko poisoning 159, 160
        Putin's seizure of Crimea 216
        and the Steele dossier 230
    and Syria 188
    and Ukraine 201, 265, 266–7
        EU membership 200
    and Yugoslavia (former) 44, 45, 46–8, 50, 51
Broek, Hans van den 45
Brzezinski, Zbigniew 16, 58, 64, 115–16, 154, 199, 207–8, 258
Bucharest summit 163–7, 170
Budapest Memorandum 167, 258–9
Bulgaria 71, 226
Burns, Nicholas 68, 135, 162–3, 165, 168, 169, 173–4
Burns, William J. 70, 88–9, 145, 178, 183–4, 214
Bush, George H.W. ('41) 9–10, 21–2, 27, 28, 30, 39, 48, 91, 95, 121, 153
    and NATO 241
    and Operation Desert Storm 124
Bush, George W. ('43) 10, 12, 14, 69, 91, 164, 179, 261

and 9/11 130, 132–3, 143–4
administration 120–8
character 120
and the crusade for democracy 157–8, 162
election as president 114
and Iraq 124–5, 139–45, 190
Obama and the Bush administration 176, 193
and Putin 118, 119–20, 124, 125–6, 128, 133–4, 157–8, 160, 174
and Rice 136
and Ukraine 156, 165–6
Bush, Jeb 120

Cambodia 53
Camdessus, Michel 35
Cameron, David 181, 200, 261
Campbell, Alistair 142, 143
Canada 108, 260, 261
Carrington, Peter, Lord 44, 45, 48
Carter, Ashton 58–9, 175, 176–7, 190, 231
Carter, Jimmy 53
Carville, James 28
Castlereagh, Lord 8
CEE (Central-East European) states and NATO enlargement 20–1, 37, 38–40, 59, 63, 79
Central Asia 62, 131–2, 191, 264
Central and Eastern Europe xvii–xviii, 19, 56
Chechnya 50, 88–9, 117, 119, 126, 127, 132, 158, 159
  Chechen terrorists in Beslan 146–7
Cheney, Dick 22, 69, 115, 120–1, 136, 139, 144, 161, 176, 194
Chernenko, Elena 239, 253
Chernomyrdin, Viktor 86, 95, 103
China 20, 107, 232, 234, 235, 243, 264, 266, 268

and the Russian invasion of Ukraine 268–9
Chirac, Jacques 15, 89–90, 135, 141
Chollet, Derek 187, 190, 214
Christopher, Warren 13, 23–4, 33, 38, 39, 40–1, 57–8, 68
  and the Partnership for Peace 61, 66
  and Yugoslavia (former) 48, 53, 86
Chubais, Anatoly 95, 97, 107, 109, 110, 112
Churchill, Winston 8, 110
Churkin, Vitalii 187
CIA (Central Intelligence Agency) 52, 85, 100, 129
  and the Russian invasion of Ukraine 3
  and Syria 187
Clark, General Wesley 60, 104, 106, 124, 125
Clarke, Richard 129
Clinton, Bill 10, 11, 12, 14, 23, 89, 120, 122, 227–8
  foreign policy 27–32, 37–8, 52, 56–8, 176
  Helsinki summit (1997) 83–4, 92
  and Islamic fundamentalism 126–7
  and Kosovo 103, 107
  and NATO expansion 13–14, 15–16, 39–41, 52–5, 60–1, 65–74, 77–82, 93, 107–8
  and NATO funding 241
  Partnership for Peace 58–65, 139
  on Putin 117
  and Russia 108–9
  and Ukraine 81, 258
  visit to NATO and Visegrád countries 63–5, 73, 74
  and Yeltsin 110

and Yugoslavia (former) 41–2, 48, 52–3
Clinton, Hillary 3, 178, 179, 183, 186, 187, 193, 234
   presidential campaign 227–8, 229, 230
Cold War xvii, 4, 9–10, 15, 16, 23, 29, 32, 57, 59, 75, 122, 123, 248
   and Kosovo 106
Collins, James 98, 138
Colour Revolutions 155–7, 155–8, 161–2, 174, 209
Comey, James 228, 232
Commonwealth of Independent States 75, 184, 223
Congo war 51
Conquest, Robert 60
Corera, Gordon 151
Corker, Bob 221
Council for Mutual Economic Assistance (Comecon) 24
Courtney, William 147
Crimea 51, 75–6, 167
   Putin's seizure of 6–7, 183, 210–13, 240, 250, 262, 266
      America and allies response to 213–17
      bridge to the Kerch peninsula 219, 262
      and economic sanctions 246–7
      and the Minsk Protocols 218–19
   Sevastapol naval base 75, 76–7, 212
Crimean Tartars 213
Croatia 41–2, 42–3, 44–5, 53, 85–6
Crompton, Paul 178
Crouch, Jack 131
CSCE (Conference on Security and Co-operation in Europe) 21, 25–7, 72, 78, 137
Cuba 260
Czech Republic 56, 63, 67, 91
and Georgia 168
Czechoslovakia 21, 24–5, 38, 54, 153, 260

Danchenko, Igor 229
Dashichev, Vyacheslav 107
Davis, David 72–3
Dayton agreement 88, 99
De Franchis, Amedeo 88
Dearlove, Richard 116, 125
Dehaene, Jean-Luc 108
democracy
   crusade of democracy in the US 27, 151–2, 157–8, 176, 178–9, 182–3, 185, 186, 194
   dismantling of in Russia 260
Denmark 169
Dienstbier, Jiří 21
Dmitriev, Major General Dmitrii 61–2
Dobbs, Michael 23
Doe, Marc 178
Dohnanyi, Klaus von 215
Dolan, Charles 229
Donfried, Karen 188
Donilon, Tom 187
Doyle, Colm 47
Dumas, Roland 14, 21

Eagleburger, Larry 30
East Germany 59
Eastern European countries xvii–xviii, 19
   communist regimes 153
   entry into the EU 56
   and NATO enlargement 20–1, 37, 38–40, 59, 63, 79, 83, 126
Eastern Partnership 171, 173
EBRD (European Bank for Reconstruction and Development) 33
economic crisis (2008) 168, 234

Edelman, Eric 27
Egypt 180, 190
Eisenhower, Dwight D. 16, 240
Elkin, Ze'ev 265
Eppler, Erhard 215
Erdogan, Recep 266
Ermath, Fritz 7, 179
Estonia 145, 146
ethnic cleansing 42–3
Eurasian economic union 186, 195, 197, 262
European Economic Community 20, 36
    and Yugoslavia 45
European Union xviii, 55–6, 70–1
    and the Eastern Partnership 171
    Maastricht Treaty 45, 55
    and Putin 5, 172–3, 186, 215–16
    and Russian oil and gas 249, 250
    and Syria 225
    and Trump 241–2, 245
    and Ukraine 7, 46, 157, 194–200, 209, 261, 262
    and Yugoslavia 45, 46
Exxon 233

Fabius, Laurent 206
Falkland Islands 8
Farkas, Emily 215
Fink, Brian 201
Finland 208
Fleming, Andy 178
Florus the Epitomist 257
Flynn, Michael 230–1, 232, 238
France xviii, 247
    and German unification 41, 43
    and the Iraq war 141, 164
    and the Kosovo war 106
    loss of empire 8
    and NATO enlargement 14, 17, 18–19, 21–2, 43, 72, 78, 89–90
    and Putin's seizure of Crimea 216
    and Ukraine 165, 198, 206, 265
Fried, Daniel 68, 126
Friedman, Thomas 29
Fritsch, Rüdiger von 211, 223, 224
Frost, David 118

G-7 countries 35–6, 132
G20 summits 188
Gabriel, Sigmar 251–2
Gaddafi, Muammar 180, 181–2, 231, 261
Gaidar, Yegor 30, 95
Gatehouse, Gabriel 205
Gates, Robert 9, 182
Gaulle, Charles de 8, 22
Genscher, Hans-Dietrich 16, 18, 20–1, 37, 39, 44, 45, 55
Georgia 147
    and NATO membership 163, 164, 169, 170–1, 173
    Rose Revolution 154–5, 156, 162, 167
    war with Russia 168–71
Gerasimov, Valerii 210
Germany
    Berlin Wall 214, 255
    and Bulgaria 226
    collapse of (1918) 8
    and Croatia 42, 43, 44–5
    and the European Union 55–6
    and Georgia 168–9
    and the Iraq war 141, 164
    and Kosovo 102, 164
    and NATO expansion 16–17, 18–19, 38–9, 71–2, 78
    Nazi Germany 4, 32, 42, 43
    and nuclear energy 249
    and the Paris Peace Conference (1919) 59
    reunification xviii, 9, 17, 23, 41, 43, 44, 55, 107, 243
    and Russia 19–20, 72, 121, 257

annexation of Crimea 215–16
Nordstream gas pipelines 215–16, 218, 241, 244, 247–53
Putin 19–20, 110, 111, 246–53, 255
and Ukraine 46, 165–6, 168–9, 198, 201, 206, 265
and the United States 257
Trump 241, 242–3, 245
and Yugoslavia 42, 43, 44–5, 46
Gershman, Carl 199–200
Glaz'ev, Sergei 204
Goldgeier, Jim 69
Goldman Sachs 234
Gorbachev, Mikhail 16–17, 20, 24, 30, 50, 112, 152
Gordon, Philip 188
Gore, Al 52, 73–4, 102, 114, 120
Grachev, Pavel 87, 104
Graham, Thomas 123, 138, 144–5, 147
Greece 85
Greenstock, Jeremy 89, 140
Grinda, José 160
Gulf War 124
Gusinsky, Vladimir 89

Hadley, Stephen 10, 126, 161–2
Hagel, Chuck 188
Haiti 52
Hall, Sir Peter 42–3
Halper, Stefan 230
Hartman, Arthur 16
Havel, Václav 24–5, 38, 39, 40, 64, 65
Helsinki Accords/Declaration (1975) 21, 153, 178
Helsinki summit (1997) 83–4, 92–3
Herbst, John 156
Heusgen, Christoph 198, 215–16
Hezbollah 187
Hill, Fiona 238
Hitler, Adolf 19, 59

Hochstein, Amos 250
Holbrooke, Richard 66–7, 83, 100, 102
Hollande, François 215
Hoon, Geoff 132
Hoover, Herbert 29
Horelick, Arnold 80–2, 88, 123, 179
Horn, Gyuia 83
Hungary 38, 43, 63, 67, 91, 153
Hunter, Robert 23, 38, 101, 122, 202
Hurd, Douglas 23, 45, 50, 58, 85, 99, 116

Ibn Al-Khattab 127, 159
Ilyushin, Viktor 87
IMF (International Monetary Fund) 33, 35, 36, 95, 96, 107, 198
India 20, 122, 269
International Renaissance Foundation 201
Iran 122, 125, 152, 153, 180, 225, 226, 235, 245
and Bosnia 53, 85
and nuclear weapons 193
and Syria 187, 223, 237
Iraq 124–5, 129, 139–47, 152, 155, 158, 160, 177, 181, 190, 194, 234, 243
and ISIS 190–1, 238
ISIS/IGIL 190–1, 221–2, 223, 236, 238
Islamic fundamentalism 117, 152, 153
and Afghanistan 153–4
Islamic terrorism 126–7, 145
see also al-Qaeda
Israel 85, 143, 222, 225, 239, 265
Italy 99
Ivanov, Igor 103, 104
Ivanov, Sergei 127, 130–1, 132, 136, 145–6, 223
Ivashov, Leonid 13

Jackson, General Mike 104, 106
Japan
Fukushima nuclear plant 249

Jefferson, Thomas 28
John Paul II, Pope 43
Johnson, Boris 265, 266–7
Johnson, Lyndon 22
J.P. Morgan 234

Kagan, Robert 194
Karabel'nikov, Valentin 104–5
Karadžić, Radovan 46–7
Karimov, Islam 131–2, 147
Kazakhstan 147, 186, 269
Kelin, Andrei 139, 258
Kelly, Ian 214
Kennan, George 9, 15, 69–70
Kennedy, John F. 176
Kerry, John 188, 191, 193
Keynes, John Maynard 8
Khodorkovsky, Mikhail 95, 196
Khrushchev, Nikita 57
Kim Jong Un 244
Kislyak, Sergei 139, 230, 232
Kissinger, Henry 53, 58, 173, 177, 195, 239
  and Trump 231–2, 233
KLA (Kosovan Albanian Liberation Army) 100, 101
Kohl, Helmut 17, 19–20, 39, 43, 45, 55–6, 65, 67, 71, 71–2, 90, 102, 137
Korbel, Josef 121
Kortunov, Andrei 13, 226, 267, 268
Kosovo 99–107, 110, 117, 140, 162, 213
  independence 164
  Slatina airport seizure 104–6, 109
Kozyrev, Andrei 25–7, 31, 32, 62, 63, 73, 86, 87, 88
Kramp-Karrenbauer, Annegret 251
Krasheninnikova, Veronika 184–5, 235
Kravchuk, Leonid 75, 77
Kruzel, Joseph, Major-General 59, 66
Kuchma, Leonid 77, 81, 116

Kudrin, Alexei 111–12, 247
Kupchan, Charles 215
Kuvaldin, Viktor 98
Kuwait 124
Kuznetsov, A. 246
Kvashnin, Anatoly 104
Kyrgyzstan 132

Lajolo, Cardinal Giovanni 43
Lake, Tony 16, 24, 28, 40, 53–4, 56–7, 63, 65, 66, 67–8, 81
  memorandum ("Moving Toward NATO Expansion") 74–5
Latin America 60, 239
Latvia 146
Lavrov, Sergei 101, 169, 179, 223, 238
Lebanon 125
Leont'ev, Mikhail 185
Leslie, Dame Alison 216
Levada, Yuri 90
Levin-Utikin, Anatoly 111
Lewinsky, Monica 127
Libby, Lewis "Scooter" 120
Libya 180–3, 188, 189, 190, 226, 231, 235, 238, 261
Lithuania 24, 146, 248
Litvinov, Maxim 268
Litvinenko, Alexandr 159, 160
Loskutov, Dmitry 203
Lugar, Richard 37, 59
Lugovoi, Andrei 159, 160
Lukin, Vladimir 206
Luzhkov, Yuri 98
Lyne, Sir Roderick 132, 170

McCain, John 201
Macedonia 220–1
McFaul, Mike 177, 178–9, 183–5, 186, 187, 194, 204
Machiavelli, N. 12, 20
McMaster, General H.R. 232, 233, 238, 239–40, 244

McNamara, Robert 16
Macron, Emmanuel 265
Major, John 17, 36, 48, 91, 95
Mamedov, Georgii 60
Mandela, Nelson 214
Manning, Sir David 260
Matlock, Jack 16
Mattis, James 233, 236, 250
Medinskii, Vladimir 256, 262, 266
Medvedev, Dmitrii 11, 162, 172, 173, 175, 178–9, 189, 196
   and the Arab Spring 180–1, 182, 183
   and Trump 236
Merkel, Angela 5, 165, 166, 198, 200, 215–16, 242–3, 244
   and the Nordstream gas pipelines 247–8, 250–1
   and Trump 245, 246
Mertz, Friedrich 250
Mexico 260
Meyer, Steven 47–8
Middle East 122, 142, 225–6
   the Arab Spring 179–83
   and regime change 151, 157
   and Russia 190–1
Miller, Alexei 111
Milošević, Slobodan 44, 46, 47, 85, 86, 99, 100, 102
Minsk Protocols 218–19
Mitterrand, François 17, 21–2, 23, 55
Moldova 171
Montenegro 47, 220–1
Musharraf, Pervez 126
Muslims
   and Kosovo 99–100

Naryshkin, Sergei 130, 210
NATO (North Atlantic Treaty Organization) xviii
   creation of 16
   and Crimea 212
   and Czechoslovakia 24–5
   and the Kosovo war 102–3
   NATO-EU strategic partnership 173
   NATO-Russia Council (NATO at twenty) 134–9, 145–6, 210
   NATO-Russia Final Act 92, 93
   NATO-Russia Founding Act (1997) 93–4
   and Putin 117–18, 244, 256–61
   and Russian seizure of Crimea 210, 211, 212–13
   and Russia's war with Georgia 168–70
   and Trump 240–5
   and Ukraine 7
   and Yugoslavia (former) 48, 50, 85–7
NATO (North Atlantic Treaty Organization) expansion
   and the Baltic states 54, 68, 73, 74, 91, 93, 108, 133, 145, 146
   and Central and Eastern European states 20–1, 37, 38–40, 59, 63, 79, 83, 126
   and Georgia 163, 164, 169, 170–1, 173
   and the Partnership for Peace (PfP) 60–1, 62–3, 64, 78, 139
   and Russia 11, 14, 15, 17–18, 41, 54–5, 66–75, 68, 77–9, 89–93, 94, 107–8, 108–9, 116, 219, 220–1
   Putin 118, 145, 158, 161, 256–61
   Western reassurances to 16–20, 106–7
   and Ukraine 68, 73, 74, 81, 91, 93, 115, 156, 173, 209, 217, 258–60, 262, 264–5
   invasion of 266
   Membership Action Plan 162–3, 164–8, 169

and the United States 13–15, 18,
    21–4, 37–8
  Bush administration 123–4
  Clinton presidency 13–14,
    15–16, 39–41, 52–5, 60–1,
    65–74, 77–82
Navalny, Alexei 254–5, 263
Nazi Germany 4, 32
Nemtsov, Boris 97
Netherlands 247
  and the shooting down of the
    Malaysian airliner MH-17
    217–18
Neville-Jones, Pauline 73, 99
Nicholas II, Tsar 270
Nikel, Rolf 166
Nitze, Paul 16
Nixon, Richard M. 120, 123
Nordstream II gas pipeline 215–16,
  218, 241, 247–52
North Korea 122, 244
Northern Ireland 144
nuclear energy 249
nuclear weapons
  National Missile Defense (NMD)
    145
  and NATO enlargement 92,
    123–4
  Putin on military balance 258
  Russia 28, 58, 69, 73, 76, 109,
    123–4
  Soviet Union 39
  and Ukraine 72, 76, 81
Nuland, Victoria 4, 194, 201–2, 203,
  204–5, 207, 215, 219, 250
Nunn, Sam 15–16
Nusra Front 221

Obama, Barack 6, 14, 173, 175–8, 240,
  245, 250, 251
  the Arab Spring and Libya 179–83,
    190, 236
  and the Bush administration 176,
    193
  and Europe 180
  foreign policy 177–8, 180, 182,
    191
  Moscow summit (2009) 174
  and Putin 175, 176–7, 178, 191–2,
    261
    seizure of Crimea 213–15, 216,
      232
  and Syria 187–9, 191, 221, 225, 235
  and Trump 228, 230–1, 232, 233–4,
    235, 236, 243
Odling-Smee, John 35–6
OSCE (Organization for Security
  and Co-operation in Europe)
  137, 219
Ottoman Empire 49
Owen, David 48, 52, 53, 86

Paet, Urmas 205
Pakistan 85, 126, 143
Panetta, Leon 28, 33
Partnership for Peace (PfP) 58–66,
  73, 78, 139
Patrushev, Nikolai 141, 159, 220–1,
  233, 238, 239
Pendergast, Tom 244
Pérez de Cuéllar, Javier 45
Perry, Bill 11–12, 39, 48, 58, 69, 79
Peter the Great, Tsar of Russia 256,
  262
Pickering, Thomas 70
Pirt, Christopher 178
Ploetz, Hans 18
Poland 63, 67, 258
  and Croatia 43
  and the European Union 5, 197
  and Georgia 168, 170–1
  and NATO 21, 38, 54, 56, 91,
    163–4, 165, 240
  and Ukraine 197–8, 206

Politkovskaya, Anna 158, 160
Portugal 154
Powell, Colin 39, 121, 122, 125, 135, 137
Prado, Ric 127, 129
Prigozhin, Yevgeny 223, 237, 243
    assassination 255
    Internet Research Agency 217, 227
Primakov, Yevgeny 18, 62, 83–4, 91–2, 97–8
    and the Kosovo war 101, 102–3
Prodi, Romano 197
Putin, Vladimir 5–8, 27, 34, 114–47
    and the Arab Spring 180–1, 182, 183
        Syria 187, 188–9
    and the Blair government 116–20, 121, 121–2, 128, 142–4
    and Chechen terrorists 146–7
    and the collapse of the Soviet Union 9
    Crimea seizure 6–7, 183, 210–13, 240, 246, 250, 266
    and democracy in Russia 157–8, 255–6
    Eurasian economic union 186, 195, 197, 262
    and the European Union 5, 172–3, 186
    and Georgia 156
    and Germany 19–20, 110, 111, 246–53, 255
        Nordstream gas pipelines 248–52
    and the Iraq war 140–3, 144–5
    and Islamic fundamentalism 126–7
    and Kissinger 231–2
    and the Kosovo war 104
    and the Middle East 190–1
    and NATO 117–18, 244, 256–61
        expansion 118, 145, 158, 161, 256–61
    and Navalny 254–5, 263
    popularity in Russia 239
    rise to power 5–6, 107, 109–13
    and the Russian petro-dollar economy 133
    and the Russian political system 254–5
    Russian presidential elections 114–16, 185
    Syrian intervention 221–6
    threat perceptions of 7–8
    and Ukraine 166–7, 173, 186, 254, 256
        EU membership 195–7, 198–9, 200
        invasion of 3–4, 5, 6, 12–13, 14, 168, 255–6, 265–70
        Maidan 203, 206–7, 211
        Orange Revolution 155, 156–7
    and the United States 160–1, 173–4, 176–7, 256–8
        9/11 130–1, 132–4, 174
        Biden 253
        Bush ('43) 118, 119–20, 124, 125–6, 128, 133–4, 157–8, 160, 174
        Obama 175, 176–7, 178, 191–2
        Trump 234–7, 243
    and the war of the Russian succession 269–70
Pyatt 202

Quayle, Dan 69

Rambouillet agreement 100–1, 102
Rapallo Pact (1922) 19
Rasmussen, General Anders 247
Raymond, Walter 199
Reagan, Ronald 7, 16, 28, 57, 58, 69, 123, 153, 199, 232, 243
Rice, Condoleezza 14, 121, 122–3, 126, 127, 128, 161

and 9/11 128, 129
and the colour revolutions 157
on the Middle East 151
and NATO at 20 135–7
Rice, Susan 188, 232
Rifkind, Malcolm 89, 91–2
Robertson, Lord 117–18, 134
Rohrabacher, Dana 204–5
Romania 71, 258
Roosevelt, Franklin D. 110
Rosenthal, Andrew 189
Röttgen, Norbert 249–50
Rove, Karl 120
Rueda, Luis 125, 139
Ruehe, Volker 38–9
Rumer, Eugene 6–7
Rumsfeld, Donald 121, 122, 125, 129, 162, 176, 194, 260
and the NATO-Russia Council idea 134–7, 139
Ruryikov, Dmitrii 87–8
Russia
as an empire XVII, 8, 9
Chechen war 50, 88–9
and the Commonwealth of Independent States 75
and Crimea 51, 75–6, 167
Putin's annexation of 6–7, 183, 210–17
and Eastern European states 20–1
and the Eastern Partnership 171, 173
economy 56, 94–8, 269
Euro-Asiatic Union 5
FSB (Federal Security Service) 3–4
Georgian war 168–71
and Germany 19–20, 72, 121, 257
annexation of Crimea 215–16
Nordstream gas pipelines 215–16, 218, 241, 244

invasion of Ukraine 3–4, 5, 6, 12–13, 14, 168, 255–6, 265–8
and the Russian economy 268–70
and Iran 180
and the Kosovo war 101, 102–6, 107, 109, 110
and the Middle East 190–1
and NATO enlargement 11, 14, 15, 16–20, 17–18, 41, 54–5, 66–75, 68, 77–9, 89–93, 94, 106–7, 107–8, 108–9, 116, 220–1
and the NATO-Russia Council idea 134–9
NGOs (non-governmental organizations) 178
nuclear weapons 28, 58, 69, 73, 76, 109, 122
oligarchs 89
and the Partnership for Peace (PfP) 58–65, 73, 78
Project Lakhta 230
St Petersburg 110–11, 262
Security Council 4, 220–1
and Serbia 102–3
the *siloviki* (deep state) 107, 153, 260
Sochi Winter Olympics (2014) 172
SVR (civilian Foreign Intelligence) 62, 63
and Trump 232–3, 243–5
and Ukraine 75–6, 262
Maidan 200–1, 208–9
NATO membership 163, 164–8, 209
and the United States 11–12, 20, 32–6, 252–3
election meddling 238–9
Jackson-Vanik amendment 35
Nordstream gas pipelines 240–1

Partnership for Peace (PfP) 58–65
and Yugoslavia (former) 48–51, 85, 87
see also Putin, Vladimir, Yeltsin, Boris
Rutskoi, Alexander 50–1, 75
Ryabkov, Sergei 264, 265
Rybkin, Valery 105

Saakashvili, Mikheil 154–5, 166, 168, 169
Sachs, Jeffrey 30–1
Saddam Hussein 125–7, 139, 140, 141, 142, 152
Sal'ya, Marina 111
Sarajevo 47, 50, 85, 86
Saratov, Georgii 97
Sarkozy, Nicolas 165, 181, 261, 270
Saudi Arabia 85, 126, 129, 143, 152, 190, 268
Sawers, John 116, 119
Schmid, Helga 196, 202–3, 215
Schmidt, Helmut 39
Scholz, Olaf 265
Schröder, Gerhard 46, 135, 141, 211, 215, 251
Scowcroft, Brent 17, 23, 24, 55, 121
Sechin, Igor 111
Second World War
and Croatia 42, 43
Serbia 44, 47, 48, 51, 53, 68, 85, 99, 164, 221
Kosovo war 100–6
and Ukraine 201
Serbs in Croatia 42–3, 44
Sergeev, Igor 118–19
Shalikashvili, John 58, 59, 69, 79
Sherman, Wendy 264
Shevardnadze, Eduard 16, 154
Shevtsov, Leontii 69
Shoigu, Sergei 210

Shokin, Viktor 219
Shultz, George 232
Shuvalev, Igor 203
Sikorski, Radoslaw (Radek) 5, 163, 170–1, 173, 206
Slocombe, Walter 24, 29
Slovakia 63
Slovenia 41–2, 46
Smolyakov, Leonid 77
Snowden, Edward 253
Sobchak, Anatoly 110, 111
Sochi Winter Olympics (2014) 172
Solana, Javier 50, 93, 167–8
Somali civil war 51, 52
Somalia 125
Soros, George 201, 205
Soviet Union (former) 115
and Afghanistan 153–4
collapse xvii, 7–8, 9–12, 30, 152, 178, 234
and Crimea 75–6
and Eastern European states xvii
former republics 50, 115, 162, 171
and NATO 18–19, 19
Nazi invasion of 4
nuclear weapons 39
Red Army 49
Treaty on Conventional Armed Forces in Europe 146
and Ukraine 258
and the US 15
and Yugoslavia 49
Spain 159, 173
Srebrenica massacre 85
SRY (Socialist Republic of Yugoslavia) 26
Stalin, Josef 12–13, 19, 60, 76, 268
Stanišic, Joven 85
Steele, Christopher
dossier of 228–30

Steinberg, James 40, 66, 72
Steinmeier, Frank-Walter 163, 206, 215, 251
Stepashin, Sergei 113
Stephanopoulos, George 33
Strzok, Peter 228
Sudan 125
Summers, Larry 31, 33, 57
Surkov, Vladislav 179, 196–7
Sweden 211
Syria 12, 125, 174, 186–90, 191, 209, 221–6, 231, 235–6, 237, 244

Tajikistan 162
Talbott, Strobe 13–14, 31, 32, 39, 56–8, 65–6, 67, 68, 72–3, 74, 77–8, 78–9, 86, 89–91, 92
    and the Kosovo war 103, 105
Tarnoff, Peter 39–40, 53
Teft, John 164
terrorism 144, 177–8, 190–1
    Hezbollah 187
    in Syria 224, 238
    see also al-Qaeda
Thailand
    Tom Yum crisis 96
Thatcher, Margaret 8, 55
Tillerson, Rex 233, 237–8
Timmermans, Frans 218
Tombiński, Jan 197–8, 202–3
Torricelli, Senator Robert 131
Tracey, Lynn 164
Trenin, Dmitrii 167
Trubnikov, Vyacheslav 62
Truman, Harry S. 244
Trump, Donald 14, 69, 227–45
    and Europe 241–2
    and Germany 241, 242–3, 245
    and Kissinger 231–2, 233
    and NATO 240–5
    and Obama 228, 230–1, 232, 233–4, 235, 236, 243
    and Russia 232–3, 234–40, 243–5, 253
        Putin 234–7, 243
    and the Steele dossier 228–30
    and Syria 225, 235–6
Tsarev, Oleg 201
Tunisia 180
Turkey 85, 195, 225, 268

Ukraine xviii, 75–7, 193–219
    and the Balkans 85
    and Crimea 51, 75–6, 167
        Putin's annexation of 6–7, 183, 210–17, 212
    Donbas region 75, 216–17, 248
    Donetsk region 34, 217, 218, 219
    and the Eastern Partnership 171
    and the European Union 7, 46, 157, 164, 194–200, 209, 261, 262
    and irredentism 268
    Luhansk region 217, 219
    Maidan 200–7, 209, 211
    and the Minsk Protocols 218–19
    and NATO enlargement 68, 73, 74, 81, 91, 93, 115, 156, 173, 194, 195, 209, 217, 258–60, 262
        Membership Action Plan 162–3, 164–8, 169, 170
    and nuclear weapons 72, 76, 81
    Orange Revolution 155–7, 160, 167, 178, 199, 210
    and the Partnership for Peace (PfP) 64, 65
    political changes in 6–7
    and Putin 186, 259–62
        invasion of 3–4, 5, 6, 12–13, 14, 168, 255–6, 260, 265–8
    and the Russian empire 115–16
    and Russian gas 199, 248
    Russian language in 76, 77
    Russian-speaking regions 156, 194, 216–17

and Trump 236
see also Yanukovych, Viktor
United Nations
   and Kosovo 104
   Protection Force (UNPROFOR) 51, 53
   and Russia 54–5, 78
   Security Council resolution on Libya 180–1, 181–2
   and Trump 245
   and Yugoslavia (former) 43–4, 50, 51, 85
United States xviii, 3–36
   9/11 15, 121, 125, 128–34, 143–4, 152, 174
   Agency for International Development (USAID) 156, 186, 199, 201
   and Blair 143–4
   and the collapse of the Soviet Union 9–12
   democracy crusade 27, 151–2, 157–8, 176, 178–9, 182–3, 185, 186, 194
   FBI 129
   Foreign Agents Registration Act (FARA) 185
   General Motors 216
   and Georgia 154–5
   Hoover Institution 177
   and the IMF 36
   and Iraq 124–5, 129, 139–47, 155, 253
   Monroe Doctrine 60
   National Endowment for Democracy (NED) 153, 199, 200, 201
   National Security Council (NSC) 120, 121, 128, 138, 144, 238
   and NATO enlargement 13–16, 18, 21–4, 38–41, 52–5, 65–74, 69, 77–82
   regime change in foreign policy 151–3, 261
   and Russia 11–12, 20, 32–6, 252–3
      election meddling 238–9
      the Jackson-Vanik amendment 35
      Nordstream gas pipelines 240–1
      Partnership for Peace (PfP) 58–65
      Putin 160–1, 173–4, 176–7, 256–8, 263–5
   and Ukraine 116
      Maidan 204, 207–8, 209–10
      Minsk Protocols 218–19
      NATO membership 164–6
      Putin's invasion of 4, 263
   and Yugoslavia 41–2, 43–4, 46, 47–8, 50, 52–3, 84–6
      Vance-Owen plan 48, 52, 53, 86
   see also under individual presidents
USAID (United States Agency for International Development) 156, 186, 199, 201
Uzbekistan 131–2, 147

Vance, Cyrus 48, 52, 53, 86
the Vatican 43, 44
Venediktov, Alexei 159
Vershbow, Alexander (Sandy) 68, 122, 156–7, 167, 172
Vietnam War 53, 224, 269
Visegrád countries 38, 63, 64, 83
Volker, Kurt 138, 169, 170
Voloshin, Alexander 103
Voshchanov, Pavel 50

Wagner Group
   in Syria 223, 237
Wałęsa, Lech 39, 40

Walker, Bill 100
Walker, Jenonne 65, 67–8
Warnig, Matthias 241
Warsaw Pact 24, 38, 54, 56, 81, 108, 153, 161
Wayne, John 69
WikiLeaks 253
Wilkerson, Colonel Larry 125
Wilson, Charles 216
Wilson, Woodrow 151
Wolfowitz, Paul 22, 124–5, 129, 139
World Bank 33, 35
World Trade Organization 35, 196
Wörner, Manfred 18, 50, 60–1, 62–3, 161
Xi Jinping 244

Yalta conference 110
Yanukovych, Viktor 7, 155–6, 157, 194, 199, 200, 201, 202, 203–4, 205, 206–7, 211, 262
Yates, Sally 232
Yegorov 112
Yeltsin, Boris 28, 31–2, 36, 82, 109–10
   Chechen war 88–9
   and Crimea 77
   and economic reform 94–8
   and the Kosovo war 102–3, 107
   and NATO 54, 54–5, 83
   enlargement 61, 62, 70, 71, 72, 73–4, 89–90, 92–3
   and the oligarchs 89, 95, 97
   and Putin 109–10, 112–13, 257
   and Ukraine 75
   and Yugoslavia (former) 50, 87
Yemen 190
Yugoslavia (former) 12, 28, 29, 31, 41–51, 52–3, 69, 85–8, 99–106, 253
   Bosnian war 84–9
   Croatia 41–2, 42–3, 44–5, 53, 85–6
   Dayton agreement 88, 99
   Federal Republic of 47
   JNA (Yugoslav People's Army) 47
   Kosovo 99–106
   see also Bosnia Herzegovina; Serbia
Yumashev, Valentin 112, 113
Yushchenko, Viktor 155–6, 157, 164
Yushenkov, Sergei 111

Zakaria, Fareed 205
Zapatero, José Luis 173
Zavarzin, Viktor 105–6
Zelensky, Volodomyr 3, 265–6, 267
Zhukov, Marshall 107
Zoellick, Robert 20
Zubov, Viktor 111

About the Author

JONATHAN HASLAM is a leading scholar and writer, specializing in the history of the Soviet Union. He was the George F. Kennan Professor at the Institute for Advanced Study, Princeton from 2015 to 2021. He is a Fellow of the British Academy, Emeritus Professor of the History of International Relations, Cambridge University and Life Fellow of Corpus Christi College, Cambridge. Haslam is the author of many celebrated books, including *The Spectre of War* and *Near and Distant Neighbours*.